dynamics of
CURRICULUM
IMPROVEMENT

PHILO T. PRITZKAU

Director of Curriculum Center
Associate Professor of Education
University of Connecticut
Storrs, Connecticut

1959
PRENTICE-HALL, Inc. *Englewood Cliffs, N.J.*

PRENTICE-HALL EDUCATION SERIES

Harold Spear, Editor

LIBRARY OF CONGRESS
CATALOG CARD NO.: 59-6958

PRINTED IN THE UNITED STATES OF AMERICA

22193

To Madonna
and Patti

Preface

THE REAL TEST OF THE EFFECTIVENESS OF THE CURRICULUM IS THE constructive difference it makes at the level of teacher-pupil interaction. The curriculum comes into focus at the place where unity and direction is attained between teacher, children, subject matter, and other resources.

In line with this concept, a guiding principle of most of the thinking developed in this book is that curriculum improvement is equated with teaching. The responsibility of the curriculum worker is to promote the conditions for high quality teaching and learning. Throughout the book an attempt has been made to provide some direction to these conditions.

Questions such as the following have been approached: How can leadership be generated to help individuals and groups toward high quality learning? What are some of the conditions needed to develop a compelling need on the part of teachers and children to search for new meanings? At what points is it possible to penetrate conditions associated with "pet" and time-honored "systems" of teaching and learning? Is the launching of curriculum improvement programs on a system-wide basis rewarding at the level of classroom practice? What are some initial steps in the development of the machinery for continuous curriculum improvement? How can the curriculum worker help teachers to avoid such pitfalls as oversimplification of meanings and rigid allegiance to one particular system? In what ways may an understanding of the simple relationships and values of people be used to promote learning?

Along with an approach to the type of questions indicated, the discussion revolves around issues related to many concepts and problems. A concept which receives high priority is that of inclusiveness in learning. Questions and problems relative to the provision for a wide range of ideas and meanings in the learning environment are considered in detail.

Another concept which is at the heart of the ideas developed in the book is the admission of the values of all children and young people into the setting for learning. In order to promote high level learning it is important for all children and youth to gain meanings about their own behavior as well as that of other people. The matter of selectivity of content and the development of conditions for the analysis and appraisal of values is also considered. The question of becoming analytical about one's behavior is pursued. A high quality of dynamics for curriculum improvement resides in the values of children.

The extracting of meanings about intangibles is examined rather fully in connection with curriculum improvement tasks. This, of course, is related to the whole question of feelings and their possible meanings. Children and young people are beset with intangibles every day in many of their activities. Yet few attempts are made in the schools to help them to discover the meanings in these intangibles.

We cite the need for the development of a new stability in learning—for more thinking which will move into higher meanings in science, social and international relations, mathematics, communications, and other areas. The curriculum must have provisions for "charging" the school environment with this new sense of inquiry. Children and young people cannot escape from tension; indeed, they must use it to give themselves a new sense of stability.

Additional questions pursued are the development of centers of learning, the provision for educating beyond "surprises," the establishment of conditions for inquiry into the periphery of ideas, the promotion of unity in learning, and others.

It is the hope of the author that the book will stimulate the thinking and efforts of all educators of children—classroom teachers, administrators, curriculum workers, supervisors, along with students involved in advanced and graduate study. Classes in "foundations" should find the ideas examined pertinent to a more complete understanding of that field of study. Teachers and parents working together for curriculum improvement should find the book useful. Also, many ideas are designed to contribute to teacher-pupil curriculum development.

The author wishes to acknowledge his debt to the help given by Dr. Arthur W. Goldberg, Vice Principal, The E. O. Smith Laboratory School, University of Connecticut, in preparing this edition. Dr. Goldberg read much of the manuscript and offered many valuable suggestions. The material of the book was discussed at different times with Dean Vernon E. Anderson, College of Education, University of Maryland, and Mr. John O. Goodman, Associate Professor of Education, University of Connecticut. These discussions proved to be of major value in the development of many of the ideas in the book. Significant suggestions were contributed to the thinking in the book by Mr. Raymond Houghton, instructor in Education, University of Connecticut, and Miss Maureen Lapan, graduate assistant at the University of Connecticut, who read several chapters. Helpful ideas were suggested by Dr. Harvey L. Saxton of the Teachers College, Towson, Maryland, and Dr. Stephen A. August, Assistant Superintendent of Schools, Cheshire, Connecticut. Mrs. Eleanor Antan, Consultant, Curriculum Laboratory, University of Connecticut, was very helpful in reading and criticizing portions of the material. The author wishes to acknowledge with deepest gratitude the many questions raised about curriculum practices and the many problems approached by the hundreds of graduate students in his classes over the past years. These have been the basis of many of the points and concepts developed in the book.

PHILO T. PRITZKAU

Contents

·1·

Some Principles of
Curriculum Improvement

EVERY SCHOOL SYSTEM HAS SOME KIND OF LEARNING EXPERIENCES. In one school system this program may be a rather rigid prescription of learning experiences through which it is hoped that children will grow in competences for effective living. In another school system, the program may be based on a statement of objectives and general procedures sometimes called a "guide to learning experiences." It is hoped that this guide will provide some direction to many learning experiences which are over and above those suggested. Still other systems may have suggested resources and excerpts of experiences designed to promote a continual study and examination of ideas toward expanded meanings and understandings. In some school systems, rather complete bulletins or courses of study have been developed. In some schools, teachers are expected to use the content of the courses of study to develop learning experiences for children. In other schools, the courses of study contain many suggestions from which the teacher may choose in promoting learning with children. Within the prevailing pattern, whatever it may be, the teacher is the prime motivator of the direct conditions for learning.

THE TEACHER STRUCTURES FOR LEARNING

The structuring for learning may take several forms. In one form the teacher plans the entire learning experiences of the children. Another more or less rigid practice is that of following

1

a prescribed course of study. Still another form of rigid structuring involves the teacher prescribing the subject matter of a textbook as material set out to be learned. Whatever discussion there is is based on the material of the teacher's plans, the course of study, or the textbook. Writing activities usually relate to the subject matter as prescribed in the above methods. If ventures are permitted beyond the rigid prescriptions, they are usually offered as "special reports" which connote isolated digressions from the "regular" and "important" work.

In the more flexible arrangement, many experiences are developed by the children or by the teacher and children in terms of what are conceived to be their purposes and interests. The teacher, of course, is a member of the various groups which are planning the experiences. He will attempt to provide suggestions and guidance in the planning. Depending on the imagination and influence of the teacher with children, this arrangement can be very productive.

Both rigid and flexible structuring needed for learning

Structuring may be alternately rigid and flexible, depending on the nature of the learning experiences which the teacher needs to develop with children. For example, a teacher may use a reading series in a certain way to develop reading skills. This means that he will more or less structure the procedures. At the same time, he will make accessible to the children a wide variety of readings for expanded meanings in science, biography, and behavior. He will also work with the children to establish centers of interest for science reading and experimentation, the study of behavior, and the graphic portrayal of ideas. He will do many other things to stimulate a sense of inquiry and an excitement about the development of ideas. The children or youth, in turn, will bring new and expanded meanings to the setting for learning. The teacher and children here are providing for a wide range of experiences without losing sight of goals and direction.

Curriculum improvement tasks relate to both rigid and flexible programs. The programs and structuring of learning experiences as described do not, of course, give a complete picture of the curriculum. The structuring cannot be put into "slots," as the description might suggest. Rigid programs, for example, are as inclusive and exclusive of intensity and depth of meanings as the powers of insight and imagination which are peculiar to different teachers. A rigid structuring for learning may put some limits on the development of powers of insight and extension of meanings. The less rigid programs, too, may be rich or impoverished as to quality of learning experiences, depending upon the understanding, imagination, and resourcefulness of teachers. Furthermore, the type of leadership provided by the administration and other personnel will have a great effect on the type of programs and learning experiences which are developed. The attitude of the community toward the schools will, of course, also make a difference in the attitude of teachers and other personnel in their approach to the tasks of curriculum improvement and teaching.

The curriculum improvement tasks must relate to all programs whether rigid or flexible. The teacher who has developed with children a high quality of learning experiences must be just as completely involved in curriculum improvement with regard to his practices as the teacher who has not attained the competence to carry on this degree of performance. Everyone should have the opportunity to help develop the conditions which will lead to improved instructional practices—hence, curriculum improvement.

CURRICULUM IMPROVEMENT EQUATED WITH TEACHING

Too often teacher education has been carried on in such a way as to make it appear that curriculum improvement work is something apart from teaching. The administration also has approached the curriculum work in such a manner as to make it appear different from teaching. As a result, when teachers are employed in school systems, they regard teaching as the major task and curriculum tasks as something above and beyond. Some teachers, therefore, regard themselves as burdened by "extras" when they find themselves becoming increasingly involved in tasks and duties concerned with improvement of the curriculum.

Curriculum improvement involved with teaching tasks

Curriculum improvement can be carried on almost with every act of teaching—in fact, it happens whenever a teacher is concerned about how a child learns. Curriculum improvement takes place whenever a teacher discusses with other teachers or with the principal the appropriate uses of certain types of materials. The curriculum is improved when there is a consideration of better ways of communicating to parents about the progress of children in school. Curriculum change occurs when teachers request more shelving for the placing of books and other materials to use with learning experiences. The improvement of lighting conditions in a classroom is an important step to curriculum development. Any set of conditions which is provided by teachers, children, principal, and citizens to improve learning experiences for children can be classified as curriculum development.

Many other acts of teaching contribute to curriculum change. A teacher may begin curriculum change, for example, by expanding his system of evaluation beyond standardized tests. Another teacher may initiate curriculum change by developing a "Questions asked by people in this room" corner. As he makes books and materials accessible so that children may do research on the questions he expands their opportunities to acquire meanings and ideas. This, in turn, will challenge the efforts of the teacher to become more resourceful. In the search for ideas, the teacher will talk with other teachers, parents, the principal, and the children. As people begin to exchange ideas and arrive at decisions about instructional practices, a real beginning has been made in curriculum improvement.

In some school systems, the staff has already equated the task of curriculum development to teaching. Teachers have recognized and accepted the responsibility of curriculum improvement as an essential and integral part of professional services. It is hoped that the leadership in teacher education institutions and school systems develop the conditions which will encourage all teachers to facilitate this unity of tasks in the teaching profession.

CURRICULUM IMPROVEMENT IN THE CONTEXT
OF CLASSROOM PROCEDURE

Curriculum improvement should be undertaken at the level of the teacher's understanding about instructional practices. Since the teacher is already involved with children in the classroom, it would seem that any questions about improving the curriculum would need to come in this context. The practice of involving the teacher in curriculum work at the level of his classroom assures a degree of security and clarity in direction.

In the approach to curriculum improvement, it is necessary for the curriculum workers to keep in mind the limitations of the human organism. Most people move rather slowly and cautiously from one practice to a somewhat different one. Many people are not immediately able to establish the connection between a high level verbalism and the related practice. Some will not make the connection for a long time. Others, experiencing a sense of frustration, will escape from the task of making any connections whatsoever. If this happens, a feeling of distrust for anything different from the ordinary routine is liable to develop. This has the effect of crystallizing the instructional pattern at "dead center." A further result may be a deterioration of practice.

Mechanical committee arrangements may separate ideas from classroom

A mistake often made by administrators and other staff members of a school system is the launching of a system-wide curriculum improvement program out of context with the level of classroom practice. The sudden impact and overwhelming nature of this procedure has a devastating effect on the perspective which teachers entertain relative to instruction. This effect is further accentuated by the oft-indulged-in practice of setting up committee machinery to facilitate action on curriculum improvement. This may tend to create a frantic response which culminates in the decision to "get something ready for them." Under this condition, thinking is not on a high level relationship to real learning because the emphasis is on "getting something done." This may eventuate into a "ground-out" document so as to have "something to show" as evidence of industrious application by the participants. What is hailed as an accomplishment by the instigators of the curriculum improvement program may not be an accomplishment at all.

The mechanical committee system so frequently used to promote curriculum improvement is a questionable approach at best and is liable to prove particularly unrewarding not only to the teachers but to the school system as a whole if it is fashioned apart from an immediate identity with needs and practices. Before teachers function effectively in any form of organization there must be a body of substance to function about. The substance, further, must be of the type with which the teachers feel some unity. They need to feel sufficiently familiar with it so that they can take hold of it in a feeling of confidence and with a sense of realization. Before people are ready to be productive in committees, there needs to be a period of "warming up" with respect to ideas about teaching and learning. This has to be done in the locale of the classroom setting where teachers and children are daily planning the learning experiences as they see them in terms of their goals and objectives. The mechanical arrangement frequently represented by the committee system of curriculum development tends to effect a separation between ideas as they appear in classroom practice and the isolated level of committee deliberation.

Hierarchical committee system may promote unrealistic meanings. Another deleterious effect which may be occasioned by the committee system of curriculum improvement is the tendency to arrange ideas in a rather subtle hierarchy relative to decision and action. This condition rests on the assumption that committee deliberation will be productive of better ideas than the deliberation of an individual with his neighbors in practice. This assumption is, of course, debatable. It is highly questionable whether the deliberation of members in the committees will result in greater productiveness with respect to curriculum improvement than that of the individual who has attained the attitude of asking questions about his practices and has made provisions in his classroom to test ideas in terms of those questions. Furthermore, it cannot be logically assumed that members participating on the committee level will come out with more workable ideas of high quality than individuals examining ideas together informally but intensively at the classroom level and in the classroom context. The hierarchical tendency of a mechanical committee system is further accentuated if there exists a steering or coordinating committee with strict definitions of responsibility. Rather than becoming a body which related its efforts to the realization of considered goals of teaching, the steering or coordinating committee may assume a restrictive role in curriculum improvement. In other words, if a "steering" committee takes its label literally, the results may be a promulgation of unrealistic meanings.

Since committees are usually constituted as bodies having decision-making and rather final recommendation responsibilities, there is a danger that in the zeal to promote action, major emphasis might be given to the "good of the order" or to further the interests of the "organization" rather than to the development of vital learning experiences for children. When committees are formed, it means that action of some kind is expected. Often action is precipitated before the members become sufficiently involved in the exchange and examination of ideas to establish a sense of security with the handling of the ideas. This may result in an artificial product devoid of real meanings for instructional practices.

Perhaps we are being somewhat too critical about the committee system approach to curriculum improvement. It should be noted that the critical references are mainly to a mechanical committee arrangement. Committees should grow out of the handling of ideas. Furthermore, at certain stages of a program of curriculum improvement, it is probably necessary to have stated committees. The question of timing comes in here. That brings us to a very important consideration in curriculum development—that is, the location of responsibility for curriculum improvement.

LOCATION OF RESPONSIBILITY FOR CURRICULUM IMPROVEMENT

Although curriculum improvement may be initiated by any individual connected with the school system, it is, nevertheless, important to consider the question of responsibility in curriculum development. As indicated before, it is hoped that everyone in the school system will consider curriculum improvement an integral phase of his position. Since the development of the conditions for learning experiences is the responsibility of every individual in the school, it follows that curriculum improvement is everyone's responsibility. It is necessary, however, for someone to provide the impetus for these initial attempts.

Relating leadership roles of curriculum workers

The top administration can, of course, provide for the conditions which will make it possible for leadership in curriculum development to evolve. The curriculum director or coordinator would be more directly responsible in providing the over-all conditions for curriculum development. Teacher representatives chosen by the various local school units of the system would, of course, be involved in essential roles relative to the conditions.

With reference to the involvement of directors, consultants, and others attention should be directed to the thinking which conceives of curriculum improvement as within the context of the classroom. This means that there exists no hierarchical arrangement in the approach to curriculum questions.

The direct attempts at curriculum development must take place in a local setting, preferably the school unit. Within the school unit it must have its initial beginnings in the setting of familiarity for the teacher, the classrooms. It seems, then, that the principal is the key person to provide the conditions for these beginnings of curriculum development.

Roles of director and other curriculum workers must maintain classroom flavor. The director, curriculum consultants, and others must find their true roles of resourcefulness in relationship to the local setting for curriculum development. All machinery for the channeling of ideas must assume a "horizontal" position. Whatever meetings or conditions for the handling of curriculum questions are arranged must maintain the thread of familiarity with the classroom. It should be noted, then, that the discussion which continues through the remainder of the chapter suggests the role of the director and other curriculum workers as paralleling that of the principal and teachers. The terms "curriculum worker" and "curriculum leader" could apply at different times to the director, principal, consultant, and teacher, depending on the location of leadership.

ESTABLISHING INITIAL CONDITIONS FOR LEADERSHIP IN CURRICULUM IMPROVEMENT

It is assumed that the principal has some vision with regard to the nature of curriculum improvement, the frame of reference within which it must take place, and the tasks incident to it. At the same time, he must recognize that teachers in the school, in varying degrees, possess potential vision and competence relative to the needs and direct tasks of curriculum similar to and possibly more extensive than those of the curriculum leader himself.

As has been suggested, curriculum improvement must be approached at the level of the teacher's understanding about instructional practices. People usually approach tasks on the basis of their present knowledge and experiences. Some may extend themselves and try to reach somewhat beyond their current knowledge about practices. Also, some may carry on practices which are below their present knowledge and experience. Assuming that the principal initiates leadership in curriculum improvement, he needs to consider his steps with insight and understanding.

Establishing working relationships with teachers

Although it is assumed that the principal, as leader, has certain goals in mind as well as vision and understanding with regard to the nature of curriculum development and implementation, *he must establish a position of mutual operation by relating his vision and understanding to that of the teachers.* Mackenzie, Corey, and others[1] give emphasis to this position in indicating alternative roles of the leader as follows:

> (1) the leader's goals must be those of the group, and he must be seen by the group as helping or potentially helping it to achieve its goals; (2) the leader's goals must be sufficiently compatible with

[1] Gordon N. Mackenzie and Stephen M. Corey and Associates, *Instructional Leadership* (New York: Bureau of Publications, Teachers College, Columbia University, 1954), p. 23.

those of the group so that the group sees him as helping or potentially helping to achieve its goals; (3) the group must recognize
the leader as helping to avoid destruction of a desired *status quo*
or offering the least threat to its goal achievement; (4) the goals
toward which the leader is viewed by the group as being able to
contribute essential help must be important enough to effect or
outweigh his refusal or inability to help the group achieve some of
its other goals.

Curriculum leader must provide for teacher goal realization.
One way in which the principal can exert leadership which is
recognized by teachers is to see to it that their suggestions or
proposals are realized. His position with teachers or other individuals would be jeopardized if he provides the occasions for
hearing suggestions and does nothing more. Such a condition
would lead to a withholding of suggestions or ideas in the
future. It is, therefore, highly important for the principal to
develop the conditions whereby there is decision and action
relative to at least some of the ideas furnished by teachers. He
is thus indicating an understanding and insight relative to the
goals of the teachers. This strengthens their confidence in him
not only with respect to his sympathetic consideration of their
goals but also regarding his ability to bring about a fulfillment
of them.

*Curriculum leader must provide for recognition and exami-
nation of limited understandings.* As the curriculum worker
views his tasks he should begin to recognize his limitations.
He just does not know about certain functions which may relate
to leadership. He needs to seek the resources of others to promote leadership. As he indicates his limitations he is being
honest with himself and with others.

As indicated above, the principal is not able to carry through
with all the suggestions offered by teachers. Having implemented some of the suggestions, however, he is then on much
safer ground to indicate his limitations. He can discuss why
he is unable to bring about action on some suggestions and
can indicate a rather frank expression of his thinking regarding them. Furthermore, having indicated a favorable disposition
with respect to their goals, teachers will feel safe to express
what they consider their limitations with respect to questions

which they harbor. They will also be more favorably inclined to the leader's (principal's) goals.

As the principal has shown an understanding and a sensitivity to the problems and ideas of others, he has taken an important step toward the initiation of curriculum improvement. This is especially so when teachers indicate a feeling of understanding and insight regarding his goals and problems. As the principal and teacher approach this condition, they are in the position of learners together. As people are learners together, they will come to recognize the competences which each one has. These competences will then be utilized to help attain individual and group goals.

As we indicated, it is important to ascertain what different people (teachers and others) regard as their limitations. In other words, in the approach to curriculum improvement tasks, people need to operate initially within their limitations. This gives them a sense of security. It follows that in working within their limitations, they will maintain a clarity of purpose and direction. This condition has the effect of providing a consolidation of gains. To consolidate seems advisable and necessary. The attendant condition, however, in the consolidation of definite gains is the establishment of the route toward higher goals. The assurance of a sense of security and clarity in direction should not be permitted to congeal or solidify on a certain level. On the contrary, if real understanding has been established, there will be no rigid stopping places on the route to new meanings. As there develops an understanding of powers of different individuals as well as a degree of consonance in meanings, there will also develop a regard for differences. It should be emphasized that understanding and consonance with respect to powers and meanings must not be equated with blind conformity. Rather, in the development of conditions to learn and work together, it is most essential to provide the impetus for the expression of uniqueness on the part of each individual.

Developing conditions for analyzing instructional practices

The curriculum worker should make every effort to develop the conditions which will stimulate the type of questioning of practices which will move people into action on the points considered. Since the curriculum worker has recognized and accepted his limitations relative to certain tasks, he tries to ascertain what questions he should be asking about those tasks. This may be an important step in providing the setting for "question asking" on the part of those concerned about learning practices.

Raising questions about learning procedures may promote curriculum improvement. As he considers his questions, he seeks the aid of other individuals in the steps to solution. These exchanges of ideas, it is hoped, will lead into further questions raised by others as well as himself. Let's say, for example, that a teacher feels that his classroom organization does not make adequate provision for the development of individual powers of children. He feels, however, that he has developed a satisfactory procedure in the improvement of reading skills by arranging for ability grouping. Someone else may question whether ability grouping is a sufficient step in promoting individual potentialities of children. Although the children may experience a feeling of success and security by reading on levels of their understanding, their efforts may become crystallized on those levels. The process of reading may become a routine which, if continued over a long period of time, may deaden any efforts at greater resourcefulness on the part of children.

As the teacher discusses his problem with other teachers, further questions such as the following may arise: Can one become so obsessed with the convenience of grouping as to regard it as the final answer for fulfilling individual differences in children? Are the different groups dynamic—that is, are children being stimulated to express unique potential and push individual inquiry beyond the group? Are the relationships of children in the groups on a one-to-one basis with the teacher or have provisions been made for multiple child-to-child relationships? Is there an opportunity in this class for communicative stimulation between the groups toward higher levels of individual thinking and performance? Are children asking questions about ideas beyond the immediate reading circle? Have the learning tasks in the group been of such a nature as to provide a self-seeking freedom of inquiry relative to the larger

environment? Have the children been stimulated to create an environment of ideas? Has the teacher been instrumental in developing with children the conditions to further an excitement about, and quest for, knowledge?

As these and other questions are considered together, teachers will tend to examine their practices and test ideas for altering some and introducing new ones. When one begins to ask questions of the type indicated above, he already is developing ideas about his practices. It is reasonable to assume that he would not be asking the questions if he did not already have some ideas about improving the practices he is questioning. For example, in questioning whether his practices contribute to the fulfillment of the potential of children, he is already probably thinking about making accessible for the groups a variety of books on science and other areas of study, simple materials for experimentation, and other resources to develop a wide range of learning experiences. As he exchanges his ideas with other teachers, he is helping to stimulate a questioning attitude in them with regard to their practices. Thus, some vital initial attempts at curriculum improvement have been established.

Locating signs of static instructional performance. Some teachers may raise questions mainly to gain approval of others with respect to practices they are presently using. In other words, the questions are designed for self-justification of the practices which they carry on. Evidence of this will become clear when the teachers do not attempt any changes whatever in their classroom practices. It is clear that the purposes of their questions are to perpetuate the *status quo.* The attitude is one of closed-mindedness with respect to ideas.

The teachers who throw up barriers against ideas other than their own with respect to classroom practices have, perhaps, never experienced any excitement about ideas. Teaching to them might be thought of as a "settling down" situation. They have developed a "grooved" pattern of practices and brook no interference with it. They fight efforts to examine other ideas because they feel secure in a fixed routine. If they do find themselves in a situation where other ideas are offered, they may invent all types of reasons to show why the ideas "won't work."

Detecting points of direction out of static instructional prac-

tices. There are, of course, no clear answers as to the approach toward promoting change in these situations. The task becomes especially difficult when people throw up defenses against ideas other than their own. A possible point of penetration behind the defenses is the pride which people have relative to their performance of a task. The teachers who raise questions of self-justification may lack security but must possess some sense of pride in what they are doing. Also, some teachers may wish to improve their performance with respect to some particular task but feel that by requesting help, they reveal inadequacies.

The curriculum worker should make every effort to locate the points of pride which teachers feel with regard to certain tasks. This he might do by truly becoming a learner about instructional practices. He might call attention to some practice or procedure which the teacher is using rather aptly. The principal might elicit help from a teacher in his efforts to secure better and more teaching materials for the school. The development of interest in ideas about instruction will have a better chance of realization if the conditions for curriculum improvement takes into account that (a) everybody possesses personal worth and resourcefulness, (b) everybody feels a sense of pride with respect to some particular task or tasks which he is pursuing, (c) everybody must have a feeling of status with one or more fellow workers, and (d) that everybody has the freedom to make mistakes.

Developing conditions for eliciting the resourcefulness of all effected by curriculum change. The curriculum worker must become a learner along with others about the nature of the learning experiences which are carried on. He should develop with teachers the conditions for action on many of their suggestions. As pointed out before, he will look at his own limitations and practices and seek to determine what questions he should be asking about them. In all probability he should be asking the same questions that were indicated previously relative to the teacher who was concerned about fulfilling the potential of children. He will seek answers to these and other questions with the help of the teachers and children in the school. Furthermore, he will arrange to make accessible the counsel and wisdom of parents and other citizens in the pursuit

of better learning experiences for children and young people. A similar pattern should eventuate in the whole school as teachers assemble the wisdom and counsel of each other, the children, the parents and other citizens, relative to the improvement of the conditions for learning.

An important responsibility of the principal is to utilize the special strengths which teachers have in promoting resourcefulness in curriculum change. One teacher will, for example, have considerable knowledge about science and can, therefore, be helpful to other teachers in furthering science learnings. Another teacher will have many ideas about improving reading. His counsel will certainly be solicited. Social studies is the particular strength of another teacher. In his classroom he has many examples of approach to expanded meanings in this area. Still another teacher exhibits great resourcefulness in promoting mathematical meanings. His ideas will certainly be welcomed by other teachers.

The principal with the help of the teachers should make the necessary arrangements for the exchange of ideas for the purpose of improving learning experiences. He and the teachers will evaluate together at various meetings the nature of the curriculum improvement taking place as a result of the exchange of ideas and resources. It will be noted what ideas are being developed by the children as a result of the learning experiences ventured. Through the contacts made by teachers and principal at parent nights, parent-teacher association meetings, parent-teacher conferences, and other forms of communication, different individuals will be brought into the exchange of ideas arrangement to help establish and refine the goals in learning. Once or twice a year, there might be a little White House Conference designed to develop some new meanings and refine others in terms of contemporary needs and societal direction. This conference will be conducted in the familiar setting of learning—the classrooms of the school. At subsequent meetings of groups of teachers and the principal, these meanings will be analyzed and incorporated in curriculum planning.

The discussion in the previous pages has indicated a pattern for the initiation of curriculum improvement. The approach emphasized is informal but intensive and within the familiarity of the classroom setting. The principal was designated as the leader who has the responsibility of initiating the beginnings in curriculum improvement. As the process develops, leadership should come from teachers and other individuals. The conditions must be developed where teachers and the principal began to ask questions about the instructional practices and seek to implement these in curriculum improvement. They seek further to determine what other questions they should be asking and develop the resources for action on the questions. Through the arrangements for exchange of ideas will develop that eagerness and courage on the part of individuals which will tend to enhance the conditions for learning to ever higher and more productive levels.

TRANSITION INTO CONDITIONS FOR A HIGHER LEVEL OF CURRICULUM IMPROVEMENT

Having developed the conditions for learning together and exchanging ideas regarding instructional practices, the initial approach to curriculum development has been established. The initial conditions, however, are not enough. The curriculum workers (teachers, principal, curriculum consultant, and others) must constantly build upon these conditions so as to provide for the maximum levels of curriculum improvement. Throughout this book it is emphasized that teachers tend to treat ideas with children and young people in a manner which parallels the conditions under which they learned to treat ideas with other adults. It is important, then, to develop those conditions which will stimulate that treatment of ideas consistent with the highest level of human understanding and competence in terms of contemporary needs.

Developing freedom for competition in evolvement of ideas

It is important, first of all, for curriculum workers to bring about those conditions wherein individuals attain such a degree of compulsiveness toward evolving ideas that face-saving behavior is eliminated from the scene. Someone has said, "Individuals could bring about great achievements if they did not care who received credit for them." The conditions for evolvement of ideas should promote that freedom of inquiry within which individuals welcome competition in ideas. Under these conditions they do not fear individuals whose ideas may be better than their own. The "loss of face" feeling which regards ideas as threats under certain conditions becomes altered into a new status achieved in total productivity of knowledge under the conditions of freedom of inquiry. In other words, dislodgment from one's status level becomes a victory of ideas in which he shares.

Providing for unrestricted flow of ideas. Under the conditions which effect a shift from face-saving behavior to provision for inclusiveness of ideas, individuals approach other individuals as people rather than artificial creatures. It is necessary to develop that freedom where individuals will exhibit their resourcefulness in a sense of release. We have too many schools where a condition of inhibition rather than release of ideas seems to prevail. This condition often emanates from the *top*. The channels of idea production are downward and, to a degree, upward in anticipated responses. Idea production under these conditions is limited to the "bosses" and the "key" individuals. This is curriculum making by directive and response. It is a narrow-sighted view and operates to limit idea production to a confined pattern.

Real leadership provides for the production of ideas through "horizontal" channels. This means that ideas evolve as freely and are considered as important at one place in the channel as any other place. The communication system is such that everyone draws strength through the unrestricted flow of ideas. The process of ideas does not limit other ideas. Consequently, the resourcefulness of every individual is provided for. Furthermore, the impact provided by the unrestricted flow of ideas causes a voluntary compulsiveness for intelligent action on them.

When the sense of release has been provided which makes people shed the inhibitions which characterize the face-saving type of status feelings, they begin to respect each other's personality and potential. When teachers work with each other in the light of these conditions, they begin to respect the great potential and resourcefulness residing in every individual. They will use this sense of freedom in examining questions and ideas relating to their tasks. Since there are no limitations in their efforts to test ideas designed to improve instructional practices, they accept this responsibility and will act on it. They will approach children as people just as they approach each other as people. The pattern which has been developed in their relationships with each other—that is, that wisdom comes not from afar but from your co-workers—will be carried on with the children and young people.

Developing conditions for individuals to pursue ideas beyond themselves

Curriculum workers should make possible those conditions which intensify the efforts of individuals to inquire into and study ideas beyond the curriculum workers and themselves.

When people operate under conditions which have provided the channels for freedom of inquiry, egocentrism is eliminated. In place of egocentric attitudes will develop an intensification of the quest for knowledge beyond the familiar confines of operation. Real leadership is evident when individuals are stimulated to develop ideas which are beyond those of the leader. A great teacher is one who has freed the conditions of learning from the limitations of embarrassment and shame when the learner exhibits an enthusiasm for ideas. Another characteristic of a great teacher is the ability to stimulate children to go beyond him in their learning. A curriculum worker should encourage individuals to pursue problems and test ideas which they cannot readily conceive. An example of this is the study of the factors which operate in integration and disintegration of family living. One may hypothesize from a position of logic that integration is characterized by an absence of conflict and that the reverse is true with disintegration. A study of individuals and groups may fail to lend support to the hypothesis. Thus further study is needed and new meanings are discovered. Perhaps conflict must be accentuated in promoting integration. Perhaps the suppression of conflict is a disintegrating factor. Under what conditions could conflict become a force in bringing about a positive understanding of family living? When does conflict constitute a threat to well-being? What other factors are involved in bringing about integration in family living? Whatever direction the study of the factors take, the effective leader welcomes and encourages deviations and findings contrary to expectations which he entertained.

Intensifying conditions for inquiry into periphery of knowledge

A very important condition which should be brought about by curriculum workers and others is to intensify the learning environment in such a way as to cause individuals to inquire into the periphery of knowledge. It will be noted that we are now equating the learning environment with the setting for action on curriculum improvement. A great deal has been stated about the conditions for the development of ideas which, in turn, raise the quality of learning experiences for children.

In order to establish the dynamics for curriculum change and development, it is necessary to promote that impact on thinking which will take ideas beyond the immediate perspective or dimensions. The process may be illustrated in connection with the development of content in science. Let's take, for example, the topic of balance. Many science books for children and young people speak about how the balance of nature has been disturbed by people. One aspect of this which is frequently mentioned is the exploitation of the forest lands of this country. Although there have been measures taken toward reforestation, this has not occurred at the same pace as the removal of trees. The depletion of vast forest areas has resulted in erosion, making much of the land useless for future growth of any form of vegetation. Many facts are available to substantiate the type of unbalancing of nature described above. Frequently, however, the study of balance stops here. The study of balance needs to go much farther than has been indicated. It should be considered, for example, whether the unbalancing which takes place in the depletion of forests in one instance is outweighed by the restoration of balance somewhere else. The thousands of building developments taking place all over the country have contributed to some degree in promoting a balance in living for some people. As a result of this, more and more people are having the opportunity of moving out of congested living areas into more ample quarters and more suitable communities. Thus, a new balance in living is being realized.

Taking ideas into new and enlarged dimensions of understanding. It is suggested from the above that ideas are being taken from one perspective or dimension into new and enlarged understandings. The new understandings can be used in establishing still other relationships of ideas and meanings. It is important, therefore, for the staff and other curriculum workers to develop the conditions which will lead into a more penetrating analysis and testing of the ideas of balance. It is conceivable, for example, that balance as related to human beings means the promotion of the welfare of the individual. The question then arises, What is meant by providing for the welfare of the individual? Other questions which might arise are the following: How is welfare related to balance in living? Is the welfare, as popularly conceived, equated with that of comfort and security? Are there limitations to this meaning? As the result of newfound needs and wants of people throughout the world and development of wider horizons of world understanding, are the original meanings about welfare being superseded by new ones? Has the atomic age ushered in new concepts of balance? Is the question of survival demanding the development of new dimensions with respect to balance? Must the ideas of sacrifice, self-denial, empathy, and strategic understanding become weapons in effecting a new sense of balance? Does the realization of a new sense of balance demand a new personality structure? What is the relation of balance to certainty? What are the components of the personality structure which tend to contribute to uncertainty? To certainty?

Making the classroom a laboratory for peripheral inquiry. The pursuit of meanings into the peripheral areas of inquiry suggests that each classroom must in a sense become a laboratory of ideas. It becomes obvious as one looks at the above questions that, as the topic of balance is pursued into the peripheral area of inquiry, it assumes new dimensions of meanings. The questions as they are developed demand study, research, and an attitude which is a far cry from the simple insights needed in connection with the familiar concept of balance. There are no upper limits in the peripheral areas of inquiry. It is suggested, therefore, that in addition to each classroom becoming a laboratory of ideas, one classroom or a separate room should be made into a laboratory for the study, research, and analysis of an extended range of meanings.

The curriculum workers and staff should exert leadership in making graphically available an abundance of resources in the laboratory for the handling of ideas. A useful supply of professional and content materials should be made accessible in each school unit. Besides this, there should be a sizeable library of professional and content materials with provisions for easy and prompt accessibility for use. Resource materials on recent research as well as research in process should be available for curriculum workers and staff. Universities and colleges have a responsibility to make known and available services in personnel and materials to improve the conditions for learning in schools. The School of Education of the University of Connecticut through a Curriculum Center makes available to school systems over twelve thousand pamphlets, guides, research studies, and descriptions of practices carried on in schools all over the country. Besides these services, curriculum laboratories, designed to improve the conditions for learning in school systems in the state of Connecticut, are conducted on request. Many states, universities, and colleges over the country have curriculum centers and other services which may be utilized for the improvement of instructional practices.

In addition to the types of services indicated above, it is extremely important to bring into the laboratory of ideas resource people representative of the fields of sociology, psychology, history, English, science, mathematics, and others. Just as important is the utilization of local and regional resource people from labor, industry, professions and various service occupations and institutions. Some of these resource people should be present as much as possible as ideas are being examined for the improvement of learning experiences. The conditions should be such as will utilize the services of these resource people not as experts but as learners together with the staff in bringing about curriculum improvement. Since the curriculum extends meanings and understandings throughout the community, the people in the community will be in a favorable position to evaluate the effectiveness of learning if they are continuously involved in helping provide direction to that learning with the professional school personnel.

Many of the subsequent sections of this book deal more elaborately with the development of the conditions for productiveness in ideas. As individuals approach the study and examination of ideas in terms of the types of questions indicated, there will develop an excitement about ideas. This excitement should have the effect of producing a feeling of compulsiveness in the pursuit of questions, together with the many relationships involved, toward their ultimate meanings. Within these conditions there will be stages for the consolidation and synthesis of meanings and ideas to be incorporated into instructional practices with children and youth.

It will be noted that the approach described is a far cry from some of the popular conceptions of curriculum improvement. It is vastly more far-reaching than the development of a guide to curriculum experiences, the making of a course of study, the revision of the book list for English, the changing of a reading series, the production of a resource unit in social studies, the preparation of a list of community resources, and the derivation of a new curriculum design. In a sense, the approach indicated incorporates features of each of the activities noted above. It goes much farther, however, in that the selection of content is based on the integration of past and contemporary meanings with the new dimensions in thinking derived by individuals in a laboratory for the handling of ideas. This laboratory gives rise to the ongoing experiences of children and youth as well as the staff and other curriculum workers. The laboratory for curriculum improvement needs, in most respects, to be the same for both the pupils, staff, special curriculum personnel, parents and other citizens, and the administration, because (a) they are all learners together about instructional practices and (b) the idea-producing setting of the teachers must find a counterpart in the instructional setting with children and youth.

Accentuating differences in people for resourcefulness in high-level meanings

The conditions for evolving ideas should accentuate the importance of differences in people so that resources will be brought to bear toward a high level of meanings. An accentuation of differences with respect to ideas will develop a unified feeling about the differences on the part of individuals. In other words, when the conditions for a freedom toward differences are provided, there will be an accompanying respect for the ideas of the different individuals. Thus, there will be a more receptive attitude because ideas are in competition without the preconceived conditions of prejudice. The conditions for individual resourcefulness should facilitate production of high-level ideas and action as well as strengthened powers of individual curiosity with respect to knowledge.

Valuing differences in international scene should elevate quality in ideas and understanding. When individuals come to respect and seek to encourage differences, they will increasingly tend to recognize the waste and futility associated with the traditional practice of mentally and physically dividing people. The valuing of differences in people is treated in other chapters of the book with particular emphasis on it in Chapter 6.

The importance of accentuating and valuing differences may be illustrated by referring to the evolving international scene. At this writing there is a clamor from many quarters for more emphasis on science and mathematics in the schools. The hue and cry about the inclusion of more science and mathematics stems from some successes of the scientists in the U.S.S.R. which seem to surpass the successes of scientists in the United States. Without intending to be critical of well-intentioned individuals, the argument for more science and mathematics in the curriculum overlooks or disregards an important aspect—that of differences. It is just as important for scientists in the United States to value and understand the differences in scientists in the U.S.S.R. as to emulate their performance. The differences then should be used to elevate quality in science in this country but, perhaps, of rather a different character than that obtaining in the U.S.S.R. We hasten to say, also, that development and performance in science should not be geared by a face-saving type of behavior.

Utilizing differences for the development of new meanings. The idea of including more science and mathematics *per se* or because of an incident is an oversimplification. The idea, in effect, indicates that more mathematics and science will take care of the difficulties. That "more of the same" will be a remedy is questionable, especially in view of the present international scene. If a clamor for something is to be made, it should be made for an examination of the present content of curriculum, for new dimensions in ideas. A further inquiry should be to ascertain what conditions have been developed with staffs and citizens to provide for a free flow of ideas relative to the world scene. The conditions should have the ingredients to intensify the efforts of individuals to ask and examine new questions regarding the content to be developed and handled in the curriculum so that all areas of study will function in promoting understanding, competences, and action relative to the evolving international scene.

Utilizing differences to promote incentives for greater scholarship. The respect accorded differences will tend to act as an incentive for greater scholarship on the part of individuals. As people of the community become involved with a staff which has set for itself the task of seeking knowledge with respect to ideas, they too will assume the attitude of search with respect to meanings. This, in turn, will tend to establish confidence in the differences in individuals as well as public confidence in teaching. The analysis of meanings from many sources together with a location of the circumstances which produced the meanings should find a parallel condition in the classroom as students work toward logical and sound conclusions relative to problems and issues. We hasten to emphasize that the handling of ideas must establish the route to decision. The arrival at logical and sound conclusions as a result of study and research is not only rewarding to individuals but, also, productive of new ideas as well as being conducive to the development of renewed and strengthened efforts in the direction of constructive implementation.

Developing conditions for weighing of issues

The conditions providing for the production of ideas should develop a careful weighing of issues before decision. The absence of these conditions frequently results in a "slanted" decision—that is, it is based on facts dealing with one phase of the question. This might be illustrated in connection with articles expressing belief that family solidarity may be impaired when both the father and mother work. Some writers feel that a child's potential growth and development may be interrupted by both parents working. Others contend that this is not necessarily true. Still others contend that this condition is, perhaps, one of the greatest factors in promoting delinquency.

In a study of this question, it is important to analyze many factors before drawing a conclusion. Some of the questions which might be raised in connection with a study of this problem would be as follows: What are some of the basic needs of children at different age levels? How does the culture influence the parent-child relationship? Do the basic needs necessitate a shorter or longer period of dependence in our culture as compared to others? Do the studies on wayward children reveal a positive correlation between behavior and both parents' employment? What constitutes neglect of children? Are some children given an overdose of attention? What are some different patterns of relationships which exist between children and parents? What are some of the ties which are built between parents and children? How may ties be strengthened? What are the types of behavior on the part of parents which are designed to relax some ties for the purpose of promoting independence in children? Is there a difference between some "ties" and "having an understanding?"

These and many other questions would lead to a rather intensive study of parent-child relationships. In all probability the subject matter derived from a study of the relationships of children to parents in our culture would lead to more far-reaching and significant conclusions than those revealed in some articles in magazines. Furthermore, the ideas about family living could be instrumental in promoting valuable competences in young people relative to this institution.

Developing conditions for thinking beyond "surprises"

The conditions for curriculum improvement should be so intense with respect to the advances of knowledge on the frontier of thinking that there will be no occasion for "suprises." New areas of inquiry must be examined. The environment of the curriculum worker should be so replete with advanced ideas and facts that the individuals operate in that speculative state as to be beyond "surprises." This is in line with the idea that the curriculum workers and staff operate on the principle of inclusiveness of knowledge. The highest forms of inquiry need not be reserved to a few individuals but may become the province of all people. An imperative in a pluralistic society is that all people be informed about issues so that each individual may become resourceful about them.

An event which illustrates the importance of the principle of operating beyond "surprises" is the successful launching of "Sputnik" by the U.S.S.R. This occasioned a surprise and feeling of consternation in people which, in some instances, almost approached a state of hysteria. This occasion also gave rise to a feeling of "loss of face" on the part of some people in high places, to say nothing of others. If the conditions for curriculum improvement make provision for the pursuit of ideas into higher realms of inquiry, sharp "surprises" are not apt to occur. The frontier thinkers in science do not experience the impact of surprises. Their thinking penetrates beyond the element of surprise.

Analyzing directional questions of frontier thinking in science and other areas for ideas. Frontier thinking needs to be injected into the conditions for curriculum development so that directional questions will be analyzed for ideas. Many of the learning experiences in science programs in some elementary and secondary schools are devoid of the meanings which are giving direction to people in the world today. The same condition exists in some schools in connection with the other areas of study. On the other hand, some schools have had programs which were always in the vanguard of scientific thinking. Some schools, also, have been in the forefront of educational effectiveness in the humanities, mathematics, and the social studies. In many cases, these same schools have certainly advanced beyond the thinking of the people in the communities with respect to new ideas in the sciences, international understanding, and social issues. This, of course, has been aided by the enlistment of the leadership of frontier thinkers in various fields to work cooperatively with the staff, administration and students.

Curriculum workers must continuously provide the conditions for extending the area of inquiry beyond the familiar dimensions of ideas. This means, of course, that elements of the most advanced thinking beyond the familiar dimensions must be brought into the conditions for learning. The ideas about new sources of energy should be translated into meanings which can be handled by children and youth. The latest discoveries about man's adaptability to different conditions should be accessible in the child's laboratory of ideas. Topics, such as the relation of behavior to different temperatures, should be examined and tested for facts and ideas. Meanings relative to the topic of defense should be analyzed for high-level understandings. For example, questions such as the following need to be pursued into high levels of inquiry: Are weapons designed to destroy the physical body or to impair mental stability? What is meant by the statement, "Bombs hit life 'whole' "? Is it possible to equate bombs with ideas? What is your theory about what constitutes destruction? Construction? In view of the above questions what might be the beginnings of a plausible theory about defense?

Questions such as those indicated, along with many others in different fields, should develop meanings which take people beyond the possibilities of "sharp surprises" in knowledge. Certainly, as curriculum people work with ideas in the manner indicated, there should be no lack of excitement about learning or the compulsiveness for ever greater understanding.

Concluding statement

It is hoped that the various principles developed in this chapter will provide some suggestions to teachers, administrators, curriculum consultants, and others for further steps in promoting better learning experiences with children and young people. The ideas presented are certainly not exhaustive. Many schools are proceeding with curriculum development programs using these and other principles and ideas effectively. The dynamics which lie in the conditions for the handling of ideas have been experienced by many groups. The experiences should not be confined. They should be extended to others. It is rewarding to sense the realization of new understandings which comes from the handling of ideas, from learning together about new meanings and relationships. It is even more rewarding to know that those with whom we have been associated in the pursuit of high-level thinking have advanced way beyond us in the realm of inquiry. When this condition obtains, one can truly say that he has been a participant in great teaching. In the continuance of this level of operation are the dynamics of curriculum improvement.

◦2◦

Conditions for Continuous
Curriculum Improvement

THIS CHAPTER IS MORE OR LESS A DESCRIPTION OF THE CONSOLIDAT-
ing conditions for the principles of curriculum improvement
which have been developed in the previous chapter. The discussion will center mostly on a description of the machinery
which evolves out of the conditions for curriculum change and
development which must already be provided. An attempt will
be made to indicate how this machinery becomes self-perpetuat-
ing.

The organization for perpetual curriculum improvement
might be likened to a centrifugal force. Curriculum development begins in the classroom and proceeds to involve other
classrooms and the school unit. From the school unit the channels of communication and interaction extend outward and
around to encompass the developments in the other classrooms
and schools of the system. At the same time, the base of operation never leaves the familiar setting of the classroom. The different classrooms constitute a sort of network of transmitters
and antennae. The air waves which are transmitted and received
are ideas. As ideas are incorporated in the instructional setting,
this fact is transmitted, together with other ideas already contemplated, throughout the system. The ideas which are transmitted will originate in as many "studios" as there are classrooms. At times, as ideas are sifted and synthesized, several
"studios" will broadcast as a unit.

This analogous description is intended to provide a type of prelude to the development of the machinery for continuous curriculum improvement. For example, studios may be equated to study and resource committees. In each school unit there may be as many committees as there are laboratories or centers for idea development in connection with particular areas of learning. A combination of studios are the same as representatives from committees of school units combining into a system-wide or regional committee necessary especially in larger school systems. One difference must be emphasized from actual broadcasting studios—that is, that the curriculum studios also have antennae and make as much use of those as they do of the transmitters.

Since it is assumed that curriculum improvement is an integral phase of every staff member's responsibility, it follows that the conditions for the development of improved learning experiences will be promoted in each classroom and school unit. The approach to curriculum improvement together with the initial conditions and the transition to higher levels of implementation of ideas has already been described in the previous chapter. The nature of the leadership evolved has also been indicated.

An obvious observation about any school is that it has some kind of ongoing curriculum. Most schools have what is referred to as a subject curriculum. As was indicated at the outset of the chapter, some curriculums, regardless of the type, are better than others. The difference lies in the manner in which ideas are handled within the subject, the core, or whatever form the curriculum may assume. This is so, granted that no restricting limitations to freedom for inquiry have been imposed by the administration. As was indicated in previous sections, no attempt will be made to indicate any revolutionary pattern as to the type of subjects which should be included in the curriculum. It is our contention, however, that the ultimate in educational effectiveness cannot be realized if the subject or field of study is handled in such a manner as to restrict the productiveness of ideas. Stated in another way, *every subject or field of study, in order to provide the ultimate opportunities for children and young people to approach meanings with intelligence, must be freed for the handling of ideas.*

The handling of ideas is a correlate of curriculum improvement. By the same token, curriculum improvement must find its counterpart in the production and handling of ideas with children and young people in the classroom. This leads into the conditions for the evolvement of the machinery for continuous curriculum development.

MACHINERY FOR CONTINUOUS CURRICULUM IMPROVEMENT IN THE ELEMENTARY SCHOOL

Most elementary schools have subject area patterns somewhat as follows: language arts, arithmetic or elementary mathematics, science or nature study, music, art, physical education or playground activities, and social studies or history and geography. Some elementary schools separate the language arts into reading, spelling, and language or English. Some elementary schools combine the art program with arts and crafts. In the previous sections, the rationale of curriculum development through a process of idea evolvement has been discussed so it will not be developed further here. As leadership has been generated in the staff toward the development and analysis of ideas, this pattern will assume a continuum of operation. The conditions have come to be charged with those elements which have promoted an excitement and compulsiveness on the part of individuals with respect to idea evolvement in the various subject areas.

Making the classroom a laboratory or center for handling ideas

Since the classroom is the laboratory for the handling of ideas, the curriculum workers, staff, children, parents and other citizens will function together in this center. The several class rooms then become the laboratories or centers for curriculum improvement. It was indicated in Chapter 1 that different teachers have different backgrounds and strengths relative to ideas. Although there is no intention to advocate departmentalism, it is, nevertheless, reasonable to assume that individual teachers are often more effective in working with one subject than another. It is proposed that every classroom become some kind of center or laboratory for ideas. It is extremely important, also, that there be unity in ideas as between one subject area and others. It is perfectly logical and conducive to resourcefulness, however, to encourage individual staff members to expand the laboratory of ideas in terms of the special strengths and capabilities. For example, one teacher may have a fine background and special interest in the area of science. It would make good sense to encourage this teacher to emphasize science in his laboratory of ideas. Another teacher would show an emphasis in mathematics. Still another would have a comprehensive portrayal of ideas in connection with social studies. Unity of ideas and knowledge would be promoted as the staff and curriculum workers met together at different times in the various rooms for study, research, and discussion. Each teacher, in connection with the responsibility for a self-contained classroom, would have all areas represented even though a particular area is emphasized.

Developing conditions for unity and quality in learning experiences. Each classroom would become an "idea" room for the purpose of promoting quality with respect to the learning experiences of children. Each room, of course, would be used at different times by a group of teachers and other curriculum workers to develop and examine ideas and add to, and raise, the quality of experiences for children. Children and individuals other than teachers may also be participants and learners in these settings for curriculum development.

It is envisioned that the various bulletin boards, tables, and bookshelves will be constituted as centers for the portrayal of ideas in relation to learning experiences. Since it is assumed that the classrooms are self-contained units, the bulletin boards, tables, and so on, will carry ideas and meanings relative to different learning areas. For example, one part of the room will be developed into a center for science, another for social studies, another for arithmetic, and so on. If the teacher in this classroom has considerable background and interest in social studies, that area may occupy the most prominent place in the room. It may be that this classroom will come to be the meeting place for the development of ideas to improve instructional practices in the social studies. In another classroom, the teacher's interests and special capabilities may have pointed the major emphasis toward science. This room may be the best meeting place for the handling of ideas to bring about better learning experiences in science.

Another room may be the best place for the development of meanings relative to elementary mathematics. The groups of teachers and other workers in curriculum that meet in the different rooms will not be segregated in terms of subject areas. The group, meeting for the purpose of handling ideas about science, will be composed of teachers and others who will have varied interests and strengths. The people of this group who have backgrounds and capabilities in connection with study areas other than science will tend to bring unity to the ideas designed to improve science experiences with children. The same would be true with the groups meeting in the other classrooms.

All through this book, much emphasis is directed to the development of the conditions for learning. The conditions for learning are equated with curriculum development. It has been emphasized, further, that the conditions should provide for an intensified learning environment which would create a compulsiveness and excitement about ideas. In other words, it is important for the staff and other curriculum workers to provide the impact which will produce a free flow of ideas. In addition, the impact should promote an intensity of action sufficiently strong and continuous as to affect extended levels of learning with individuals and groups. The process of promoting the conditions for idea development has been dealt with at considerable length in the previous pages and in other chapters of the book. It might be helpful to indicate how the conditions could be developed in connection with one of the idea classrooms suggested.

Developing the approach to science ideas in one classroom center. For illustrative purposes, let's assume that a group of teachers who have been working for some time in the manner just described are planning the next meeting to be devoted to the study and discussion of ideas about the topic of "balance" as developed in science. It is decided that the meeting will be held in the classroom of the teacher who has *given particular attention* to the science phase of the centers of interest. It is decided, further, that this teacher and two others will prepare the setting for the meeting. These two other teachers are, of course, interested in science but their interests and capabilities tend toward social studies and language arts respectively.

The three teachers have two or three meetings to decide on ideas about the meeting. Their planning could be done in connection with questions such as the following: What can we do to get the thinking beyond the point of considering the topic of balance as related only to nature, conservation, and erosion? How might we produce the effect of stimulation of ideas beyond the point of topical outlines and lists? How can we provide the impact for relationships of ideas? As the three staff members ponder these questions, they arrive at four tasks which they consider at least a partial answer to the questions. They will secure an opaque projector. They will try to secure several pictures, cartoons, and drawings which they feel might provide the stimulus for ideas about the topic or idea of *"balance."* They will enlist the interest of the children and, perhaps, the art teacher in preparing cardboard strips carrying the captions indicated below.

MAN DISTURBS THE BALANCE OF NATURE
A STORY OF BIOLOGICAL CONSERVATION
BALANCE AND PROTECTIVE COLORATION
THE RELATIONSHIP OF EXPLOITATION TO BALANCE
BALANCE AS RELATED TO EROSION OF RESOURCES, HUMAN AND NATURAL
BALANCE AS "SURVIVAL OF THE FITTEST"
"WEIGHED IN THE BALANCE AND FOUND WANTING"
BALANCE AND THE ROUTINE OF LIVING
BALANCE AS A CRITERION IN THE ANALYSIS OF THE CONSEQUENCES OF
    FEELINGS
BALANCE OF POWER
BALANCE AS RELATED TO CERTAINTY
THE STORY OF BALANCE AND ENVIRONMENTAL CONDITIONS
BALANCE AND HUMAN UNDERSTANDING

Another task which the teachers set for themselves is to use the pictures, cartoons, and drawings and the captions indicated above with children in developing ideas about "balance." The captions indicated will be tacked up in prominent places in the room where the meeting is to be held. Most of the pictures, cartoons, and drawings will also be put on bulletin boards. Several of these, however, will be used for projection purposes at the outset of the meeting. Suitable pictures or drawings which they might select for projection are an erosion scene, a scene representing people in conflict, a blueprint representing plans for a housing development together with the surrounding areas, a picture of a street with large and beautiful houses showing an air of leisure and friendliness, a pastoral scene containing many cows, and possibly one or two others.

As the members of the group arrive, they might find, for example, a prominent visualization of the pastoral scene. Since man disturbs the balance of nature by bringing in an animal that has not been there before or bringing into the habitat too many plants or animals of one kind, the scene will be approached on the basis of these facts. The many cows in the habitat would, of course, furnish a clue to some meanings about balance as related to nature. Nature will be disturbed if the cows rely for sustenance on the grass growing in the area. Soon the grass will be depleted and the cows will have to be moved to another area. This might give the grass a chance to be recovered in the former area. If, however, rains come, serious erosion may result, thus lessening the chance for growth to be restored.

The discussion would relate to the lack of foresight on the part of the owner of the cows to allow this condition to come to pass. Suggestions would be ventured as to what the owner should have done. He probably should have supplemented the feed supply of the cows in the form of ensilage or in some other way. Furthermore, he probably should have acquired more grass areas so that no particular area would have been so seriously affected. The discussion might go in other directions, such as providing a cornfield to supplement the feed supply for the cows.

Having provoked some discussion relative to simple concepts about balance, the other scenes and pictures would be projected. Discussion following the erosion scene would resemble pretty much the pattern indicated above. The questions raised would be in connection with ideas about reclamation of eroded areas, and the substitutions developed by the frontiers of scientific thinking.

The ideas relative to the scene representing people in conflict would lead to a somewhat abstract thinking in dealing with questions of balance. The blueprint of plans for a housing development should lead into many questions about balance in living. Congested housing certainly contributes to unbalanced conditions regarding living. On the other hand, plans which take into consideration the needs for recreation and other aspects of living would tend to promote balance. The picture of the street with the large and beautiful houses would indicate some sense of balance which, for economic reasons, could not be realized by many people. The pictures and scenes projected would certainly open up many points of inquiry and analysis regarding the topic of "balance." The ideas that would evolve as a result of the projected scenes would range all the way from the effects of erosion on the lives of people to the new sense of balance developed by them as they take up residence in a new neighborhood.

It is evident that if the pictures and scenes would provoke discussion and study such as indicated above, the purposes which the three teachers had in mind with respect to this meeting could well be realized. As the ideas of balance are related to integration, equilibrium, and sense of stability in people, the thinking should in all probability go beyond the development of lists and topical outlines. Furthermore, as the topic of balance is pursued into the many relationships of ideas incident to it, a unity of knowledge and understanding will be furthered. It is hoped that some impact for evolving new ideas about the topic of balance would be established.

Extending the approach to science ideas with children. The pictures and scenes projected could very well constitute the subject matter or agenda for one meeting. The questions raised and the ideas which are developed would be used in bringing quality to the learning experiences carried on with children in the classroom. No doubt, some of the ideas which are discussed in this meeting have already been considered with children on their level of understanding. The captions appearing on another page have also been used with children. This, of course, is in accord with the principle that curriculum improvement must be carried on in the familiar setting of the classrooms of the curriculum workers.

Children are always involved with the curriculum improvement tasks in the actual learning situation and, frequently, in the development of ideas with groups of adults. To illustrate, let's take one of the captions—BALANCE AS RELATED TO CERTAINTY. With children, one might establish some meaning relative to this caption by discussing the daily routines people go through in carrying on with the activities of living. The conditions for the initial evolvement of ideas about balance and certainty may be established by tacking the cardboard strip on a bulletin board. In connection with the discussion about routine, the thinking about the relation of balance to certainty could be developed somewhat as follows:

Our daily routines.

Unsatisfactory phases of the routine.
Satisfying phases of the routine.

Happenings about which we are always sure.

Happenings about which we are not sure.

What is it that we would like to see happen?

What are some of the things now happening which we would like to avoid?

Unwanted experiences.
What types of unwanted experiences seem necessary?
What types seem unnecessary?

Let's examine our routine again.
What can we do about our routines to make them more satisfying and useful?

Relating science ideas to other areas of study. The above headings and questions are, of course, only possibilities. Others, or different ones, may develop as teachers and children discuss and study together the topic of BALANCE AS RELATED TO CERTAINTY. The study, research, and discussion by the children and teacher will serve to provide ideas related to the headings and questions. It is hoped, of course, that as a result of handling ideas about the topic of balance and certainty, the thinking will be expanded into meaningful abstract concepts, especially as they relate to conflict and international understanding. It should be noted that the learning experiences about balance and certainty could not be confined to science alone. Many of the ideas would be dealt with in the social studies, language arts, the arts, mathematics, and other areas of study. The classrooms would be constituted as laboratories for the handling of ideas. Every field of study would be used in connection with the ideas. With these conditions a thread of unity with respect to ideas and knowledge would be furthered.

The suggested plan in the previous pages dealt with a meeting to study and examine ideas relative to the topic of balance. The plan was to initiate the study in terms of science emphases. As the plan developed, however, it became evident that the ideas about balance are related to other fields of study. The group of curriculum workers who dealt with the topic of balance would, in all probability, need to have several meetings to treat the related topics for learning experiences. It could be, of course, that two or three groups would be working with the topic of balance. Then, too, some of the groups would be handling ideas in connection with other topics related to such headings as communications, social understanding, and behavior.

It was suggested that the various classrooms be constituted as "idea rooms" or laboratories for the handling of ideas. An alternative arrangement would be to establish curriculum development centers or laboratories in other places than classrooms. For example, the library could be arranged so that one or two sections of it could be used by groups to study and develop ideas relative to certain topics. The lunchroom and teachers' lounge could be arranged so as to provide settings for the analysis of ideas for learning experiences. The alternative conditions suggested are treated in other chapters of the book so will not be developed here. These separate centers should, of course, not be designed to reduce the classrooms as functioning "idea" rooms and laboratories for the development of high quality learning experiences. In other words, the separate centers should serve rather to supplement or extend the study, research, and analysis of ideas which emanate from the classrooms as laboratories.

MACHINERY FOR CONTINUOUS CURRICULUM IMPROVEMENT IN THE SECONDARY SCHOOL

The machinery for curriculum improvement in the secondary schools would follow rather closely the pattern of the elementary schools. Perhaps the main differences in the development of the conditions for curriculum improvement in the secondary schools lie in the more advanced and abstract treatment of ideas and the more or less compartmentalized arrangement of subject areas. The major unifying topics would, in most respects, be similar to those used in connection with curriculum improvement tasks in the elementary school.

Problems in unity in development of learning experiences

Although the various classrooms in the secondary school may be constituted as "idea" rooms or laboratories for the study and analysis of ideas, the problem of unity in the development of learning experiences is somewhat greater on this level than in the elementary school. For example, it is much easier to bring about unification toward ideas in the areas of social studies, English, and art than in the areas of chemistry, physics, and mathematics. This is due to the nature of the subject content, as it is usually conceived.

There seems to be a feeling among some educators that the conditions for a unified approach to ideas may lead to a relaxation of intensity and thoroughness of treatment of the specific subjects which furnish the resources for the ideas. This feeling is well founded if the organization for unity in subject matter is more or less mechanical. If the main emphasis on unity seems to be the task of effecting a combination of two or more subject areas into a stated block of time, there exists a possible danger of superficial treatment of ideas. The reason is that the teacher feels he has to serve two "masters"; that is, the "mechanism" and "unity." Chances are that both "masters" will suffer. Furthermore, if the conditions for the handling of ideas tend toward an emphasis on consensus to the point of a loss in individual resourcefulness, the effectiveness of unification is reduced. These conditions would also tend to interfere with the dynamics of curriculum improvement.

One of the mistakes that usually accompanies the launching of a curriculum improvement program is the initial tendency to alter the existing curriculum design or subject pattern. The difficulty here lies in an "either-or" definition of curriculum problems. This is noted in the conflict often precipitated between the subject matter enthusiasts and the advocates of the "unified areas" approach to teaching and learning. The debate continues apace without any real clarification of issues and, hence, without any development of ideas toward improved instructional practices. This ultimately may result in a "dead-center" condition of the curriculum improvement attempt. Everyone has gone through an excitement which finds its counterpart in frustration. Such an experience may have a debilitating effect on any future attempts at curriculum change.

Handling ideas within subject necessitates content from other areas

Since unity comes about through the relating of ideas in thinking toward more mature meanings and understandings, neither the subject matter nor the "unified studies" enthusiasts have a premium on its attainment. Unity of knowledge may well result from an intensive handling of ideas by the teacher and students, within a subject such as history, English, or chemistry. As a teacher develops the conditions for an intensive handling of ideas in a particular subject, however, he will be impelled to draw on the content of other subjects. To treat ideas in a comprehensive manner, he will find it rewarding to solicit the resources of other subject matter teachers.

The proponent of the unified studies approach will need to have a good background of knowledge in several subjects and will also have to draw on the resources of other subject matter teachers. He will find that before the conditions for the development of relationships in ideas can be established, it is essential to know and have accessible the subject matter for ideas. Unity of knowledge and understanding and an intelligent grasp of the content of subject fields go hand in hand in the development of high quality learning experiences with youth.

The factors in curriculum improvement indicated above may be illustrated in connection with a teacher of chemistry. The teacher may be fully aware of the make-up of substances and the changes that take place in them. He may know that the changes can be controlled to produce new substances, such as plastics, drugs, clothing, and others, for man's use. Through instruction in the classroom and laboratory, he might guide young people to an understanding of these facts. The chemistry teacher has access to a vast array of facts and ideas which have changed the way of living of people throughout the world. These facts and ideas make it incumbent on him to relate himself to other scientists, to sociologists, to government officials, to philosophers, to engineers, and others to promote competences and social intelligence in the use of them. He must see that chemistry is related to problems of health, housing, employment, energy, and many others. In order that the chemistry teacher may become intelligent regarding the relationship of ideas in his classroom, he needs to solicit the resources of teachers of social studies, mathematics, health, English, art, industrial arts, and other subjects. Furthermore, he must put himself in the position of being helpful to the other teachers. He must become intelligent in the development of the unity of knowledge. He develops the conditions for new and expanded meanings.

Developing conditions for study, research, and handling
of ideas for improved practices

It was stated that the teacher who has not developed the attitude or attained an understanding of the relationship of ideas was ill-equipped to promote adequate learning experiences with children. To go a step further, the school that has not generated the leadership to bring about the conditions where individuals together handle ideas to promote high quality learning experiences is failing in its responsibility for educational effectiveness. It is suggested, therefore, that the secondary school provide for continuous curriculum improvement by developing "idea" rooms or laboratories for the handling of ideas, similar to the pattern suggested for the elementary school. Before this happens, there needs to be a "warming up" period of simple changes as teachers begin to ask questions about instructional practices.

The preliminary conditions are rather fully described in Chapter 1 so it would be superfluous to go into them again.

As has been stated before, teachers, curriculum consultants, administrators, students, and citizens must be involved in the conditions for curriculum improvement. Curriculum improvement, as the term is used in this book, is to be equated with the development of high quality learning experiences in the classroom. As teachers are asking questions about present instructional practices, they consult with each other for an approach to some answers. Each classroom, then, becomes a center or laboratory for the handling of ideas. The handling of ideas implies, of course, that students, teachers, and others will be engaged in the tasks of developing relationships in ideas. Each classroom, then, is a center for the development of unity of knowledge and understanding. In addition to the procedures of curriculum improvement in the context of the classroom and student-teacher relationships, each classroom will be a center or laboratory for study, research, and the handling of ideas by the teachers and others. Thus, everyone—students, teachers, and other staff members—are engaged in becoming increasingly more conversant with content and the unity of knowledge.

Arranging for exchange of resources between staff. As indicated before, curriculum development tasks are equated with the learning experiences of young people. The plan proposed suggests no revolutionary changes in the pattern of subjects. It does suggest continued study and attention to the treatment of ideas in each classroom so that high quality learning conditions will be provided. The plan further proposes that a definite place be provided by the teacher for the handling of ideas with respect to topics which would cut across possible subject barriers.

The topics would grow out of the conditions which the teacher has developed with students and in consultation and exchange with other teachers and curriculum workers for the intensive treatment of related ideas in the subject at hand. Let's suppose, for example, a topic such as "The Meaning of Success As Conceived in the American Culture" has emerged prominently as the result of the work in a class in literature. At the same time, topics and questions which cut across subject lines have arisen in the other classes. The teacher of each one of the classes usually will try to pursue ideas with his students in connection with the topic or question. The teacher and students may feel, however, that their knowledge about the topic does not do full justice to it. It might be helpful, therefore, to draw on the resources of a teacher of another subject. To facilitate this opportunity, it might be helpful for the staff to designate one or two periods a week where this exchange of resources may be made possible. This arrangement should, of course, be made by the staff and should be flexible. Since the topics usually will develop out of the learning experiences carried on in the classrooms, a sharp break in the schedule for consideration of the topics in isolation might tend to work against the very principle of unity which the arrangement is supposed to serve.

Developing intracommunication as well as intercommunication for idea evolvement. The type of scheduling to be effected for the development of greater resourcefulness relative to unity of ideas should grow out of the curriculum improvement tasks of the teachers and other curriculum consultants. To this end leadership should be exerted by all the staff to evolve the working machinery for intercommunication as well as intracommunication of teachers in relation to their subjects.

As indicated before, it is highly important to develop the conditions for an intensive handling of ideas relative to a subject so that the content and instructional procedures will be of the highest possible quality. It is important, for example, for the science teachers to work as a group to improve the quality of learning experiences in their respective areas. The same is true of the social studies staff, the mathematics group, the English teachers, the industrial arts teachers, and the other subject groups. Besides this, there should be intra-subject groups. These groups should handle ideas relative to areas or topics which cut across subject lines. Examples of these are communications, behavioral science, science and man, social relationships, mathematics and the environment.

As has been indicated, the subject groups as well as the inter-subject groups, would develop the conditions for study, research, and discussion to bring about a high quality of learning experiences. All resources possible should be made accessible to the groups. Provisions should be made for utilizing the services of resource people from colleges and universities as well as from the lay public. Ample audio-visual materials should be provided.

"Charging" the environment for ideas. The rooms in which the groups meet should be developed into a "charged" environment of ideas. Bulletin boards would carry high level questions, descriptive facts, a portrayal of frontier thinking, and other items of inquiry. The groups would work on ideas to take learning into the peripheral areas of knowledge envisaged by new discoveries and ventures in science, new frontiers of human relations, the dynamics of change, and other fields of inquiry. Many of the clues for "charging" the conditions for the study and analysis of ideas by the groups would come from the learning relationship between students and the teacher. For example, the social studies people, meeting in one of the social studies rooms, would build on many of the ideas already developed with students. Much of the thinking of the students would be prominently portrayed in the room in the form of questions, graphs, pictographs, cartoons, pictures, and other forms of representation. It is, of course, always advisable to have representative students working with the adult curriculum improvement groups.

The inter-subject groups would, of course, meet at different times from the subject groups since many, if not all, of the teachers will be involved in both types of groups. The inter-subject groups would work very much the same as the subject groups on areas and topics such as indicated in the previous pages. The results of the meetings of the subject groups would, of course, be used in the approach to the handling of ideas in connection with the topics which cut across the subject lines. The conditions for the study and examination of ideas would be "charged" with vital questions and facts about contemporary trends, new frontiers in international relationships, the "growing edge" of meanings as to today's problems, and many other pressing and deep-seated issues. The great thinking of men both in the past and present on these issues and problems will be made accessible and prominently portrayed to generate ideas. Resource people from industry, business, labor, the professions, and other lines of endeavor should be used. Students should also be involved in the task of handling ideas.

Developing leadership for high quality learning. It should be noted again that the machinery and the process for curriculum improvement as described in the previous pages does not happen all at once. The reader is referred to the preliminary conditions which are developed in Chapter 1. A type of leadership which demonstrates an acceptance and realization of the ideas of individuals must be present at all times. The curriculum leader must open up the channels for free inquiry, must value differences, and provide the conditions which will involve everyone in the examination and appraisal of ideas to promote high quality in learning.

Good leadership provides the avenues for resourcefulness to be developed by all individuals in the curriculum setting. This resourcefulness, starting with pride in some tasks, the raising of questions about instructional practices, and the production of that impact which intensifies the approach to ideas, will generate recognized leadership in all the centers of the school unit and system. The impact provided by the conditions for freedom of inquiry, the accentuation and valuing of differences, the questions which have evolved as a result of critical appraisal of instructional practices, will develop a type of absorbing excitement about ideas which will make curriculum tasks self-propellent.

Under the conditions of respect and acceptance of individuals indicated above, the teacher will not have to stop and ponder whether he should depart from the book or course of study to pursue questions raised by students which have meaning for them. The conditions will remove the state of compartmentalized thinking which regards the book, the course of study, and students' questions as separate entities. The only condition which will be considered is that the teacher and students appraise the questions raised as to structure, value association, and peripheral meanings. In other words, a distinction should be made between "whims" and the "hard nerve" core of ideas. It should be cautioned, however, that the veil which separates "whims" from ideas is often very thin.

As the teacher and students pursue ideas together, they will remove the top limit of achievement with respect to subject matter. They will be developing high level learning experiences. The teacher will teach so that the students will go beyond him. Ideas will be in competition without the danger of "loss of face" on the part of the teacher or students. Subject matter will be approached in a more intensive and higher level manner than before. Curriculum improvement is bound to follow. It is obvious, also, that the intensiveness and extensiveness of ideas and instruction developed in this classroom will extend to other individuals and the other classrooms. The more an individual discovers about ideas, the more he tends to become involved with other individuals in the examination and handling of ideas for the production of better ones. Each individual also develops better understanding of his own subject as he involves his thinking with that of others.

Developing conditions for thinking beyond regular pattern of inquiry

Certain conditions and arrangements are entailed to promote high quality learning experiences for all students. It has been suggested from time to time that the spread and intensity of learning should proceed on the basis of inclusiveness of people. At the same time, there must be a recognition of the uniqueness of every individual. The study, research, analysis, and discussion carried on in the subject and inter-subject groups should lead to, or enlarge on, the development of the conditions for a wide range of learning experiences in each classroom. Within this range, each student should be encouraged to find meanings and understandings within his potential. Furthermore, he should be encouraged to go beyond himself. Extraordinary resourcefulness and potential powers exist in "ordinary" people if the "points of contact" can be located for their release. The range of experiences must provide these points of contact for students. The ways of doing this are discussed at length in subsequent chapters.

Stimulating conditions for continuous occupation with ideas. In any program of curriculum development, it is important that the experiences be of such high quality that a saturation point in stimuli for ideas is never reached. This should be true both for students and teachers. The teachers and other curriculum workers meeting at different times as subject and as inter-subject groups will tend to generate a continuous absorption with, and excitement about, ideas as they pursue them farther into the peripheral areas of knowledge. As they are occupied with research, study, and examination of ideas, they will come to detect certain salient features which stimulate the progression of thought into higher areas of inquiry. For example, a topic dealing with what is known about human adaptability would furnish many ideas which could be pursued into peripheral areas of inquiry. A study of the extent to which man's environmental conditioning can be overcome would most certainly lead into the periphery of knowledge and understanding.

The development of relationships of ideas about more simple topics can, of course, also be exciting and directional. For example, a study and analysis of questions such as the following would tend to develop a compulsiveness for inquiry: What is the meaning of emotional deprivation? Is it possible to be deprived emotionally and not physically? Under what conditions does an individual suffer mental deprivation? What are the conditions which could be equated with physical deprivation? Mental? Emotional? Social?

Another topic which could lead to an interesting development of ideas is the formulation of ways in which equations in mathematics might be used to gain understandings of some phases of the environment. There are, of course, many other topics emanating from the content of subjects which would furnish substance for ideas. Enough have been indicated, however, to illustrate high level procedures in curriculum improvement.

As teachers, other curriculum workers, and youth proceed to develop high quality learning experiences, there will come about an increased sense of recognition of the tremendous responsibilities entailed in providing the conditions for the seeking of knowledge. As the various individuals and groups handle ideas about the subject areas and the many topics, there will develop a greater eagerness to study and inquire further, as well as more intensively, about the ideas. Certainly, if there exists this eagerness and excitement about learning and understanding, the school must do everything possible to expand opportunities for this quest for knowledge. The staff of the school has the responsibility to develop those conditions which will make possible increased opportunity for fulfillment, to the utmost, of the potential of students.

The staff and other curriculum people who have been involved with the development and expansion of ideas will, of course, constantly work to improve learning experience with students in the classroom. The provision for a wide range of learning experiences will tend to promote the intensive and extensive pursuit of ideas by the students. This very provision will lead to a discovery of potential of students which may demand some additional conditions for intensive inquiry, study, and research in the subject areas and with the many topics and questions which have evolved in the classrooms. It is suggested, therefore, that additional centers of learning or laboratories be developed where extensive study and examination of ideas, over and above that which takes place in the classrooms, may be carried on. Not only should students be encouraged to go beyond the learning experiences in the classroom, but the provisions should be for them to be able to do so.

Providing facilities and equipment for advanced study and research. In Chapter 3 it is suggested that instead of study halls, schools should have several extra rooms which could be constituted as centers or laboratories for expanded learning opportunities. The library could serve as an important center for study, research, and the pursuit of ideas into higher realms of inquiry. New buildings should be planned to have several classrooms designed for seminar groups and intensive study and research beyond the usual program of learning. Some of the classrooms should have sections designed to provide these additional opportunities for students.

Many or, perhaps, most of the classrooms devoted to these extra intensive learning opportunities would be the same ones occupied by students for the regular program. This would be especially true with the studies in science so that not too many new science laboratories would have to be installed. The daily schedule would, of course, have to be extended for most of the students working with the extra studies. Additional staff would be needed to carry on these opportunities.

In order to carry on study, research, and high quality learning experiences, it is necessary to have the best equipment possible. It is assumed that the members of a staff, curriculum consultants, administrators, and students who have been operating in a pattern of curriculum improvement such as described in Chapter 1 and this chapter, will function most persuasively in securing the best equipment, supplies, books, and other materials needed for the classrooms.

The rooms should be well-stocked with all types of books and pamphlets. The library should have facilities for transferring books and resource materials for use with topics which evolve in the classrooms. The science laboratories should have the type of equipment and apparatus which can be used for an advanced form of experimentation and study. Projectors for films, slides, pictures, and film strips should be available for the asking. There should be plenty of space and facilities for storage of equipment and supplies. The rooms should have many stationary and movable bulletin boards, chart-holders, easels, a book-cart, and other usable features. Lastly, but exceedingly important, is a good professional library for use by the staff.

Using additional centers to further ideas and launch new ones. Some of the classrooms for the additional work will be used to carry on more intensive studies in the various subjects. Many of the ideas for the extra studies will already have been started in the regular classroom programs. In that case, extra time will be devoted to supplemental studies. As stated before, however, many of the learning experiences to be undertaken in these special centers will either originate here or will assume directions in advance of the regular classroom studies. It should be noted, however, that "regular" does not mean mediocre. With the involvement of staff and others in the curriculum improvement tasks already described, the regular program should be one of high quality learning experiences. The additional centers are designed to give more time for students to follow through in an intensive study and analysis of high level ideas already started as well as the launching of others.

Some of the centers will be used for study, research, and discussion of topics which cut across subject lines. Areas of study or topics to be dealt with in these centers would carry captions such as Man and Science, The Role of Communications for Intercultural Understanding, Why People Behave as They Do, An Intelligent Approach to the Realignment in International Loyalties, A Study of the Personality Structures Needed for the Development of a Sense of Certainty, and others. The students working on topics of the type indicated should gain a depth of understanding as to relationships of ideas. The centers or laboratories designed to deal with these topics will be "charged" with questions and ideas which should lead to a greater unity of knowledge on the part of students. It is not, of course, to be assumed that the subject centers and the "unified studies" centers can be sharply separated as to functions in promoting unity of knowledge. Ever so many aspects of relationships of ideas will, no doubt, be developed in the subject centers. The functions of the two types of centers are really interrelated in the pursuit of high level ideas. It would be desirable, therefore, if students could work in both.

Additional staff members should be procured to work with the students in these extra centers for learning. These staff members would be needed because the regular schedule for many students would be extended at least one period for part or all of the week. Besides the additional staff members, resource people from industry, labor, the professions, and various trades and occupations should be brought in as consultants in the centers. From time to time the services of consultants from colleges, universities, and technical institutions should be utilized in promoting high level learning experiences. People from the various disciplines such as psychology, sociology, English, and others, should be invited to serve both as staff consultants and with students. The services of supervisors and curriculum consultants should be used freely.

It is the belief of the writer that when organized efforts and plans are made to involve people in the community as participants and resource assistants in curriculum improvement, their cooperation in the development of these centers will be forthcoming. Concrete evidence that additional expenditures will be used for the procuring of additional staff and the development of centers for students to pursue higher levels of learning will provide some real incentives for support on the part of the people of the community. People will come to regard with pride a school system which not only places high value on the belief that there lies great potential in all children and youth but which also provides a workable plan for the realization of that potential in a high level of learning.

SELECTED READINGS FOR CHAPTERS 1 AND 2

Anderson, Veron E., *Principles and Procedures of Curriculum Improvement*. New York: The Ronald Press Co., 1956. Chapters 2, 4, 8, 9, 15, 16, 17. A description of methods of initiating curriculum improvement at the classroom level and system-wide.

Anderson, Vivienne and Daniel R. Davies, *Patterns of Educational Leadership*. Englewood Cliffs, N. J.: Prentice-Hall, Inc., 1956. Chapters 1 and 2. Interesting and most valuable guides to the development of staff leadership in curriculum improvement tasks.

Association for Supervision and Curriculum Development, *Research for Curriculum Improvement*. 1957 Yearbook. Washington, D. C.: The Association, 1957.

Bush, Robert Nelson, *The Teacher-Pupil Relationship*. Englewood Cliffs, N. J.: Prentice-Hall, Inc., 1954, pp. 143-169. Shows the effect of the administrator-teacher on the teacher-pupil relationship.

Corey, Stephen M., *Action Research to Improve School Practices*. New York: Bureau of Publications, Teachers College, Columbia University, 1954.

Faunce, Roland C. and Nelson L. Bossing, *Developing the Core Curriculum*, Second Edition. Englewood Cliffs, N. J.: Prentice-Hall, Inc., 1958. A most valuable guide to teachers, curriculum workers, and administrators in approaching the tasks of unity in learning.

Frank, Lawrence K., *Nature and Human Nature*. New Brunswick, N. J.: Rutgers University Press, 1951, pp. 3-15. Some direction as to a new climate of opinion.

Hicks, William V. and Jameson, Marshall C., *The Elementary School Principal at Work*. Englewood Cliffs, N. J.: Prentice Hall, Inc., 1957. Chapters 2, 3, and 11. Practical suggestions for principals in developing channels of communication and helping improve instruction.

Intelligence in the Modern World—John Dewey's Philosophy. Edited by Joseph Ratner. New York: The Modern Library-Random House, Inc., 1939. pp. 811-835. Deals with the relationship of mind and consciousness and a discussion by Dewey on the unity of the human being. See also *The Quest for Certainty*, pp. 275-291.

Lane, Howard and Mary Beauchamp, *Human Relations in Teaching*. Englewood Cliffs, N. J.: Prentice-Hall, Inc., 1955, pp. 201-247. Some valuable concepts on leadership for curriculum improvement.

Mackenzie, Gordon N., and Stephen M. Corey and Associates, *Instructional Leadership*. New York: Bureau of Publications, Columbia University. pp. 3-96, 137-168. An analysis of conceptions of leadership; also a discussion of various types of approach to leadership with the staff. Should have much value to the curriculum worker and teacher.

Miel, Alice and Associates, *Cooperative Procedures in Learning*. New York: Bureau of Publications, Teachers College, Columbia University, 1952, pp. 13-257. Many examples of experiences of teachers in cooperative procedures.

Prescott, Daniel A., *The Child in the Educative Process*. New York: McGraw-Hill Book Co., 1957. Part I, II, and IV. Very valuable resource for teachers in their efforts to understand children and to develop learning experiences. Book is based on a longitudinal study of the child and the educative process. Thousands of teachers have been involved in producing the ideas found in the book.

Smith, B. Othanel, William O. Stanley, and J. Harlan Shores, *Fundamentals of Curriculum Development*, Revised Edition. Yonkers-on-Hudson, N. Y.: World Book Co., 1957, pp. 3-24. Also Parts II, III, and IV. Deals with the curriculum in relation to the culture. Parts Two and Three deal rather completely with educational objectives, subject matter selection, other phases of curriculum development, and the various patterns and designs of curriculum organization. Part Four treats the problems of human relations in curriculum development.

Spears, Harold, *The Teacher and Curriculum Planning*. Englewood Cliffs, N. J.: Prentice-Hall, Inc., 1951. A concise statement of fundamental principles of curriculum planning. Focuses on the classroom level of curriculum planning.

————, *Curriculum Planning Through In-Service Programs*. Englewood Cliffs, N. J.: Prentice-Hall, Inc., 1957. Excellent suggestions in planning with teachers in the handling of ideas for curriculum improvement.

Superintendent as Instructional Leader, The. Thirty-fifth Yearbook. Washington, D. C.: American Association of School Administrators, 1957. Many ideas and suggestions are provided for administrators in the approach to the tasks of instructional improvement. The approach is classroom-oriented.

Toward Improved Curriculum Theory. Supplementary Educational Monographs Number 71, ed. by Virgil E. Herrick and Ralph W. Tyler. Chicago: University of Chicago Press, March, 1950.

Yauch, Wilbur A., *Helping Teachers Understand Principals*. New York: Appleton-Century-Crofts, Inc. Many suggestions on what teachers might do to help the principal in promoting instructional improvement.

·3·

Developing Conditions for Learning

THE CONDITIONS FOR LEARNING AS DEVELOPED IN THE PAGES OF this book carry beyond those that are usually conceived in typical learning situations. They are designed to provide an environment charged with those ingredients which tend to create a voluntary compulsiveness for learning on the part of children and youth. They might be thought of as the stage or setting where learning takes place, yet that conception is too limited. One might conceive of the conditions as an atmosphere conducive to learning; but that conception may be vacuous.

A popular conception of the conditions for learning is that the environment must be structured. This conception could have considerable merit if the implementation of it is designed to expand opportunities for learning. Still another idea about the conditions for learning is that there is provision for freedom of inquiry. That idea, although a vital essential, is only one element of the conditions for learning. Physical features conducive to flexibility in the pursuit of goals are strongly advocated by educators. Again, that is one of the conditions contributory to learning, but it is not adequate by itself.

CONDITIONS FOR LEARNING—DEFINED

It is impossible to attempt to derive a clear-cut definition of the conditions for learning out of context with the learning situations with which teachers and children become involved. A clue to a definition may be that the ingredients of the setting for learning are of such impact as will cause the participant to

53

assess his behavior against the meanings which unfold in the process of basic thinking, study, and research. This definition obviously is not complete nor can any definition be complete since there are many forces operating in the conditions which promote learning.

FACTORS INVOLVED IN CONDITIONS FOR LEARNING

The culture exerts great pressures on the individual to behave in a certain manner even when an examination of operating values produces some question as to their adequacy for modern living. Every day an individual encounters situations where he has to make decisions. Is he free to make these decisions in terms of basic thinking, study, and research? Not altogether. In some situations, he might make his decisions on the pattern which he has established as a result of considered and basic thinking. Other decisions must be made on the basis of the pattern which prevails in the group with which he is associated.

A group exerts great pressures on decisions by the individual especially when they affect the welfare of the group. An individual has to weigh the opinions of the members of the group and decide in terms of the apparent consensus. Otherwise he loses status with the group. This is true especially where he has been placed in a position of responsibility by the group. Conformity to certain traditions is a powerful factor in enforcing ways of behavior on the part of individuals. The phrase "When in Rome do as the Romans do" becomes a significant one with respect to behavior in terms of tradition. To decide on an issue in terms of the framework provided by research, study, and basic thinking, if not in accord with tradition, is often a sure way to cut oneself off from the group. It is a sure way to become socially ostracized and inactivated as far as group membership is concerned.

The problem of developing direction within a framework of "opposites" in values

It is apparent from the above discussion that the conditions for learning must entertain an all-inclusiveness with respect to the nature of behavior constituting the social forces. At the same time they must contain elements of constructive direction as provided by the substance and process of basic thinking, study, and research.

The conditions for learning must provide for a reconciliation of possible opposites in values and, at the same time, develop a degree of constructive selectivity toward choice of direction in the value field. Some of the opposites in values which must be included in curriculum development toward educational direction are the following: the school environment for learning and the many learning environments in the community; the setting for learning in the school and the settings prevalent in the community; the school atmosphere and the various atmospheres surrounding the school; the structuring for direction in learning in the school and the structuring represented by the values in the community; the development of the conditions for freedom of inquiry in the school and classroom and the limiting factors dictated by certain values in the peripheral area; the provision in the school for an understanding of intangibles and the uncertainty often developed about them in the out-of-school environments.

Additional opposites which exist are: the provision for, and arrangement of, physical features to contribute to flexible conditions for learning and the formal conception of learning prevailing in the outside community; the principle of unification of learning and the compartmentalization represented in a confined approach to ideas and subject matter; the admission of all values into the instructional setting and the practice of ignoring some and accepting others as they conform to the preconceived patterns of a small group of individuals; the development of flexibility in the organization of the school so that the whole range of abilities will be served and a static organization serving an exclusive pattern of standards.

DEVELOPING THE LEARNING ENVIRONMENT

The ambivalences or contradictions in possible values which are prevalent in the society make the task of developing the conditions for learning one which requires extensive knowledge and a tremendous degree of insight on the part of the teacher. The curriculum worker or teacher who proceeds to develop an environment for learning, apart from the operating forces involved, is naturally inclined to include in it those elements which conform to sound constructive values as he conceives them to be. In doing so, he may not be preparing an environment of learners at all. He may just be structuring the school pattern of learning in terms of his preconceived notions as to what that pattern should be.

Is he then supposed to disregard his inclinations and purposes in developing a learning environment for children? Not at all. He would certainly create confusion and flounder in his efforts if he didn't have ideas and a plan to get them into the learning situation. He must, however, in the process recognize that his thinking represents only a portion of the ideas which will be in the learning situation. To go further, he would be wise to make specific provisions for other ideas to become operative in the conditions for learning. For a time, in fact, all related ideas should at least have a fair hearing so that he will know that they exist. Then it will be possible for him to help structure the conditions in such a way as to cause the holders of the ideas to study and appraise them in terms of the consequences which they might entail. The structuring should encompass the conditions which will stimulate young people to go beyond curriculum worker and teacher in pursuing the tasks of learning.

Learning environment must be inclusive of values of children

The wise teacher will make every effort to build an environment for learning which is inclusive of the values of children. The learning environment then becomes a laboratory for the study and critical analysis of the values of children and young people toward constructive choice. As values are clearly portrayed through an analytic process, some will be denied and others accepted as being contributory to constructive living. It should be emphasized that the teacher and the school do not develop the environment, but they facilitate the conditions for learning within all environments in school and out.

Conditions of inclusiveness of values will help children relate to many environments. When the teacher brings about the conditions for learning which will develop intensive identification on the part of children with the values they have chosen as being constructive, the behavior in all environments will be affected. Accordingly, there gradually develops a sense of direction and understanding as to which values exhibit a unity and which show degrees of diversity as between the school and community. At the same time, the conditions have brought about selectivity on the part of the participants as to constructive elements in living in the total environment. Environments then change because the components of the behavior in the environments have been examined, selection of values has been made, and a process has been identified for activating the selected values wherever the holder of them may associate with others.

In view of the above discussion, it would follow that the conditions for learning must include those ingredients which give understanding relative to the many settings for learning in the community. That is true, also, of the atmospheres for learning, the structuring represented in the settings and atmospheres, the conditions for inquiry, and all the other elements prevalent in the opposites in values. The fact that the various settings for learning, the various patterns for induction of the young into the society, and the other conceptions represented by the opposites are brought into the conditions for learning does not mean that all values incident to the conceptions are condoned or accepted. Again, it should be emphasized that the values are brought in to be studied and examined as to their components or possible consequences for choice and decision.

The values brought into the classroom and school represent the various behaviors residing in the total environment. As the patterns of behavior are portrayed as to their context and intensity of meaning in the conditions for learning in the classroom, children develop concern as to the position which they occupy in these patterns. They will think about their beliefs in connection with the patterns of behavior, accepting some if the consequences envisioned are constructive, questioning some in view of the values which they have accepted, and clearly rejecting others where the possible consequences indicate definite negative features.

Environment must provide for basic thinking about behavior

The whole question of developing the conditions for concern about behavior patterns and a child's recognition of his place in them is so involved that a few illustrations might serve to clarify it. The setting for recognition of behavior patterns on the part of children in the early elementary years of school is that which involves parent-child and child-to-child relationships.

The question of a child's responsibility in the home might arise in the course of the work in school. Some of the children might relate how their mothers keep telling them to keep their rooms clean and to pick up things after they are through with them. As is well known, children neglect these tasks either because they do not care or because they know that their parents will do them if they fail to. Now, a child may entertain the belief that he should do his part, but evidently is not too concerned about whether or not he follows through on his belief. He might say he knows it is right for him to do his part, but the facts reveal that he does it largely under compulsion. Either his belief that he has certain responsibilities is not very strong, or he does not identify with the responsibilities at all. He probably is always ready to state that he knows it is right for him to do his part because he feels that is what the teacher wants him to say.

Environment must have provisions for basic thinking and research about behavior. The question arises, Where does basic thinking, study, and research come in with respect to this behavior? Basic thinking for a child is implied in the discussion about his belief, his so-called recognition of his responsibility, and his actual performance in terms of his belief. Questions around which basic thinking may arise are such as the following: What happens if you do not do your part? How does it make you feel when you constantly have to be reminded about your responsibility? Suppose your parents did not do what you failed to do—what would happen? People care for other people. What is meant by caring for one? What are the things that make you love your parents? What happens when one child in a group doesn't do his part? What happens if half of the children do not do their part? How do you find out what is your part in a task to be done?

The questions above could provide some real leads to basic thinking on the part of young children. Research and experimentation may also be carried on with respect to the questions. For example, the teacher may suggest that the children think of ways by which the real meaning of the questions might be presented. Either a child or the teacher may come up with the idea, for example, that certain children in the class should refrain from doing what they considered their part for a whole day to see what would happen. Then the same situation might be repeated with the whole class. Of course, it should be made clear that this is an experiment in responsible behavior. It is needless to say that the impact of some such experiment would provide valuable concepts about responsibility and one's behavior with respect to it. It would also furnish clues to the children as well as to the teacher regarding the strength of identification between beliefs and the responsibilities entailed relative to tasks which have to be performed. Furthermore, an experiment of the type, carefully planned, could reveal whether one actually knew what his part was in a task. It would tend to point up degrees of recognition of tasks on the part of some children and evasion of responsibility on the part of others.

Environment must provide for understandings beyond moral responsibility. With regard to the questions indicated above, it should be emphasized that the understandings to be developed should carry beyond the importance of responsibility in participation. Although the discussion is related to moral questions, the study of the questions will interpret to the child logical and scientific considerations in the approach to his individual purposes and tasks.

A study of the questions will necessitate readings of all types in the conditions for instruction. Some of the readings will deal with the tasks different people have to perform in the process of producing needed articles and goods for living. Other readings will deal with the parts different members of a family need to take in making living more satisfying in a home. Still others will reveal the successive steps one has to take in thinking to get at answers to one's problems. There will be readings about people who are doing tasks of all types, and about other people they must relate to in connection with the tasks. Some readings will reveal how many people were involved in helping someone to attain his objectives. There will be stories about friends, neighbors, playmates, and people in other lands. Certainly many of the books and materials will reveal much about the thinking of people in other times and places. The background of our present ways of behavior will be revealed in many of the readings.

An illustration which points up in a somewhat different way than the one above the need for inclusion of the patterns of behavior in the community in the conditions for learning is the use of number. Almost every activity in the community is related to the use of number in one way or another. The grocer makes use of the processes of addition, subtraction, multiplication, division, fractions, measurement and possibly some others. It is important, for school purposes, to know how he uses these processes. It is important, too, to know how he makes calculations with the use of scales and cash registers.

The engineer uses a more advanced type of number in his calculations. It is necessary to make accessible to children how number is used by the engineer in his preliminary thinking as well as in the more precise calculations he has to make in connection with a project. Then there are, of course, the uses of number by bankers, restaurant owners, service station operators, and by people in innumerable occupations. The various uses of number must be made available in such a manner as to indicate relationships to the behavior of people in a society.

The fact that number is used by people in their everyday tasks, in their social relationships, in casual conversations, and in human understanding, should be clearly portrayed in the provisions for learning. This will serve to point up in the minds of children that the use of number is an integral part of the system of thinking as carried on in our society. In its more advanced stages, number will be seen as a process or tool which is tied up with the advance of civilization. History, philosophy, political developments, and science cannot be understood apart from the thinking which is involved with number. Thus it is clear that number is part and parcel of the whole field of knowledge. It cannot, therefore, be isolated, from the settings designed to develop an understanding of behavior in the community and outside world.

DEVELOPING CONDITIONS FOR FREEDOM OF INQUIRY

A helpful approach to the development of the conditions for freedom of inquiry in the face of the limiting factors dictated by certain values, is the initiation of situations with the participants for the establishment of meanings about freedom. First of all, it is necessary to dispose of the most obvious concept of what is not freedom, that is, doing what one pleases under any circumstances. It does not take too much insight to recognize that if everyone did as he felt, freedom would disappear. It is logical, then, that in order to achieve a state of freedom in a group, individuals must limit action on some of their feelings as well as expand action on others.

Freedom for inquiry built on positive conditions for its achievement

Freedom for inquiry is not built on permissiveness but rather on the positive achievement and development of the conditions for its attainment. In other words, the conditions must have the ingredients for the evolvement and activation of freedom on the part of individuals. A small child has to be prevented from exercising certain types of freedom to keep him from being hurt. In all probability an exercise of extreme "freedom" by a child would destroy him.

In the process of induction of the child into the environment, the parent attempts at every step to help him clarify his limitations. At the same time, the parent clarifies to the child those actions which may be exercised without any restrictions attached. As the child grows up, he is gradually learning to recognize the consequences which may result when exercising unlimited freedom at the same time that he is learning to recognize the consequences of undue limitations on freedom.

It is comparatively simple to develop the meaning of freedom when dealing with tangibles. One begins quickly to recognize what is possible to do and what is not. In the matter of dealing with intangibles, however, difficulties are encountered in developing the meanings of freedom. For example, a twelve-year-old child may well learn how to drive a car. The practice, however, of permitting youngsters of this age to drive cars would not be wise because of their immaturity in recognizing their limitations—physical and mental—in connection with the operation of a vehicle designed for adults. Experience has indicated that youngsters of this age lack the maturity to recognize the limitations to freedom as well as potential powers in certain situations. They haven't had sufficient experience to understand and exercise choice with respect to the consequences in unrestricted freedom.

Conditions for freedom of inquiry in classroom essential to understanding. The clue to the definition of conditions of learning, indicated in the previous pages as assessing behavior in terms of the patterns evolved from basic thinking, study, and research, is extremely valuable in developing meanings about the nature of freedom, especially as it pertains to inquiry. In this connection it is vitally important to deal with topics and events which are integrally related to freedom, its nature and perpetuation. One wonders to what extent this is done in the classrooms.

An example of an event where many topics about freedom and its meanings were involved was the Summit Conference on World Problems held in Geneva, Switzerland, in 1955. In assessing the importance of a conference of this magnitude with regard to world understanding, it is essential that there be developed freedom of inquiry in the conditions for learning in the classroom. What does this mean? It means, first of all, that the conditions for learning be established to consider to what extent and in what connections the questions involved in the conference relate to the extension of freedom and to what extent to the restriction of it. Secondly, it is extremely important that all types of materials be made available to students so that they may obtain some background for basic thinking relative to the problems considered at the conference. Third, and more important, it is most valuable to understanding to provide the setting for much basic thinking regarding the motives involved in the behavior of the various representatives at the conference.

Conditions must provide experiences with criteria for ascer-

taining meaning of freedom. It should be most emphatically emphasized that the conditions for learning should provide for complete freedom of inquiry, such as reading and discussing communistic literature, among other things, to obtain some understanding about the state of mind and the motives of the proponents and writers involved in the conference mentioned above. As children and teacher study the values by which people function in a state of real freedom, they provide for themselves certain patterns which they accept as criteria for living. Among these are ample provision for the advancement of the dignity of man, his uniqueness, his right to promote the welfare of others, his opportunity for social and intellectual mobility, and his right to express himself ethically and spiritually.

The conditions under which youngsters study all types of literature having to do with the thinking of people need to be charged with those elements which will enable the youngsters to ascertain whether the behavior produced is in accord with the above criteria. It is important, then, to assess the behavior of people against the principles of freedom indicated. It is the responsibility of the teacher to promote broad opportunities for freedom of inquiry so that students may gain an understanding of the thinking back of behavior. The development of this freedom will lead to the establishment of patterns of values to guide thinking. In other words, students must have freedom through basic thinking, study, and research to develop limitations as to what they will accept as true principles of living. Even more important are the conditions which will help students to detect and develop plans to remove the constricting limitations to freedom. The schools must develop those conditions which will enable pupils to achieve the freedom to exercise intelligent choice regarding different value patterns in living. Again this necessitates the conditions for study, research, and basic thinking as inherent in the process to decision.

Developing understandings about freedom with elementary school children

All through this book there appear direct applications of the principles of freedom of inquiry and implications of freedom in many of its aspects. In connection with the development of a concept regarding the nature of freedom, it might be helpful to clarify the approaches to an understanding of freedom with children of different age and maturity levels.

With young children, the problem of freedom may be approached through the question, What would happen if every one of us were always allowed to do what he wanted to do? It is obvious that a careful analysis of the problems which would arise in connection with this question would reveal some real meanings about what is freedom and what is not freedom. A simple example would be the use of a certain toy. Several children might want to use it at the same time. The children would immediately recognize that this is impossible. They would find it necessary to schedule the use of the toy so that each one would get to use it. In other words, the individuals would have to take turns at using it. Another example would be the necessity of standing in line to buy a ticket to the movies. Children would quite readily determine the consequences if everyone would try to buy his ticket at the same time.

With children in the fourth through the sixth grades, the thinking with regard to the meaning of freedom could be moved into a more abstract vein. An example which may be used is one in which the selection of a chairman or leader of a group is involved. What are the qualifications that the leader should have? Children might wish to consider for leader the type of person who could help them most in their work. Would it be the one that would help them agree on a plan or the one that would tell each one to do what he wanted to do? Would the group be free if everyone did as he pleased? Or would this condition keep others from being free? As the children analyze the ways in which a chairman or leader could be most helpful, they are beginning to learn a great deal about freedom. They are beginning to recognize that in the achievement of true freedom certain restrictions must be imposed on behavior. They are also beginning to recognize that some restrictions limit the realization of responsible freedom. They begin to understand that if one person operates in terms of his own conception of freedom without regard to the others, freedom is destroyed for the others.

Developing understandings of freedom with children
in junior high school

The meanings of freedom as developed with children in the middle grades may be dealt with on a more advanced level with children in the junior high school. On this level, the achievement of freedom may be studied more intensively both in connection with the responsibilities and limitations that it imposes on individuals and the arrangements for their release to achieve it. Good examples to use as a springboard toward the establishment of the meanings of freedom might be found in the following questions: Do you believe that the actions of some of the colonists in the events leading to the Revolutionary War were reckless? What signs of calm deliberation do you detect? What limitations were imposed on the colonists by England which were considered as an infringement on their rights? By what patterns did the colonists judge these limitations as an infringement on freedom? Were the people who participated in the decisions previous to the Revolution aware of the consequences? What do you feel would have happened if the colonists would have accepted the limitations put on their freedom rather than go to war about them?

The basic thinking, study, and research relative to these questions would tend to clarify many meanings about the nature of freedom. Other questions relating to united efforts in the struggle, the sacrifices of people, and the principles of freedom reaffirmed in the Declaration of Independence would be studied for profound meanings of the nature of liberty and its gifts. Still other questions of a more abstract nature would develop in connection with the study about the establishment of our nation through the Constitution. Some of these questions would deal with the unlimited type of freedom established by each state for itself through the Articles of Confederation as against the limitations imposed by the Constitution.

There would arise some discussion relative to the restricting effects of ill-conceived notions of freedom. Much would be made of the difficulties encountered by the efforts of men to advance the cause of freedom through the establishment of a Constitution. Most, if not all, of the questions relative to the Revolution and establishment of the Constitution could give rise to questions relating to the efforts of men to advance the principles of freedom today.

Developing understandings of freedom with high school students

In the high school, similar but more penetrating questions would be dealt with in connection with the development of meanings with respect to freedom. In the high school every effort should be made to bring into the conditions for learning the thinking about freedom as conceived in the great literature throughout the span of history. The different concepts of freedom must be brought before the students for analysis through study, research, and basic thinking. The conditions must contain those elements, also, which will lead to generalizations on the value patterns of freedom as derived from the analysis of the literature. These generalizations should contribute to a synthesis of the thinking which will guide the actions of the students in their everyday living. This synthesis would be basic as a guide to behavior which conceives of each individual as unique, as having personal worth, as possessing human dignity, and as the embodiment of moral attributes.

Responsible freedom essential in promoting learning

The concept of freedom as developed in the previous pages, that is, freedom with responsibility, is essential in the promotion of opportunities for learning. All subject areas, to become meaningful and productive of intensive thinking on the part of students, must be approached on a basis of freedom. For example, in the study of the science areas it is necessary to establish those conditions for inquiry which will stimulate children and young people to go way beyond the "canned" experiments indicated in some textbooks and lab manuals. As a matter of fact, textbooks and manuals should be developed in such a way as will promote a studied penetration into the peripheral areas of scientific inquiry. This contention is supported by the fact that at the present time scientists are operating with concepts deemed impossible of realization twenty years ago. In other words, "stargazing" activities are being replaced by "satellite" ventures in the area of scientific inquiry. Whenever the pursuit of knowledge is confined to a constricted area of operation, the uniqueness, personal worth, and human dignity of individuals is denied recognition.

We have tried to develop some of the positive conditions for freedom of inquiry. As indicated earlier in this chapter there exist some "opposites" to freedom of inquiry in the peripheral area. They were described as limiting factors to freedom of inquiry. As long as the limiting factors are those imposed in the interest of freedom, the opposites as between the school and peripheral area may be reconciled. As has been emphasized time and again, the resultant products of freedom of inquiry are shaped into the value patterns consistent with the dignity, uniqueness, worthiness, and ethical and spiritual expression of the individual. This means that in the establishment of true meanings of freedom, limitations and restrictions must be imposed in terms of those value patterns. If, however, the "opposites" remove the right of freedom of inquiry, the patterns of values are dictated and the recipient operates in ignorance and on a faith that is shaky in its foundation.

A removal of the conditions for freedom of inquiry denies to the individual his dignity, uniqueness, worthiness, and a completeness of ethical and spiritual expression. These are the conditions which exist in communistic and other totalitarian systems and cannot, therefore, be reconciled with the true responsibility of the school to educate for freedom.

PROVIDING FOR AN UNDERSTANDING OF INTANGIBLES

Opposites as between the school and community which are of tremendous significance in developing the conditions for learning are those involved with the meaning of intangibles. It is the responsibility of the school to make provisions whereby children may gain some understanding relative to the intangible elements in their lives. It is important that children be concerned about such intangibles as anger, fear, guilt, and other emotions.

People are perhaps guided in their actions more by feelings that they do not understand than any other elements which are a part of their living. Yet very little effort is made by people to understand their emotions and the other intangible forces which affect their lives. Frequently, individuals do things without knowing why they do them. Yet they do not seek to understand their actions. They are bothered by the uncertainties with regard to their behavior but do not seek to establish the conditions which will provide a degree of insight into the meanings of the uncertainties. Frequently, the intangible elements are explained away as conditions that will exist as long as people are human, or as strange phenomena that have to be accepted in the course of living.

Other explanations of intangibles are that they are guides to the conscience, that they are supernatural, and that if one lives "right" he will be free of their negative effects. When an attempt is made to help children in school to assess their feelings as to origin and meaning, it is frequently frowned on as being something beyond the proper role of the school.

Intangible elements in living are closely tied up with values. Since education is involved with behavior, it is extremely important that the school make ample provision for children to understand and assess their behavior in terms of the prevailing values of the community. This will give the children some meanings with respect to their daily behavior. The approach to the development of meanings with regard to intangibles does not come by itself. The conditions must be established which will contain the ingredients for gaining meanings from intangibles. How is this done?

Providing for induction of children to intangible meanings

In modern schools, when children first enter them, an attempt is made to acquaint them with the new environment. Different induction processes are planned by different teachers for children first entering school. Since school is associated with books, and parents have frequently mentioned to the child that he will read books, teachers will usually have them available in the classrooms. At first the books will be viewed casually, but as time goes on their importance will gradually be recognized. The induction process, however, includes many types of activities which are not directly related to books.

Some of the induction activities will be those centered on

getting children familiar with the classroom and some of the jobs that will have to be done by everybody. Other activities will be getting acquainted with one another through games of all types. The teacher might make children familiar with the organization of the school, the principal and his office, other teachers, older children, and the routine of the daily activities.

As the preliminary induction process is completed, school to the teacher and children settles into a form of routine. This routine with kindergarten children is somewhat as follows: opening exercises, sharing or telling time, story period, mid-period snack, rest, play in rhythmic and other games, work period, painting, drawing, and clay modeling, clean-up and dismissal early in the day. If the school does not have a kindergarten but starts children in the first grade, the routine is quite similar except that reading and, perhaps, some number work would be added and the children would be in school all day.

Conditions for induction to school should provide clues to intangibles. The induction process leading to a settled routine should operate mostly in terms of tangible meanings. The routine, however, is structured usually in terms of a tangible approach toward gaining meanings about other tangibles. Whatever intangible elements appear usually do so in painting, drawing, playing, and other tasks which the child does. Alert teachers will make use of some of the intangible elements observed in gaining a clearer understanding of the children who have indicated these elements in their tasks.

One objective which the teacher usually holds with young children is that they learn to get along with one another and that they get ready to adjust to the routine of the school. One way that is emphasized is to learn to read. This might be stated as a second objective and, in the usual pattern of thinking about school, is perhaps regarded as the most important one. Learning to read is, no doubt, *one* of the most important objectives of the school but not *the most* important one, especially in the initial phases of school experiences.

Conditions for initial induction should give child some meanings about items of wonder. When a child first comes to school, the greatest responsibility which the teacher has is to develop the conditions wherein the child will gain meanings about the things that he is wondering about. This cannot be done by putting a book before him. He is not wondering about books. His mind is filled not only with the tangible things that he sees or plays with but also with fears, anger feelings, how others react to him, and the phenomena around him.

Many of the intangibles which exist in a child's mind have, of course, been planted there as a result of his experiences at home and in his total environment. He has also discovered that if he is kind to someone, he will usually be treated with kindness. He has developed fears and is often unable to distinguish between those that are designed to protect him and those that are unwarranted. He has observed in his own mind that he gets very angry sometimes and afterward feels sorry about this feeling. He does not, however, seem to learn from this feeling, for he has repeated spells of anger in similar situations. He lacks insight with regard to the intangibles of crying. The whole question of living is not understood. He may have pangs of jealous feelings which come and go without his being wiser about them.

It is, of course, true that most of the feelings indicated above remain latent as to meanings. In the meantime, the child has satisfying feelings in the school routine. Many of these feelings, however, are frequently overshadowed by those which encompass the child in his relationship with others. Satisfying experiences in the routine will not alter the fact that his behavior will be affected by some real feelings involved with fears, anger, jealousy, and concern with the reactions of others to him. Learning to read or adjusting to the school routine will usually not give the child meanings relative to his behavior.

Conditions to help children understand themselves— their capabilities, powers, limitations

Too frequently the only approach made in the school toward action on a child's behavior is that of suppression of overtness in behavior and praise for conformity to the routine. Outside of the school environment, the approach is more of the same. Unless the overtness in behavior is of an extreme type, no real effort is made in the school to develop the conditions wherein the child will be led to examine behavior symptoms. Outside of school, parents usually look at the changes in behavior manifestations as something that "comes and goes." It is taken for granted that eventually a balance will be effected in the personality of the child. A similar attitude toward the behavior of children is generally assumed in the school.

The conditions for learning which make provisions for a child to gain meanings about the ways of his behavior must be built on a philosophy which regards behavior as important in a positive way. In the first place, the school must be associated with a function which is more than making a child literate. The school must be associated with that thinking which helps an individual to gain an understanding of himself—his capabilities, his powers, his limitations.

Very early in the child's school life, the conditions for learning must be of the type which clarify to him what he is able to do and what tasks must be postponed. For example, he cannot drive a car but he should have the opportunity to sense what strengths in mind and body are needed to drive a car. He has the powers to think and visualize which clarify to him his limitations. He has the ability very early in life to gain a general appreciation of the tasks which adults perform and, through analysis with the teacher and parents, to recognize that he cannot at present bring his mind and body to function coordinately in performing those tasks. The child does, however, have the strengths to perform certain tasks which are also performed by adults. For example, he is able to clean up his room and to go to the grocery store for his mother to buy some things for her.

In order to develop meanings with respect to the points which have been mentioned, it is clear that the conditions for learning might include much more than is indicated by the routine described in a previous section. These conditions might be labeled as "Thinking About What We and Our Parents Do." In the course of a work session in the kindergarten or first grade, questions might be raised as to the work done by adults and the work done by children. The questions should be amply portrayed with pictures on bulletin boards or experience charts so that the thinking of children will be encouraged. Much can be done in sessions of this type to develop constructive ideas with children about responsibility, understanding of their role in the family, and moral questions about love and care. More important is the fact that in this situation children are gaining meanings with regard to their behavior.

Conditions must help children understand feelings and their consequences. A second element of the philosophy operative in the conditions for making intangibles meaningful for the child is that of self-derivation of values in behavior. The function of the school must be associated with value-building by the child. The emphasis in learning here is not on *telling* by the teacher, but rather on the mutual setting of the stage for behaviors to develop. In other words, the emphasis is on the development of those conditions which will enable the child to derive some meanings relative to those feelings which have baffled him. One of these intangible feelings may be anger. A child experiences anger from time to time, the consequences of which may at some times be satisfying and at other times distasteful to him. Since the culture accepts these conditions of behavior as part of the make-up of people, the child gives them either a passing thought or no thought at all.

In school, the emphasis in learning usually has little or no relationship to feelings. Although the teacher would find it difficult to explain to a child about his feelings, he could initiate the arrangements which would tend to point up the consequences of those feelings. Meaning as to the nature of the feelings can, therefore, be approached through the conditions which envision the consequences which may ensue if the feelings are acted on. With particular reference to promoting understanding with regard to the feeling of anger, the conditions may carry a portrayal of the following process to induce concern about it: Type of anger, what caused it, what was done about it, and what happened.

Conditions must provide for resourceful experiences about feelings. The analysis of feelings of anger might initially take the form indicated above. Children will offer innumerable examples of feelings of anger that they have harbored and what they did with the feelings. The examples will also be very valuable as they analyze the results of their action on the feelings. At this point, the children will evaluate the process of the feelings from the inception to the culmination of them. Some of the results prove to be satisfying and constructive. Other results appear to be satisfying to some children but raise questions in their minds as to whether the effects were constructive. Some children would be able to distinguish the questionable results from the constructive ones. One or two children might reveal that they were so angry that they couldn't think. A number of children might express regret for having done what they did when they were angry. A few children would suggest that they were angry but got over it.

As the teacher and children study anger in terms of the leads furnished, they will introduce several new elements into the conditions for understanding feelings. One of the elements would be that of thinking as to what caused the feelings. The child would begin to consider the people toward whom his feelings are directed. He would also attempt to analyze the feelings of the other people toward him. Thus the child would try to determine what he said or did which might have been regarded as a threat by the other person or persons. This will lead to the introduction of another element into the situation—that of caring about what happens to the other person's feelings.

Another element which might be suggested as influencing the conditions for understanding of behavior is thinking about the consequences before one acts on feelings. This, in turn, may suggest the study and thinking about those prior elements of action on feelings which were satisfying both to the actor in the situation and the recipient of the action.

All the elements suggested as becoming part of the conditions for learning about intangibles in behavior might be portrayed in drawings, cartoons, or pictures with captions such as the following:

HOW ANGER HELPS
ANGER AS A DESTRUCTIVE FORCE
WAYS IN WHICH PEOPLE SHOW FEELINGS
STORIES WHICH DESCRIBE THE FEELINGS OF PEOPLE
WAYS IN WHICH PEOPLE THINK ABOUT FEELINGS

As suggested, meanings with regard to the above topics may be developed with young children through drawings which they make to represent feelings. As a child finishes his drawing, he hangs his picture under the appropriate topic on a bulletin board. Pictures and cartoons may also be selected from magazines, newspapers, and other sources and placed under the captions which are to be represented. From the stories which the teacher reads and which are developed together with the children in the kindergarten, the ones describing feelings are selected and placed on tables under the proper headings. In first and second grades, as children are gaining initial strengths in reading, they will pick out the stories which represent the feelings indicated by the different headings. Time is taken to analyze for meanings their drawings, the pictures they have selected, and the stories they have chosen. In the process of identification with the feelings analyzed, the children may arrive at certain generalizations which will serve effectively in subsequent situations where feelings are involved.

Developing meanings about intangibles with older elementary and secondary school students

The pattern of developing meanings with regard to intangibles indicated in the previous pages may be continued with older children and through the high school. The opportunities, of course, in studying behavior with older children would be expanded to include the literature of the great thinkers of the present and of other times and places. The process, summarized, would be somewhat as follows: The development of the conditions for evoking concern about elements of behavior which are felt but not understood, structuring the conditons so as to enable children to identify themselves with the feelings, analyzing the feelings in terms of possible consequences, evaluating the results, and generalizing in terms of the results and the incorporation of choices into the value pattern.

The steps indicated in the process do not necessarily follow each other but may occur simultaneously. Also, as children grow older, more and more reading materials are used in the analysis and study of the intangibles. Basic thinking is inherent in the process, especially where readings are used, of analyzing the consequences of different types of fear, anger, and other feelings. This will frequently result in incorporating into the behavior pattern those alternatives in feelings which show promise in human understanding. Basic thinking gradually produces a revised criteria for the acceptance of values into one's behavior pattern. Research could aid in the development of the criteria. A good example of research which could be carried on is an assessment of reactions of children as statements displaying various degrees of aggressiveness are presented.

Conditions might provide for center of behavior study. In the elementary school, much use is made of bulletin boards for graphic picture representation of consequences of intangible feelings. In the secondary school the graphic representations take on more abstract meanings. These meanings could be analyzed in connection with the development of a center for behavior study. By center for behavior study is meant the designation in the school of a place and the development of conditions where young people might study and analyze the intangible elements in such topics as incentives, status, and security.

The center for behavior study might be developed in a section of the library, in the classroom, or an extra room in the building. The center would be supplied with all types of books and materials related to such topics as indicated above and to significant issues in history and contemporary times. With the use of all types of literature encompassing the thinking of men in the present as well as of other times and places, students will be led into a study of the processes of behavior which shaped the ideas for great events. A study of the motives and other factors involved in the thinking of men who exerted much influence on events of the past and today will reveal many meanings relative to intangible concepts. It will also be discovered that much of the thinking and action of other people is not unlike that which is operative in the immediate local situation.

Concluding observation about school's role in intangible meanings

An attempt has been made to present some of the ways by which children will gain meanings about the intangible feelings in their behavior. This topic will be developed in detail in a separate chapter of this book. The whole thread of the relationship between intangibles and tangibles continues more or less throughout the book. It has been suggested that the function of the school is primarily that of creating the conditions for children, when they first enter school and on through, to learn about those feelings which they do not understand. As they gain meanings about the intangible feelings which they have, they will be better equipped to act intelligently on those feelings in the subsequent establishment of value patterns.

The school should develop the conditions whereby it operates as a partner with the parents and community. The conditions for meaningful development should first include those feelings which are involved in responsibility, love, and care as between child and parent. To the parent, school then should become associated with thinking about oneself—one's purposes, role, powers, and responsibility as a person. The school exists to generate thinking before action and to provide the resources and conditions for the formation of a higher quality of value patterns. The heart of the school's function is to charge the learning environment in such a manner as to enable children and youth to understand their behavior sufficiently well to generate constructive decisions relative to the problems of living which they encounter.

THE ADMISSION OF ALL VALUES INTO THE INSTRUCTIONAL SETTING

Most learning situations are structured in such a manner as to admit the values of only a part of the students into the instructional setting. Under these conditions, one's own values as well as those of others will only be partially understood. In order to have a comprehensive setting for learning, it is essential that all values be admitted into the learning situation. It is necessary to do this to broaden and refine the existing values of some pupils as well as to cause a change in the values of others. Value direction has usually been enforced by suppression. This has the effect of causing the possessors of certain values to practice them where the suppressing agent cannot operate. No real change takes place because the possessors had no opportunity to match values in thinking about them with others. They have not recognized the existence of any satisfactory alternative values because the conditions were not provided where they could examine them.

Learning conditions must provide for the analysis
of values of people

Values, in order to be understood, must be brought under analysis and examination. Under the conditions where a clear portrayal of all values is developed, the possible consequences of them can be tested. As these consequences are envisioned by the students, the facts will help them in a studied appraisal of the relative merits of different values. It is the responsibility of the school to make provision for the development of studied insight into the nature of the different values held by people. The classroom is the most natural laboratory for value development. The courageous and resourceful teacher will try to bring all the values held by children into the conditions for learning so that real constructive decisions in behavior will be brought about. An entire chapter on the admission of values is developed in this book so it is unnecessary to discuss it further here.

PROVISIONS FOR FLEXIBLE CONDITIONS
FOR LEARNING

Since the provision for flexibility in the conditions for learning is implied in the discussion on the previous pages and will continue in connection with the development of the other topics, the matter of physical features mainly will be considered here. The studies on group dynamics have demonstrated quite conclusively that the arrangement of physical features in school and other groups makes a difference in the learning process. By flexible is meant that arrangements are adaptable to different situations. If, for example, the learning occasion is the presentation of a lecture, the physical arrangements can be more or less formal because each individual is listening to the lecturer. The individual's relationship here, for the time being, is with the speaker and no one else. If, however, there is a period for raising questions or comments, an attempt should be made to relax the rigidity of the occasion.

One thing that could be done to involve more people as participants in the question period is for the audience to be grouped into several sections with each section asking one or two questions which would be common to the section. A better way, if the lecturer could be available for a period of time, is for groups to spend a part of a day digesting the various points of the lecture and formulating questions and comments which may be dwelt on in another session.

Conditions should contribute to intercommunication for high level thinking

Depending on their various purposes individuals, no doubt, need to hear lectures frequently so as to assess their own thinking compared to the thinking of specialists who have made an intensive study of certain questions. The assessment of the thinking by individuals against the thinking of the lecturers is, however, not complete without an opportunity to become conversant with the reaction of other individuals to the thinking of the lecturers. It is important, then, to make arrangements for a more complete learning situation—that of providing the facilities where individuals may gather in face-to-face informal relationships to assess the thinking on the topics presented by the lecturers.

Conditions must facilitate pupil intercommunication for high level meanings. It is indeed regrettable that in most learning situations the opportunities for real understanding and higher levels of thinking are denied to individuals because of the thoughtlessness or ignorance relative to proper provision for facilities and arrangement. Unfortunately, this is just as true in school situations as in community groups. In most schools which the author has visited, a child usually learns about how other children think about a question or problem outside of the classroom setting. Children get to know each other more often outside of the school situation than in it. This, of course, is due to the rigidity and regimentation which often characterizes the philosophy of school as conceived by the public as well as certain educators. Part of this condition is due to the rigidity of school schedules. Often, however, it is due to the formality of arrangements within the class schedules. Granted that the instructor has a certain amount of material to cover, he should give much thought to the fact that by covering it he might have done no more than expose students to it.

In any school system it is the responsibility of the administration to develop the arrangements whereby all the children are served in terms of their background and understanding. This necessitates the development of the conditions for the utilization of the resourcefulness of all staff members in expanding and intensifying opportunities for learning. This would mean the setting up of facilities where children could learn from each other, where advanced thinking could be developed through the establishment of centers of selected resources, and where scheduling would be responsive to individualization of opportunities for learning. Most important of all, these teachers would see to it that arrangements are made for students to become acquainted with each other's reactions and thinking relative to important questions.

The charge is often made that teachers and parents, acting on the assumption that youth is interested only in social affairs and passive diversions, make provision only for those functions. At the same time, they frequently lament over the lack of responsibility of youth in the approach to serious matters. With the exception of a few isolated instances, this writer has yet to witness a real effort on the part of most school administrators, teachers, and parents to establish centers apart from classrooms where youth might enter into a serious study of behavior through the humanities, sciences, and arts in such a manner as to be able to identify with these fields of knowledge.

Conditions must provide new conceptions about the classroom

It is assumed in this discussion that all classrooms from kindergarten through graduate school should be equipped with the best type of movable furniture. Also, rooms should be so equipped as to make arrangements quickly for different situations, such as use of visual aids and opportunity for group work. With all types of evidence from research and literature on group dynamics it seems rather obvious that there should be very little question, if any, as to the need of the above facilities. It is appalling to witness the prevalence of the limited conception which prevails in many communities with regard to the arrangements of classrooms. This conception almost invariably associates school with rows of desks and chairs frequently screwed to the floor. Other associations with school as conceived by the public in a passive manner are the gymnasium, lunchroom, and library.

Sometimes an auditorium is recognized as a phase of school but, often, it is combined with the gymnasium or lunchroom, especially in elementary schools. It seems regrettable that the faith of the public is so entrenched in the association of the schools with classrooms that the question of education has become really secondary in importance. More often than not the thinking is so patterned with respect to schools and classrooms that the question of how education could be best provided becomes submerged in the pattern.

It is not the intention of the discussion to convey the impression that classrooms are unnecessary. Classrooms are necessary and no school could operate effectively without them. It is important, however, that the emphasis on the classroom be critically examined. It is imperative that the conditions for learning be developed in such a manner that the arrangements in the classroom will be within those conditions. Therefore, in every step of planning the school building and facilities, the conditions which are to be developed for learning should take precedence.

Providing flexible room arrangements in elementary school. The room for kindergarten children should be in one unit and large with ample space for group and individual play and work. There should be sufficient space in the center of the room for rhythmic and group games. Besides this, there should be various nooks within the room which would lend themselves to planning in terms of ideas which children develop. They may wish to plan a book center, a home center, a science center, and other areas of learning experiences. Within the nooks and around the wall should be shelves, storage space, and facilities to make materials accessible and to exhibit work which children have completed.

The room should be arranged in such a way as to make it possible to work out ideas which go beyond the regular routine. For example, there should be an opportunity for children to portray in painting and drawing what they think about things. This would give the teacher some degree of insight about the concepts of children and their efforts in solving problems. This is one way of enabling the teacher to discover some of the values which young children hold. Many of the feelings and attitudes of children will be revealed when they are released to think about the things which appear in their painting, drawing, and clay modeling.

The rooms for children above the age of kindergarten should also be spacious. There need not be as many nooks and special arrangements in the rooms of older children because it is important that they become more independent in improvising the facilities for learning. For example, instead of the teacher taking the major initiative in arrangements, the children must become more responsible in developing their centers of interest in terms of the questions which are raised.

The teacher will, of course, play a major part in structuring the environment for learning so that ideas and questions will arise. The children, however, acting on many questions and ideas which have emerged in the classroom would proceed with the development of arrangements which would make it possible to facilitate an understanding about them. At times these questions would have to be studied individually. In that case, the conditions should be such that children will not be disturbed by each other. This calls for a more or less formal arrangement of seating. At other times, it is essential that children study the questions and ideas together by working in groups. For that purpose, it would be helpful if the room could be blocked off into compartments where the different groups could work without disturbing each other. To facilitate the opportunities for group study, it would be helpful either to have rooms other than the classroom available or to have lightweight sliding doors so that the room could be arranged into several sections.

Providing equipment appropriate to expansion of ideas. It is assumed that if learning is to develop into the utmost completeness, the classroom should be equipped accordingly. Among other common items needed to promote learning, there should be sufficient large size paper so that children will have an opportunity to visualize their ideas in picture and graphic form.

Each learning center—science, social understanding, communications, arts, and arithmetic—should have an ample supply of slides, film strips, and pictures which portray the meanings to be derived from the center. Equipment such as a camera, film, and other materials should be available so that children might learn to visualize an idea from its inception to its completion. Maps of all types should be made available so that children may identify the places in the nation and world where different types of thinking are developing. It is extremely important to have many maps which are not filled in so that children might portray in various places on maps the international trouble spots, underdeveloped countries, conflict within countries, means of livelihood in different countries, and other items of international interest.

Classrooms should be equipped with plenty of bulletin board space, several easels, three or four chart holders, and exhibit tables or cases so that the process and results of study and thinking may be visually represented. There are, of course, many other items which should be included to promote effectiveness in learning. Enough, however, have been indicated to illustrate the importance of ample equipment in the classroom.

Contributions of library to the conditions for learning

An attempt has been made to show the development of physical arrangements and facilities so as to provide the conditions for learning which will enable the pupil to engage in basic thinking, study, and research on questions and problems which affect him and others. The discussion up to this point has dealt with the classroom of the elementary school. It is implied that the classroom becomes a laboratory for the development of ideas. The physical arrangements must be adapted to the development of the conditions where thinking and decision will evolve relative to ideas which influence the value pattern of people. The classroom, however, is just one facet of the conditions to promote completeness in learning both in the elementary and secondary school.

Library must develop concern about knowledge. That the library is an important adjunct to the conditions for learning is more or less accepted in educational planning. Frequently, however, the library is just another room, perhaps a little larger than a classroom. Although size of the library is important so that sufficient space may be available for books and reading tables it is, however, not the most important feature of a library room. The most important feature of a library is personnel who understand the function of the library in developing concern about knowledge on the part of children. The arrangements should be such as will help to establish in the learning environment those ingredients which will cause children and youth to seek knowledge. How are these ingredients manifested in the physical arrangements? In the case of elementary children, as they enter the library they should be greeted by signs in different sections of the room, some of which might read as follows:

DO YOU KNOW YOURSELF? DO YOU BELIEVE THAT THESE BOOKS MIGHT
GIVE YOU SOME THOUGHTS ABOUT YOURSELF?

THESE BOOKS HELP YOU UNDERSTAND OTHER PEOPLE.

HERE YOU WILL LEARN ABOUT THE SCIENCE OF MACHINES.

HERE YOU WILL FIND THE BOOKS WHICH TELL ABOUT NATURE.

THESE BOOKS TELL HOW PEOPLE HAVE BUILT THINGS THAT HELP US.

THESE BOOKS TELL HOW TO MAKE SIMPLE THINGS.

THESE BOOKS HAVE STORIES ABOUT HOW CHILDREN IN OTHER LANDS
WORK AND PLAY.

WOULD YOU LIKE TO KNOW ABOUT THE GREAT EVENTS IN HISTORY?

WHY NOT BECOME A STUDENT OF HISTORY?

WOULD YOU LIKE TO JOIN OTHERS IN THINKING ABOUT THE WAYS IN
WHICH PEOPLE BEHAVE?

THESE BOOKS WILL HELP YOU HAVE FUN WITH YOUR FAMILY AND
FRIENDS.

THESE BOOKS GIVE YOU IDEAS ABOUT HOW TO PROTECT YOURSELF AND
OTHERS.

IN THIS SECTION YOU WILL DISCOVER MORE ABOUT THE PROBLEMS OF
PEOPLE IN DIFFERENT LANDS.

ON THIS SHELF ARE BOOKS WHICH TELL ABOUT FEELINGS AND HOW
DIFFERENT PEOPLE HAVE THOUGHT ABOUT THEM.

Library an adjunct to classroom as a resource and service center. It would be very helpful if the library shelves were low and, if possible, on wheels so that sections could be moved into a classroom. The library should be a resource and service unit of the entire educational program. It should, therefore, have the facilities to transmit sections of shelves of books as needed to the various classrooms of the school. If it is impossible to put the shelves on wheels, then there should be a number of mobile sections and movable carts available so that books can be taken from the library to the classrooms. The books would, of course, be checked out so that there would be an accurate record as to the location of each book.

In connection with the suggestions indicated above, we wish to emphasize again that the function of the library is to promote concern for knowledge on the part of children. Accordingly, it must become a resource and service center for the promotion of study, research, and basic learning. To be truly resourceful in facilitating learning, the library must be an adjunct to the classroom.

The library should be sufficiently large, especially in the elementary school, so that the librarian will be able to discuss the books and materials with about thirty children at a time. Another reason for ample room is to make it possible to display the books in terms of such topics as are suggested on the previous page. There must be sufficient room, too, so that groups of children might come in to select one, two, or more shelves of materials which they need to take to the classrooms. The point that should be made, however, is that a library should never be used as a study hall. Too frequently it is used mainly for that purpose in many secondary schools. As a matter of fact, there is no reason for a special study hall in a constructive educational program.

In a school where real educational leadership exists, every room is used for study, research, thought generation, and other processes essential to constructive learning. Every room in the building is in a sense a library. If every room is not another library, then it is the function of the main library to make it so. By extending the library throughout the school, the librarian is fulfilling a major responsibility in promoting concern and quest for knowledge.

In the junior high school, library services should be developed very much in the same manner as in the elementary school. Again it is emphasized that the library should not be a study hall, but rather a place where a class or groups of children are helped to use books and other materials in gaining meanings and understandings.

In the senior high school, the library must be even more resourceful and serviceable than with younger children. The library should contain sufficient space so that it may be stocked well with books and materials in the humanities, sciences, and the arts. Many of the shelves should carry labels of materials in terms of the various subjects. Some of the shelves should carry books and materials which serve to unify the meanings developed in the various subject areas. There should be several shelves stocked with books on communications. Many shelves should carry books and materials on unifying areas such as behavior, scientific development, the arts and man, international understanding, social understanding, and others. Either the shelves should be made mobile or carts should be provided so that books and other materials may be moved in quantity to classrooms and learning centers.

Planning cafeterias as service units

Another feature of the secondary school where more imagination might be exercised in planning is in connection with the cafeteria. Most secondary schools have immense cafeterias. What purpose is served by hundreds of students eating together? Wouldn't it be better to have smaller cafeterias and have, instead, the facilities for food to be transferred to classrooms or other rooms where students might take their lunch and continue their discussions in smaller groups? The lunch hour plus some additional time might well be used by students in carrying on in the centers of learning. A few schools over the country have been planned with less cafeteria space but most of them still have large cafeterias.

Instead of building an expensive cafeteria, the money might be better expended in providing food-moving facilities and additional rooms where some students can meet to plan and carry through in connection with their various clubs, and others can work in the learning centers. The learning centers are discussed in the next sections. The additional rooms should be constructed where they are close to the kitchen so that the food wouldn't have to be moved very far. There should, of course, still be a small cafeteria where some of the pupils might have their lunch and where meals might be planned for groups larger than those contained in a classroom.

Concluding observations about importance of flexible conditions

An attempt has been made to indicate some of the physical features in schools which contribute to flexible conditions of learning as opposed to the formal conception of classrooms. It should be noted that the proposals which have been made do not carry any sign of superficialities in arrangements for better learning conditions. In brief, for elementary schools some of the provisions suggested are adequate equipment and facilities for the development of centers of learning which will enhance the pupil's concern for knowledge. There should be maps, files, charts, bulletin board space, and other features for pupils to portray their thinking and learning. It also means that rooms should have movable desks, tables, library carts and facilities to make a room into compartments where groups might work together at certain times.

If it is thought impractical to have movable walls to adjust classrooms for different purposes, then other small rooms should be made available for groups to carry on plans for work and research together. In any event, the classrooms are to be considered the real laboratories for learning, and libraries should be developed mainly as service units for the classrooms. This means that the library of an elementary school should either have movable shelves stocked with materials arranged in terms of topics which might be transferred to classrooms when needed, or movable carts or miniature bookmobiles to move books which are needed to the classrooms and study centers.

In the secondary schools, similar facilities should be provided with the addition of rooms to serve as interdisciplinary centers. The libraries should arrange the materials in broad fields such as humanities, arts, and the sciences with some subdivisions carrying such titles as communication, man and his behavior, man creates opportunities through science, thinking through literature, and others. Provisions should be made for students to transfer the materials to convenient centers for study, discussion, research, and basic thinking.

Although we have gone to considerable length in discussing some of the physical arrangements which we consider important in promoting effective conditions for learning, we will be the first to admit that we have only approached a partial coverage of the topic. The auditorium, gymnasium, music rooms, and dramatic and speech facilities are other features which play a most important phase in the development of the conditions for learning. To deal with all these features would contribute nothing new, however, to the theme which is attempted in this book, that is, the development of the conditions for learning. In dealing with the classroom, we feel we have projected the conditions for learning as they would be dealt with in the auditorium, little theatre, or any of the other adjuncts to a full-fledged educational program. We shall leave the rest then to the enlightened administrators and educational planners who are doing much of what is advocated in the discussion.

PROVIDING FOR UNITY OF LEARNING

The term, unity of learning, may mean different things to different people. We prefer to treat the term as the conditions in learning which bring about the use of resources as derived in the different disciplines toward a unity of knowledge in the student. Since this topic is dealt with at considerable length in several chapters of this book, only a brief discussion will be attempted here.

Although everyone has more or less designed for himself a special function to perform as his means of achieving a livelihood, he finds that his responsibilities are many and, to a large degree, unlimited. An example of this is the engineer who has as his special function the duties of developing and operating a flood-control dam. Although it is essential that he possess a good background and knowhow regarding his special duties, his responsibilities do not end there. He must be able to communicate about his specialty in such a manner as to reach different groups of people. He must know much about conservation. He must become conversant with the processes of governmental operation which are often involved with the development of dams. He must know something about politics. He needs to become familiar with the matters of finance involved in the construction and operation of the dam. Last but not least, he must be cognizant of his responsibilities as a citizen in the community in which he resides. In other words, to be truly resorceful in his capacity, he has to be more than a specialist. He works with people and thus must operate in terms of the thinking and behavior of people.

Conditions for unity advance human resourcefulness

In view of the above example, it is rather obvious that the development of human resourcefulness necessitates a unified approach to knowledge. Subjects, of course, are necessary in the process of obtaining a degree of insight into the various disciplines and the acquisition of skills for one's chosen profession or occupation. A unification of knowledge where the various subjects become resources in that knowledge provide direction to living in the wider sense. Mathematics and science may establish background in the pursuit of a specialized knowledge of engineering. As the engineer, however, envisions his total role, he will recognize that literature and other studies relating to an understanding of behavior of people are vital in the fulfillment of that role.

Although only one example relative to the need for a unified approach to learning is given, the same principle would apply to the other professions and occupations carried on by people. It seems plausible and logical, then, that the conditions for learning in the elementary, secondary, and on through the graduate school in the university should make provisions for unification of knowledge. Without detracting in the least from the subjects in the curriculum, definite provisions should be made for students to study, do research, and think basically in such areas as communication, behavior of people, science and man, and the arts and man. This means that method and content as well as the various disciplines must operate as a unity in the development of learning with students. Real opportunity must be provided for students to identify with the resources of knowledge in terms of ideas. Method is part and parcel of the content for ideas. It cannot be developed separately. It must grow out of the analysis of content as related to ideas. Content is not important by itself but becomes important only when treated in such a manner as to give the student some insight into the behavior of people. The teacher has a definite responsibility in structuring the learning conditions so that the subject is freed and made available to the student for the purposes of self-identification.

Developing centers to promote unity of knowledge

Frequent reference is made throughout the book to the development of centers of interest or learning. Perhaps the greatest function of educators is to initiate the conditions to promote concern on the part of children to understand themselves basically—their feelings, processes of thinking toward action on the feelings, and the synthesis of the results in terms of a pattern of values. The physical arrangements of a school have much to do with the development of these conditions. As pointed out before, the school is usually associated with classrooms. This has become more or less a pattern in the thinking relative to physical features of the school. A further pattern which has developed throughout the years is that classrooms are associated with subjects—chemistry, English, history, and others. The discussion which carries throughout this book is designed to broaden the thinking about the treatment of subject matter. In order to do this, the emphasis on thinking relative to subject matter must be on its comprehensiveness. Each subject may be dealt with in such a manner as to promote a unity of knowledge. That means that the subject matter, when properly developed, will be identified with the process of living—the thought and action of man.

Centers help children gain unity with subject matter. The development of centers of interest is a means to the identification of the learner with the subject matter. In the elementary school, the centers of interest and learning may be established within the classroom. In connection with the study of English, the centers may revolve around topics such as the following: Saying What You Mean, Conveying Your Feelings, Finding Words for Your Thoughts and Feelings. Bulletin boards are provided where thoughts and feelings are expressed in writing and in pictures as children conceived them. These are evaluated together with the teacher. Then, as children are learning how to express their thoughts, they are at the same time learning much about themselves and the values they hold. As a result, they are identifying with the subject in more than a superficial manner. They have a working familiarity with it or, to say it another way, attain a sense of unity with it. Thus a unity of knowledge is being effected. As children are beginning to gain greater insight with respect to their ideas and how to express them, they are recognizing the need for more background relative to their tasks. It is important then to bring in books, pictures, and other materials and make them accessible in connection with the particular tasks at hand. Children may want to represent their feelings about ideas both before and after thinking about the consequences. Equipment such as bulletin boards, easels, chart holders, book and magazine racks, shelves and exhibit sections must be made available so that this can be done.

Centers help youth approach thinking and research on basic questions. In the secondary school, the maturity of the student necessitates, of course, a somewhat different use of the centers of interest and learning than in the elementary school. One type of approach to the unity of knowledge in a high school subject might be illustrated in connection with the study of the Civil War in American history. Centers of learning with respect to this area of American history might be represented by the following questions: What were the seeds which generated this conflict? What were the patterns of thinking which eventuated in war? Do you recognize alternative patterns of thinking which were overlooked? Do you discern some conciliatory elements in the thought processes which led to decisions previous to the Civil War? What basic principles were involved? Did the consequences of the conflict serve these prinples?

As one views the above questions, it becomes increasingly clear that in the study of the Civil War, the student must identify with the motives of people and their behavior in serving the motives. This means that the student must make use of all types of resources to do research and basic thinking relative to the questions. Thus it is necessary to make shelves of books and magazines available to the students. Furthermore, the facilities must be provided where students might gather in face-to-face relationships to help each other toward a mutual sense of understanding and insight relative to the questions at hand. It is important then to have arrangements which will enable students to deal with these questions within the classroom, during lunch, and in the library where groups of students might meet for discussion. Furthermore, there should be at hand movable blackboards, bulletin boards, and chart holders on which a running development of the thinking may be recorded.

Centers provide expanded conditions for insight and understanding. It was suggested that centers of learning to bring out unity of knowledge within a subject should be developed to promote expanded conditions for insight and understanding. These centers, it was pointed out, might be developed in the classrooms and such other areas in the building as are available. It is valuable, in addition to these centers, to establish the conditions to develop an interdisciplinary approach to learning. Educators, in planning buildings to house secondary pupils, should go beyond the concept of a classroom for each subject.

In order to provide for truly needed educational effectiveness in a secondary school, there should be several rooms which would be used to develop learning with respect to such areas as the following: Communication, Science and Man, Social Understanding, Man and His Behavior, Great Ideas, and possibly others. In providing these facilities, there is no intention to minimize the importance of the subject fields such as history, English, chemistry, biology, and mathematics. On the contrary, the development of these centers will tend to point up the importance on the part of students of understanding the subject field. For example, to understand the area of communication, it is necessary for the student to know history, English, literature, and science.

The centers will help the teachers and students to bring the subject matter of all the areas of knowledge into a unitary focus. Furthermore, the centers will tend to develop a concern for learning which goes far beyond a simple preparation for college. The true function of the secondary school is to enable the student to view the sequence of preparation as the acquisition of powers of skills and understanding in the quest for knowledge. The sequence then is adaptation to college plus. The college becomes one of the milestones in the process of becoming identified with the heritage and the horizons of knowledge and understanding.

SELECTED READINGS

Beck, Robert H., Walter W. Cook, and Nolan C. Kearney, *Curriculum in the Modern Elementary School.* Englewood Cliffs, N. J.: Prentice-Hall, Inc., 1955, pp. 49-225.

Brameld, Theodore, *Cultural Foundations of Education.* New York: Harper & Bros., 1957. The importance of this book lies in the interdisciplinary approach to the foundations of education. The book should guide one into an attempt to unify the understanding of the culture and its sub-components—environment, values, social forces, and idea patterns. Especially pertinent to the discussion is the section entitled "Human Freedom as Cultural Goal," Chapter 12.

Brogan, Peggy and Lorene K. Fox, *Helping Children Learn.* Yonkers-on-Hudson, N. Y.: World Book Co., Chapter 1. Very valuable discussion on the required conditions for learning.

Education for American Freedom, Washington: Bulletin Association for Supervision and Curriculum Development, National Education Association, 1954. Many clues to the development of meanings relative to freedom.

Gilmer, B. Von Haller. *How to Help Your Child Develop Successfully.* Englewood Cliffs, N. J.: Prentice-Hall, Inc., 1951. pp. 73-98. Valuable discussion about fears, anger, and other emotional factors.

Kelley, Earl C. and Marie I. Rasey, *Education and the Nature of Man.* New York: Harper & Bros., 1952, 205 pp. Entire book is highly relative to developing conditions for learning. The reader's attention is directed especially to Chapter 2, "The Dynamics of Change," Chapter 3, "Man's Structure and Method," Chapter 5, "Man and His Environment," Chapter 10, "Freedom," and Chapter 14, "The Next Development in Man."

Lee, Elizabeth Bryant and Alfred McClune Lee, *Social Problems in America.* Part I, Chapters 1, 2, 3. Part II, Chapter 4. A source book. New York: Henry Holt & Co. Revised Edition, 1955.

Whitehead, Alfred North, *The Aims of Education and Other Essays.* New York: Mentor Books, 1952, pp. 40-52. The reader is directed to the late Professor Whitehead's rather penetrating discourse in the essay, "The Rhythmic Claims of Freedom and Discipline."

❖4❖

Developing Direction
in Instruction

AS STATED IN CHAPTER 1, IT IS THE BELIEF OF THIS WRITER THAT
the approach to curriculum improvement should take place
within the context of the classroom. It is in the classroom where
the child and curriculum come together. It is here where the
vital questions about instructional practices find a natural and
functional habitat. Some of the most important signals for
the initiation of curriculum improvement are the expressions
of concern over instructional problems. Some of these expressions run something like this:

"Yes, some are ready to learn and interested, but it is like pulling
eye teeth to get others interested."

"It is a pleasure to work with the youngsters in the second period
class, but I am at my wit's ends to know what to do with my fifth
period class."

"The group I had last year learned to read so quickly, but my
group this year is really slow."

"I dare not leave this group a minute but what they are all over
the place."

"What can I do to get these children interested in something?"

"What makes these people so noisy and quarrelsome?"

"I just don't feel that I can let these youngsters work in groups
because they get out of hand."

"The mental ages of most of these children are above their chronological ages, and yet they have trouble with everything."

"The slow children take so much of my time that I cannot do justice to the fast learners."

"I think the fast-learning children are getting a poor deal."

"There just isn't time to do all the things that we should do according to the course of study."

"These children want to talk all the time about what they do outside of school."

"I have to spend too much time every morning with chores such as lunch money, tickets, announcements, and other administrative matters. Couldn't something be done about this?"

"We do not seem to finish the jobs we begin because of the shortage of time."

"I do not have time to work on problems with children because of the many necessary things they have to do."

"Why doesn't the principal tell us what he wants?"

"It sounds all right in theory, but it doesn't work out in practice."

One could go on indefinitely enumerating expressions of anxiety and concern by teachers, but the above are sufficient to indicate the type of questions which are bothering them. Furthermore, the anxieties could be multiplied manyfold by hearing the expressions of pupils, administrators, and others engaged in the work of instruction.

SOME CONSEQUENCES OF ANXIETY

It is important to hasten to say at this point that the fact that anxieties exist does not mean that the educational process is ineffective. A mistake made by some curriculum workers, administrators, and others is to interpret the expression as indicative of inability to cope adequately with instructional problems. On the contrary, it is rather wholesome that teachers are concerned with the nature of instructional problems. The effective teacher is not only concerned and anxious with regard to the problems of instruction but usually has more problems than the ineffective teacher. One criterion for judging teaching effectiveness should be the number of problems which a teacher identifies. A good teacher identifies many problems whereas a poor teacher frequently does not identify any. Identification of problems, however, will not by itself guarantee effectiveness in teaching. Effectiveness of teaching is related to what one does with the problems which are identified. The effective teacher will devise ways of approaching the problems whereas the ineffective teacher will view problems as something one either sidesteps or forgets. A very possible difference is that the effective teacher is asking questions about his problems so as to point to answers, whereas the ineffective one has already concluded that since there are no answers any questions would be useless.

Failure to act on problems may bring deterioration in learning

It is easy to talk about effective and ineffective teaching. It is often extremely difficult to get at the basis of effectiveness or ineffectiveness in promoting learning. Similarly, it is difficult to develop the conditions where real action will result with respect to the problems of instruction which have been identified. Action on problems is vitally necessary once the problems have been found. If action does not occur, disturbances are multiplied. When this happens, the mental health of people is impaired. In teaching this is especially significant. If problems and disturbances remain unresolved, the results might be reflected in instruction in one or more of the following ways:

(1) Frustration may develop to such an extent that learning may gradually deteriorate for all children.
(2) Learning will be considered as an attribute only of the faster learners.
(3) Learning will be carried on in independent preconceived patterns regardless of the needs of children.
(4) Learning will be considered synonymous with conformity, "being good."
(5) Disproportionate amounts of attention are given to the slow learners on the belief that the others will get along anyway.
(6) Learning will be conceived as the recalling of structured and isolated information with no thought given to identification with ideas on the part of the children.

Unresolved teacher anxiety hurts people involved

As learning takes one of the above directions, something is happening to the people who are involved. Some youngsters will glide through the experiences so easily that they will develop little real respect for school. Others, failing to grasp meanings, will be frustrated and come to regard school with an attitude of indifference. Still others will just consider it a place you have to go nine months or so during the year. Most of the children come to realize that they can at least "get by" by doing the assignments and responding in the manner that is desired by the teacher. Education to them might become a "package deal" in which they learn to recognize the different size "packages" which are expected. Very few, if any, of the children will regard their school work as a satisfying undertaking. That the classroom should be a center of great and many ideas of life and the world is farthest from their thinking. Children in this situation have met few problems which are at the same time both baffling and challenging. They have little or no opportunity to participate in working out the conditions which would develop an intelligent curiosity relative to the vast store of knowledge residing in the world. They have developed no real incentive to become seekers of knowledge, but have instead complied blindly with patterns with which they have not become identified.

DEVELOPING CONDITIONS FOR DIRECTION
IN INSTRUCTIONAL CHANGE

As indicated previously, the effective teacher usually has more problems and asks more questions about his instructional practices than the ineffective one. Some teachers never seem to have any problems and carry on without any worries or disturbances. Within this group are some effective teachers. Others in this group are proceeding ahead without any apparent difficulties. A closer look at what is happening, however, may reveal some rather impoverished conditions of learning. These teachers apparently have assumed a pattern of practices about which they ask no questions; nor do they invite questions from others.

The group that is carrying on with rather impoverished learning experiences for children is taking one or more of the directions indicated on page 95. This, of course, might not occasion any surprise. Narrow as it may be, these teachers have carefully designed their instructional route. Efforts to effect a questioning attitude on the part of these people may meet with opposition and be fraught with difficulties. Any proposals for curriculum change would be viewed with suspicion.

Conditions for expression of anxiety may constitute "nerve center" for change

The teachers who are asking questions or making comments of the type indicated at the beginning of the chapter possess great potential resourcefulness for curriculum improvement. They constitute a "nerve center" for curriculum change. Yet, lacking the conditions to work on the problems expressed, many of these teachers, too, will tend to settle into a more or less impoverished routine of instruction. It is hoped that curriculum workers will be intelligently alert to develop the conditions which will prevent these unrewarding and tragic consequences.

The principles indicated in Chapter 1 are directly applicable in helping teachers develop direction in instruction. The concerns indicated at the beginning of this chapter must be dealt with at the familiar level of the classrooms. Within the context of the classroom, the teacher is more apt to begin questioning his practices. This questioning attitude is at first the prelude but later becomes part and parcel of curriculum improvement procedures. The questions and expressions of concern regarding instructional problems should become the substance for the handling of ideas by groups of teachers.

Conditions must avoid oversimplification of learning

As the curriculum worker approaches the task of developing the conditions in which teachers will handle ideas toward improved practices, he must take care that he does not oversimplify the content and process of learning experiences. Too often a teacher has somehow gotten the impression that his job is to "keep school." Perhaps some administrators, in the difficulties which they have faced in staffing schools, have unwittingly lent support to that impression. The teacher, going on the assumption that something will happen in the classroom which might be called education, avoids questions about the content and process of learning and concentrates on having a neat-appearing room. The emphasis is on making it appear to all comers that interesting things are going on. There is no questioning in the mind of the teacher as to what is happening. This teacher just more or less proceeds with the routine of teaching as usual. His idea of success in teaching is to carry through with the routine on schedule and without incident. The whole situation may look good. Children are probably busy, order prevails, and the teacher seems interested in what he is doing. He never offers any suggestions or asks any questions about practices. He apparently is not much excited about anything. Attempts to engage him in conversation on educational problems somehow yield very little.

It is obvious that the curriculum worker needs to tread softly with this teacher. If one takes the position that classroom practices are synonymous with curriculum improvement, he finds little resourcefulness here. Yet the teacher may be potentially resourceful. Perhaps the curriculum worker needs to ask himself questions as to what produces constructive involvement in the handling of ideas. Perhaps this teacher can be approached on points of pride relative to his tasks. In any event, it appears that this teacher is leaving many problems untouched. He is acting as if they did not exist. Somehow, concern about ideas and a sense of compulsiveness about high quality learning experiences is not apparent.

There are other teachers who also just "keep school" but talk about it. In these situations, it is much easier for the curriculum worker to work on the problem of oversimplification regarding educational tasks. As people begin talking about their tasks, they usually begin doing something about them. As they are brought into situations where people are asking questions, they will begin to see relationships to their own problems. Thus a degree of involvement with the handling of ideas toward curriculum improvement may be assured.

Statements covering problems should be presented in context with related questions and practices. Frequently, confusion and frustration with regard to learning conditions and curriculum improvement result from the "blanket" coverage of teaching problems conveyed by some educational phrases. Many of these phrases are given out as if they were axioms in learning. The statements, for the most part, are educationally significant; but, when presented out of context with basic and related questions and practices, they are meaningless. As a result, they are fraught with consequences of anxiety on the part of people engaged in teaching. Some of the statements the writer has reference to are as follows:

"Make the work interesting to children."
"Base your instruction on the needs of youngsters."
"Adapt instruction to individual differences."
"Find out what the interests of youngsters are."
"Take the child where he is."
"Learning is creative activity."
"Develop independence in learning."
"Use the principle of discovery in promoting learning."
"Help children identify with problems."
"Make the learning experiences real."
"Develop direct learning experiences."
"Create the freedom to learn."
"Develop a permissive atmosphere."

This list could be vastly extended, but it is sufficient to illustrate a possible reason for the development of questionable conditions in learning. Having digested, on a verbal basis, some of these educational "truths," the teachers will invariably go back to the classroom with mixed feelings. There exists a feeling of distressing uncertainty as to how to implement the intent of the statements in terms of instructional procedures. Due to the rather "surface" treatment of the statements, the basic meanings have not been identified. No curriculum worker should be allowed to get away with these statements out of context with practices and the establishment of basic meanings regarding them.

Educational concepts must be analyzed for deeper meanings. Some teachers, in attempting to implement certain meanings of the statements in the classroom, will often do so with fear and trembling because of their feelings of uncertainty regarding the statements. Some will try to make the work with children interesting by using various devices such as displays, dramatizations, and discussions. In this process, however, some of the teachers may disregard many questions which should have been dealt with in connection with the statement on making the work interesting. Some of the questions may be as follows: Will the emphasis be on the interests of children regardless of social goals? Can interest be equated with needed competences? Should richness of content or expressed interests of children receive priority in learning experiences? What psychological principles are involved in the relation of displays to direction in learning? To what extent and in what manner must the conditions for learning provide for the development of new interests beyond the expressed and felt needs? How does one know where the child "is"? The teacher who is mindful of these questions will have to conclude that making the work interesting to children is not all there is to it. Furthermore, he gathers that building experiences on expressed interests and felt needs of children might pose some serious limitations to learning. These interests and needs may not be constructive nor very far-reaching in the development of competences needed by children. Thus the teacher finds that this one approach, making the work interesting through displays, dramatizations, discussions, and others, has implications and relationships which go *way beyond just making the work interesting.* The fear and trembling which accompanies this instructional attempt may be increased as the tasks and competences involved loom much larger than they appeared on the surface.

As the instructional situation indicated above is viewed by the teacher, he will be confronted with a kind of dilemma. Either he will try to keep the work interesting, come what may, or he will try to bring the high quality implied by the basic questions which have arisen in his mind into his instructional practices. If he decides on the first alternative, he will devote his efforts to keeping the interest high. This may become the prime consideration in anything he undertakes to do with children. If he decides on the latter alternative, he realizes that he must redesign his thinking and study relative to the question of interests of children. He will need to gain new competences as to the basis of children's interests, the forces which motivate the interests, the conditions needed in instruction for the analysis of interests, and so on. In connection with these efforts, however, there may exist certain conditions which limit the realization of his goals.

Curriculum worker must provide conditions to bolster instructional attempts

Frequently, in school systems, no provisions have been made for the cooperative study and improvement of the curriculum by the staff. The teacher may have to redesign his thinking all by himself. Other teachers may have their own ideas about practices which may range all the way from a casual attempt at the implementation of the meanings of the statements to a complete disregard of them. This would put the teacher, who is trying to approach the question of interests of children with a comprehensiveness of understanding, in the position of pioneering in improved instructional practices. It is obvious that his is no easy road. Frustrations may ensue which may leave him somewhat "scarred." In view of the attitudes of many other teachers, the support of his efforts by the administration may be more or less passive.

The task of the curriculum worker in the above situation becomes quite clear. He must anticipate the fact that the lack of any well-conceived machinery and provisions for the mutual study of the problems of teaching will tend to limit the process of instructional improvement on the part of individuals. Where this condition exists, serious efforts on the part of a few individuals to expand the quality of teaching practices will be more or less nullified by the regimen of the *status quo*. Gradually, quality in teaching may be crystallized at a level where uniformity is the guiding pattern. The whole instructional pattern becomes such an oversimplified routine that teachers tend to approach a state of immunity to educational ideas designed to promote quality.

Other examples revealing limited concepts about educational problems are the approach to individual differences, direct learning experiences, and parent-teacher interviews. In order to adapt instruction to what they conceive to be individual differences of children, some teachers develop more ability groups. At best, this is only a partial answer to the question of individual differences. Direct learning experiences are often in-terpreted as all types of field trips. That direct learning experi-ences can take place with an analysis of children's satisfactions and dissatisfactions regarding tasks undertaken in the classroom has never entered the minds of some educators. Since the edu-cational literature advocates parent-teacher interviews as a de-vice to learn about the needs of children, some schools arrange for twenty minute interviews with each set of parents once or twice a year. Where this is done, it is frequently arranged without basic preparation in the dynamics of face-to-face re-lationships and out of context with the child's environment. Role-playing and sociograms are often used for no other reason than that they have been suggested in educational courses and in some of the educational literature. One could go on and on indicating the rather perfunctory treatment of basic and in-volved educational principles in instruction but enough has been described to illustrate the points to be made.

The efforts by teachers as described above alternately dis-close clarity and confusion with regard to purposes. Many of the practices indicated are those which are implicit with the de-velopment of a "façade of learning." The setting for learning looks good, but one wonders if something is happening and whether it is important. The disturbances are often resolved by arrangements which put appearance before actuality. Questions arise in the minds of teachers and others in education as to whether the appearance that "school keeps and keeps well" is enough and whether a "happy and permissive atmosphere" is necessarily directional.

It is important to emphasize again that the curriculum worker must proide for the conditions in which meanings about content and processes of learning are carefully analyzed. He must provide for those situations where teachers will have the opportunity to appraise their anxieties about educational prob-lems together. The conditions must carry elements of impact for establishing meaningful relationships between concerns and procedures. Most important of all, the setting should make graphically accessible the "pioneering" ideas of teachers so that they may be carefully examined for expanded practice. Chapter 1 carries many suggestions for the initiation of these conditions. Chapters 2 and 3 contribute suggestions about the expansion of meanings. It is hoped that the ideas advanced by the suggestions in those chapters and in the following pages will help curriculum workers and teachers move toward improved learning conditions.

THE SCHOOL SHOULD HELP THE INDIVIDUAL UNDERSTAND HIS ENVIRONMENT

All types of forces in the environment are operating on the individual, as has been so clearly pointed out time and time again by social psychologists and sociologists. Parents, of course, are the most important teachers as the home is the primary institution. Parents, however, are those citizens who were and are responsible for the development of schools for the purpose of perpetuating and strengthening the values founded in the home and community. If one looks carefully, he will find another purpose in the founding and development of the school. That purpose is concerned with the individual and his environment. The individual has either been ignorant of or somewhat awed and perplexed at the workings of the environment in shaping patterns of living. To lessen this perplexity and awesomeness, the school has the effect of placing the individual into a condition which may be described as a disciplined arrangement. Within this condition, he begins to detect signs of orderliness and direction in the environment. It should be noted that the disciplined arrangement which the school effects with the individual is not exclusive. On the contrary, the arrangement develops within a condition replete with environmental acts and forces. In other words, the forces operating in the environment are brought under surveillance in the school so that their effects can be more clearly analyzed. The presence of other individuals in this area of surveillance with differing values presents complications which, at the same time, are rewarding. The condition which is developed is that of taking the environment from one context into another where it can be visualized microscopically. The context is the classroom, which has clearly been endowed by the home and community as a mutually operative institution in promoting clarification of direction in the environment.

*Conditions must provide connecting links between
school and environment*

It is reasonable to assume that one of the most important
objectives of education is to develop intelligence on the part
of individuals and groups in their approach to an understanding of their environment and culture. This objective of education has been stated over and over in much of the literature
on education. This means that the teacher and curriculum
worker have a responsibility which at first appears overwhelming, that of making the environment available for close appraisal and study. The real function of the school, then, is to
provide the opportunity for individuals to acquire competence
and understanding as to their relationship to the many influences operating on people in the environment. This suggests
that the classrooms must become laboratories which maintain
points of contact with the environment. Through the examination in thinking and action of the influences residing in the
points of contact, it is hoped that insight and direction will be
established as to dynamic roles in that environment.

In the process of developing understanding with respect to
the environment, a great many more factors are involved than
are indicated. Most of these factors will be developed in other
sections of this book. The point to make here is that the conditions must be established by curriculum workers whereby
the implementation of the principles of learning will become
clarified in the minds of the teacher so that he will approach the
task of instruction with confidence and imagination. The curriculum worker needs to initiate the conditions which will
bring about a clarification for teachers of those forces in the
environment with which they can identify as being operative
in providing clues for instructional direction. The tasks are
by no means easy.

HELPING TEACHERS CLARIFY DIRECTION IN TASKS

A very important point for the curriculum worker to consider when embarking on a program of improvement is to
make certain that the involvement of people carries with it a
clear identification with purposes and goals. His efforts should

be devoted to helping people clarify the purposes in the task which they are undertaking. More important, he should try to ascertain to what degree teachers and children have experienced a favorable balance as to satisfactions and dissatisfactions in past curriculum improvement undertakings. If teachers have done what they conceive to be relatively useless tasks in connection with the improvement of curriculum experiences in the past, they might be very apprehensive to approach another curriculum task. If they are veritably swept into another venture of curriculum development without a clear identification with the purposes, they will tend to be mechanistic in the tasks involved.

Conditions must involve all teachers in clarifying purposes and goals

A corollary to the point indicated above and to which the curriculum worker must give utmost study and attention is that which is related to the behavior of people. He must assess his resources against those which are revealed by the behavior of teachers and children in their experiences in the classroom and school environment. It is true, of course, that teachers are already doing tasks in the classroom which are important to them. There are, however, some experiences which are carried on in the classroom about which teachers are not so sure.

As the curriculum worker is able to ascertain a lack of clarity in purposes and goals on the part of some teachers, he has a clue to some next steps in his responsibility. He needs to develop those conditions which will tend to enhance the concern of the teachers relative to this lack of clarity. Just as important, however, are his efforts to involve those people who seem to be clear about purposes and procedures. These people do not wish to be left alone. The resources of all the teachers are indispensable in curriculum improvement. The conditions should be charged with those elements which will evoke a type of questioning toward identifying the real problems involved in the establishment of purposes and goals. Provision should also be made for a continuing reappraisal of purposes and goals in the light of new values and direction.

The conditions which may be initiated by the curriculum

worker in promoting the questioning of certain practices may be illustrated in an attempt by a teacher to develop an understanding on the part of high school pupils of improving their "style" in expression. The teacher felt that it was essential to develop certain fundamentals before increasing degrees of excellence in style would be attained by the students. The purpose here was to develop a better understanding of style on the part of students. The goal was to establish the habits and attitudes to study and practice better forms of expression and to increase facility toward better speaking and writing. The teacher was clear about these purposes and goals. To facilitate the improvement of style in expression, an accepted textbook with exercises and examples was used. The exercises were studied and discussed and the assignments were prepared. Some of the students did quite well. Others prepared the assignments rather reluctantly and showed no clear identification with the contents. The teacher became quite concerned about the latter group, in spite of the fact that he was probably following a guide to curriculum experiences developed some time ago.

It was clear that the teacher was beginning to question the goals, especially since some of the students did not identify with them. The teacher raised questions about the goals with other teachers and the curriculum worker. The curriculum worker suggested that the questions be raised in a staff meeting by the group concerned. The questions with some accompanying suggestions were developed as part of the agenda for the staff meeting which was devoted to curriculum problems to be faced during the year.

Conditions must promote a convergence and redirection relative to curriculum tasks. It is assumed that the principal will exert the leadership which will cause this problem to be isolated for study, and the development of resources for an improved approach. At the same time, the resources of the principal (the curriculum worker in this case) should be brought to bear toward a unifying approach to the development of style in expression and writing. By unifying is meant that he will, in his conversations with various members of the staff, bring to bear the resources of the teachers in the areas of science, social studies, English, and other fields, to the questions raised relative to style. More important, the forces and values operating in different groups of students will be brought into the conditions for learning.

It will be noted that the approach indicated goes beyond a reconsideration of the adequacy of the guide and the textbook. This points up the idea that curriculum development is much more than a revision of a guide to experiences or the replacement of a textbook. The teachers here are dealing with problems and ideas that transcend revision of a curriculum guide. They are dealing with many questions among which may be the following: Why are the pupils disinterested? How may we get at the real goals of the pupils? Have we separated the purposes and goals from the values of the students? Should the fundamentals of sentence and paragraph structure precede the development of style? What are the psychological factors involved in the development of concern on the part of pupils with respect to style and expression? Have we disregarded the indigenous characteristics of pupils? In the case of those pupils who seem to be interested in improving their style of expression, are the experiences provided ministering to their greatest potential? Since the topic of style in expression is just one element of the whole process of communication, doesn't that open up a clue to the approach needed for real identification with purposes on the part of the pupil?

As the teachers from the various fields come together on such questions as indicated, valuable ideas about curriculum improvement will take shape. Hunches which various teachers had will be tested, plans will be developed, and the quality of thinking about the improvement of curriculum experiences will be expanded. The effect of different forms of communication on the behavior of individuals will be studied. The whole question of the relationship of behavior to communication will be analyzed in different settings for learning. Samples of communication will be taken from magazines, newspapers, television, advertising and other media and studied and analyzed for probable effectiveness. The use of language as an instrument of threat, persuasion, beauty, and status will be critically examined. As teachers approach the problem of improving style of expression, it will become increasingly apparent that there is no end of possibilities in the employment of forms of language. The conditions for learning will have a range of such latitude as will serve the potential of all pupils.

Curriculum worker as learner develops clearer perspective regarding conditions for change

When the curriculum worker has taken stock of himself in the comprehensive manner indicated, he will be in the position to approach the curriculum improvement tasks in a sense of humility and understanding. As a learner along with other staff members, he will gain insight into the meanings of curriculum improvement as they are seen by each individual. He will arrive at a clearer perspective regarding the nature of curriculum change. This, in turn, will tend to give the basis for the development of new anticipations of behavior so essential in the promotion of high level learning experiences with children and young people. The teacher, being assured of a sense of direction and compatibility as to goals, will look to many sources for answers to his questions regarding present instructional practices. The teacher, then, will tend to assess his questions and answers in relation to the thinking of the present as well as other times and places on the nature of learning, and, also, in relation to the children who live and move in terms of the values with which they have identified.

Teacher as learner probes for basic and composite elements of educational problems

In the process of discovering himself and the bases of his reaction to the thinking that he has examined and studied, the teacher will tend to become more sensitive to, and conversant with, the responses of children. Content, then, is not limited to any particular resource developed in some particular course. Content, to adequately fill the vacuities in the process of learning, will be derived from those who are now behaving as well as those whose thinking on behavior has been recorded in books.

The teacher who is approaching an understanding of greatness in teaching will seek to ascertain the composite attributes of all axioms to which he gives expression. When he says that education is change of behavior, he will be able to show the route and the vehicles which are designed to produce the change. More important than that, the teacher will be discriminative with regard to the conditions provided to produce the change. He will set up the conditions wherein children will have the opportunity to help structure the plan of learning experiences in such a manner as will preserve and perpetuate for them the dignity, selfhood, and human welfare of every individual. The learning situation will promote an opportunity to experience the feelings of personal dignity, worthiness, and personable understanding in a degree of intensity sufficient to produce in the participants a real sense of cognition as to the nature of those feelings as they are encountered in subsequent situations. At the same time, the learning situation will provide the ingredients or stimulation for continuous accomplishment, productiveness, and creativity. Good teaching creates a unity between practical self-realization and the maintenance of personal dignity and human understanding.

◦5◦

Developing an Understanding
of Needs

THE IDEAS PRESENTED IN THIS CHAPTER GO BEYOND ANY "NEEDS" theory. Although the idea of needs is useful in promoting curriculum improvement, it is so mainly in opening up related areas of knowledge and understanding. An attempt will be made to analyze in some detail the study and tasks involved in the development of constructive learning with respect to the needs of children. Statements about relating instruction to the needs of children are frequently used in educational materials, by instructors in educational institutions, by some of the curriculum workers, by administrators, by parents, and others. Some of the needs of youngsters that are usually thought of are those of love, affection, self-confidence, feelings of success and status, belongingness, emotional security, and freedom from devastating fears.

CONDITIONS MUST BE ESTABLISHED TO FEEL THE IMPACT OF MEANINGS OF NEEDS

Some of the conditions for the fulfillment of the needs as far as the classroom is concerned are provided in connection with school subjects, playground, teacher relationship with pupils, creative activities, and so on. The goal is to provide happy conditions for achievement. This, of course, is important. Very infrequently, however, are the conditions developed which will charge the learning environment with a full impact of meanings with regard to needs. For instance, one of the needs

110

of the pupil who has always belonged and had security might be to feel rejection so that he will be sensitive to its effects on himself and other people. It may be valuable also to have the setting depict the consequences of hate in such a manner as will cause an analysis of feelings which one holds with respect to that category of behavior.

The whole question of needs is related to the culture within which one finds himself. It is related to the behavior of people in that culture. Since a rather high estimation is placed on social adjustment and conformity in the culture, does it mean, then, that the need to "keep up with the Joneses" is a false need, especially if the Joneses are spoken of with great admiration? Must the values of the individuals in a peer group be alike? If so, does that mean that each one's needs are the same as those of every other member in the group? These and other questions must be dealt with in order to approach an understanding of needs in a going culture.

Curriculum must provide opportunities for children
to understand problems of people

Perhaps, in order to arrive at a true recognition of needs, it will be necessary to create the setting whereby the wants of people will be appraised in terms of what should be rather than what is. Children and the teacher, for example, could analyze to what extent the school is creating opportunities to understand the motives and aspirations of people now as well as throughout the span of history. At the same time, the situation could be structured in such a manner as to bring about a study of the thinking of needs of people as revealed in the story of history in relation to the thinking about needs today.

One approach to the question of determining the needs of people today is to study a section of a newspaper and magazine and observe the problems with which they are confronted. Many observations about the needs and problems of people and institutions can be made with respect to television programs. Most events and stories as related in newspapers, magazines, and television graphically reveal many of the needs and problems of people. If provisions are made in the classroom to point up the relationships of people in the news and other media of communication, children will in turn often see themselves in those same relationships. As children identify with the problems of other people, they will tend to identify some of their own problems. Furthermore, they will begin to discriminate between real needs and false ones.

Curriculum worker and teacher must learn to recognize how the child relates to adults

As one thinks about this whole question of needs, the factors involved loom increasingly larger and more complex. Love and affection are indispensable ingredients in the growth process of children. As the child grows older, he will become increasingly more conversant with the meanings of love and affection. He will begin to relate these meanings to values. He accordingly will recognize, in his relationships with other people, when expressions of love and affection are genuine and when they are merely patterns of propriety. In other words, he is gaining the capacity of recognizing when and where the expressions of love and affection are true. For example, a parent may love his children very much as long as they are very young and "cute." A simple expression of love here seems true and adequate. As the children grow older and their interests change and expand as they should, the parent may still proffer his love very much as he did when they were small. This, to older children, is inadequate. They expect the parent to visualize the changing interests and to have an understanding regarding them. The children will easily recognize whether the parent identifies genuinely or is just acting.

Teacher must identify with changing needs of children. As the child grows older, the terms love and affection take on a somewhat different and expanded meaning which may be interpreted as "caring." It doesn't take an observant person long to recognize those classrooms in which teachers care and those in which this characteristic is absent. In either case, this quality of behavior in teachers will be reflected in the whole classroom atmosphere. To express that one cares is important to children, but it is not enough. True caring about a situation where needs of children are involved is exemplified in a teacher's identification with those needs. The only difference between the teacher and the children as persons is that the teacher is supposed to have greater maturity and experience. This means, then, that the teacher must begin the behavior in the process of learning. When the teacher is a learner with the children, he brings into play the behavior qualities exemplified in caring for others. These qualities take shape in the cooperative analysis of learning situations and ideas, evaluation of plans and developments, teacher-pupil conferences, and a critical appraisal of processes and outcomes.

It is often stated that teachers should not criticize children. On the contrary, criticism is necessary. Children want to be criticized. As a matter of fact, criticism is an attendant quality to caring. It is important, of course, that criticism be administered in a constructive manner. It should be given in a climate of understanding and should generally be directed to the situation rather than the person.

There is a difference between genuine criticism and deflation of selfhood. An example of this occurs when the teacher gives his opinion with respect to some work a group of children are doing. A statement of genuine criticism would be somewhat as follows: "I am somewhat disappointed with the way the plans are shaping up. The work which was considered as necessary to the completion of the plans seems to be falling short in the following respect. . . ." An egocentric form of criticism is revealed in the following: "The work you are doing is very unsatisfactory to me." In the former statement, the teacher is identifying with the plans of the children and specifying points of shortcomings with respect to the work attempted. In the latter statement, the criticism is based entirely on the teacher's preconceptions or patterns. Furthermore, no way out is specified in the criticism. Constructive criticism serves a need which many youngsters have. It is clear, then, that caring as conceived by children must have positive discriminating elements. The curriculum must give direction toward the realization of meanings about these elements.

The discussion on love and affection as needs of children is, of course, involved with many more factors than have been indicated. The above, however, is sufficient to illustrate that the blanket statement, "Children need love and affection," when used as a simple method, is woefully inadequate when approaching the development of the conditions for need fulfillment of children. The next section, which deals with the need of developing self-confidence in children, is a more complete discussion of the approach to an understanding of needs.

MANY FACTORS INVOLVED IN BUILDING SELF-CONFIDENCE IN CHILDREN

A need which is frequently considered important to a child is the development of self-confidence. Some children underestimate themselves. They have the feeling that someone else usually will do a particular task better than they would be able to do it. Often a child will begin a task and be so concerned about another child doing it better that he fails to become sufficiently absorbed to do a good job or to finish it. Some children will give up on a task before they even try it. The conditions in a classroom which tend to encourage this pattern of approach are damaging to the child's personality. A teacher should frequently take a good look at the classroom environment and try to develop it in terms of the potentialities of children.

Factors which may adversely affect building self-confidence

Several factors are involved in developing the conditions which will tend to fulfill the need for self-confidence. The provisions for confidence-building should answer the questions, "Are there any factors in the learning conditions of this room that would make it difficult to build self-confidence in every child?" "What factors exist which provide encouragement for children to achieve with the utmost feeling of security and understanding?" "Is the feeling which exists in this classroom of such a nature as will help a child to accept his limitations without losing face with others?"

Competitive practices may affect self-confidence in children. Some of the factors which retard self-confidence are found in the culture within which the child operates. There exist some distorted values and many extremities of values which tend to make it difficult for some children to develop self-confidence. Some of these factors are involved with the idea of competition.

In the culture, competition is frequently viewed as a sort of cover-all panacea for progress. Youngsters are told that they have to face a rather "cruel world" where they must compete with others to get ahead. This type of thinking is very prevalent in our society. The extreme operation of this factor is related to a "survival of the fittest" pattern of thinking. This pattern of thinking evaluates "quality" as the possession of those who are able to do a task the best. There is, to be sure, a respect for differences, but it is confined to those differences which produce the most or the best.

The real tragedy about competition is that the appraisal of quality often leaves out certain values which should be regarded as important in assessing the true meaning of success. The restrictions imposed by some competitive practices are very confining. The top of the ladder of success accordingly is kept very narrow. Success, as viewed by those who are extremists in the competition pattern of thinking, is the almost wholesale acceptance of the factors which were instrumental in the process of elevating certain individuals to the top of the ladder. How one gets to the top of the competitive ladder is frequently not considered important in the process. The sole objective seems to be to climb regardless of the means employed in doing so.

An example of this in the classroom is apparent in some of the speed tests in arithmetic. From time to time, children are asked to do a certain set of examples or problems in arithmetic while the teacher keeps time on the rate of performance. Usually the same ones repeatedly finish first. Once in a while, another child reaches the winning group. The winning group is, of course, usually rated high, whereas the others are considered second rate even if, when given time, they do the examples or problems correctly. Although the slower group has done a task in an effective manner, its members are usually rated in a second or third class category.

By the nature of the conditions established by competitive practices, criteria for success frequently limit status feelings as accruing to the fast group. This is a definite blow to the development of self-confidence. There exists a degree of unfairness in this type of competition. The unfairness is not in the fact that certain children are able to finish certain tasks faster than others. Rather, it exists in the overwhelming estimation accorded the fast worker.

There is no question as to the merit of work done well and completed quickly. If one works efficiently and speedily, he should be admired for it. On the other hand, the child who works slower but reaches the same objective as the fast worker also deserves due credit for his performance. If this credit is not forthcoming in terms of himself, his behavior might be affected in the direction of a lowering of self-confidence.

The value of conformity may affect self-confidence. A value which is accorded high priority in our culture is that of conformity. A person wants for his friend someone who has similar ideas and who likes to do the same things. A speaker usually is favorably regarded when he emphasizes those ideas which are already largely held by the audience. A clergyman is on safe ground when he dwells on topics which have already been digested by the congregation. The superintendent of schools makes it a point to approach the community in terms of the values which are most commonly held by its members. The teacher, more often than not, expects the members of the class to respond to the assignment in terms of the textbook.

When the teacher and pupils plan learning experiences together, the results arrived at are frequently in terms of the preconceived pattern of thinking of the teacher or on the basis of few and confining alternatives. If a group of children decide to do a puppet show on a favorite story, the two or three individuals who suggested a diorama or mural will usually give in quite easily to the majority. If one of the three persists in the opportunity to give his idea a chance, he is often labeled as "stubborn" or "never wanting to do what we decided." Frequently the person who suggests an idea which is different or proposes a re-evaluation of the customary pattern is rejected along with his ideas. In schools, it is a very rare occurrence when a student has the opportunity to suggest an approach in the subject of history, for example, which might be different from that of the teacher, and have it accepted by the class. In most classrooms a powerful criterion for a high rating is conformity to the assignments. Pupils are marked largely on their response to the requests of the teacher. In most cases, any deviation from the established pattern, regardless of its effectiveness, is considered secondary in importance. It is clear that conformity is regarded highly in society.

There are, of course, many other factors which interfere with the conditions for the developing of self-confidence as well as the fulfillment of other needs. The above are sufficient, however, to indicate some of the problems that have to be dealt with in curriculum improvement tasks relative to the understanding of needs.

QUESTIONS FACED IN DEVELOPING DIRECTION IN SERVING NEEDS

It is one of the responsibilities of curriculum workers to help develop the conditions which will result in considered thinking relative to the direction the teacher will take in serving needs such as promoting self-confidence in each child. The teacher cannot be fully blamed for unwittingly practicing unfair methods of competition in promoting learning. He is told by one system that this is a world marked by highly competitive practices. He is told by educators that he should strive to build self-confidence in children, to consider each child as having personal worth, and to develop the learning environment in such a manner that all the potentialities of children will have a chance of being fulfilled. Perhaps these same educators espouse views which favor competitive practices. The teacher, however, is quite clear about the fact that competitive elements exist in our society. He has observed the operation of competition in his high school days and in his college work. The professional educators, on the other hand, have spoken of cooperation, selfhood, personal worth, and other qualities which should be developed with people.

The dichotomy represented, on the one hand, by many who operate in a competitive set of values and, on the other hand, by those who espouse the noncompetitive elements poses a rather perplexing problem of choice for the teacher in his efforts to promote the conditions for learning. The dichotomy of values is made even more complex when people who emphasize the noncompetitive approach to learning have either shied from, or have been unable to change the system of, rating and marks which prevail in schools. In other words, those who emphasize the noncompetitive approach to education are content to go along with a marking and rating system which is based on the comparison of pupils and which is thus competitive in nature. Thus the contradiction in values prevails, and the teacher is in a constant dilemma as to the alternatives which confront him as he tries to develop self-confidence in individual children. The course he takes will make a difference in educational effectiveness.

Becoming involved with culture-related questions

In making his choice, the teacher should become involved with several questions. Some of them are as follows: To what extent is competition a system in the world outside the classroom? Is it possible that the historical relationship of the idea of competition with the economy has perpetuated the concept, whereas the practices are really taking on a neocompetitive flavor? Is it not true that factors other than competition are at work in the economy of our society which for want of an historical base have not been clearly labeled by economists? In view of the high regard that tradition has placed on speed of performance, is it possible to provide the conditions for alternative estimations of effectiveness in learning? Is it possible that children in a complex society may view second or third place as established by tradition as satisfying for themselves? Should the limitations of children be clarified with them in terms of traditional levels? Is it enough for a child to be helped to recognize his limitations and leave it at that juncture? Have we fully studied and recognized substitute and alternative values which are prevalent in the society or culture? Are we making the mistake of confining the pattern of growth and development of children to a preconceived stereotype of learning? Is it possible that many educators have confined themselves so narrowly to their area of specialization that they have overlooked the comprehensive range and field of learning?

It would be dangerous indeed to provide set answers to the questions which have been indicated, for the simple reason that it is impossible for any one person to have the infinite knowledge which is embodied in their implications. There is, however, a definite responsibility on the part of those engaged in curriculum development, and those who ponder the question of learning, to suggest certain signposts of direction with regard to the questions. In view of this responsibility, this writer will venture several suggestions which, it is hoped, will lead to the development of conditions that will promote concern and action with respect to the questions which have been presented.

Analyzing the practices held in high esteem by members of the society. In the first place, it is important that educators provide the setting which will enable teachers to view many of the practices prevailing in society which are held in high esteem by its members in general, and those practices which are highly regarded by segments of the society. This means that people in education will try to detect those practices in a moving society which are constant and those that are variable. It means, also, that a special effort should be made to ascertain those forces which are accorded high priority and those which are relegated to a secondary position. The attributes which cause people to be held in high esteem as well as those elements which tend to rejection should be fully fathomed by the person who wants to become, or already is, a teacher. In other words, it is important to know what values, when accepted, provide smooth sailing and those which, if accepted, tend to bring considerable rejection and throw up barriers to the devotees.

Studying alternatives in the approach to needs. Granted that the teacher has at least a reasonable amount of freedom to teach, the manner in which he uses the elements of status inherent in his position will make a difference in the degree of self-confidence developed with children. Assuming that the teacher is a student of the social patterns and values prevailing in a community, he will have to make certain choices relative to his beliefs and his responsibilities. Recognizing that one of his beliefs is that he should help children and adults to attain a considerable degree of self-confidence, what is he going to do? What are some of the alternatives in the procedures he may choose? He could choose to structure the teaching process in terms of those forces which are accorded high priority in the culture. He could choose a textbook and develop a plan of assignments to coincide with it and expect the children to show proficiency in performance relative to the plan. He might reason that conformity is a very important factor in fitting a person for the society which holds that value important. His rating of proficiency on the part of the children would have to conform to the pattern of degrees of performance on the assignments. The quality of performance would be judged in terms of the textbook.

The above is one alternative. If he chooses to reject this alternative as a procedure, he may reason as follows: A textbook contains the considered thinking of one, two, or possibly a dozen people. It is important to have a textbook as a springboard for the development of thought and action. It is essential to provide, in addition to the textbook, a "charged" environment for learning. By a "charged" environment is meant the emergence on the scene of learning of those elements which will disturb the children concerning their roles and responsibilities. Furthermore, a "charged" environment provides certain signals designed to produce direction relative to the roles and responsibilities.

The teacher now begins to feel a somewhat different responsibility than was envisioned in the alternative, described as a structured pattern of assignments coinciding with the textbook. He is thinking now of the expanded opportunities for children. He, therefore, decides to consider seriously a different procedure.

He ponders this whole question of conformity. He is not a skeptic. He recognizes the importance of some degree of conformity in developing a unity of approach to problems of learning. He has, however, witnessed and studied the extreme applications of the value of conformity and is questioning it as a universal pattern. He has been bothered by the humiliation heaped on underclassmen by upperclassmen in colleges. He has noticed the ridiculous lengths certain organizations, such as fraternities, have gone to in exacting conformance to a past practice. He has observed that an important goal of many students is to find out what the teacher wants. He recognizes that there may be real intelligent differences espoused by minorities or by two or three individuals in a group. Consequently, he makes up his mind to do everything possible to develop those conditions for learning which will not only elicit the responses of all individuals but will view them as necessary elements in the learning process. The conditions for experiences in learning which he envisions would tend to utilize the responses of each individual in the total pattern of education.

IMPORTANCE OF DEVELOPING STATUS FEELINGS IN CHILDREN

In a previous discussion, some reference was made to the status elements inherent in the position of teacher. With respect to the needs of children, status is an important factor. Everyone needs to have a degree of status. Self-confidence is a need related to status. If a child experiences some feelings of success, he is gaining self-confidence and, accordingly, a degree of status. It is very satisfying indeed for a child to reach a point where he is able to recognize the elements of a situation which appeared extremely puzzling a short time ago. Chances are that in the attempt to gain insight into a puzzling situation the child frequently felt discouraged. Somehow, however, something happened that made him stay with the tasks involved. Others may have run away from the situation feeling themselves incapable to perform the tasks involved in the mastery of the problems. As a result of retreating from the situation, these children were feeling pangs of dissatisfaction within themselves.

Some consequences of failure to achieve status

When a child once retreats from a task, it somehow becomes more difficult for him to undertake other tasks. A loss of self-confidence discourages one from undertaking new tasks. After he becomes accustomed to repeated failures in tasks, he experiences a reluctance to tackle anything and gets to the point where he simply doesn't care for the accepted pattern of operation into which he has been thrown. As an alternative, he may resort to unaccepted performance outside of the realm of normal operation. He is seeking status and is going to those places and becoming involved with those people who give it to him. Depending on where he finally finds a degree of status, his action may result in dire consequences.

The teacher and curriculum worker, in developing the conditions for learning experiences, must consider carefully the possibilities related to the status feelings of children. When a teacher structures the learning situation in terms of a textbook alone, he has not considered clearly these feelings. When a teacher structures the setting for learning entirely on his preconceptions of what it should be, he has failed to consider the potential powers of children. The teacher's action here may be regarded as using his status position unwisely. The responses which children make are judged by him and him alone. Whatever status feelings revert to children, come as a result of the teacher's satisfaction with their work.

In other words, those children who are able to do the assignments have status as a result of the teacher's feelings rather than satisfaction in the work which they have completed. Self-confidence for the child under this condition comes about through pleasing the teacher. Pleasing the teacher means to conform to the assignments which have been laid out for the children. Some of the children will do the assignments satisfactorily for the teacher. Others will do the best they are capable of. The nature of the performance will be rated all the way from acceptable to poor and unacceptable. Most children in this category will have few feelings of success. Few will develop self-confidence under this set of conditions. A repetition of performance which is considered unsuccessful may eventually threaten the normal growth and development of the child.

Status feelings may result from insight into
the processes of accomplishment

Self-confidence does not happen by itself. When people speak about someone possessing a great deal of confidence in himself, they often view it as an inherent characteristic of the person. This concept of self-confidence is a result of surface thinking. As has been indicated in the discussion above and in much of the literature on personality, self-confidence develops with success in accomplishment. That does not mean that one should always experience success in order to develop self-confidence. It is important, in fact, to experience failure in order to actually appreciate success. To make mistakes is a freedom which is necessary for true learning. When making mistakes, however, becomes a pattern of performance, then it is serious. If this happens, the one who makes the mistakes is not learning from them.

Failure to learn from mistakes is due to a lack of insight into the elements of the mistake. Experiencing failure without recognizing the nature of the failure results in a clear loss of effectiveness in performance. If failures continue, the result may be injurious to personality development. An important phase of the process, then, of developing self-confidence is experiencing success and recognizing what caused the failures that were encountered. One is gradually assured of self-confidence and feelings of status as he increasingly gains more insight into the processes which make for accomplishment.

Status feelings develop when teacher and children are learners together

When a teacher strives to develop the conditions which will give young people the opportunity to gain self-confidence, he has to consider all the aspects of the learning environment. As has been indicated before, he must initially provide the conditions which will elicit responses from all individuals. The conditions must also contain those ingredients which will enable children to observe that the responses of all individuals are necessary elements of the total work of the class.

Children participants in developing conditions for learning. The teacher who would create the opportunity for the need of self-confidence will see the need for help from the children. He recognizes that their behavior must necessarily form the nucleus of the learning environment. The children become participants in preparing the conditions for learning. This will have the effect of expanding as well as intensifying the opportunities for learning. Participation on the part of children will open up many vistas in the scene of learning and achievement. Children will, in the experiences of planning and evaluating, begin to be more sure of their goals. Furthermore, with the help of the teacher, they will create new and more farsighted goals than they previously had.

All this time the teacher as a leader is learning along with the children. He raises many questions himself which will charge the learning conditions with elements of concern, which in turn produce an intelligent questioning attitude on the part of the children. This should make it necessary for more and more books and materials to be brought into use. Children come to recognize the need for greater skill in approaching the many questions and problems. Time is taken out to plan for improving and developing more effective skills in reading and communicating.

Teacher and children facilitate resourcefulness in learning. The class will be organized so children will be able to help each other in small groups. In the small groups, they might be able to dwell more intensively on their special needs than when the response is to the teacher alone. In smaller groups, children will have greater opportunity to experience and weigh the ideas which the individuals hold. From time to time, the class will meet as a whole group and attempt to evaluate the total productiveness of the group. New light will be brought to the plans and achievements of the small groups so that they will have the incentive to advance to higher levels of performance. Periodically, too, the teacher will give lectures to the group on more effective ways of learning and about the new ideas which have emerged from the small groups.

When the small groups are in session, the teacher gives his services as a consultant either by sitting in with the groups or by establishing a consultation center to which children may come for aid on various questions. The teacher and children will plan this center together, arranging the schedule so that all groups will have an opportunity to take advantage of it. Since the teacher will find it difficult to serve all the groups himself, assistants will be chosen from among the pupils who will help keep the consultation center operating as a real answer to the many needs of the children.

Status feelings related to personal worth

Self-confidence is a need which is integrally related to personal worth. In the structured classroom where achievement is judged by a single pattern such as the textbook and the limiting preconceptions of the teacher, children come to accept progress as something apart from themselves. The pattern is there, and if they find it impossible to meet the requirements laid down in the pattern, they feel themselves as inferior. They think of themselves as not being good enough to do the work. These same children who are unable to cope with the pattern have pals and friends who think a great deal of them. They go to and from school together, eat lunch together, and have many pleasant experiences in each other's companionship. Learning appears to them, however, to be something different, something quite apart from this companionship which they enjoy with their friends. It is tragic that this condition so frequently exists. It is destructive to true resourcefulness.

Developing conditions for realization of personal worth. Learning is not something which happens in only one place. It happens everywhere. To be truly effective, it must have consistent continuity in, and be related to, the child's whole environment. Learning, to be really effective, must not only be as absorbing to children as their friendships but must also bring about a true respect for the personal worth of every individual in the classroom. It is the responsibility of the curriculum worker and the teacher to constantly study, discover, and plan how this condition can be brought about in the school.

As a springboard for the conditions which will promote a realization of self-confidence and a respect for personal worth, we suggest the development of the classroom as a laboratory or center of learning which will amply portray the meanings of these qualities. The conditions will relate to all the needs of children and constitute a continuous pattern of living. This, of course, is not the complete answer to the question of need fulfillment of children. It is not the intention to develop a pattern which others might imitate. The suggestion of the center of learning is made primarily to emphasize the importance of expanding the opportunities for children to achieve status through exciting achievement. Within this center, provision should be made for children to not only become acquainted with exciting ideas but also to test the ideas for expanded meanings and uses.

TEACHING DEMANDS MANY COMPETENCES AND RESOURCES

As the teacher proceeds wholeheartedly into the task of developing learning experiences with children, it becomes increasingly clear that it is anything but simple. In an environment which is becoming more and more complex with more and more forces exercising influences on the individual, the knowledge and competences needed by the teacher in developing direction in instruction loom in almost overwhelming proportions. The teacher needs to become conversant with a vast body of content regarding human growth and development. Regardless of the area or age level with which his tasks are involved, the teacher needs to gain a great understanding of the various disciplines and their relationship to people and the culture. He needs to develop competences in relating the thinking of men in other times and places to the contemporary scene. No less essential is his responsibility of keeping abreast with contemporary thought.

The teacher needs to develop competences in providing the conditions for learning. In order to gain these competences, it is necessary for him to know much about how children learn. The content with which he works must be treated in such a manner as to develop identification with it on the part of children and youth. The degree to which meaningful relationships have been established between the student and the content indicates the degree to which the methods employed have been successful.

Curriculum must provide for expansion of incentives for learning

In the promotion of direction in instruction, it is most important that the curriculum provide for the conditions which will enable teachers to develop objectives and goals that are not only realizable but will expand the incentives for learning. Furthermore, the content must be made accessible in such a manner as to produce an eagerness in learning which will go far beyond the initial recognition of needs. The teacher usually expects to develop an eagerness to learn on the part of the pupils. In any classroom, there are those pupils who satisfactorily complete all assignments all the time. Frequently the teacher concludes that these pupils are eager to learn. This assumption may be erroneous. These pupils may just be conforming to the system by which they can satisfy the requirements of the teacher and school.

The appraisal of the completed assignments should be no more than a clue to the possibilities of learning. To illustrate, let's consider a topic such as Power and Its Meanings. Pupils might be asked to talk and write about power—how it is produced and the results of it. Some of the topics may deal with water and heat, others with mechanical devices, and still others with the power of words and language. The topics are developed through much reading and discussion. Too often, however, the ideas advanced with the topics are those which already are known. The area of idea development is more or less confined to academic perusal and discussion. For example, the ideas about the power of water revolve around floods, power-producing dams, and so on. The thinking about power has been channeled with no real provisions for the impact of relationships.

Curriculum should provide laboratory conditions for idea evolvement. To cause the unfolding of relationships of ideas as well as the expansion of inquiry relative to power, it is necessary to develop laboratory conditions which are charged with the interconnective elements of thought evolvement. Water as a force will then be seen as related to human incentives and motivation, social conflicts, and control.

Human incentives and motivations may be seen at work when a river or stream is harnessed for the purpose of operating the machinery which will produce electricity. Social conflicts may be observed in operation in connection with the allocation of water rights on irrigation projects in the western regions of the United States. Priority in control of water rights becomes an issue between states. The matter of conservation of water and flood control is an important social issue which has occupied the attention and ingenuity of engineers, politicians, and other groups in our society. Water, of course, has many other relationships to human activity and the needs of people. Among these are its cleansing quality, the power of buoyancy, and its use in hydraulics.

The laboratory conditions for idea evolvement relative to different types of power and their meaning should be developed in such a manner as to provide for a wide range of learning experiences so that every child may have a degree of realization. Every pupil, within his level of understanding, should be stimulated to formulate hypotheses for the testing of ideas. The teacher should consult with the children in such a manner as will give them a full realization of discovery. This means that the children should have at least an equal opportunity with that of the teacher to initiate plans and experiments with respect to the logical study and the scientific testing of facts and ideas. Pupils should think through the type of experimentation needed to test their hypotheses and to plan it themselves. The thrill of initiating the processes to test their thinking, as well as following through, will go a long way in producing eagerness in learning on the part of children. They will be excited about knowledge when they see it in action. Consequently, they may go far beyond the completed assignments.

Curriculum should provide for a wide range of learning experiences. The illustration about power and its meanings as given above was based on the furtherance of learning experiences with those pupils who almost always complete their assignments. There was no intention to suggest that the process indicated is for these pupils only. In every classroom, there are pupils who fail to complete the required work for various reasons. Some may have a difficult time perceiving meanings. Others may use slipshod work methods because of a lack of interest. Still others may not have the ability to gain insight into meanings of the type suggested in the illustration.

Children are different and, therefore, learn at different rates and with varying degrees of insight and understanding. It is essential, therefore, that the curriculum have provisions for a wide range of learning experiences wherein all pupils may approach the development of meaningful ideas in terms of goals which they can envision as possible of realization. Furthermore, the conditions must be provided whereby the routes of meaning perception are varied so as to enable different pupils to identify with them in terms of their previous experiences and present knowledge. There are always causes for lack of interest on the part of pupils. Among the causes is the rigidity of practice prevailing in many classrooms relative to the modes of response of the pupils. As suggested in some of the previous discussions, the conditions for learning are often confining. This gives pupils the idea that there is only one way of getting at meaning. As a result, learning to them becomes monotonous and deadening. Some resign themselves to conformity as the way to learn while others resign from learning itself.

Conditions for learning should generate opportunities for all children. It is important to emphasize that most pupils who are performing effectively in terms of supposedly high standards established by teachers are not fulfilling the potential they possess. Children and young people should not be limited in their efforts by so-called standards. There has frequently been a tendency in schools to "level off" on standards. Perhaps a wrongful use and interpretation of tests has been responsible for this. Tests are only a partial indication of learning and should not be used to dictate the routes of development in insight and understanding. They should never serve as a deterrent to the development of ideas. On the contrary, the curriculum must develop the conditions where the routes of learning are open-ended. There will, of course, be plateaus of goal realization where the gains of learning will be consolidated. The consolidation, however, is a means of stimulating the development of new routes of learning demanding a greater intensity of effort than before.

The process of open-endedness in exploring for ideas must be provided for all children and young people. The only difference to be observed is timing, momentum, and difficulty of content. To illustrate, the study of power may vary in intensity all the way from the development of meanings relative to such abstract concepts as power and the will, power and human motivation, power and status, to those meanings associated with tools, physical stamina, and commonplace forms of energy. One should be careful, however, to refrain from rigid assumptions as to which pupils are able and which are not. The teacher who considers his task more than just another job will be open-minded about the power resources of children and youth. He will recognize the aspects of superior thought resourcefulness in the so-called average people. As a curriculum worker, he will develop the conditions for a manifold approach to meanings. As an operator with students, he will be instrumental in developing the foundations designed not only to uncover, but to generate into resourcefulness, all forms of latency.

The individual must retain his identity in mass education

The tasks which have been indicated for the curriculum worker and teacher have great implications for the American dream of mass education. One of the dangers which might lie in mass education is the allegiance to a concept of total production regardless of the individual and his destiny. The zeal and the need for construction of school buildings should not overshadow the fact that in these buildings will be thousands of individuals who should have an opportunity to understand themselves and their potential in a dynamic culture and society. It is extremely vital that the individual retain his identity in mass participation.

Another serious danger which has somehow grown with the mass concept of education lies in the rigid organization of the school. This organization establishes a series of barriers which students must hurdle in order to be considered educated. Mass education is provided in hours—so many hours of *this* and so many hours of *that*. The student is placed in the position of being a receiver of education pure and simple. The question of acquisition of knowledge and the development of an attitude for the pursuit of wisdom and understanding is frequently passed over or taken for granted. In order for learning to be effective, there must be a continuous effort on the part of people in education to provide for the accessibility of content to the student. Furthermore, the conditions for learning with respect to the content must be so charged with meanings that each individual approaches his optimum degree of realization.

The curriculum must make provisions for the portrayal of

meanings in such a manner as to cause the student to voluntarily approach learning with a deep sense of concern about consequences and direction. This provision for the portrayal of meanings provides the method through which the individual in his interaction with others experiences the dynamics in learning.

School structure must be continuously examined for educational effectiveness for the individual

The curriculum worker's task is to bring about the conditions wherein all the staff continuously examine the school structure to determine its provisions for the utmost realization of the potential of every individual. It is important, then, to make sure that the school organization does not create a static arrangement for learning. The curriculum design should be sufficiently flexible to enable individuals to identify with the culture and society in particular ways so that a wholeness of learning will emerge for them. In the process of identification, the individual conceives of learning as a capacity to gain satisfaction and excitement out of evolving ideas in the companionship of different individuals.

This relationship should be disturbing as well as supporting. The disturbance, however, should be distinguished from frustration. It is rather the challenging type—the ideas incident thereto not being threatening but sufficiently strange as to logical meanings to evoke new bases of perceptiveness. An example of this may be an individual trying to construct a picture of an opposite condition to his actual pattern of living, to put himself in that picture, and to react to the actual pattern. Perhaps a somewhat more concrete example would be to construct for oneself the whole constellation of meanings which hold importance, for example, for a "Rock-and-Roll" addict. Then, one might try to examine the reactions to those who somehow do not have "insight" to our (Rock-and-Roll) meanings. An identification of this type might convey a better understanding of what different individuals regard and why. It might also lead to a more intelligent approach to individuals in helping them examine their values in terms of human principles.

*Curriculum must provide for pursuit of learning
in the periphery*

Learning is not confined to a classroom or school but exists everywhere in the peripheral area of the school. The classroom may be the center where thinking is tested for possible consequences, but most of the observable uses are distributed in the total surrounding environment. The classrooms must have the conditions which develop the competences for obtaining knowledge from the environment.

In order that educational experience may become truly effective and far-reaching, we suggest again that the classroom be developed so as to penetrate the peripheral areas of the confines of learning. Space education, the processes of mind control, and other ideas must be examined for negative as well as positive elements. This means that the conditions for the pursuit of knowledge are provided. The conditions must make the whole mass of knowledge available in such a manner as will enable the child to identify with it. This means that he must have access to it with confidence and security. The child will approach knowledge with these attitudes only when it appears in understandable form. He understands ideas when he has sufficient insight to relate them to himself. When the curriculum worker recognizes the importance of the identification of children with ideas, he is taking a big step in providing the conditions for true learning.

Having taken the initial step in promoting the conditions for learning, that is, accepting the premise that children must encounter a clear identification with ideas, the teacher will ask, "What does one do from here on out?" As he ponders this question, he is at the same time formulating clues which will establish some answers. As he seeks answers, many new questions will arise. They will cause him to continuously examine the conditions for learning to ascertain whether they relate to the development of basic as well as emergent purposes of young people. We hope that the succeeding chapters will help the teacher to identify himself, at least in part, with the experiences which will tend to direct young people toward an enthusiastic responsibility in connection with the competences needed for individual and societal effectiveness.

SELECTED READINGS FOR CHAPTERS 4 AND 5

Association for Supervision and Curriculum Development, *A Look at Continuity in the School Program.* 1958 Yearbook. Washington, D. C.: National Education Association. An exploration of the present situation of continuity as viewed by children. There is also a discussion of some fundamental considerations upon which continuity can be based. Several examples of current efforts are presented.

————,*Creating a Good Environment for Learning.* 1954 Yearbook, pp. 15-150. Washington, D. C.: National Education Association. Examples of practices in developing a good environment for learning.

Beck, Robert H., Walter W. Cook, and Nolan C. Kearney, *Curriculum in the Modern Elementary School.* Englewood Cliffs, N. J.: Prentice-Hall, Inc., 1953, pp. 269-573. Very helpful guide to teaching the subject areas in the elementary school. Especially significant is Chapter 16, "Beyond the Earth Sciences." Several interesting cases of teachers in action are described.

Bush, Robert Nelson, *The Teacher-Pupil Relationship.* Englewood Cliffs, N. J.: Prentice-Hall, Inc., 1954, pp. 20-61. Case studies of teacher-pupil relationships.

Fromm, Erich, *The Sane Society.* New York: Rinehart & Co., Inc., 1955, pp. 3-78. This book should stimulate thinking on some fundamental questions regarding the nature of our society. Many of the questions are basic to an approach to the understanding of present-day behavior.

Havighurst, Robert J., Myra Z. Robinson, and Mildred Dorr, "The Development of the Ideal Self in Childhood and Adolescence," *The Adolescent.* Ed. by Jerome M. Seidman. New York: The Dryden Press, 1953, pp. 300-314. Interesting discussion of the development and importance of ideals in directing behavior.

Havighurst, Robert J. and Bernice L. Neugarten, *Society and Education.* Boston: Allyn & Bacon, Inc., 1957, Part IV. Discusses the teacher as to social origin and roles, as a socializing agent and leader and as to economic status and professionalization.

Miel, Alice and Associates, *Cooperative Procedures in Learning.* New York: Bureau of Publications, Teachers College, Columbia University, 1952, pp. 257-481. Some real tangible attempts to help teachers use cooperative procedures in learning. Many examples of actual practices are given.

Prescott, Daniel A., *The Child in the Educative Process.* New York: McGraw-Hill Book Co., Inc., 1957, pp. 3-26. Indicates some of the complex responsibilities of teaching. Several cases are presented.

Symonds, Percival M., "Development of the Ego and of the Self," *The Adolescent.* Ed. by Jerome M. Seidman. New York: The Dryden Press, 1953, pp. 222-230. Author discusses the need of the child to gain satisfaction and status and to avoid anxiety and the lowering of self-esteem.

Taba, Hilda, "The Moral Beliefs of Sixteen-Year Olds," *The Adolescent.* Ed. by Jerome M. Seidman. New York: The Dryden Press, 1953, pp. 314-319. Gives some understanding of the adolescent's code of morals with respect to the qualities of friendliness, honesty, loyalty, moral courage, and responsibility.

Witty, Paul, "Television and the High-School Student," *The Adolescent.* Ed. by Jerome M. Seidman. New York: The Dryden Press, 1953, pp. 230-242. Some answers to questions about the effect of television on the high school students are attempted.

⟡6⟡

Simple Relationships and Values

VOLUMES HAVE BEEN WRITTEN ABOUT PEOPLE AND THE VALUES they hold. It is, therefore, impossible to deal adequately with the nature of values in a short space. An attempt will be made, however, to deal with them sufficiently to show how they are involved in practically every learning situation. In the following pages, some of the simple values will be indicated. This is done in the hope that the teacher and curriculum worker will consider the importance of them in the promotion of learning experiences. The simple situations described should provide a point of departure toward the development of the conditions designed to enable children to understand their values as well as those of others, to promote a refinement of certain values held, and to help set direction toward the evolvement of new values.

It should be emphasized that many of the most obvious everyday experiences of children and adults are fraught with fundamental meanings. The very fact that things are obvious may cause them to be approached in such a casual state that the rich meanings inherent in them are never identified. Furthermore, this oversight with regard to the obvious might have the effect of obscuring many of the meanings in connection with more abstract learning. Meanings of democracy, status feelings, and conflicts of people will be more readily understood if the conditions for learning provide for a study of the simple face-to-face relationships of people.

The understanding of abstract relationships of values is ex-

135

tremely important in the whole process of education. The tendency, however, to view these relationships from afar and outside of the operational context of classroom experiences has the effect of supplying an incomplete sense of identification on the part of both the teacher and learners. An attempt, then, to assemble values into an instructional setting must be on the basis of a realistic look at the nature of things and the acts of men in the identifiable area of the learner. That we will try to do in the sections following.

SIMPLE FACE-TO-FACE RELATIONSHIPS

A major part of the satisfactions of people are a result of close relationships with other people. This relationship is highly esteemed and thus constitutes a working value. This will be more clear by indicating a number of typical face-to-face relationships in varying situations. These are developed below.

Everyday commonplace happenings contain ingredients for high-level learning experiences

A face-to-face relationship of a common everyday type is that of the daily transactions as between owner or sales clerk of a business establishment and the customer. If it is a neighborhood business, the personal relationship is more in evidence perhaps than in a metropolitan center, especially if the seller and customer have been carrying on transactions for some time. The relationship may be so close as to invoke mutual concern over such matters as each other's health, possible success at some new venture, the new school building that is going to be put up, and how the children are enjoying their school work. This type of relationship is highly esteemed because of the ease of manner within which it can be daily renewed, the comfort derived from the concern expressed over one's problems, the friendly give-and-take quality which prevails, and the helpfulness displayed by one person for another. In this relationship, the product purchased may be a decidedly secondary matter of value since it is assumed that this extrinsic consideration is bound up in the total situation.

The setting which is indicated as between the owner or clerk of a business establishment and the customer appears very wholesome and productive of a sound value pattern. In other words, the situation appears so satisfying and proper that any further consideration of it might be dismissed. Such a finality of thinking, however, terminates the opportunity for the assessment of the values residing in the situation. The owner or clerk and the customer have had a satisfying experience which is repeated frequently. It is taken for granted that the experience could not be otherwise.

Casual human relationships furnish clues to educational direction. The conditions which provide continuing face-to-face relationships are usually taken for granted by the participants. Wirth[1] senses a point for direction relative to these conditions when he says:

> We have learned that the most important thing to know about a person is what he takes for granted, and the most important thing to know about a people is what it takes for granted. We have also learned that we cannot always believe what people say, but what they say is nevertheless important. This suggests that the values by which people live can be more effectively inferred from what they do rather than from what they say.

The very fact that an experience is repeatedly satisfying can lead to an easy forgetfulness of the consequences of the experience. The elements operating in the experiences of face-to-face relationships are not readily visualized. The only condition which might emphasize the elements of the relationships would be one where the relationships would be removed. In other words, a sudden absence of a casual relationship is the only condition which would bring it to attention. That points up the tragedy; that is, the real gifts which free the spirit of man are indulged too lightly.

It should become increasingly clear to the student of society (the teacher as the student) that in a relationship, which is representative of the commonplace things, lie the ingredients which may be the most productive in human understanding. It constitutes part of the subject matter of human relations. Here is truly a sample of something which has real meanings

---

[1] Louis Wirth, "Freedom, Power and Values in Our Present Crisis," in *Toward Better Human Relations,* edited by Lloyd Allen Cook (Detroit: Wayne University Press, 1952), p. 12.

for the participants but, due to the consistency of the pattern, the dynamic qualities operating in it are actually ignored for value purposes.

It is important for people to think about the value ingredients of commonplace and everyday happenings. In these happenings reside the substance for the development of resourcefulness when encountering new social situations. Some of the elements in this substance are friendliness, acceptance, understanding, freedom of ideas, evaluation or sizing up of progress, and the release of the human spirit for attainment of satisfying experiences.

It is imperative that the school recognize these elements and utilize their real potential in building values with children. A studied recognition of the social situations embodied in the commonplace happenings provide one springboard in the repossession of the values in face-to-face relationships under more impersonal conditions. Children in school are in a particularly advantageous position to work in an atmosphere of face-to-face relationships under both personal and impersonal conditions. The curriculum must provide for the conditions which will emphasize the values of face-to-face relationships as they operate both in childhood and the adult world. The adult world is, for the most part, also the child world. It is highly important, then, that the child learn from the simple experiences in this world to be cognizant of the ingredients residing in face-to-face situations so that those same ingredients may be refined and productive of greater potential for community living.

Neighborliness contains many possibilities for building values

A face-to-face relationship which is of the utmost importance in the lives of men is that of neighborliness. Neighborliness is a universal value. Everyone has friends in the block or along the road. Each one is more or less concerned with what is happening to the other. There is a sort of sharing of events of all types such as a new baby in the family, a minor or major accident, a building project undertaken, successes both large and small, a recognition of some accomplishment, the "ups and downs" of daily living.

It is simply natural to chat with one's neighbors about all

types of events. Some of the chats may take the form of gossip which, although undesirable as a means of communication, is integrally related to the values of a community. Frequently neighbors may help each other with many individual undertakings, such as digging a cellar, building a house, loaning a truck, loaning chairs and dishes for a party, and in many other ways. It may seem that the mention of such mundane ways of neighborly interaction may be considered trivial but, for purposes of the value field, they are highly significant in assessing value patterns of people in a community. Of course, it may be contended that the help which one person gives to another may be on the condition that there is reciprocity. Even so, it is evident that in the arrangement there is a degree of mutuality which is in itself a value of no small measure. It is often said that as long as people discuss, interact, and even "quibble," some common bond of satisfaction with each other exists.

An interesting illustration of neighborliness is revealed by the approach that an eleven-year-old boy made to his father's neighbor in connection with mowing his lawn. The boy said to the neighbor, "I would like to mow your lawn whenever it is necessary at regular intervals." The neighbor asked how much he wanted for the job. The boy replied, "What is it worth?" The neighbor said that he would be willing to remunerate the boy in terms of the prevailing wage. The boy investigated and found that the fee would be $1.50 an hour. He added, however, that since he was doing this for his neighbor, he would mow the lawn at a fee of $1.00 an hour.

This is very interesting, indeed, and also significant when viewing values. The situation gives rise to several questions which must be resolved in terms of values which have come to be accepted. The questions would run somewhat as follows: Is a neighbor supposed to merit greater status than someone else? Is status really a consideration here or is it something deeper which cannot be described by the term? Has the parent of the boy cautioned him to take into consideration the fact that he is doing this for a neighbor? Does the boy or parent expect something in return? If so, is it a short-term or long-term return? It is obvious that some thought-provoking values are prevalent in the situation. The whole process indicated by the questions deserves a scrutinizing examination and appraisal.

In examining the questions for values one has to take into account the boy as a minor, the use of his dad's lawn mower, the ability of the boy to do an adequate job and, most important, the values of this culture. The boy as a minor, who has approached the adult neighbor on a man-to-man proposal, should for value purposes be dealt with as an adult. Legally, of course, he is a minor. For a testing of values, however, the situation rises above legality and should be viewed as such on its merits as respects the boy and the neighbor. The relationship is entered into on the basis of faith in human dignity and personal worth. The odds are contributory to real value-building. If the odds indicate that the confidence was misplaced, the experience is still significant in that misplacement. Whatever may happen, the illustration of the lawn-mowing experience is obviously rich in value-building.

The church may promote understanding of the concept of neighbor. In the face-to-face relationships of neighborliness, the church is a very significant example. To many regular church-going people, neighborliness is a satisfying routine productive of supremely important values. Although the meditation of people together may be rewarding to those who participate, equally important, perhaps, is the gathering outside of the church before and after service. On this occasion, the outgoing spirit of men is communicated in a form of momentary involvement which may have some of the most satisfying consequences. Here one asks about how one is faring in a situation and how his neighbor is doing. This is especially true in smaller communities where the church is not built right next to a sidewalk. The fact that a sidewalk fronting the church entrance may nullify the gathering before and after church is highly significant to the whole problem of face-to-face relationships.

It may be contended that the purpose of church is for worship and, although this contention is granted, the true spirit of worship is only culminated in the concern for the welfare of one's fellowmen. Accordingly, this concern must take place in a meeting place of its own which gives an opportunity for casual informality of expression. Thus occurs that face-to-face relationship which is value-seeking as well as value-productive. *The "back fence" relationship may be productive of meanings for educational direction.* A form of face-to-face relationship which is all too frequently lost sight of and which seems to be disappearing from the neighborhood scene, is that of the "back fence" relationship. This is a situation wherein one person casually at work with some backyard duties looks and observes that his neighbor is engaged in a similar occupation. After some effort with these duties, one or the other senses that a breaking point is in order. Consequently, one or the other goes to the fence and throws out some casual remark which eventuates in a sort of "passing the time of day" chatter. In all probability, before this casual conversation is concluded, some weighty problems are tackled. This may even result in one inviting the other in to look over some newer ways of developing roses or some other kind of flower. As the concern over plants or some other idea continues, one can conceive of a situation of complete absorption which may result in the expansion of interests which can be pursued together. In any event, it is obvious that there are in this neighbor relationship some ingredients for mutual productiveness of ideas and satisfying value patterns.

There is no doubt but that this type of neighborliness affects the daily routine of living not only of the two individuals involved in the situation but also their families. The values, of course, speak for themselves as is clear in the description of the situation. The elements of satisfaction, however, deserve study and appraisal in a learning situation because they are possible only under a rather distinctive way of life. By distinctive is meant the free latitude of conversation which can take place in this situation. Topics all the way from the growth of the tulip bulb to the local meaning of national politics may be discussed with complete candor. People must become cognizant of the reasons for conditions which give rise to satisfying elements of neighborly living. It is important for them to know why they cherish certain values, for therein are discovered the ingredients for more positive and resourceful face-to-face relationships.

RELATIONSHIPS BETWEEN CHILDREN AND ADULTS

Most thinking people are interested and concerned about the conditions which promote the development of values with respect to children. They want their children to grow up in an environment which will encourage them to take on the constructive values of adults. Accordingly, it will be clear to thoughtful parents that more is needed to encourage constructive practices in children than mere exposure to the environment. In short, they want children to have a better opportunity than that exemplified in the "growing up like Topsy" environment.

Roles and responsibilities between adults and children contribute to values

Many parents will do everything they can to create family relationships which will make every member recognize that he is both needed and desired in this body. Every member will recognize a definite and important role in the family. Many opportunities will be specifically arranged where all the members of the family will participate in the conversation relating to plans and aspirations. When any improvements are made, everyone is involved. Mary's room is painted or papered only after she had made known her wishes as to these improvements. John's requests relative to some of his needs are made without fear of consequences, whether granted or not. He has no apprehension as to the outcome because his past experiences have indicated a complete sense of fairness. Many families try to develop an understanding between the members. There is no doubt but what many constructive values relating to personal worth, care, regard, clear purpose, security, and a feeling of confidence and fulfillment of needs, will develop for those who participate in family conditions such as indicated above.

Other examples of conditions developed by people to facilitate value-building opportunities for children and youth are the following: family get-togethers in a neighborhood to help children and young people fulfill the need for friends and companionship; the establishment of social centers for young people of high school age; the development of well-planned recreation and expanded learning facilities for all children by many communities. More and more churches are developing social centers for young people and employing staff to work with them through recreational and educational activities.

Involvement of youth helps identify their values. The above examples represent some of the usual types of opportunities provided by people in neighborhoods and communities to enable young people to fulfill certain needs and acquire constructive values. That youth will tend to build some new values and strengthen others in the opportunities provided in these situations is attested to by those who have worked with them. Whether the potential for the specific development of values in these situations is recognized is something else. In many instances, the conditions are established by anybody but the youth themselves. In other words, many of the centers for youth activities have been handed to the young people. Thus, perhaps the greatest potential for the recognition of, and identification with, the values on the part of youth is initially denied. This also goes for the development of the activities and programs in the centers.

Very important considerations, too, in the development of centers and other facilities for youth, are the attitudes and objectives which prompted them. When people attempt to create opportunities for youth without consulting them and taking them along in the projects, they are showing a disregard of values which youth hold. If the facilities for recreation and other activities are provided so as to in effect separate youth from adults, then the values which were considered operative in the activities envisioned are negated by the very nature of that objective.

Importance of interfamily relationships

An example of relationships in which there is great potential for the development of constructive values with children is when two or three families go together for an outing or picnic. This situation sometimes involves a great deal of planning and effort on the part of the adults. If the adults are of the "outing" type, they have a vested interest in this kind of diversion and will readily enter into it. Other adults would just as soon stay at home and have a more quiet weekend. They feel, however, that they owe this occasion to their children. Some feel it as a responsibility. Others consider it an opportunity to promote greater understanding between adults and children. Some parents recognize in the occasion an opportunity to promote the value of true freedom. In other words, they recognize that freedom is something which must accrue to all. The measure of responsibility lies in the fact that what one desires for oneself is realized more fully in creating the conditions of fulfillment of desires of others. As parents and children learn to understand and accept each other's feelings in terms of respective maturities, a constructive regard for differences will become established.

There are, also, those adults who are so concerned about their own comfort and feelings that they will try to dissuade children from the fulfillment of reasonable desires. They might simply tell their children that it is better to stay home and "read a book" or, if the persistence is too strong, suggest that they go to a movie with their friends. Still other parents will grudgingly accede to the wishes of youngsters to do something together. Somehow these adults cannot hide their feelings of discomfort. Clearly, a degree of this discomfort will be reflected in the children, too, and may result in a form of negativism or passive friction. It is doubtful if this condition will contribute to constructive values.

Many other relationships involving children are prevalent in most communities. Perhaps, through the assessment of interests of various members of the family and neighbors, activities will be evolved so that all may have opportunities to enjoy particular experiences at different times. It is quite obvious that the face-to-face relationships of parents, children and neighbors have great value-making ingredients. It is important, therefore, that these relationships be reflected in the development of ideas with children. Furthermore, these relationships must become a part of the conditions for learning in the school. The curriculum must make provisions for a richness of value development in these conditions.

COMMUNITY RELATIONSHIPS

It is really quite difficult to distinguish between face-to-face relationships as discussed in the previous sections and community relationships. A person becomes a member of a community largely through casual face-to-face relationships. For example, when a person moves into a community, he is often introduced to some of the ways of the community by neighbors who at different times may go and call on "the new people living in the brown house." Then, on the other hand, no one may call on the new people. In that case, the new people would enter into the community life more gradually. There are situations, too, where people do not consider the place they live as their community. About the only membership they have is that which is incurred through legal obligations such as paying taxes for support of certain community services. Otherwise, their community may be with those associated in the place where they work. It seems that there is such a great variation in types of communities that cannot be labeled that it is well to describe certain features about some of them. Along with this description, an attempt will be made to point up some of the values apparent in different communities, as well as to portray some possibilities of community action relative to the values.

Relationships in a typical traditional community

The typical traditional community contains certain elements which are common to all communities. For purposes of this description as well as those of other communities, the community will be considered as an area of habitation where people are not too far removed in distance from each other. In a community of this type, people know each other or know about each other through face-to-face relationships as neighbors. People have gotten acquainted in various centers such as churches, service clubs, parent-teacher organizations, transactions with town officials, grange meetings, community clubs, the neighborhood grocery store, school programs, group picnics, and many other ways. In all these gathering places, one may not meet all the people but a sort of common acquaintanceship develops through casual free contact. This contact has the effect of

spreading information as to *what* happens in the community
and *who* is causing it to happen. The elements of control are
apparent to almost everyone since the community members retain a close knit face-to-face relationship.

In any kind of acquaintanceship, feelings are generated.
These feelings are, for the most part, a form of reflection on
simple problems together. Feelings as indicated here come
about as a result of what is often called "small talk," that which
is carried on over the simple affairs of everyday living. The
talk hinges around such problems as what is stunting the growth
of a certain flower, the common illnesses of children, the distance to the bus stop, the neglect of a road, and others. Casually
arrived at, people just as casually return from this simple type
of intercommunication with no real problems solved and with
no special concern over the failure of solution. There exists,
however, in this casualness a simple feeling of satisfaction which
tends to perpetuate the contact.

One may wonder in this connection as to the worth of these
casual contacts. One may inquire into the quality of dynamics
in this type of community contact. One might seriously question the efficacy of the typical traditional community. Again, it
is pertinent to draw the attention to a possible danger in the
lack of recognition of the dynamics in this casual concern which
prevails so frequently in communities. That danger is the
casualness which leaves satisfying feelings in a state of complacency and inaction. There is a tendency to overlook the
potential for real progress.

City community may cause shift to centralization

In order to assess the potential in the communities, it is
well to describe a different type of community, that of a large
city. A city, in the broadest sense of the term, is the community
composed of smaller communities. In order to clarify this, it is
important to indicate the relationship of the city organization
to a smaller community of the city. Through the process of
developing services for the city, the people have established a
governmental structure to make the services available. As a
result, there develops a type of central leadership which influences direction, modification, and increase or decrease of

services. More often than not, this leadership splits into two or more opposing camps which vie for the attention of the individuals in the community in promoting their particular brand of service.

Now, if the small community retains the complacent characteristics described earlier, it may, in all probability, keep on in its casual ways and at stated times lend its support to one or another of the opposing camps of central leadership. As the true effects of the services dispensed, however, are becoming more clearly felt by individuals, elements of dissatisfaction will arise with respect to some of the services. This dissatisfaction will develop into real concern on the part of some individuals. These individuals will express that concern to other individuals who previously fulfilled the role of simple casualness. Provided that the typical casual arrangements have existed in the community, the question is: Will the people now take up this concern and seek unified action or will they be gripped by the nostalgia of the former pleasantries and take the attitude of "leaving well enough alone"? As between the two positions lie the dynamics of autonomous community development or surrender to another power of control.

Centralization in control must provide release for leadership in people. The assumption up to this point has been that there existed in the smaller community of the city certain arrangements for casual intercommunication. The contention further is that there are possibilities for potential action in a casual arrangement because it exemplifies a face-to-face relationship, individual to individual, neighbor to neighbor. To assume, however, that this potential action always occurs is an overstatement. In large cities, and even in small cities, frequently there is no appreciable arrangement of intercommunication. People frequently do not know their next-door neighbor. Real face-to-face relationships in many places are practically nonexistent. This vacuity may produce such a degree of isolated centralization of control that people become pawns in the hands of unscrupulous manipulators.

For fear that the trend of the discussion may be misunderstood, it is necessary to clarify some concepts about centralization with regard to the welfare of a community. The type of centralization in which the release for resourcefulness is provided to a few is faulty in that all the needs are never really fathomed. On the other hand, where centralization is developed through channels of release available to all the people for leadership relative to their problems, then ministration to most needs is more likely to prevail. In the latter form of centralization, services will be modified, increased or decreased as a result of the concern about the services which is indicated by the individuals and groups in the community. In this form of centralization, the responsibility to minister to the needs of individuals and groups is derived as a result of decision on the part of community groups.

The distinction which is made between two types of centralization presents some very important operational factors with regard to communities. The control which operates irrespective of needs of people is more liable to develop where there is no community intercommunication among individuals and groups. This type of control often occurs in large cities where there is a lack of face-to-face opportunities for the evolvement of concern on common problems. It may, of course, also happen where there are opportunities for face-to-face relationships, especially if the face-to-face arrangements produce only a degree of casualness of concern with respect to problems. A casual approach to problems in a community may be desirable at first, but if the casualness continues, no real action toward services results. When these conditions prevail over a considerable period of time, people lose interest, and all semblance of action disappears. Then, what is left is the type of face-to-face relationships in which people simply keep talking about what is wrong with situations. It is doubtful whether any real constructive action results from this condition.

PROVIDING IDENTIFICATION WITH PROBLEMS AND DYNAMICS OF INDIVIDUALS AND GROUPS

It is important that the curriculum develop the conditions with children which will not only promote understandings but provide points of identity with problems and the dynamics of face-to-face and group relationships in communities. By dynamics in this connection is meant those forces of interaction among people which tend to retard or enhance action on community problems. Face-to-face relationships have potential for the solution of real community problems if they do not remain in a casual state. It is important, therefore, that the curriculum make provision to point up the many values and alternatives of these relationships so that intelligent choice on the part of the students may emerge. The teacher must recognize that most discussion is of the informal and casual type. He must also recognize the steps or processes necessary to take the thinking out of the casual conditions into a situation where real plans for action may develop.

Moving informality into analysis and appraisal

Informality characterizes practically all types of communication in a community. The difference in the degree of informality depends on the sense of need developed for action. Some of the types of communication have reached a kind of planning stage especially if it is agreed that "the matter be brought up at the council meeting." At this stage, informality may still prevail but it tends to be more intensive and compulsive.

All parties to the intercommunicating groups are identified with some problem. The identification may be with a common problem or with several problems. In some cases, each individual is expressing himself on his particular problem. Some individuals may be for or against something because someone else is for or against the same thing. Some individuals seemingly may exhibit a form of identification which is influenced by a condition outside of the general information of the group. They may express themselves as being against a proposal which they really favor but are "smarting" within because their selfhood has been threatened. The threat may be occasioned by some aggressive individual who is feared because of the power he may inherit and use in the consequences which may ensue if the proposal made becomes an accomplished fact.

Ascertaining motives in identification. The teacher must cultivate an awareness of the different ways in which people identify with a problem or situation.

Many motives are at work in the matter of identification.

The big task is to develop the conditions where all the motives might operate in a learning situation. Under these conditions, the motives can be analyzed and appraised by the motivators themselves—in this case, the children and teachers. It is hoped that from the type of analysis which takes place in the learning situation motives may be appraised as to feasibility, practicality, and direction. He who sets up the conditions in which each individual can be resourceful in terms of his identification to disclose meanings relative to operational values, will have performed a great act of curriculum development. Out of a clear recognition of the identification one has with a problem will come a new perception of the problem which will alter the original views he had regarding it. In the process of analysis of the different concepts of the problem, a new pattern of planning may emerge encompassing the common points of view held by the several parties identifying with the problem.

The analysis of ways in which individuals and groups identify with problems should help develop competence in promoting action in community situations. The object is to take the informal and casual intercommunication of community groups into the realm of analysis and appraisal so that identification may develop into real concern and, subsequently, into action on problems.

Utilizing identification indicated by various reactions for meanings

Types and intensity of identification with problems on the part of groups may be indicated by typical expressions regarding a topic such as the thoughts and action of so-called modern high school youth. The fact that this topic has been dealt with through commentaries in newspapers, "letters to the editor," magazine articles, small town newspapers, and numerous other sources to the point of boredom is all the more reason to present some of the reactions with a possible refreshing approach. The expressions indicated are stated substantially as they were heard and read about by the writer on various occasions. They are as follows:

"Do they drive! Your life isn't safe after school lets out."

"Where are the parents today? That Smith boy and girl are out every night till all hours of the morning."

"My kid talks over the telephone all the time. Why don't they have some homework?"

"I hired Bill's boy to cut my lawn. You should see the job he did and then charged me a dollar and a half an hour. What is it coming to?"

"You should see how these kids spell. I have had one working for me. I know. Why don't they teach them something!"

"All they do at school is have a good time, go to games, and never do any work. Why don't they make them work?"

"My boy was supposed to write a composition on some topic in which he was interested. He did. He got out an encyclopedia and copied it. He showed me his paper after the instructor returned it. He gloated over his A."

"What we need is some good old-fashioned discipline."

"Have you noticed Jim's boy? He certainly has improved, has twice as much ability as Jim ever had. That boy has something!"

"What do you expect of kids? We haven't anything for them. Why don't we organize a Little League? Baseball makes a man out of a kid!"

"We should have more things to keep these teenagers busy. They have so much energy."

"I like Mamie's girl. She is so polite about everything. She has respect for people."

"I guess it's her upbringing. The parents are dead-beats. What can you expect of the kid?"

"In my day, if a youngster did not get his lessons he would be flunked and no questions asked."

"Did you see that Blair boy? Imagine, him getting through high school! He can't do anything."

"Did you see where Kitty is going to college? More power to her! She really deserves it."

"Why do kids always cut across lawns? Couldn't the school do something about this?"

"I have a hard time going to sleep because of the kids congregating next door and playing games into the night. Why don't parents have hours for their youngsters?"

"When I was a boy I didn't have time to play. Why do youngsters have so much time to do everything except important things?"

"You know that Farrell boy? He talks just like a man. He seems to know a great deal about what is happening in the world."

"Yes, my girl is just like that. She leaves her room in a mess, but, after so long, she does something about it. Perhaps, it is better not to be too disturbed about everything!"

"Why worry so much about your girl! She was over the other night and, believe me, she has some mighty interesting answers to some weighty questions! Better find out more about her yourself."

"What do you do with your youngster? I tell Jane to do things till I am blue in the face and get no results. I am at my wits' end to know what to do with that child."

Many more observations of reactions of parents and other adults to youngsters could be recorded. Enough have been indicated, however, to show various types of identification of people with the problems of youth. Reactions of the type indicated may be given in some cases with intense feelings and in others only in a casual manner. Usually nothing really happens about the reactions and the meanings underlying them. As a result, no one is wiser for having heard or read them.

It is important for the curriculum worker to develop the conditions where children and youth may critically examine the reactions for the many meanings which are inherent in them. In this manner, an opportunity is provided for youth to develop competencies in using intelligence in the approach to problems. One might challenge many of the reactions as recorded in the observations above as being representative of the real problems of youth. They might be considered by some as impulsive reactions which show no real understanding of the problem. This challenge is accepted as an honest appraisal certainly of some of the observations. There are, however, some reservations with regard to the anticipated challenge, especially in connection with (1) the concern exhibited in the reactions, (2) the substance for value-building which the reactions provide, and (3) the potential for action.

Conditions for learning must relate to reactions as between youth and adults

The reactions as to the behavior of youth reflect mainly adult values. These may be at variance with what youth regard as *their* values. It would be well to provide for situations where youth could give their reactions to youth problems. Let's take, for example, the observation made by an adult about Kitty going to college and being deserving of it. Kitty, perhaps, has never thought of herself as being especially deserving as compared to others. Then, of course, there is the question: What is meant by deserving the opportunity to go to college. What criteria were being considered by the one who said, "She really deserves it"? An analysis of these questions would reveal much about differences in values and provide clues for direction in value-building.

Some interesting simple relationships and values might be discovered in the following observation: "Why worry so much about your girl? She was over the other night and, believe me, she has some mighty interesting answers to rather weighty questions. Better find out more about her yourself."

Questions such as the following may provide clues to values: What are the forms of behavior which are at variance here? Should the values of children always be the same as those of the parents? Might the provision for the expression of differences be a value? Is the problem of behavior indicated by this observation one-sided? Many other questions, no doubt, would develop to provide clues to answers by adults and youth. It is very possible that many values would be revealed. The analysis of interesting answers to weighty questions might provide the approach to a wide area of inquiry and greater quality in thinking.

In the development of the thinking with regard to the reservations which might be held relative to the reactions, it might be well to consider that of carelessness in driving. Some questions which might be developed are such as the following: As you have heard people talking about carelessness in driving, what impressions did you form relative to their observations? Were the drivers youths of high school age or were they older people? How did these people learn to drive? Is there some relationship between reckless driving and the sales emphasis on possible power and speed of a car? Is the problem of recklessness related to the close scheduling in the pattern of modern living, that is, everyone in a hurry to be on time?

There are, of course, many other factors which are closely related to the problems and values associated with the reactions and situations indicated. It is hoped that the conditions for an analysis of the reactions and situations may point up (a) various ways in which people identify with particular problems, (b) some underlying feelings and motives in the identifications, (c) the nature and intensity of concern relative to the problems, and (d) some insight with regard to intelligent action on the problems. Furthermore, a careful study and appraisal of the clues to thinking revealed by the questions should produce some of the dynamics prevalent in the problem.

DYNAMICS OF COMMUNITY RELATIONS SUMMARIZED

An attempt has been made to point up the importance of the development of understanding on the part of teachers of (a) varied forms of community relationships, (b) how the relationships may be present or absent due to the nature of the community, (c) some of the consequences resulting from the degree of intensity inherent in the relationships. In the approach to the development of understanding of community relationships, it was suggested that the program of education must provide for the conditions where learning experiences relative to the dynamics in a community may operate in a realistic manner. It was suggested further that the conditions for learning must be such as will enable the teacher to recognize the ways and the degree of intensity with which people in a community identify with problems. It is also necessary to gain insight relative to the causation of identification with problems. An illustration of identification is entered in connection with the question: How responsible is modern youth? Typical questions relative to the illustration are indicated showing various ways in which people identify with youth problems depending on individual experiences and circumstances.

SIMPLE RELATIONSHIPS AND CURRICULUM TASKS

Curriculum workers have responsibilities in providing the conditions whereby the participants will become resourceful relative to the use of simple relationships in curriculum experiences. They will utilize many phases of the simple relationships discussed in the preceding pages to develop learning experiences with children and young people. Many or, perhaps, most of the ideas for the use of simple relationships of people in the improvement of learning experiences will come from the teachers and the children. An elementary school teacher, in planning with the children for a field trip to a market, for example, might arrive at such questions or suggestions as the following: What are the different ways in which people go about the task of shopping? How did the clerks help the people? Do the many items one sees in a market give rise to thoughts about the needs and wants of people? As you looked around, did you notice whether the shoppers were mostly men or women? Did you feel that the clerks were giving the types of service which you consider important? What kind of experiment could one do to determine the difference between needs and wants? What other relationships as between needs and wants could be found through experimentation? Do you see any relationship between research and the variety of products found in a market? What competences are needed by people who operate the market? What types of competences are needed by people in the whole process of making available to the consumer the products found in a market? Do the shoppers need certain competences?

*Using simple relationships in learning leads
to expanded meanings*

There would probably be some other questions, suggestions and proposals but the above will suffice to indicate the reservoir of resourcefulness of the teacher and children in promoting a high quality of curriculum improvement through the utilization of even one aspect of simple relationships of people. As teachers and other curriculum workers study, analyze and discuss these questions along with others, all will tend to promote better learning experiences with children. Taking just one of the questions, "What kind of experiment could one do to determine the differences between needs and wants?" one can easily see the potential for high quality learning experiences in the pursuit of it. Many valuable experiences would accrue to children as they pondered the question of wants and needs. It might be suggested, for example, that twenty or thirty children make lists respectively of their needs and wants and note which list is the longer. In a study dealing with needs and wants of elementary school children, Houle[2] showed the "wants" list for most items exceeding the "needs" list by almost a hundred per cent. An exception was clothes. Evidently, appearance was rated high as a value by these children. Many children had difficulty aligning their wants with their needs. Some tended to impoverish the needs list possibly because of admonitions from home and from teachers.

Developing meanings about different roles in fulfilling wants and needs. As one pursues this question, more and more relationships become obvious. A visualization of the possible consequences in partial or full realization of wants should give some valuable clues to intelligent choice with respect to values and the pursuit of ideas. If, for example, a child would have the chance to follow through on the acquisition of wants, his relationships would be affected in several directions. Certainly his parents would be concerned. His status with companions would be altered. His role in peer relationships might under different conditions take conflicting courses. Some values may have to be satisfied to attain the others. All this would affect him as a person.

As an individual is experiencing changed relationships with peers, his wants and needs alignments are shifting into the nonmaterial aspects of living. For example, one may want to have more friends, to be liked by certain people, to attract attention to statements or remarks, to be free from loneliness, and have other more or less intangible forms of realization. As the teacher and children examine their wants in terms of the more intangible needs, the experiences which are envisioned would tend to give rise to new questions. Some of the questions might be as follows: In what way would my present relationships with others change? What changes would this make in the manner of behavior which others would entertain toward me? What does it mean to be lonely? Is loneliness something to be avoided at all costs? Is it possible to envision a situation where an individual might be lonely among many friends? Do you know of instances from your readings where

[2] Therese Marguerite Houle, "An Analysis of the Needs and Interests of Children in Grades One Through Six," unpublished report. Storrs: University of Connecticut, 1953.

lonely individuals experienced a sense of satisfaction and realization? How do we go about testing these questions? Have your best ideas come about when you were with friends or when you were alone? What is it that makes you say at different times, "This is a good idea." "That is not a good idea." What would you consider to be a simple idea? How, in your mind, do you evaluate ideas as being simple or complex? As you examine simple and complex ideas, what feelings do you experience relative to each?

Providing meanings through analysis and testing of relationships of people under different arrangements and conditions. The questions indicated are not nearly exhaustive as individuals and groups pursue the problems of wants and needs. The simple relationships and their connection with values as described in the previous pages will provide most ample substance for the development of conditions of learning which have no limit in possibilities. An analysis of face-to-face relationships as they relate to behavior of people under varying circumstances will establish the conditions for the testing of many ideas which will be productive and directional. As these relationships are tested, many consolidation points which give strength and intellectual excitement to individuals will be ascertained. The understanding of neighborliness will give new avenues of resourcefulness to people. The roles that people play in community relations provide a most valuable source of meanings to children and young people. The work people do and the vast array of activities in which they engage give meaning as to their incentives, motives, aspirations, and other signs of behavior.

As one proceeds into the testing of ideas with respect to simple face-to-face and community relationships, the conditions for a point of departure for expanded meanings will be provided. As the problems of people become the conditions for learning, the related phenomena will serve as the richest resources for endless inquiry and the development of ideas and understandings. Such topics as the balance of nature in relation to the balance of man's constructed environment, the nature of man and space, the enlarging conception of the components of survival, the relation of ethics and man's pattern of selectivity from the heritage, the story of incentives of individuals through history, become in large part the substance for the conditions of learning.

Many of the tasks of curriculum workers are apparent as they proceed to develop the conditions which will promote meanings with children and young people with respect to the above topics. Other tasks are obvious from the many questions and ideas which have been indicated in the preceding pages. Again, we wish to emphasize that the dynamics of curriculum improvement must function primarily at the level of the learner. By learner is meant everyone engaged in the development of the conditions for the realization of meanings and ideas. The teacher, curriculum specialist, principal, supervisor, and children are all learners. Learners have the task and responsibility to develop relationships in meanings to promote an environment of ideas and to generate leadership in each other to continually extend the area of inquiry and understanding. What the teacher and children do in the classroom to promote learning should also be done on, perhaps, a somewhat different level by the teacher and other curriculum workers. Therefore, the tasks of the curriculum workers become quite clear. They promote leadership toward the development of conditions for learning in the classroom. They study, analyze, and attempt to improve and extend the conditions in seminars, committees, and by individual and group resourcefulness. They return to the classroom with expanded ideas and renewed resources to give greater quality to the conditions for learning. In this process lie the dynamics of curriculum improvement.

SELECTED READINGS

Department of Elementary School Principals, *Human Values in the Elementary School*. Washington, D. C.: National Education Association, 1952. Parts 2 and 3 are especially interesting as simple statements of values and illustrative experiences in developing values.

Educational Policies Commission, *The Education of Free Men in American Democracy*. Washington, D. C.: National Education Association of the United States and the American Association of School Administrators, 1941. Although this was published in 1941, it provides some valuable criteria for value-building.

Freeman, Beatrice, "Not Our Property—But Our Responsibility," *Childhood Education*. Washington, D. C.: The Association for Childhood Educational International, Vol. XXXII, No. 1; September, 1955, pp. 14-15.

Hartford, Ellis F., "Emphasizing Values in Five Kentucky Schools," *Bulletin of the Bureau of School Service*. Lexington, Ky.: University of Kentucky, Vol. XXVI, No. 4; June, 1954. This bulletin gives numerous examples of how values may be emphasized in every aspect of the school program.

Jackson, Ann Hill, "We Are Constantly on the Move," *Childhood Education*. Washington, D. C.: The Association for Childhood Education International, Vol. XXXII, No. 1; September, 1955, pp. 12-14.

Smith, B. Othanel, William O. Stanley, and J. Harlan Shores, *Fundamentals of Curriculum Development*, Revised Edition. Yonkers-on-Hudson, N. Y.: World Book Company, 1957, pp. 45-52. Points out changes taking place in family life and occupations and employment.

7

Using Children's Values
to Promote Learning

ALL CHILDREN HAVE VALUES. VALUES ARE BELIEFS WHICH HAVE been derived by experiences. Most of the values have been formed in the home. This is, of course, as it should be since the home is the primary institution which exists for the purpose of building values. The home, however, is part of a larger environment known variously as a community, section, district, ward, neighborhood, town, country, or village. The names which indicate the environment more or less circumscribe an area of commonality of operations. The home interacting with the environment is the production center of the values of children.

The environment and home, functioning as the production centers for values, have a heritage or background of values. The people in any particular locality came originally from other environments which contributed to the value-making ingredients of the present environments. Thus it is obvious that present values have come about through the experience of men throughout the whole span of civilization. Values have been passed on from generation to generation, from country to country, and from community to community.

DISCOVERING THE SOURCES AND VARIATIONS OF VALUES

It is clear that value-building never reaches a stopping place but goes on and on. It is important to face the fact that individuals, consciously or unconsciously, continue to develop

160

value judgments concerning all elements of their existence —themselves, the people with whom they come in contact personally or vicariously, the physical world surrounding them. Some value judgments, though having reality as they become focused in the minds of individuals, perhaps have meaning only in a metaphysical sense.

Many values appear to be held in common by most people. For example, most individuals value steady work and income. There are, however, many variations employed by individuals in attaining realization within the framework of their values. Some are satisfied to work in a factory or other establishment for an hourly wage. Others will find their opportunities in government work. Many engage in the professions. Still others are employed in various types of service occupations ranging all the way from operating a grocery store to running a gambling establishment. What they do contributes to adequate care for themselves and their families. All of the individuals, no doubt, feel that they are fulfilling criteria of service in the community. Doubtless individuals of alleged antisocial tendencies through the psychological devices of rationalization, sublimation, substitution, and others, likewise maintain this feeling.

Factors influencing direction of values

The fact that all value steady work and income makes that a common value. Other common values would relate to the high esteem placed on the freedom and right to work. Within the framework of these values, however, other values are taking shape, some common and others peculiar to individuals and groups. In the process of goal-seeking, the values tend to ramify and go in different directions. For example, one individual may be interested mainly in having his bank account grow without any special purpose in his efforts to save money. This individual might feel a kind of independent glow over the fact of just having the "means" to do without doing. Then, too, he may feel a satisfying sense of power in possession. Another individual saves so that he will be able to build a home, enlarge his present home, or purchase some conveniences for the kitchen. He values the happiness, perhaps, which goes with greater comfort for himself and his family. Then, too, he may improve his living situation so that he can gain the plaudits of friends for his initiative and planning. In other words, he relishes the status feelings which a certain type of achievement has given him.

Almost every community has its "four hundred," "gold coast," "right side of the tracks." The form of social stratification which is implicit in these terms may carry all types of values besides the common value of belonging in this group. Some of the members in this group may have been more happy to live in another part of the community but were somehow pressured into "keeping up with the Joneses" for business reasons. They gave in to the forces operating in the culture with respect to class status. The values held by many in the culture were strong enough to draw these unwilling members along with the class level.

In any community, there are individuals who have entirely different values from those indicated above. One individual may be fully aware in terms of neighbor patterns that the physical living facilities for him and his family leave considerable to be desired. This individual and his family, however, consider several alternatives as to where they should use their money. After some deliberation in the weighing of the alternatives, they might decide to use the money they have accumulated to travel.

Another family may decide to buy a television set instead of making needed repairs on their house. Still another family chooses to use extra money to buy books. Some families make special sacrifices to see that the children have special opportunities in music, art, and other phases of education and choose to use the money accordingly. In some homes, there is great emphasis on saving money, whereas in other homes that is not an important factor in living. What some people regard as luxuries, others regard as necessities.

It is clear from the discussion that there are all types of ramifications of values among people in a community. It would naturally follow that most, if not all, the values are reflected in the children. The teacher and curriculum worker, in dealing with children, must be cognizant of the fact that all these values and others are the normal behavior patterns of the children that come to school.

Developing conditions for ascertaining and changing values of children

Some interesting developments with regard to values being held or changed were observed in a classroom of ten- and eleven-year-old children. It was apparent in this classroom that an honest attempt had been made by the teacher to admit all the values of children into the learning situation. The developments were really initiated by a resourceful teacher who had placed on the bulletin board some clippings about newsboys. The clippings told what routes were covered by certain newsboys and how much money they made. Many of the newsboys mentioned in the clippings were members of this classroom.

As the children first looked at the clippings, one would hear such remarks as "He carries papers," "He looks just like you," "Let's go up and look at it closer," "I have a long route. I go all the way from A Street to D Street," "Where is your route ?" As the conversation continued more and more children were drawn to the bulletin board. General discussion followed in which the facts brought out by the clippings were verified, challenged and compared with the experience of those newsboys in the classroom. Some of the boys began to talk about how much money they made. Others in the room were drawn into the discussion and began to tell about ways in which they made money.

Assessing incentives of children and other people. The teacher urged the discussion on to reasons for earning money. One child said, "I have to pay for my bicycle." Another said, "I buy some of my own clothes." One child said, "Our family is large, and my dad says it helps him out if I earn money." The discussion continued on the question, "Why is it important for people to earn money?" There followed answers all the way from buying groceries to paying for the family car. It was brought out by someone that children work in school and do not get money for it. Others said they helped at home and did not receive money for it.

From this developed discussion about ways in which people

are paid and rewarded. Some of the children told about things they liked to do, for which they had no intention of receiving pay. From this developed the fact that people do not spend all their time making money. The teacher observed that an important recognition of values grew out of this. One value which was quite clearly revealed is that money is just one of the many forms of individual realization. Services which are satisfying to the individual are often rendered with no thought of reward in the form of money. Furthermore, most of the activities in which people engage and find satisfaction are not rewarded in a pecuniary manner.

Centers of interest to expand ideas about incentives of people. In view of the many side issues which arose from the discussion on earning money, it was suggested that two interest centers be established, one containing clippings, books, and materials pertaining to earning money, and another containing news items, books, and materials which showed what people did without receiving money. The interest centers were expanded as more and more news items were coming in to stock them with meaningful ideas. It was important to observe that following the initial clippings brought by the teacher, the children hastened to expand the interest center daily with clippings, news items, and other resources which they secured on their own initiative.

The interest centers drew children into other areas more or less related to money and other values. It seems that someone had found a story on buying what one needs. This was pursued in further discussion until another angle arose when someone said, "But some people get things they do not need." From this developed the use of the term, luxury. It was pointed out by the children that some luxuries are good for people and some are not. A group decided that the members should ask their parents about different luxuries. Following this, it was brought out that some luxuries make one's house nicer to live in. The observation was made that wallpaper, paint and decorations were luxuries, but they were really needed because people wanted things to look nice. Children told about pictures, collections of beautiful trinkets, and other items they had in their rooms. One boy said that he bought himself tools to do carving; another said he had bought a leather tooling set. They explained that they liked to work with them.

The discussion on needs and luxuries led into a decided form of action on the development of values. The question arose, How many of the things that one gets should be luxuries? Many different ideas were advanced with respect to this question. Some said that one luxury article a week should be added, while others thought that would be extravagant.

According to the teacher's observation, several types of values developed out of the ideas of earning money. It will be noted that one idea which grew in importance with the children was, as previously mentioned, that money is negligible as a factor in some types of service. A generalization which came out of the study was that some luxuries were needed by all people to make their living brighter and happier. It was contended, that one should exercise choice in terms of what he could afford and what would help him to live better. The youngsters cited the qualities of usefulness, beautification and opportunity for creativeness as some of the criteria upon which to base the choice of luxuries.

A third idea or generalization which either arose from or was strengthened by the classroom experiences was that saving money was not always a good thing to do. The children gave, as examples, decisions one would have to make as between saving or buying such things as a picture, a violin or other musical instrument, a baseball mitt, or a fishing pole. They placed some limiting factors on these decisions such as whether one already had many pictures he liked, how often he went fishing, and how many musical instruments he had purchased before. In other words, one should not buy on "whims."

PROMOTING UNDERSTANDING OF BEHAVIOR

The approach to an understanding of behavior necessitates the conditions wherein all values are admitted to the classroom. The conditions must provide for the most challenging questions and portrayal of facts in the environment which will promote the opportunity for children to examine and appraise their values. Some valuable ingredients of the conditions are the development of alternatives with respect to ideas. Important, also, are the opportunities to study the consequences of the alternatives.

Providing for evaluation in terms of children's values

It is important to retain the idea that with the admission of all values, it becomes the task of the teacher to provide for the analysis of alternative values identified by children. This does not mean that there is a difference between held values of children and teacher; nor does it necessarily mean that there is difference in degree. There is primacy in time and place with respect to values. A teacher who says, "Children, let's discuss the value of honesty in taking tests," even though he admits all shades of value judgment for examination, fails before he starts. At the moment the students may not be concerned with this issue but, with his mention of it, their own value judgments freeze as they say to themselves, "Whoops! Somebody's been cheating." It is an artificial approach to value considerations which pose threats. When people are threatened, even with assurance and later permissiveness, their judgments tend to become static.

This again shoulders the teacher and curriculum worker with a tremendous responsibility with respect to leadership and understanding. As leaders, they have to see that conditions are under control so that antisocial values may not predominate in the value-seeking operation. They need to, at the same time, make sure that all values are exposed so that the alternatives emerge in the setting for learning. They have to be very astute, therefore, in bringing their point of view to the situation without excluding any other points of view. If a point of view or value held by a child fails to emerge in the setting of alternatives, that value fails to be examined for its consequences. As a result, the holder of that value continues to hold it regardless of how dangerous it may be.

Structuring for children to become analytic about their behavior. Action with regard to behavior problems has frequently been ill conceived and misdirected. Behavior is frequently conceived of as an overt manifestation. An example of this is stealing. The method of treatment with respect to stealing is usually some form of arbitrary punishment. Similarly, in a group where there is a manifestation of stubbornness on the part of some member in clinging to an idea when the rest of the group has disallowed it, there is a tendency to heap blame and denunciation on this member. This treatment reveals that behavior has been considered only as it looks from the outside, something one should not do. The treatment should go much farther than dealing with symptoms. It should deal with causes.

The structuring process for determining causes of behavior should be such as will urge the participants in a group to be analytic with regard to their behavior. It is a process of developing consciousness, of becoming aware of one's self, of knowing the stimuli to which he himself will respond. It is, in a sense, an establishment of communication with himself. In short, it becomes self-analysis toward insight.

There is increasing evidence to indicate that learning to look at human behavior in an analytical way is fundamental to the development of social understanding and cooperation. In one study by Ojemann and Morgan,[1] a group of young persons were taught to think of their own behavior and that of their parents, teachers, employers, and classmates in an analytical way. The experimental groups were paralleled by carefully matched control groups who were not given special training. The results indicated significant reductions of conflicts for the experimental groups. Various types of qualitative data also indicated significant changes in attitudes and actions toward others when behavior was understood in an analytical sense.

In another study by Ojemann, Nugent, and Corry,[2] it was indicated that there is ample evidence from experimental and clinical studies to show that overt behavior, such as noncooperation, destructiveness, shyness, aggressiveness, discrimination and prejudiced behavior may be produced by many different causes. It follows then that one will not have a functional

[1] Ralph H. Ojemann and Mildred I. Morgan, "The Effect of a Learning Program Designed to Assist Youth in an Understanding of Behavior and Its Development," *Child Development*, Vol. XIII (Sept. 1942), pp. 181-194.

[2] Ralph H. Ojemann, Anne Nugent, and Martha Corry, "Study of Human Behavior in the Social Science Program," *Social Education II* (Jan. 1947), pp. 25-28.

understanding of the behavior nor will one know how to react toward it or change it until the causes operating in particular cases are known.

Observing children in climates of action may furnish clues for behavior analysis. Clues to a real analysis of behavior can be developed by observing children in a variety of climates of action. The clues derived from such observation will serve the teacher in helping children to analyze their own behavior. The following illustration will reveal some guiding clues. In a certain classroom, there had been considerable fighting between children on the playground. The teacher was at a loss to know what to do about it. A clue was offered by a little girl when she said, "Some people never fight and get along much better." The teacher took this lead and decided with the children to determine what causes differences which lead to conflict. The group together decided to look at these causes carefully and to point them up in any way they could. Some drew cartoons, others studied differences of people as revealed in books and still others perused the newspapers for clippings showing differences of opinions on issues. The cartoons drew the most attention because they most nearly reflected the differences in the classroom.

There followed a discussion of what to do with these lists and illustrations of causes of differences. The decision arrived at was to have the members of the group indicate various types of solutions. The solutions were to be rated as highest, passable, and lowest types. It was interesting to observe the efforts and ratings. The highest types of solutions usually were connected with intelligence, good will and self-possession. The solutions receiving the lowest ratings were invariably those connected with brute force, such as giving two contenders gloves to fight it out. Others that received either lowest or passable ratings were punishment by the teacher and staying after school. A few recommended arbitration by a court.

Some of the most important gains by the type of structuring indicated above accrued to the offenders who gave rise to this project. Almost everyone of them rated "fighting it out" in the lowest category. As a matter of fact, the same offenders gave some of the most plausible suggestions for resolving conflict. It is apparent that real social action toward constructive value-building was taking place in this process. A great deal of change was effected in the children. They were developing insights and skills which would serve them most effectively in the approach to action on problems which had meaning to them. The new insights and skills learned would help them also to look at problems in terms of causation, background, and self-identification.

Making sure that all value concerns and issues are in the learning environment. It is hoped that the previous discussion and illustrations will give some meaning with regard to the value systems of children and how they attempt to resolve them. Yet an analysis of values concerned with attitudes toward overt behavior cannot be the only concern of teachers. This could become an example of teacher-directed, teacher-centered value concerns. It does not take students long to discover when a teacher is interested only in those values which relate to how students act with respect to him.

An environment must be provided for not just total value admission with respect to certain delimited areas but total value admission with respect to all value concerns and issues.

It is often difficult for a teacher to allow analysis of values in areas in which he can trace no direct personal relationship. Often the teacher fears threats from his own authorities, i.e., other teachers, principal, superintendent, school board, when he entertains discussion of issues which "are not part of the curriculum."

It must be faced, however, that no serious effective analysis of values can be initiated on a delimited basis. The value patterns which operate in schools and the environment are developed in detail in Chapter 8.

❖8❖

How Environment
Can Help Learning

AT FIRST SIGHT, IT APPEARS PARADOXICAL TO DISCUSS THE MATTER
of availability of the environment in schools because it is always
present. Children are largely products of their environment.
It would seem, then, that their presence in the school and classroom would make the environment available for learning. Since
the children carry the effects of the environment into the school
setting, it would appear that its availability would be clearly
assured.

It is true, of course, that the effects of the environment are
brought into the school setting by the children. These effects
constitute the values of the children, that is, those standards
which guide children toward making adjustments to problems
encountered in everyday living. These values have developed
during the child's process of growing up. Some of these values
are common to all children. Many, however, vary according to
individuals. The variety of values evolve as the result of influences exerted by religious backgrounds, ethnic origins, social
strata, and diversified social relationships. As a result of circumstances influenced by the environment, some children hold
values commonly attributed to the middle class level of society.
Some children come to school with a set of lower class values.
Still others possess values indigenous to the upper class.

SCHOOL LIMITS VALUE ADMISSION INTO SETTING FOR LEARNING

As children come to school, all are physically admitted. In terms of the values which they hold, however, some of the children are admitted, others are partially admitted, and a number are refused admission.

Perpetuation of outmoded practices limits value admission

The admission of the values of children is limited by the perpetuation of outmoded practices. The school, through the years, has had to fulfill different functions at different periods in its history. Established in the beginning to teach children to read the Bible so that they would be properly inducted into the faith, the school has gradually assumed more and other roles to aid in inducting the young into the culture. Although the school is generally representative of the culture of which it is a part, it has had to continue to carry into the present a considerable number of ideas and practices of the past. Some of these ideas and practices can be identified with today's problems. Others are outmoded, having no apparent connection with the needs of the day. An illustration of an outmoded practice is a somewhat typical geography lesson on the New England states. In many instances, the New England states are still studied on the regional basis apart from their relationships to other parts of the country. Another item pursued in the study of New England is that, due to its land surface, it became a manufacturing region. Nothing much is done with population centers and their effects on industry and the problems resulting from industrialization.

Another illustration in which the school frequently exists as the repository of an outmoded practice is the manner in which language is taught. The approach to language teaching is usually through a prescribed format in which grammar is disguised. The approach is through grammar, pure and simple, notwithstanding all the embellishments designed to give it a communicative pattern.

How does this all relate to the admission of values of children? In the first place, the practices together with the ideas to be developed with children are already resident in the school curriculum when they arrive in the classroom. Most children contribute little or nothing to the curriculum. The multiplicity of values which they bring to school find no clear-cut identity with the typical presentations of geography and language, not to mention other areas. In other words, the approach to learning in connection with these subjects is frequently quite unrelated to what children experience in their environment.

Since the approaches to the various areas of study are established before the children arrive on the scene, there is no effort to consider the values indigenous to the environments of the children. This constitutes, in effect, a clear exclusion of the values of children.

Reluctance to alter established organization limits admission of children's values

A way in which the admission of children's values into the school is limited is through the reluctance of the school people to alter the established pattern of organization. The school is still largely organized on a rigid pattern. This organization is influenced somewhat by the historical background of the establishment of the school, and to a considerable degree by dominant school people and by economic, political, and religious minority groups in the community. Bonner[1] expresses the prevailing conditions quite emphatically when he says,

> A limited survey of the enormous quantity of literature on the American school system, and an impartial examination of the degree of its success in preparing children and youth to understand and cope with the changing problems of life, leads one to the sad conclusion that on the whole the forces of obscurantism and reaction are in the saddle.

Dominant groups limit value admission. Although the schools are supposed to belong to all the people to be used by them to perpetuate some values, refine others, and evolve new ones adaptable to changes in the culture, they too frequently function in consonance with the dominant groups. This contention is emphasized by Bonner[2] as he goes on to say:

[1] Hubert Bonner, *Social Psychology—an Interdisciplinary Approach* (New York: American Book Co., 1953), p. 321.
[2] *Ibid.*, p. 322.

The administrative machinery, the curriculum, and the method of instruction reflect the values of the dominant groups, whose chief objective is not education in the sense of enabling every child and youth to grow into an independent and thinking individual, but the preservation and transmission of their own prejudices.

It is quite obvious that under these conditions only those values are admitted into the instructional setting which tend to reflect the thinking of the dominant and controlling groups. As was indicated earlier in this discussion, the school was organized largely for the purpose of inducting the young into the values of the culture. This will work quite effectively if a culture is stable. In a changing society, however, alternative values present themselves which create many demands on the curriculum. Changes in the home, occupations of people, the community life, and the social structure brought about largely by technology have more or less upset the rules or values to which people had become accustomed. If school people are sensitive to these conditions, they will attempt to adjust the curriculum to serve the needs of children in terms of the new values taking shape. The school organization, however, is already firmly established, this organization being effected in a time when the culture was more or less stable in a simple society. It has come about partly through historical concepts of what constitutes a school and partly through the reluctance of people to break with the past.

Rigid induction to culture limits value admission. Induction into a culture means that one becomes disciplined in its requirements. The school is supposedly organized in terms of that objective. Subjects have been developed in the curriculum which are supposed to fit the young for the requirements of the culture. As long as the society remains simple, this curriculum serves the school's part in the induction process. In time, however, as society becomes more complex and some of the old rules and associations are broken down, the older requirements are no longer adequate.

As the individual seeks answers to this condition, he is confronted with many conflicts. Finding no definite clue to answers, he begins to blame some individuals or groups. In all probability, a major part of the blame is heaped on the schools.

This, in turn, gives rise to concern on the part of some of the school people. In their efforts to do something about it, some changes are suggested relative to the school curriculum.

Other members of the school are reluctant to change. They fear change. In fact, they are opposed to any innovation which may disturb the existing equilibrium. More often than not, this latter group will have the support of the school administration and a considerable segment of the community. In all probability, one of the arguments which will be advanced by a considerable number of people is that the school has changed too much already, that it has gotten away from the fundamentals. The group which advocates a "return to fundamentals" really means a "return to the 3 r's." The group further means by a "return to the 3 r's" that they be taught by the same methods which prevailed when its members were in school. They submit that since the school program of the past served to bring them success it will do so for the youth of today. The proponents of the "return to fundamentals" philosophy do not attempt to relate the content and process of the school program logically to the problems of living. A possible exception to this is the value that is placed on hard work *per se*—doing the requirements of the school without raising any question about them. As a result, the original organization remains. If anything, it may be even more rigid than previously.

Rigid curriculum excludes values by avoiding innovations of change. One example of a change in society is the almost universal acceptance of television as a medium of recreation and information. Much of the leisure time of the majority of the people of the United States is occupied with indiscriminate television viewing and listening. Similar conditions, perhaps to a lesser degree, prevailed in connection with radio. Little was done by the schools to develop the arts of discriminative listening and the development of tastes during the many years that radio held sway as an entertainment and communicative device. The patterns of school organization and curriculum development remained rigid and constant. This rigidity continues in most of the schools and classrooms today. English classes in both the elementary and secondary schools continue to deal with correcting mistakes in speech and composition without ascertaining the type of content and practices with which young people actually identify. The practice of drilling on the improvement of sentence and paragraph structure continues apace in the classroom whereas outside in the environment children and youth continue to ply their patterns of communication in terms of their real values. Very little real association between school practices and those which prevail in the child's environment is visible.

Curriculum must provide conditions for insight relative to change. If the school is to be considered as an institution designed to promote some degree of societal change, the curriculum must develop the conditions which will produce some degree of compulsiveness on the part of young people and teachers to gain insight relative to that change. Television must be brought into the setting for learning. The reasons for the types of programs carried by television must be ascertained with young people. Experimentation relative to communication of all types must be carried on. The conditions for learning must contain those ingredients which will enable young people to gain insight and understanding regarding the values which have demanded the enormous time given by television to rather questionable presentations throughout the day as against the rather limited time devoted to high-caliber programs. The curriculum workers have a great responsibility in providing for the opportunities of inquiry, experimentation, and practice relative to the new developments which are taking place in communication.

As indicated in the previous section, changes take place in the community, the home, occupations of people, and the social structure. With the advance in technology and science, for example, the impact of urbanization in the community brings many problems which are baffling to people. The face-to-face relationships which formerly existed have now all but disappeared. Family life has changed. In more and more cases, both the father and mother are employed. In many homes, there is no regular schedule of family living as existed before. Many families have to live in cramped quarters and congested areas. All in all, these conditions tend to threaten family solidarity.

The impact of these conditions is reflected in the children and youth. Many problems which were formerly taken care of in the home now tend to cause conflicts in the mind of boys and girls. Some of these problems, for example, relate to sex and boy-and-girl relationships. Where can these children go for answers? Where can they go to gain a point of direction as to the roles which they need to play under these changing conditions? Certainly not to the school people because they are compelled to operate in terms of established values. The conditions for learning frequently do not make provision for the study and appraisal of the new values which are producing conflicts in the children. As a result, the children seek answers wherever they are able to find them and, more often than not, the answers are not obtained in the school environment. It is clear that the nature of the school organization frequently contributes to the exclusion of the values of children.

BLOCKS TO VALUE ADMISSION

As has been indicated in the preceding pages, only a limited number of values of children are included in developing the design and content for learning. Several reasons for the limited admission of values are implied in the previous discussion. Some of these are the prevalence of a blind faith on the part of people in practices which once served a purpose and which are now outmoded, the continuation of the authoritarian pattern of school organization and instructional design and the allegiance to middle class values held by teachers. There are, however, various other reasons which relate to the behavior of teachers with reference to a limited admission of values in the classroom.

Failure of school people to understand relation of environment to individuals

One reason for the failure to admit all the values of all the children into the scene of learning is a lack of understanding of the nature of the environment on the part of school people. The environment consists of those conditions which tend to influence the behavior of an individual with respect to the activities in which he engages. The conditions may promote

or hinder, stimulate or inhibit his responses or actions relative
to his activities. These conditions largely shape the individual's
values. At various times, he assumes different roles. Some of
these roles indicate satisfaction with experiences he has encountered while others show his aversion to situations with which
he has experienced dissatisfaction. Gradually, the process of
reacting in the environment produces in him a certain system
of behavior or values which influences his action under various
circumstances. As the child comes to school, he is expected to
respond favorably to the conditions which have been established. Some of these conditions are responsive to his needs;
others are not.

Typical learning experiences may exclude values. An illustration, applying to older children, which represents a failure
to understand the environment on the part of school people is
the "limited values" study of the feudal system in medieval history indicated below. The usual procedure in the study goes
something like this:

(a) A reading of the story and a portrayal of the facts and
pictures of the feudal system.

(b) A discussion of the questions given by the textbook together with a few questions raised by members of the class and
the teacher.

(c) A convergence toward the more interesting phase of the
feudal system—that of knighthood.

(d) A departure into activities, for example, reproducing
some of the weapons and armor of the knights.

(e) Dramatization of knighthood as a possible culminating
activity.

It is difficult to say just what values are admitted by this
typical study of the feudal system. It is doubtful whether any
real values are admitted unless they are those whose possessors
regard knowledge important for its own sake. One might ask
the question: Is it within the bounds of possibility that the
values of all the children of a typical classroom might be identified in a study of the feudal system?

To answer this question, the author wishes to provide an
illustration which is a sharp contrast to the above approach to
the study of the feudal system. The situation which developed

was actually observed by him in a class of seventh grade children. One of the first points observed in the approach to the study were two bulletin boards on which were portrayed different systems of relationships between people. The feudal system was pictured in terms of its power structure, showing the controlling forces in the hierarchy of values. Alongside this was placed the rather loosely organized structure of the Greek city-states. Shown, also, were the democratic structures as well as the laissez-faire type of organization.

Some two or three children posed the inquiry as to how people felt toward one another in the different structures. One youngster brought out that it would be difficult to transplant the thoughts and feelings of another time and place and make them seem real in relation to the present. Someone suggested that the literature should be studied for the purpose of reproducing the feudal system as nearly as possible. Another agreed and added that careful research should be done so as to ascertain the feelings of people at the different levels of the feudal power structure. One of the high points was a child stating that it was necessary to find out what produced the system and adding, "We should look into the politics of the system." The children talked about how different people gained power, how it should be distributed, and about other pertinent concepts related to status. Much more transpired than has been described, but the above is sufficient to illustrate the wide range of identification of values which were obtained in this study.

It is obvious that the teacher of this class had an intelligent grasp of the nature of the environment of these children as well as considerable understanding of the values of people. It would have been impossible for this class to proceed as it did if the teacher had not made an attempt to discover the values of the children.

Entertainment of limited views about selective school environment

A reason why some teachers fail to admit all the values of children into the instructional setting is a mistaken view about selectivity in school experiences. Feeling that the school environment must be special, there is a tendency to unwittingly restrict the conditions for learning. In connection with this tendency teachers, in effect, might become censors of the learning environment. They may even find an element of support by Dewey[3] who gives weight to this philosophy by stating:

> . . . . it is the business of the school environment to eliminate, as far as possible, the unworthy features of the existing environment from influence upon mental habitudes. It establishes a purified medium of action. Selection aims not only at simplifying but at weeding out what is undesirable.

Selectivity must enable children to identify many values. It is indeed important that the school environment be simplified and selective. In the illustration of the class studying the feudal system observed by the writer, it becomes apparent that the teacher had planned for a selective environment. His approach to selectivity, however, was through the values of all the children. There is no question but what some of the values of some of the children would hardly make for a selective environment; in fact, they should not be condoned. This teacher admitted the values so that the possessor of them could see the position he occupied, for example, in the power structure. In that way, the consequences of these values could be ascertained so that a more desirable choice of values might result. In other words, all the children might have an opportunity to see and study their values beside alternative ones. The true meaning of a value can often not be ascertained until its impact is seen in relation to other values. Finally, as one views the illustration of the typical approach and practice as against the actual approach in the study of the feudal system observed by the writer, it seems safe to say that high selectivity in the learning environment is preponderantly greater in evidence in the actual approach.

Teachers' and administrators' fear to deal with some values

Another reason for refusing admission of all the values of children into the school and classroom is a fear on the part of

[3] John Dewey, *Democracy and Education* (New York: The Macmillan Company, 1916) , p. 24.

teachers and administrators that they do not have the wisdom to deal with some of the values. This reason is related to a lack of understanding of the environment in that the school people fear that they do not have the knowledge necessary to cope with some of the values which may be brought out in the open. The taboo placed on certain questions relating to such topics as sex, religion, family problems, and ways of settling disputes have kept them out of the realm of the classroom. The school continues to function as if these questions did not exist. As a result, teachers feel that they are woefully unprepared to deal with these questions. The real tragedy, however, in addition to the position of the school on some of these questions, lies in the paucity of conditions in most classrooms for real everyday experiences which are held important by children. Some of these experiences would be those associated with money problems; analysis of feelings such as hate, anger, and friendship; the appraisal of the nature of one's fears; and the resolving of conflicts with regard to guilt feelings.

Teachers often fail to deal with these experiences because they have the feeling that the questions may become too involved for them to approach with confidence. Another failure to exercise the imagination to include experiences of the type mentioned above is the fear of criticism from colleagues and the principal.

Teacher's fear that teaching "beyond" may invoke censure and loss of status

Another reason for the reluctance to develop conditions for experiences related to real and actual problems of people is that the teacher has sensed that teaching of this type is misunderstood by other school people as well as the people of the community, who might invoke censure of his efforts. The teacher might feel that a launching of a classroom program dealing with questions of feelings, conflicts, and others of this type would jeopardize his status role as conceived by other school people and the community. Tragic as it may seem, a subtle disapproval of teachers who venture beyond the bounds of the habitual pattern of teaching is a practice which is all too common in many communities.

*Resignation to "easy way out" concept of instruction
and administration*

Finally, some teachers and school administrators have resigned themselves to what might be called "the easy way out" method of keeping school going. Unfortunately, some people find their way into teaching because it is something they think they are able to do. To them, teaching is just another job, something at which they feel they can get by without exerting too much effort and imagination.

No doubt, this attitude prevails on the part of some people in any occupation. Their attitude toward performance in any occupation or profession is that it is something one has to do. Needless to say, teachers who possess this attitude lack most of the elemental understandings about child life, and refuse to make the effort to learn. It is frightening, although a fact, that a considerable number of these people are in our schools. This fact has tremendous implications for public concern with the status conditions of teachers in communities. Furthermore, this condition demands unprecedented attention on the part of colleges, universities, and school systems toward the reactivation and redirection of the whole process of teacher education, both pre-service and in-service. It is hoped that the thinking developed in the chapters and pages of this manuscript will promote and contribute substance for this attention.

Having dwelt on some of the reasons why all the values of children are not admitted into a development of the conditions for learning, an attempt will be made to discuss and graphically portray different patterns of value admission.

THE PATTERN OF LIMITED ADMISSION OF VALUES

Every child is in constant interaction with his environment, that is, he is influenced by it and in turn influences and modifies it. The environment does not exist apart from individuals. The values which a child holds result from influences exerted through his constant involvement with people whose thoughts and actions reflect the environment. His behavior is influenced, of course, by the values derived from his involvement with the environment. His responses to various situations are geared to his values. As has been stated in the previous discussion, there are extant in the environment a variety of values held by different individuals and groups. Values held by any particular child may differ from those of another child, depending on the groups or individuals that have influenced him as he is growing up. It would follow then that the response to similar situations will vary from child to child.

Limited value pattern may produce artificial response in children

As the child comes to school, he will naturally tend to respond to situations in terms of the values which he holds. He soon discovers, however, that some of his responses are accepted by the teacher and others are rejected as not conforming to the established rules or wishes of the teacher or school. Furthermore, he discovers that the responses of some children are invariably accepted and those of others rather consistently rejected. The reason for rejection is not clarified because the values which were basic to the responses are not understood by the school and are, therefore, not brought under scrutiny. Those whose responses are not accepted soon find that they must make a decision between two alternatives, to conform or be ostracized.

Most children will decide to conform. A few unwittingly do not conform. Those who decide to conform will thus operate under two sets of values as between their school life and community life. The role they perform in school becomes an artificial one as it is carried on under compulsion and not in harmony with their real values. Once they are out of school, they return to the real values. It is obvious that this dualism in response will not only tend to introduce many conflicts in these children but also fail to provide any degree of understanding of the values they hold. In other words, their opportunities for learning are severely curtailed by the school. Only a portion of the environment is made available for learning. The curriculum here is designed for a limited number of children and revolves around few ideas. The conditions for meanings are limited to the ideas used by this group.

Limited value pattern fails to relate meanings
of past and present

The conditions for learning under limited value admission to the school is represented in Figure 1. For purposes of this representation and much of the discussion which follows, the values have been placed into several categories. One category consists of those values which come from the past and with which no real relationship has been established with present values. These are represented by the long solid arrows which come from outside the circle or environment. An example of this category is the characteristic treatment and use of such literature as *Silas Marner, Ivanhoe,* and *A Tale of Two Cities.* It will be seen that this type of literature is readily admitted into the setting for learning.

One reason for admission of this literature into the learning environment is that it has been used in classrooms over a sufficiently long period of time to be considered safe. In other words, the values represented by the literature are sufficiently remote from those of the youngsters and their parents that no serious questions will be raised.

The solid arrows may, of course, also represent material which is more highly value-charged than that indicated, but the treatment is of such a nature as to leave the values in a latent form. Examples of this type of material would be some of Shakespeare's plays, such as *Macbeth* and *Hamlet,* the dialogues of Plato and more contemporary materials such as Steinbeck's *Grapes of Wrath.* The limitation of value treatment usually given to these materials naturally puts them into the category represented by the solid arrows. For example, *Macbeth* is treated as a rather brilliant work of Shakespeare. However, it is usually read and analyzed for rather innocuous meanings with little or no relationship to the subjective value elements which may link the reader to the characters and their action.

Value admission limited to prescriptions
of middle class behavior

A second category of values which are admitted into this limited learning environment are represented by the solid short

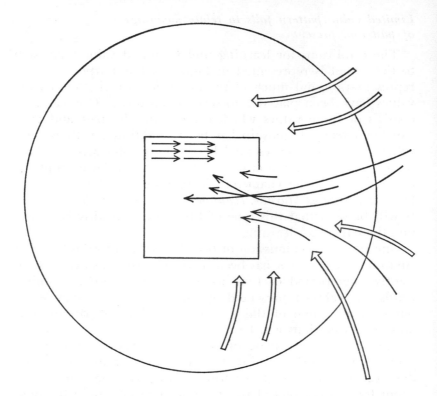

Figure 1. Pattern of limited value admission into the instructional setting.

○   The local environment

□   The school

——————→   Values from the past with treatment unrelated to present values

———→   Values having local flavor of conformity to established standards of teacher and school

════════⇒   Values having local flavor of non-conformity reinforced by similar values of the past

══⇒   Values having local flavor of non-conformity to established standards of teacher and school

arrows. These values come from the local community and might be explained as those common ways of behavior which conform to everyday middle class standards. These values dictate actions which conform to the established standards of behavior prescribed by the traditional organization of the school and the teacher of that school.

A third category of values represented in the diagram are those which exist in the local community but which do not conform to the prescribed values of the school. These are represented in the diagram by short double arrows. It will be noted that these values are not admitted into the classroom setting. Some of these values may be illustrated as those which carry considerable aggression on the part of participants to a dispute, feelings that an action is all right if one can get away with it, the absence of habits of frugality on the part of children and their parents, and others. Other values which are in this category are those related to sex and other intimate problems of youth which give rise to conflicts.

Exclusive pattern fails to provide for insight to deviational behavior. The practices in the classroom usually will ignore the deep-seated feelings of children relative to these values. A heated dispute is considered a troublesome situation in which the participants are either admonished to behave or "make up" at once. This practice ignores the fact that the aggressiveness attendant to a heated dispute is often in line with the values which are a living pattern of the parties involved. The seriousness of the practice lies in the fact that none becomes any wiser about the meaning of his behavior. There has been no opportunity to analyze and evaluate the feelings involved in the use of aggression in settling a dispute. The fact that the parties were admonished to behave and "make up" does not change the feelings of the parties. The failure to admit the values for study and analysis provides no resources of thought and action more promising than to proceed to operate in the same manner as before. Therefore, nothing has been learned by the children about their behavior.

What is true with the lack of admission of the values related to aggression is also true with the other values indicated which do not conform to the pattern of practices in the school. The feelings, for example, that go with the thought that an action is right if one can get away with it will continue as a value pattern if they are not admitted into the instructional setting for the discovery of alternative ways of behavior. A considerable number of children hold the above values and will continue to do so because the school closes the door to any real opportunity for them to develop habit resources which will point up the consequences of action on the values. The old value patterns persist as long as their holders fail to discover any new meanings regarding them.

Exclusive prescription of values tends to isolate school meanings from reality. A value which is quite safely anchored to middle class thinking is that one should live conservatively with respect to possessions. Habits of frugality are frequently encouraged without any form of assessment of possible alternatives. Thrift as a pattern of living receives a *carte blanche* in the instructional setting. An indiscriminately high estimation is attached to it. Yet many children and young people have been brought up in a hand-to-mouth existence. To them money is something that should be spent and quickly. Thus, the lack of admission of the values characterized by an absence of frugality introduces a form of dualism of practice on the part of many children. In school they verbalize the concept of thrift, whereas outside they conform to the sense of release about money and things dictated by their real values. It is doubtful whether any new meanings have been identified by these children through the indiscriminate code of frugality operating in the school.

The paucity of conditions for the development of some understanding with youth about sex and other intimate problems is well known. The instructional practice under the system of limited value admission is carried on as if sex did not exist.

A fourth category of values are represented by the long double arrows which link the present values with those of the past. These are the values which have a local flavor and are reinforced by a treatment of the thinking of the past in such a manner as to identify with contemporary behavior which is in conflict with the established standards of the school. If the treatment by the teacher and children of the material will bring out some meanings which can be ascribed to one's present behavior, it falls into this category. The treatment of the play *Macbeth*, for example, out of context with personal behavior meanings of young people, puts the classic in the category represented by the long solid arrows. In the former treatment of content materials, the values are not admitted; in the latter, they gain admission into the conditions for learning.

Many schools would come under the limited value admission type represented by Figure 1. Local, present, and past values of children which conform to the standards of the school and teacher are readily admitted to the learning setting. Values which may be different receive either limited or no admission.

Learning under limited value admission characterized by strict standardization

The type of learning carried on under the conditions of limited value admission is represented in the diagram by the neat arrangement of the arrows in the classroom. This is symbolic of the conformity, standardization, and rigidity which characterizes the curriculum in the school and classroom. There is an absence of those values which contain elements of conflicts or promote a sense of inquiry. Accordingly the conditions for learning which may lead to a resolving of conflict or study and experimentation with respect to the relationship of ideas are absent. Rather, the conditions are constricted in terms of the prevailing values of the teacher and school. These values represent and perpetuate the status quo, the deadness of the past, and much of the thinking of the upper middle class. This means that the curriculum is composed of those elements which are considered to have stood the test of time and in the teaching of which the teacher is in relatively safe territory with respect to methods and procedures.

The dynamics of curriculum development reside in the conditions for the analysis and examination of concepts and ideas. These conditions are absent when a school or classroom limits the admission of the values of people. Since the teachers, staff members, and children are the ones through whom the curriculum is changed, it is almost a truism that very little, if any, change will result under these conditions. Since the pattern of practice is confined to the constricted areas of maintenance of old ways of thinking, the possibility of curriculum change by the staff is very remote.

Curriculum improvement limited to a strictly prescribed program. It is more or less logical to conclude that whatever curriculum improvements are attempted under the conditions indicated in the previous pages will conform to the values which are admitted into the school setting for learning. Since the school program is rigid and for the most part prescribed, any attempt at curriculum improvement would be in terms of questions such as the following: Are our standards high enough? Are the children meeting the standards? Should we change textbooks? Are we giving enough time to the study of English literature? Are we teaching enough mathematics? Should American history be taught in the tenth or eleventh grade? Since the children are not reading up to grade level, should we have more drill periods in reading? Or, should we change the reading series? Does every teacher of the first and second grade children spend thirty minutes a day on phonics? Do we have enough drill in spelling? Should we work on a new "Required Reading" list in English? Should Indians be taught in the second or third grades? Should we write a new course of study? How many themes should a tenth grade student write? In what grade should compositions be taught? In what grade should we teach about our state? How many groups should one have in a reading class? Should social studies be taught by the group method?

Curriculum procedures limited to the status quo. It will be noted as one views the above questions that a rather high premium is attached to standards, textbooks, time, grade level, drill, series of readers, greater quantity of subject matter, prescriptive program, and this or that method. All these items possess some degree of importance and deserve to be considered in the process of curriculum improvement. The questions, however, as they are stated, suggest either a "yes" or "no" answer or doing more of what is already being done. The questions also indicate categories of fixed ideas. For example, the questions about reading lists suggest rather restricted limitations in the lists. Furthermore, designating the lists as "required readings" presupposes a reluctance on the part of students to read them.

Most of the questions indicate a status quo type of thinking —that is, what is, is right. Ideas are to be dealt with as they appear in the textbooks. There is no thought of questioning the categories of fixed practices. There is no conscious effort to treat subject matter in such a way as to help children and young people identify with meanings in terms of their experiences and values.

Other typical procedures in curriculum work under limited value pattern. The curriculum work which is carried on under the limited system of value admission frequently evolves out of the results of standardized testing. This approach, of course, is not without merit if it includes an analysis of basic causes of difficulties of children. To get at basic difficulties, it would be necessary to use many other phases of evaluation. Under the limited value admission pattern, however, the procedure for curriculum improvement goes something like this:

1) Standardized tests are given.

2) The results are tabulated and plotted to show high and low spots of achievement on the part of children.

3) The principal, superintendent, or some other status official looks over the scores and decides that something needs to be done with the children who do not achieve the norms.

4) Committees are appointed to work on the curriculum to "bring up" those children who are not achieving the norms.

5) A somewhat typical procedure of one of the committees would be as follows: Assuming that the committee is one dealing with the problem of "bringing up" those children who are not achieving the norms in reading, probable steps would be to (a) look over the present course of study, (b) talk about how many reading groups there should be, (c) consider the amount of time devoted to phonics, (d) decide on changes within the present pattern of reading instruction. A revision of the course of study to include more time for phonics, a statement about increasing the number of reading groups and giving more time to the slow and average readers, would probably result.

It will be noted that the above effort at curriculum improvement does not provide any conditions for the study of how children learn, how interests in reading may be developed, the use of evaluative techniques other than standardized tests, the development of a wider range of reading opportunities, the study of the child's success in terms of home conditions, and an effort to seek out and remove the causes of difficulties. All efforts in curriculum improvement are limited to the pattern of present practices. No new questions are raised as to a more comprehensive approach to the reading problems. The efforts constitute nothing more than a form of artificial tinkering.

THE PATTERN OF PSEUDO-ADMISSION OF VALUES

The practice of limited value admission of children into the instructional setting described in this section is actually related to the type described in connection with Figure 1. It is presented here, however, for the purpose of showing how, in the efforts of eliminating some of the deficiencies of the practice indicated in Figure 1, similar defects continue to be a part of the conditions for learning. Figure 2 represents an admission of values which are considered to be of immediate concern to children. As will be noted, in Figure 1 the values which are admitted are mostly those from the past. Figure 2 represents an admission of those values which are assumed to be of immediate concern to the pupil.

As one views the picture of value admission, however, of Figure 2, one is immediately struck by the similarity to the admission process as represented by Figure 1. In other words, the arrows, although coming from the local community as represented by the circle, are solid. This indicates that the values are innocuous with respect to real problems of children and are, therefore, safe. The real values of children represented by the double arrows fail to be admitted as do those of the past which reinforce the local ones. The school makes certain that those values which are admitted will fit neatly into the pattern already in the classroom—those represented by the solid arrows within the square.

Pseudo-admission gives appearance of "modernism." Regarding the value admission pattern indicated in Figure 2, one

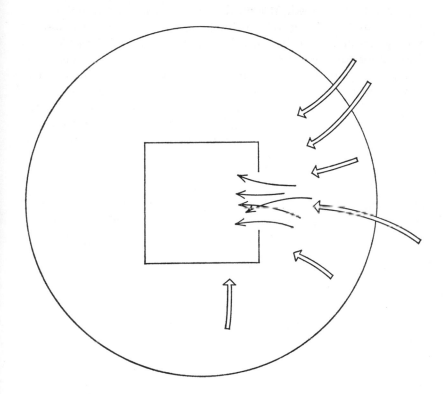

Figure 2. Pattern of pseudo-admission of values into the instructional setting.

○ The local environment

□ The school

⟶ Local values having an appearance of modernism but which have been purged to conform to established school standards

⟹ Local values representing a conflict with established school practices and standards

⟹ Local values reinforced by thinking of past in conflict with established school standards might ask the question, Could the values admitted be considered as representing the immediate concerns of children or young people? In other words, since the values admitted are innocuous, that is, purged of certain hardened reality-centered problems as dictated by the value pattern obtaining in the school, are they admitted at all? The admission process in reality presents a façade of the real values. For example, "rock-and-roll" records are permitted to be played at certain times during the classroom day, but nothing is really done to examine analytically with youngsters the basic reasons for the popularity of this type of music.

No effort is made to develop opportunities for children to study the meanings of rhythm as well as the various types of quality in music. No attempt is made to expand the interest in "rock-and-roll" into new areas of inquiry with respect to sound, rhythmic interpretations, constructive taste in emotional response, and the many alternative meanings and symbols of aesthetic expression.

The idea behind the pattern of pseudo-admission of values is an attempt to conform to what is conceived as "modernism" in school practices. This idea is not to be confused with constructive modern approaches to learning, such as learning experiences about new concepts in astronomy or outer space. Rather, the process represents a sort of resignation to what is going on. It is characterized by the thoughts: "It is going on outside of school, so why not let them have some of it here so they will like school better"; "Let them do some of this and then they will do the regular work better"; "Let them blow off steam and they will appreciate you more." It is, in effect, a form of concealed bribery. It is, also, in a sense, an admission that one is not adequate to the task of approaching an understanding of behavior and its relation to learning. It suggests a type of thinking which views behavior and learning as opposites, as operating in different compartments. The process of limited value admission representing this form of "modernism" might be considered a feeble attempt to resolve the problem of resistance to learning on the part of young people.

Some of the other practices in limited value admission are related to activities which are presumed to be in line with a so-called modern school of thought. The teacher might ask the children to tell about their interests. Next, classifications are made about their interests and the children are divided into groups to work on the interests. The children may be quite busily engaged and the situation looks rather wholesome. If one examines more closely, it may be found that there is a lack of direction. Many of the things children are doing fall in the classification of "busy work." Neither short-term nor long-term goals seem to be present. The activity is a sort of aimless self-indulgence with what are supposedly expressed interests. Obviously there is much to be desired in the situation provided here. No questions are developing, no real planning is taking place, no decision with regard to alternative concepts and ideas is evolving. It is a façade of learning behind which one finds much emptiness and uselessness.

Pseudo-admission of values characterized by perfunctory approach to children's needs

Another situation of value admission which is limiting in understanding is a perfunctory approach to children's needs. The teacher might ask children to indicate some wishes, or to state what three people they would choose for a fishing trip. The teacher might also ask the children what bothers them. Following this, the wishes and the things troubling children are classified. The responses with regard to the fishing trip may be made into a neat friendship circle or sociogram. There may develop some discussion about the wishes or problems which are bothering children. This may sound very interesting to the observer and, from all appearances, some results should develop. Viewed as a device, however, apart from attending factors in the environment, not much will happen to heighten the understanding of teachers and children relative to needs.

Purpose and direction is lacking in this isolated procedure to deal with the immediate concerns of children. The nature of this approach to the problem of needs is often quite vacuous. The learning environment suffers from a lack of basic direction which would be derived from a studied analysis of the relation of behavior and needs. In other words, the environment is not "charged" with meanings which children might identify in their own behavior and the alternatives to that behavior. Consequently, there is very little direction in behavior analysis.

The types of situations indicated above have in too many cases become patterns of instruction. There are several probable reasons for the patterns. One reason quite clearly evident is a lack of understanding on the part of workers in education as to the nature of the behavior of people. Another reason is the use of various techniques out of context with the environmental forces operating on children. A further reason is found in the application of the "bag of tricks" technique to a highly involved process of learning. The zeal to be in line with so-called trends in modern education may be another reason for the misapplication of devices in promoting learning. These are just a few of the reasons for the existence of the questionable patterns indicated. Many others will become clear as the discussion proceeds in connection with the many factors involved in the development of the conditions for learning.

Pattern of curriculum development in pseudo-admission of values

The nature of curriculum improvement which would take place under the limited value admission practices in a so-called modern situation is guided by two philosophies: (1) that described in the limited admission pattern indicated in Figure 1 and (2) that characterized by learning through indiscriminate doing. Many school practices are designed to appear modern but the instigator of the practices frequently operates in a very closed system of value admission. The teachers that carry on this practice want to appear as if they are in the "swim of things" so they provide certain embellishments to instruction.

Value admission limited by "extra" things designed to keep children happy with "regular" work. The "extra" things that are provided in instruction are simply for the purpose of encouraging children to do the regular confined and restricted program. In other words, teachers provide opportunities for games, dances, and other extra things which they feel children like for the purpose of appeasing the child's desire for these things. Having fulfilled this desire, the teachers conclude that the children can be easily talked into doing the regular work of the school. "Regular" in this case usually means that which is included in the course of study and what is detailed in the prevailing textbooks.

The process alternates between prescribed rigidity and irresponsible release. The gadgets, games, and devices are simple, a form of verbalization with respect to modernism. No attempt is made to tie the games up with the deeper sensitivities of children and youth. No attempt is made to bring about a realistic identity between the learning experiences and the problems of young people. Behavior is usually treated as an intangible unrelated to "school."

The teachers that pursue these rather extrinsic practices do curriculum work somewhat as follows: They chat with other teachers about certain devices that can be used throughout the day during short periods to cause happy breaks in the pursuit of what is conceived by pupils as a rather dull program or the things that they have to do. These teachers will also work on committees to plan what are conceived as motivating devices for regular work. This atmosphere may prevail throughout the school. The premium is on keeping people happy through extrinsic activities rather than situational tasks.

Value admission limited by narrow approach to children's wants and needs. A practice which sometimes prevails in the pseudo-admission of values pattern is the provision for many activities to satisfy so-called felt needs and interests. Planning rests on the assumption that children alone know their wants and needs. There may be some use of sociograms to obtain a picture of acceptance and rejection of children and young people. Some efforts are made to involve children toward promoting greater acceptance. The approach, however, might be criticized as that which goes with the danger of "a little learning" as to the meaning of acceptance and rejection in relation to the values which children hold and with which they have lived. An example of this is the practice of helping certain children to become accepted in a peer group even if the values of that group may be out of focus with the basic principles of acceptance.

The type of curriculum work which is done in connection with this thinking is in accord with an acceptance of the dominant upper middle class values. The focus of curriculum workers is in using various devices to determine immediate interests, felt needs, and satisfactions regardless of far-reaching purposes and promising direction. No serious effort is made to develop the condition where the whole peer problem is examined, where the nature of behavior which has evolved in peer groupings is studied and understood, and where interests and needs are expanded beyond those which are immediately felt and expressed.

THE PATTERN OF TOTAL VALUE ADMISSION

A comprehensive approach to learning demands the admission of all the values of children into the instructional setting. The type of school and classroom setting envisioned by this concept of learning raises many problems and questions basic to behavior and its direction. An attempt will be made in the following pages to develop elements of direction with respect to the questions raised. In order to try to clarify some of the problems raised by the questions, it is necessary to point out some of the conditions for a comprehensive view with regard to the process of learning. Figure 3 represents a total value admission approach to learning. A few observations relative to Figure 3 are in order to disclose the peculiar differences between the representations of Figure 3 and Figures 1 and 2. In the first place, in Figure 3, all values are admitted into the school as shown by the double arrow. In the second place, in Figure 3, there are several doors through which the values may enter. There are no restricting barriers. The close inspection, therefore, symbolized by entrance through one door, is not carried out at that point. In the third place, the values in Figure 3 are not reposing neatly in rows.

There is much for children in this school environment. The teacher has been resourceful in exhibiting many of the aspects of the environment. Children coming into this room will be able to discern elements with which they are able to identify themselves. The values with which they are already identified are, of course, brought in and will make the environment more

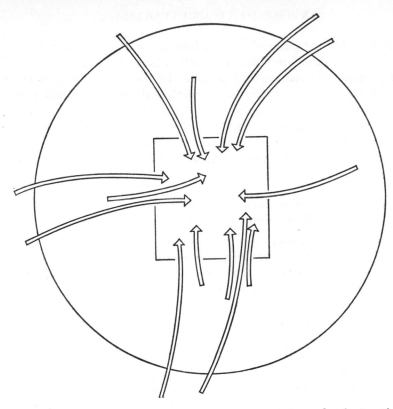

Figure 3. Pattern of total value admission into the instructional setting.

○   The local environment

□   The school

⟹   Values in the environment representing meanings indigenous to all children

⟹   Values representing a continuity of present and past with meanings indigenous to all children

Within the center for learning opportunity is provided for:
- Expanding meanings into the peripheral area of knowledge
- Appraising the alternatives on the growing edge of the cultural core of values
- Examination of what people hold important in the culture
- Centers of understanding toward resolving conflicting values
- Portrayal and examination of the consequences of different values
- Thinking translated into vocabulary having meaning for children and youth

replete with alternative values. A fourth condition which exists in Figure 3 is the interlinking of all values, old and new, past and present, immediate and remote. In the fifth place, in the pursuit of ideas, all values are revealed through the study of consequences and the evolving of decision. Accordingly, those values that cannot be reconciled with the criteria of truth and understanding as arrived at through testing against the consequence of alternative values cease to maintain an important place in the environment.

Total value admission pattern provides points of identity for all children

The teacher through the use of various types of literature and the inclusion of various questions which children raise will have built into the conditions for learning the contact points of the values of all children for critical examination. The books, bulletin boards, and other materials will portray what different people hold important in the culture. Along with this will appear many questions which are related to children's values and the resolution of which will require much research, analysis, study and discussion.

The conditions are provided whereby the thinking that children and young people do is translated into vocabulary and communication forms having meaning for children and youth. The conditions for learning in the total value admission pattern must contain various elements which promote a type of compulsiveness for learning. Children and youth will have portrayed some of the elements, for example, of integration and disintegration in social relationships. Along with this portrayal some questions might develop relative to possible steps to assess the nature of the elements which promote either harmony or disruption in social groups. Within these conditions should also appear in a rather striking manner the effects of fear, threats, and forms of status behavior. These will be examined in terms of both small social groups and the large social groups, even nations.

Total value admission provides unrestricted channels for involvement with ideas. In the total value admission pattern will be no upper limits to learning and understanding. There are no minimum standards. The "lid" to standards is off. There exists a sense of release and stimulation toward the search for meanings. Research in this total value admission pattern begins in the nursery and kindergarten. It continues throughout the whole span of childhood and youth. In order to facilitate the revelation of all types of behavior in thinking, the nature of behavior of people as portrayed through headlines and editorials of newspapers will be critically examined. Curiosity about ways of behavior will be pursued into peripheral areas of understanding. The school will have centers of understanding showing compartments of values, the attempt at reconciliation of the compartments of values, and the repossession of meanings which have been disrupted by the changing technology. There will be a portrayal of different values together with striking hints for the examination of the possible meanings which reside in them.

For fear that the symbolic representation of value admission indicated by the diagrams may be viewed as an oversimplification, an attempt will be made in the following pages to provide some clarification as to inclusiveness of value admission into the setting for learning. The discussion should also help clear up some of the questions with regard to the problem of admission of all values.

Questions involved in admitting all values into the school

In the process of making the environment available in the conditions for learning, it is important that all the values held by children be admitted to the classroom. Admission of all values does not, of course, mean indiscriminate condonement or acceptance of them. Admission simply means that the values must be brought under examination and appraisal through thinking. It also means that people are accepted. When values are exhibited under the conditions of critical thought, the exhibitors will discover many qualities about their behavior that they never knew existed. If values are brought into a setting of this type, there is a vastly greater probability of bringing about needed changes in the existing values and the evolvement of constructive new ones than if they are left to chance.

Total value admission involves testing of consequences of

behavior. Total value admission is then related to the question: What better opportunity is there for a child to develop constructive values than a classroom environment where teacher and children together explore, examine, and appraise their feelings and ideas in terms of possible resulting consequences? Under these conditions, the concepts of *good* will be both discovered and enhanced. The result will be a deeper appreciation of the consequences of certain acts. Whereas a feeling may normally seem perfectly proper to the possessor, an examination and appraisal of it under permissive and thoughtful conditions may reveal elements which might have resulted in serious consequences if it had been carried through.

The matter of admission of all values into the school and classroom gives rise to many questions. Some of the questions which, no doubt, would arise in the minds of some people are as follows: Since some values are extremely antisocial, is it not dangerous to admit all values into the classroom? Would it be possible to control a situation where values characterized as overtly antisocial are operating? If the antisocial values were admitted, would there not be danger of these values becoming predominant in the situation because of the aggressive nature of some of the children who hold them?

Total value admission reveals potential behavioral effects for critical analysis. In answer to the questions, one has to consider several elements which are inherent in the questions. In the first place, to have an extremely antisocial value exhibited in such a degree of aggressiveness as to inflict harm would be unthinkable. The conditions must be such as will reveal values in connection with questions which arise in the daily learning experiences. The important point is that the classroom atmosphere or conditions for learning are such as will exhibit varying types of behavior through examination and appraisal. There must develop that relationship between teachers and young people which will elicit in thinking their identity with types of behavior. Otherwise, one does not know that different types of behavior exist.

In the second place, regardless of whether antisocial behavior is revealed in a threatening or more subtle manner, the fact that it is curbed in its intention does not remove or alter the feelings involved. It becomes necessary, therefore, to deal with the feelings in such a manner as will show the full impact of them in terms of the possible consequences which may result from the behavior involved.

Total value admission helps teachers understand their behavior toward children. There may be various interpretations of what constitutes antisocial behavior. Teachers often regard as acceptable the behavior of the docile, introverted child and concern themselves solely with the extroverted behavior that represents a threat to their classroom routine and teaching authority. As a result, extroverted behavior may be regarded in a disapproving manner; whereas the introverted child who may be harboring suppressed grievances is overlooked. Frequently, the so-called well-behaved child may be all tied up inside with disturbances which eventually might affect his mental health. For the well-being of the extrovert, it would have been much better if he had felt it safe to "pour out" some of his disturbances so that he could have been helped toward understanding himself.

It is necessary that conditions for learning in a classroom and school bring into focus those elements of the self that one does not understand. The conditions must provide for the release that will enable pupils and teachers to look at their feelings without harboring a sense of guilt or fear. Madigan and Steadman have suggested these conditions quite aptly when they say, "Where the emotional climate of the classroom is such that children and the teacher can express their feelings, knowing that these will be accepted, and, when necessary, clarified, we find a relationship between student and teacher characterized by mutual respect and acceptance." [4]

Total value admission provides mutuality in communication between children and teacher. It is hoped that in a climate of this type the ingredients of behavior will be mutually discovered. In addition, there will be established that basis of communication between a teacher and child and among chil-

---

[4] Betty Madigan and Mary Louise Steadman, "Accepting and Clarifying the Child's Feelings," *Fostering Mental Health in Our Schools.* (Washington: Association for Supervision and Curriculum Development, National Education Association, 1950), p. 302.

dren themselves which will tend toward the acceptance and clarification of feelings of all concerned. All will relate their feelings toward situations together rather than directing them to each other. This release will in turn lead to an analysis of the components of the feelings in terms of possible consequences. As each one's perception of a situation is understood, it may become clear to individuals that certain aggressive feelings are unwarranted since they cannot be directed at anyone. It would follow then that, since there is a willingness to see a situation from each other's perspective, antisocial values would not become predominant.

Total value admission provides approach to great thinking. Some questions might be suggested relative to what is conceived as a narrow admission of values represented by Figure 1. One might ask: What is wrong with the values of the past? Has not practically all progress been based on the past? Is it possible to judge the future by any other criterion than the past? Is the new and immediate necessarily good? What is wrong with the admission of values that are safe? Are not the safe values those which have been accepted and have stood the test of utility and direction? Does not the admission of values of immediate problems and concern to the exclusion of those outside of the immediate give rise to the idea of provincialism in thinking?

The questions indicated above really furnish great insight into the whole problem of admission of values into the instructional setting. After pondering the questions and weighing the problems relative to them, one might consider some more basic ones which provide directional clues. Some of these might be somewhat along the following line of thought: What values are really basic to behavior designed to promote truth and progress? What is meant by old and new? Should one seek to identify the undesirable values in both the past and the present and the immediate and distant ones? Do the problems and concerns which children have now reflect the problems and concerns of people throughout the whole span of man's progress in the arts of civilization? Then, is it not possible to link the threads of great thought and ideas throughout the whole span of man's progress in the arts of civilization? Is not the problem really one of providing the conditions for learning that will encompass the identifiable clues of values, old and new, past and present, immediate and remote, into the art of great teaching?

These and other questions will constitute many of the learning experiences in the total value admission conditions. The questions will be related to the problems of people. The thinking behind great events will be examined. Provisions will be made for assessing this thinking against the thinking behind issues today. Literature of all types will be approached on the basis of meaningful connections with contemporary issues. The circumstances which produced certain patterns of thinking will be analyzed for relationships of ideas.

PATTERN OF CURRICULUM DEVELOPMENT
IN TOTAL VALUE ADMISSION

The pattern of curriculum development in the total value admission approach to learning is discussed and developed throughout the several chapters of the book. It is also implied in the discussion on the previous pages. In line with the development in Chapters 1 and 2, the conditions to be established for curriculum development will be those associated with the handling of ideas in the familiar context of the classroom. The instructional setting must evolve out of the "proving grounds" of learning, the classrooms.

Elements involved in curriculum of total value admission

Many elements are involved in the conditions for curriculum improvement in the pattern of total value admission. Some of the elements are an acceptant environment, the provision for release toward fulfillment of curiosity, development of the route for a wide range of experiences, and the establishment of a social mobility for ideas. Other elements relate to release from extremities of circumscription by courses of study, reading series patterns, textbook way of learning, ability grouping, programs for the "gifted," constricted child development concepts, particular methods and systems of learning, and others.

In the total value admission pattern, courses of study and

guides will be used as springboards for ideas beyond. Any decisions made should carry guarantees against crystallization of thinking on any particular level. Any consolidation points reached in the handling of ideas and issues should contain clearly described provisions for new and higher dimensions of inquiry.

Principle of extraordinary potential in every person. The total value admission pattern operates on the principle that there is extraordinary potential in every person. It is the responsibility of the curriculum worker to help establish the conditions wherein every child will find points of unity as between himself and ideas. These points of unity should carry such a degree of intensiveness as to elicit a consuming occupation with the ideas. When a child recognizes points of unity between himself and ideas, he will begin to discover relationships to other ideas. To illustrate, suppose he has read something about the nature of heat, its effect on materials and life. Under some conditions, he would react to it as something that just is. If, however, under the conditions of handling ideas toward curriculum improvement, there appear some vital questions about heat, a new curiosity may develop. In the pursuit of the new curiosity, more and more evidences of the effect of heat might appear on the scene of idea-handling. This may have to be the beginning of a chain reaction of ideas about heat. The new interests could continue into experimentation. New relationships would continue to build up. Thus new points of unity would be established with the child in his relationship to ideas.

Principle of inclusiveness of people. It should be emphasized that in the total value pattern opportunities for learning are based on the principle of inclusiveness of people. The learning experience described above would be available to all children. The responses would, of course, vary from child to child. In this sense, all children are "gifted" in different degrees and directions. It follows, then, that, in a manner of speaking, the curriculum must provide for a range of "giftedness." The curriculum worker must, therefore, continuously seek to broaden the base for high level learning experiences for all children and young people.

Issues involved in total value curriculum in secondary school

The curriculum approach in the secondary school under the total value admission pattern follows pretty much on a more advanced level that in the elementary school. There are, however, a few somewhat distinct features which apply more particularly to the secondary school. The difference lies chiefly in the handling of ideas by the students and the nature of the school organization.

In the secondary school, the conditions should provide for expanded opportunities for the pursuit of ideas into the periphery of meanings. This could be done in connection with the development of advanced centers of learning in such areas as Science and Man, Communications, International Understanding, Behavior, and Man and His Incentives. The conditions for these centers are described in detail in Chapter 2 and so will not be considered further here.

Problem of rigid scheduling and specialized subject areas. Under the total values admission pattern, it is essential that the channels of communication for meanings be established. In the secondary school, this poses a somewhat difficult problem for the curriculum worker because of the rigid scheduling which often prevails. The problem is further complicated by the nature of specialization of subject matter. For example, it may be somewhat difficult for a teacher of Latin to handle ideas in common with a teacher of industrial arts. Somewhat different conditions from those of the elementary school may, therefore, need to be developed in the handling of ideas.

Problems of crossing subject lines. The curriculum worker must help bring about teacher centers for the handling of ideas which cut across subject lines. The reader is referred to Chapter 1 for ideas about this arrangement. A point that should be stressed is that in the total value admission approach there exists no hierarchical conception as to the different subjects. Total value admission suggests that all subjects or unified studies in the secondary school must have the content to enable youth to attain high level meanings and competences. In other words, the English areas must have the same provisions for the attainment of high level understandings about industrial society as the industrial arts areas or vice versa. By the same manner, college preparation content should receive the same amount and intensity of treatment in one subject area as in another. It is just as logical, then, to suggest that industrial arts teachers, English teachers, and mathematics teachers might find an exchange of ideas together highly productive in their efforts to provide high level meanings in their respective areas.

Problem of curriculum compartmentalization. Again, the principle of inclusiveness of people in opportunities for knowledge suggests that college preparation content is equated with that of general preparation. If anything, general preparation should receive the more intensive treatment for meanings. To put it bluntly, the content which is designed to help individuals attain competence in the workaday world should, in every respect, receive the same attention and carry the same level of meanings as that which supposedly prepares one for college. To put it in another way, the separation of college-bound students from life-bound meanings constitutes a "watering down" of content for the college-bound group. The practice carried on in many high schools of maintaining strict dividing lines between different "curriculums" tends to impoverish the opportunities for college-bound students as well as the others.

Tasks of curriculum worker. In the total value admission conditions, there exist no upper limits to learning. The curriculum worker has a tremendous responsibility in pushing out the containment conditions which are a characteristic of rigid school organization patterns. He must locate the blocks to resourcefulness for higher level subject matter content. He must develop the conditions for a state of release toward questioning and examination of practices. He must help individuals and groups locate the "watered-down" conditions which are often unwittingly perpetuated by static instructional practices.

The curriculum worker must seize on every indication of practice designed to develop high level meanings with students. He needs to devote a great deal of time becoming conversant with trends and new developments in international understanding, science, mathematics, communications and other areas. As he is a student of what is happening as well as what is in the offing, he becomes a learner with others who are in the task of promoting high level meanings. In the process of being a learner, he is becoming involved with others in making accessible the literature, instructional aids, and other resources to develop relationships of ideas toward higher dimensions of meanings.

Finally, it is emphasized again that the curriculum worker must be a dealer in ideas. The evolvement of ideas holds considerable priority in the total value admission pattern of curriculum development. The principles of inclusiveness and the existence of extraordinary potential in people suggest that the handling of ideas be the province of all. It follows that the opportunity for curriculum development must be made available to everyone.

SELECTED READINGS FOR CHAPTERS 7 AND 8

Abrahamson, Stephen, "School Rewards and Social Class Status," *Educational Research Bulletin*. Ohio State University, College of Education, January 16, 1952, pp. 8-15. A study showing valuable conclusions about the relation of rewards and penalties to social class status.

Alberty, Harold and others, *Helping Teen-Agers Explore Values*. Ohio State University, Department of Education, 1956. Mimeographed report.

Association for Supervision and Curriculum Development, *What Shall the High Schools Teach?* 1956 Yearbook, Washington, D. C.: National Education Association, Chapter 2. A picture of the adolescent in his society.

Bonner, Hubert, *Social Psychology—an Interdisciplinary Approach*. New York: American Book Co., 1953. A resource helpful in gaining understanding about values, motives, attitudes, and so on.

Buhler, Charlotte, Robert Haas and Gertrude Howard, "Tools Teachers Can Use," *Childhood Education*, Vol. XXXII, No. 6. Washington, D. C.: The Association for Childhood Education International, February, 1956, pp. 262-64.

Department of Instruction. *Foundation Values of American Life*. Cincinnati, Ohio: Cincinnati Public Schools, May, 1954. Although the values are for major emphasis in the Cincinnati Public Schools, many of the ideas can be used for this chapter.

Dewey, John, *Democracy and Education*. New York: The Macmillan Co., Chapter 2. Discussion on the relationship of the school to the environment.

Fink, R. M., "How Children Tell Us They Are Afraid," *Childhood Education*, Vol. XXXII, No. 6. Washington, D. C.: The Association for Childhood Education International, February, 1956, pp. 264-266.

Getzels, J. W., "A Stable Identity in a World of Shifting Values," *Educational Leadership*, Vol. XIV, No. 4, January, 1957, pp. 237-240. A plea for the examination of values to help the child attain a stable identity in a world of shifting values.

Goldenson, Robert M., "Children Tell What Makes a Happy Family," *Childhood Education*, Vol. XXXII, No. 6. Washington, D. C.: The Association for Childhood Education International, February, 1956, pp. 267-269.

Havighurst, Robert J. and Hilda Taba, *Adolescent Character and Personality*. New York: John Wiley & Sons, Inc., 1949.

"Individual Difference and Social Class," *Educational Leadership*, Vol. XIV, No. 4. Washington, D. C.: Association for Supervision and Curriculum Development, National Education Association, January, 1957. Entire issue. These articles present many ideas relative to setting the stage for value admission.

Kluckhohn, Clyde and Florence Kluckhohn, "American Culture: Generalized Orientations and Class Patterns," in *Conflicts of Power in Modern Culture, Symposium of the Conference in Science, Philosophy, and Religion*. New York: Harper & Bros., 1947, pp. 106-28.

Marshall, James, "The Child and His Community's Values," *Childhood Education*, Vol. XXXII, No. 6. Washington, D. C.: The Association for Childhood Education International, February, 1956, pp. 270-72.

Miel, Alice and Peggy Brogan, *More Than Social Studies*. Englewood Cliffs, N. J.: Prentice-Hall, Inc., 1957, pp. 185-217. Many suggestions which will help create the conditions for the admission of values into the learning setting.

Montagu, Ashley, *Helping Children Develop Moral Values*. Chicago, Ill.: Science Research Associates, Inc., 1953.

————, *On Being Human*. New York: Henry Schuman, Inc., 1950.

Moore, Bernice Milburn, "Adults Look at Children's Values," *Childhood Education*, Vol. XXXII, No. 6. Washington, D. C.: The Association for Childhood Education International, February, 1956, pp. 257-61.

Raths, Louis E. and Stephen Abrahamson, *Student Status and Social Class*. Bronxville, N. Y.: 1950. This booklet is intended to aid teachers to locate possible social class status patterns in their own classrooms.

Smith, B. Othanel, William O. Stanley, and J. Harlan Shores, *Fundamentals of Curriculum Development*, Revised Edition. Yonkers-on-Hudson, N. Y.: World Book Co., 1957, pp. 24-45, 58-107. A discussion of community changes, an analysis of the value system and the problems involved, and a statement about curriculum tasks.

Stegner, Wallace. *The City of the Living and Other Stories*. Boston: Houghton, Mifflin Co., 1956. Stories catching manifest qualities of life in very different places and social circumstances. Good background ideas to approach an understanding of many shades of values with young people.

Taba, Hilda, *School Culture*—Studies of Participation and Leadership. Washington, D. C.: American Council on Education, 1955. *School Culture* is a most concrete study of participation, the nature of leadership, and the patterns of belonging and exclusion in school life.

"Values," *California Journal of Elementary Education*. Vol. XXIII, No. 3. Sacramento, California: California State Department of Education, February, 1955. A valuable resource for use in the understanding of values.

Yutang, Lin, *The Wisdom of America*. New York: The John Day Co., 1950, 458 pp. This journey through America's literature and culture resulting in this rather monumental volume would be a crowning extension to the reading of teachers, curriculum workers, and others who must gain a greater understanding of the values of people.

◆9◆

Developing an Environment
of Ideas

AS WAS INDICATED IN CHAPTER 1, PERHAPS THE FIRST AND FOREMOST
task of the curriculum worker is the development of conditions
for the evolvement and treatment of ideas. The curriculum assumes constructive direction as it makes provision for dealing
with data and facts, motives in behavior, values, and the
processes of relating these in the form of ideas. All this time
the curriculum worker is dealing with people. As he establishes
the conditions where people handle ideas, the curriculum becomes an environment for learning. This environment becomes
the resource for the development of the understandings and
competences needed by children and young people for social
effectiveness.

DEFINITION AND TYPES OF IDEAS

An idea is an intellectual construct relative to a fact, situation, or problem. It might be interpreted as a design in thinking. In a sense, it is composed of one or more concepts which
are ordered into a plan of action. A person will view a situation
or problem as to its parts and their interrelationships and form
a mental configuration of it. This mental configuration is a
bundle of facts. From these facts he derives suggestions, inferences, meanings, and tentative explanations. These are ideas.
They anticipate possible solutions.

There are many different types of ideas. As indicated in the
above definition, ideas are developed from data and facts. As
a result, the types of ideas that an individual or group forms

are related in direct proportion to the types of facts and data available. If the learning environment contains many facts about science, ideas will be developed relative to that area. If the environment has data and questions relating to human behavior, ideas about social attitudes and values of people will be generated by the individuals operating in the environment. They will try to ponder the question of why people behave as they do. As a result, ideas will be formed about the causes of different attitudes, how certain attitudes might be strengthened, and how changes in people may be brought about.

Depending on the nature of the conditions for learning in the environment, many ideas might be evolved relative to such questions as caring for others, the understanding and extension of responsible freedom, and the quest for spiritual realization. A study of the nature of rights, privileges, and responsibilities would be productive of ideas and their relationships toward this understanding and realization. Especially significant are the conditions which foster ideas seeking to establish understanding, harmony, and peace among the peoples of the world. Equally significant are the ideas of men which seek to improve the community so that the welfare of the people residing there will be advanced. More intangible and yet important are the ideas which men formulate in their effort to reconcile the cosmos and to understand the relationship of man to man and to a Supreme Being.

IDEAS AS PROCESSES

Any good environment for learning should contain many facts dealing with nature, soil, plants and animals, climate, water, the physical properties of the earth, the structure and function of the human body, communication, shelter, and many others. The reconstruction of the many facts in thinking will generate ideas about growth, about the development of new or different properties from a combination of properties, about behavior and its particular functions, and other phenomena.

Inferences, testing, and anticipation relative to data

Ideas in thinking will assume a certain order or process which grows out of inferences from the data, testing of the data, and the anticipation of results. To illustrate, when a child views a plant, ideas are taking place. The child begins to reconstruct experiences dealing with the plant. He begins to form ideas about it such as its growth, its health, and the life-giving elements of it. He may observe several plants and notice that they are not all growing at the same pace. From this observation will follow questions such as: Why do some plants show much sturdy growth while others barely exist? Do the seeds have something to do with the differences in growth? Could the soils in which the different seeds have been planted have something to do with the sturdiness and weakness of the growth of different plants? As he is pondering these questions, he is at the same time thinking of possible answers to them. He is thus hypothesizing with respect to the reasons for the differences in growth.

It is obvious from the above that the child would be formulating many ideas, step by step, in the approach to possible solutions for his questions. His hypotheses are the result of a process of ideas. He next formulates more ideas as he proceeds to test his hypotheses. He will now have to study the ingredients of soils. He may take samples of the different soils to an agronomist to have them examined for the ingredients. He may go further in his preparation to test his hypotheses. He may decide to try different seeds in a germination process and use those which show equivalent strength. As he proceeds to answer his questions through an orderly process of ideas, more ideas will constantly evolve in his thinking. He is thus expanding and intensifying his environment of ideas. At the same time, he is making provision for the environment of ideas to be expanded for others.

Ideas having qualities more or less visible as they evolve

The process of ideas in connection with the above illustration about growth of plants is one which relates for the most part to factors of change which are invisible. Some ideas such as those related to building something out of wood, for example, have qualities which are more or less visible in the process of development. In connection with building are many readymade facts such as blueprints. In building a house, for example, one might secure a number of plans with the blueprints, select one and proceed to build according to plan. In the reconstruction of the thinking with regard to a house, however, many ideas will emerge which are not exactly related to the plans or blueprints. These ideas will be concerned with such questions as: What type of a home should we build? Where should we secure our building site? Do we want a site which already has trees or do we want to do our own landscaping? Why is this plan better than the other one? What style would be appropriate? What are the purposes of this or that feature? As these questions are considered, there will be a regular flow of ideas, the process of which will result in a home which will, in all probability, conform to the needs which are envisioned.

Questions which may lead to assessment of the nature of people and their behavior

Other processes of idea development which are perhaps more subtle and complex than those indicated, relate to change of behavior. An individual changes in many ways, in varying rates of time, and in different degrees of intensity. Changes in human beings are baffling to the student of change. Although certain elements of the process of human change become observable, others are mystifying to the observer. Although psychologists have clarified some of the patterns of change, the deviations in human behavior remain to a considerable degree incomprehensible to those who would discover them. More and more ideas, however, are being derived relative to what makes people behave as they do.

The process of idea formation applicable to behavior change with youngsters of high school age may be illustrated in connection with the reasons for fluctuating interests with respect to friends. A teacher might make observations on the change of interests of a group of young people of secondary school age. After a period of observing he might, through the study of literature, raise some questions or issues which might lead to an assessment of quality in people. This initial step on the part of the teacher may give rise to such questions as: What is the true nature of friendship? What are the behavior qualities in others which makes them desirable as friends? What do we like in people? How has my conception as to friendship qualities changed over a period of time? Is there a difference between friendship and respect? As we choose our friends, what are the criteria upon which we base our choices? These and other questions will be instrumental in extending the base of thinking with respect to friendship and related behavior. The thinking will extend to the task of examination and appraisal of the values and feelings which are involved in the actions of young people.

The questions which are indicated above will give rise to many processes of ideas. Some of these ideas will be concerned with various points of view regarding the types of behavior in people which are considered important. Other ideas will be developed in response to needs which have become apparent to individuals as they study their own behavior and its social effects. In all probability, these ideas will lead to plans for deeper probing to arrive at a clearer understanding of the question of behavior. As a result, the learning environment will be expanded and intensified with resources which will provide direction for more as well as new ideas about friendship, values, and the nature of man and why he behaves as he does. In this act of probing for greater understanding, more readings on philosophy, psychology, sociology and other fields of study will be needed in the conditions for learning and basic thinking. It is the task of the curriculum worker to develop leadership with teachers and children in promoting the conditions to become resourceful in drawing from many fields of study for meanings.

IDEAS AND MOTIVES

The ideas which people develop are shaped largely by their motives. Motives are the habits which have been built up in the individual through early and constant involvement with social and cultural values and expectancies. Men strive for those values which are highly regarded by the culture. An individual is a social being and is, therefore, responsive to the attitudes and evaluations of other social beings. He strives for those things which give him social standing with the group. He will, therefore, constantly look to the culture and the social beings in that culture for cues for ideas which might give him a degree of social realization.

Different motives resulting from involvement with social and cultural values and expectancies give rise to different ideas on the part of individuals to serve those motives. The literature of psychology carries all types of lists and classifications of motives. Two motives which have high priority in the lists are those of security and recognition. Of all human impulses, the motive of security is perhaps the most basic. Individuals strive in every way to promote their sense of security. As a result, all types of ideas relative to security emerge not only on the part of the individual who seeks to satisfy his own needs but also on the part of those who promote schemes of security for others. An individual is beset by ideas of security through the radio, television, press, public lectures and his fellow men. Insurance companies devote a major part of their efforts to developing ideas of security for individuals and their families. Safety campaigns are carried on by organizations and agencies to reduce accident hazards for people. Investment concerns bring out plans which, if accepted by an individual, are supposed to make him more secure. Religion carries the message of security and peace for people as they relate themselves to a Supreme Being.

Ideas developed in the quest for security

Security as a motive is used by people in their relationships with others. They feel more secure when they belong to a group of their peers. Thus they strive to develop ideas on how they might get along better with others. Sometimes, individuals sacrifice values and personal beliefs in their efforts to belong to the group. Frequently, the desire for status with a group or certain individuals of the group leads some individuals to sacrifice beliefs they have cherished over a long period of time An example of this is a person joining an organization so that he might be associated with certain individuals who are in an advantageous position to serve his motives. One frequently observes opportunistic behavior in certain individuals—that is, they purposely perform the roles which they feel would be the most acceptable in given situations. They have taken the position that it is most advantageous to them to behave in this manner. It becomes rather disconcerting that after having associated with someone on a rather understanding basis one discovers that under different conditions the responses of the individual assume entirely unfamiliar directions. The quest for security on the part of some individuals leads to various types of maneuvering in the efforts to attain it. This action may become so pronounced that it is frequently difficult to discern any consistent pattern of behavior in these individuals.

The motive which has been characterized by the terms "opportunistic" and "maneuvering" may be designated as the wish for response experiences. A person wishes to be closely identified with others. He, therefore, evolves the responses which he feels makes the identification possible. He wishes to have fellowship with others, to be wanted, and to be considered as having personal worth. He contrives ways of response which will tend to have these wishes fulfilled. The development of an effective response system on the part of an individual is an approach to the satisfaction of a need for security.

A study of security with a classroom of sixth grade children

The relation of the security motive to ideas recalls to mind a study on the meaning of security which the writer observed in a classroom of sixth grade children. The teacher had gathered clippings on various topics and had tacked them to a bulletin board. Many of the clippings dealt with different ideas about security. Children added to these clippings with such topics as safety, saving money, pictures of home life, and others. The children also told about conversations which they had with their parents and friends about topics on security. They talked about some articles they read in newspapers in which "security for our children" was mentioned.

All these efforts on the part of the children led to questions as to why there was so much talk about security. This was discussed with the teacher. He detected some great possibilities in the leads which were furnished toward a study of various concepts of security. Some of these concepts were concerned with feelings, goodness, caring, peace, preparing for a "rainy day," safety, and others. The discussion finally settled on one question, "How does one become 'secure'?" The teacher and children arranged for study and discussion sessions where small groups could point up ideas about security in their own way. Some interesting observations about the concepts of security came from the group.

One group decided to work on animal security, how nature protected animals and how man protected them. The members of this group gathered and drew pictures to illustrate their ideas. They pictured the dog as an animal that protected children. Another group dwelt on national defense as a security measure. This group also worked on safety problems. Still another group developed ideas on how people promote security among themselves in working, playing, and just living together. One group conceived of security as being related to jobs. This group developed and brought in pictures of power plants, factories, trucks, markets—anything which showed people at work. Another group found their meaning of security in happy family living. They portrayed their ideas in connection with homes—the family gathered before a fireplace reading or looking at television.

One group had rather unusual and, perhaps, advanced ideas about security. This group developed a small mural with beautiful pastel coloring which to the members represented "peace of mind." The members of this group explained somewhat abstractly that security is more than protection, jobs, safety, and having possessions. They suggested that you were secure when you had "feelings which didn't hurt." Security to them consisted of the qualities which induced serenity, peace, and an absence of mental conflicts.

The reports of the various groups and the discussion which ensued revealed some interesting and valuable ideas regarding the motives of children with respect to security. Different groups and individuals equated security with the following:

Being protected by the police.
Being liked by people and friends.
Being powerful so no one might harm you.
Learning to protect yourself by practicing jiujitsu and boxing.
Having enough money so you can take care of yourself.

Saving money.

Being friendly with the right people.

Having feelings which didn't hurt you.

Having a good home and an understanding family.

Having a good job.

Having many friends.

Praying to God for help and guidance.

Making friends with people who will help you.

Trying to make people happy.

Getting a good education.

Doing your work well.

Having fun with friends.

Building a strong defense system with atomic and hydrogen bombs, and guided missiles so Russia will be afraid.

Obeying the laws.

It is clear from the above list that the security motive operates strongly in children and that they have many ideas as to how to go about obtaining security. One can readily observe from the list that there is a great desire to belong as indicated by the frequent mention of friends and being friendly. The element of discrimination and selectivity as to friends is present as revealed by the responses which indicated "the right people" and "people who will help you." Other motives are those of desire for power, responding for acceptance, and freedom from troublesome or conflicting thoughts.

Recognition motive and desire for status productive of ideas

Another motive which is closely related to security is that of recognition. This motive operates in all classes and ages of people. Everyone seeks that type of social intercourse which will give him a degree of recognition. He strives for some element of positive regard for something he does or for his ideas from those with whom he comes into contact. He may come away from a group of individuals feeling high or low. If he analyzes himself in connection with the situation he will invariably trace his low feelings either to a lack of recognition of his ideas by the others or a failure to identify with what was being said or done. In the latter case, his disappointment may stem not only from his lack of understanding but also from the fact that the others with whom he associated did not give him the recognition he desired by helping him clarify some meanings relative to what was said or done.

One of the principles of democratic operation is that everyone possesses a degree of resourcefulness or personal worth. In other words, every human being seeks to have a degree of status in the eyes of his associates. This need is deeply embedded in the people of almost all cultures. It is evident very early in life. A little child does a rather unimportant task in the home knowing that the parents will give him some recognition for it. In the process of induction into the ways of the home and the culture, he comes to know which acts will receive positive recognition and which will receive negative reactions.

Sometimes, the need for recognition will become so strong in a child that he will go to great lengths to gain it. If more fuss is made over his negative acts than the positive ones, he may persist in them to the point of questionable behavior. In other words, if parents and others seem to take for granted the positive acts of a child but react with a great deal of concern toward the negative ones, his behavior may become overbalanced in favor of the attention-getting type regardless of its merit.

The recognition motive which operates in the young child will operate in a rather similar fashion in young people and adults. The teacher and curriculum worker have tremendous responsibility and opportunity to expand the area of the conditions for learning so that the recognition motive will become productive of ideas. If, for example, they harbor a rather constricted line of thinking patterned after the values they hold, the range of ideas based on young people's motives will be confined more or less to those values. As a result, all ideas which arise within that pattern will be considered good and those outside of the pattern as questionable or bad. This does not mean, of course, that all acts on the part of young people or adults in the fulfillment of the recognition motive are to be condoned or accepted into the conditions for learning. It does mean, however, that if the conditions for learning do not provide for an analysis of all the acts which operate in pursuit of recognition, the field of idea development will be seriously curtailed. Young people must have the opportunity to study and examine the recognition motive in all the ramifications and directions in which it is used by people so that they might become intelligent with respect to their choices and decisions. The curriculum must have provisions for this opportunity.

Possible topics to use in the study of motives. A good example which might be used in the study of motives is the development of the Constitution of the United States. A study of the contrast in motives of recognition as between those who were intent on continuing the type of government carried on under the Articles of Confederation and those who favored the government envisioned by the Constitution would give great meaning to motives of men at a certain time and place. Also, the recognition motive could be studied and analyzed in the other developments of this nation. Coming to more recent times, an exciting approach to the study of the recognition motive could be in connection with such topics as the "Cold War" and political campaigns for the presidency of the United States. Other approaches to the study of desire for recognition could revolve around local questions such as the action of the members of a Board of Education in providing better school facilities and the development of a community center for study and recreation. Other useful approaches to the understanding of the recognition motives would be in connection with advertisements in magazines and on radio and television. Considerable insight regarding the motives of recognition may be gained by studying the relationships of students in a classroom.

There are, of course, other motives than the two chosen for discussion, namely, security and recognition. The two, however, are sufficient to indicate the importance of motives in the development of ideas. The resourceful teacher will find in connection with the motives of security and recognition a wealth of material in the development of an environment for constructive ideas.

IDEAS AS VALUES

Every idea is in some manner related to a value. One frequently hears such expressions as "That is a good idea," "I wouldn't go along with his ideas," "He usually comes up with good ideas," and "That idea won't work." When an individual says, "That is a good idea," he is judging the idea in terms of some value that he holds. Similarly, when he says, "I wouldn't go along with his ideas," he is indicating that the ideas are at odds with his values. When one thinks that an idea won't work, he is, perhaps, judging it by his experiences which are, in all probability, related to his values. Still another value is indicated when one neither accepts nor rejects an idea pending further study as to its meaning.

Ideas and values interrelated

Ideas and values complement each other in productiveness and intensity. This may be illustrated by using again the example of reconstructing the process of plant growth. As the teacher has contributed toward the development of the conditions for inquiry within which the children are beginning to raise questions and gain some ideas about the differences in plant growth, a value is either forming or being intensified. Children either begin to put a high estimation on the opportunity for inquiry, thus taking it as a value, or they come to regard it as more important than before, thus intensifying the value in their action behavior. As the children begin to regard opportunity for inquiry as a value, the repetitive and expanded use of the opportunity will tend to strengthen it as a value for them and, at the same time, produce an increasing number of ideas.

As they continue to develop ideas about the nature of plant growth, they will finally reach a point where many of their questions will be answered. Other important questions, however, will remain unanswered. It is essential, therefore, to provide those stimuli which will bring about further experimentation. This condition could, in turn, cause a new or related value to function, that of open-mindedness. In other words, having arrived at some facts and some clear answers and failing to arrive at others, children will hypothesize and probe further. They will tend to keep the door open for new ideas. They are, at the same time, intensifying the value of open-mindedness for themselves and others.

Conditions for inquiry and open-mindedness essential
for evolvement of ideas

It is important that teachers and curriculum workers nurture the conditions for inquiry and open-mindedness for the purpose of evolving ideas about the nature of man and his surroundings. Through the process of curriculum improvement, contact points must be established for youth to pursue meanings about man—his incentives, his motives, the many roles necessitated by his activities, and the adaptations which he has had to make to a changing world. Furthermore, the contact points should provide for an intensive pursuit of ideas about man's powers— the potential resources that reside in him as a human being. The curriculum must also provide for the extension of these meanings into the larger environment. Since man has great powers within himself, the dynamics for their constructive release toward resourcefulness must be found in the curriculum. When the curriculum by default seriously limits the opportunity for inquiry and fails to provide for the development of open-mindedness, it is constricting the birthright of children in a democracy. It is denying to children and youth the development of those values through which they gain the competences which are needed to perpetuate and improve democratic institutions. Dewey,[1] in dealing with open-mindedness as a method, says: "The worst thing about stubbornness of mind, about prejudices, is that they arrest development, they shut the mind off from new stimuli. Open-mindedness means retention of the childlike attitude; closed-mindedness means premature intellectual old age."

Conditions for open-mindedness and inquiry needed to establish relationships between the individual and his behavior. The conditions for open-mindedness and inquiry in the approach to various topics will bring into clearer perspective all the values which are held by young people. Meanings with respect to the values will have a chance to be clarified by the pupil. This may be illustrated by two types of approaches in a high school class to the question of rights and freedom. In

---

[1] John Dewey, *Democracy and Education* (New York: The Macmillan Company, 1916), p. 206.

one type of approach, this question may be dealt with in connection with the discussion of the Preamble and the Bill of Rights of the Constitution. The section of history devoted to this phase of the Constitution would be read and discussed in terms of the answers provided by the book. There would also be some treatment regarding the personalities who had a part in shaping the Preamble and Bill of Rights. Students would report on Benjamin Franklin, Alexander Hamilton, Pinckney, and others. The virtues of the great document would be extolled. Perhaps the students would be directed to read what Blackstone said about the Constitution. Perhaps, even some of the documents which influenced the men who formed the Constitution would be studied. Something would be learned by students regarding the beginnings of our government. Many important concepts about the rights and freedoms provided by the Constitution would, no doubt, be fixed in the minds of the students.

Somehow, this type of approach leaves the true values of this great achievement to other times and places. The meanings are viewed in retrospect. The approach leaves much to be desired with regard to the true meanings of rights and freedom. Another type of approach is needed to bring out the practical and verifiable concepts of rights and freedom as they relate to and affect the individual and his behavior.

A possible approach which might be used to develop meanings and values with respect to rights and freedom would be to obtain a picture of the different conceptions that the students hold regarding those qualities. Chances are that the ideas about rights and freedom uncovered by this revelation would range all the way from the "Do as I please" concept to almost complete submission to group thinking. The next step might be the representation of the perceptions of freedom as they would function in terms of behavior between individuals and between individuals and groups. In other words, the possible types of action which might result from the perceptions would be portrayed so that they could be analyzed as to varying effects on individuals and groups.

In connection with this analysis, questions such as the following might be raised: What opportunity would there be for the achievement of rights and freedom if everyone did as he pleased? What limitations does the pursuit of freedom impose on individuals and groups? What are the obstacles which must be removed in the efforts to achieve rights and freedom for people? What is our responsibility in the development of freedom of speech? Under what conditions may freedom be corrupted? Under what conditions could freedom become a liability? These questions should certainly contribute to the development of a new set of conditions for the promotion of greater understanding regarding the rights and freedoms of people.

As one studies the above questions and others, it becomes increasingly clear that new values are developed and old ones are either eliminated or altered on the basis of ideas which are bound to evolve. As ideas are developed through an initial analysis of the perceptions of students with regard to rights and freedom, further questions will arise to stimulate them to a more intensive probing of the thinking of men in other times and places on these great topics. It is the responsibility of the teacher to provide the conditions which will make accessible to the students the materials and resources which will lead to further research and study on the nature of freedom. Furthermore, it is extremely important that "grass roots" situations be provided in the conditions for learning for a living identification on the part of students with the various concepts of freedom and its antitheses.

EXTRACTING IDEAS FROM THE ENVIRONMENT

In the preceding sections, an attempt has been made to describe in some detail the nature and development of ideas. The discussion is not nearly exhaustive but it is hoped that it will serve at least partially to introduce the reader and student to the development of an environment of ideas. It is important at this point to consider an analysis of the existing environment to determine how ideas are acquired from it.

The environment has an abundance of stimuli for ideas. The previous discussion on the nature of ideas indicates many of the sources of stimuli. The discussion also carries suggestions or hints as to how ideas become a part of the thought process.

In the previous chapters a considerable part of the development and analysis has been in connection with the acquisition of ideas.

Since the environment is replete with stimuli for ideas, one could start out enumerating them and soon reach the point where they would overwhelm the individual. To do this would tend to introduce such unwieldy elements into the learning situation as to make a sound approach to the acquisition of ideas next to impossible. There is frequently a tendency in connection with some school experiences to have children make lists and lists of things without doing anything about them. This practice is questionable in that children may become so discouraged with this process that they will be too willing to be content with the other extreme, that of rigid orderliness with a few ideas. To be able to name things does not guarantee that ideas have been acquired. To overwhelm children with lists makes the ideas related to the lists practically meaningless to them. An attempt will be made, therefore, to present some feasible ways by which children acquire ideas and grow in stature in the process of relating them.

Children acquire ideas from situations with which they live

The environment is full of ideas by virtue of the resourcefulness of people in the pursuit of their activities. Accordingly, children possess many ideas because they, together with their parents and adult friends, compose this resourceful environment. It is a truism that ideas do not arise in a vacuum. They arise as individuals and groups react to the stimuli in the environment.

In order to understand how ideas are acquired, one has only to watch children at play with one another. Very young children, for example, emulate things of movement, power, and simple building. They handle blocks, put one against the other, and move them across the floor. They build by putting one block on top of another and, when a number of blocks have been so placed, they delight in knocking them down and seeing them scatter. Children feel their power by shoving one another and wrestling. This is especially true of boys. Girls display movement by playing with dolls, putting them to bed, picking them up, dressing them, undressing them, and so on. Why do children play in this manner? Because of what they see in the environment, watching things move, observing with excited expectations the power tools used in construction, and noticing parents care for babies and other living things. They see motion, the effects of mechanical power, and the tenderness of care displayed by people. Children early begin to identify themselves in play as participants in ever so many activities they see going on around them.

Feelings of children operate to increase and expand ideas

It is clear that certain elementary ideas are acquired from the situations which prevail in the environment. Now, children could go on pursuing these elementary ideas in play—that is, building and knocking down, shoving one another, grabbing things from each other and so on. Over a period of time, the ideas would become static. They would be complete in their simple state and no other ideas would be acquired. This would be similar to the practice of making "lists." In other words, nothing much would be done with the act of play if it remained in this simple stage.

The act of play develops beyond the static stage as the child experiences certain satisfactions and understandings in the process of his activities. Some of the developments come about through observations made by the child himself. Whereas, for example, he at first experiences satisfactions in playing alone, he will soon ask others to help him with the activity in which he is engaged. He will soon identify the blocks as railroad cars or aeroplanes and imitate the functions of a railroad engineer or an aeroplane pilot. He is constantly gaining more ideas in the process of play. The child makes other discoveries. He finds that if he places the blocks on top of each other a certain way, the pile will not fall down as easily as when they are piled up at random. He also discovers that the blocks, when moved across the floor, will not get out of line if they are arranged in a certain pattern.

He begins to develop the acumen to promote increased facility in play. He is growing in the process of manipulating objects for his purposes. At the same time, he is discovering more things about the objects and the ways to handle them. He may reach the point of generalizing relative to objects, their arrangement and use.

As the children are experiencing new ideas in the process of play, valuable clues are being supplied to the curriculum worker in his approach to the tasks of improving opportunities for learning. For example, the relation of different arrangements to manipulation of blocks for certain purposes may lead into an understanding and inquiry relative to simple principles of physics. Understandings can be furthered by ascertaining the reasons for differences between the construction of railroad cars and aeroplanes. Topics associated with such terms as streamlining, jet propulsion, buoyancy, and others may become part of the learning conditions. Ever so many other experiences in science could very well develop from observations made by children in their play activities. The curriculum must provide the impact for the teacher and children to pursue ever expanding and new routes to ideas.

Discovery leads to further probing for ideas. The very fact that the child is discovering more about objects and the ways they can best be handled increases the stimuli in the environment for ideas to develop. The stimuli are also increased and intensified by the resourcefulness of the teacher. The teacher provides the conditions for ever-expanding experiences so that children might acquire more ideas in their work and play. Some of the stimuli brought into the environment of play will be in the form of paints and brushes, clay, pieces of lumber, tools, toys, crayons, and other materials. The children will use these materials at first in passive play but as they observe the effects of shape, form, and color their play will take on pattern, design, and creativity. The process of thought in the use of the materials will gradually assume purposes and action in fulfilling the purposes. No longer will the children brush the paint back and forth with abandon. Instead, they will proceed to paint in terms of the ideas that they have acquired in the experiences with the paints or crayons.

As the teacher now capitalizes on children's ideas through the process of questions, suggestions, and discussion, new stimuli are produced. Children will begin to put ideas together, take them apart, and reintegrate them into a more comprehensive idea. For example, they might begin to talk about the many colors present in the room. They will observe the decorations in the room, the colors represented by the dresses and shirts worn by the children, and the colors in the pictures around the room and in books. They might wish to put all the colors into a pattern representing the children in the room. They will proceed to paint some of the blocks so as to represent the colors in a streamlined train. They begin to think of the colors of houses that they see on their way to and from school.

The children at first think of colors in terms of their occupation with them. Perhaps there isn't much thought at all except that colors are pleasing. In this connection, children express their feelings about colors in the terms "nice," "pretty," "good-looking," "I like it that way" and so forth. As they proceed in their experiences with color, they begin to think more discriminately as revealed in such expressions as "That is ugly painted that way," "That color doesn't go with the other one," "These two colors go good together," "That doesn't look good." Soon their comments lead them into what might be called higher levels of observation. They talk about how their rooms are painted, what colors their parents like, and what changes are contemplated in their homes.

Teacher promotes a sense of release in ideas about beauty. As they grow older, children talk of shades, tone, and warmth with respect to colors. Thus a whole new field of ideas about colors is being opened up to them. They are advancing beyond the stage of simple sensuousness. Their sensuousness now is taking on a higher quality and, in the process of relating the colors, they experiment with shades to produce a more satisfying quality of beauty. As youngsters reach this stage, the teacher is providing the opportunity for them to dwell on different elements of beauty. It is clear that the children are interested in producing beauty not only for itself but as something within which they wish to live. In order to heighten the sense of appreciation of the relationship of beauty to living, the teacher gradually makes provision for the expansion of the ideas of children with respect to beauty.

Some of the initial steps the teacher might take in promoting a sense of release in ideas about beauty is to provide some simple representations of beauty on a bulletin board or in a section of the room reserved as a study or experimentation center. Also, in order to develop an opportunity for children to develop meanings with respect to beauty a variety of children's concepts of beauty are introduced to the environment. A simple way to do this is to encourage children to exhibit their ideas in a section prepared by them and the teacher.

The various ideas will reveal all types of values—harmonious as well as conflicting ones. At first, children will indicate their reaction to harmony and conflict with such terms as pretty, nice, straight, ugly, bad, messy, and others. They will simply express a "dislike" or "like" to the ideas in color. As they grow older they will go into some reasons for their reactions. They will begin to think of balance, blending, symmetry, cluttering effect, emptiness, perspective, and other concepts relative to beauty. An example of this thinking was observed by the writer when a child remarked: "That picture is so full of things that I get tired looking at it." Another child was observed saying, "Those lines running back and forth and into each other are like people bothering other people." It would appear obvious from these statements that the children were moving ideas into a new perspective.

TEACHER MUST BE MINDFUL OF INFLUENCES ON CHILDREN'S THINKING

In providing for the acquisition of ideas, the teacher must be mindful of all the influences which are operating on children in their thinking. First of all, the home rightfully influences the development of ideas. This is true as the children are identifying with more and more ideas as a result of the classroom environment. The very fact that the child gives expression to an ever-increasing repertoire of ideas will evoke expression on the part of parents and other members of the family. Expression by family members will sometimes serve to influence the ideas of the child in the direction of a reconstruction on somewhat altered levels from that obtained from school experiences. If an element of conflict appears in the expression of the child as against the expression of the parents, the attempt at reconciliation of expression may result in the reduction of one set of ideas and the assumption of another set.

It would be well for parents to keep alive the ideas of children so that they may be truly analyzed for possible consequences and elements of creativity. One must hasten to state that the ideas with which children have superficially identified themselves need not be condoned. On the contrary, if they appear in opposition to basic values, every effort should be made by parents to counteract constructively by providing alternative ideas. As a matter of fact, the development of the atmosphere for sound inquiry with respect to ideas is a proper function of the home. It is indeed important that the home and school should operate in sufficiently close unison to communicate understandingly in the provision for ideas to be acquired by children.

Child's environment influenced by associations

The influences operating within the home in the development of the conditions for ideas to flourish suggests another influence, that of neighbors and friends of the child. The suggestion that the child operates in an environment may be putting it too mildly. The child really lives in many environments —as many, in fact, as the influences which are peculiarly indigenous to each of his friends and neighbors. There will, of course, be many common elements as between the child's ideas and those of some or all of his friends. On the other hand, there will be many ideas offered from the many environments which will tend to reshape at least a good share of the ideas that he brings to his own particular environment. His environment, then, is derived from a combination of environments. The child's friends, neighbors and acquaintances are the resources in the creation of his environment. Their ideas interacting in a process of mental reconstruction with his own ideas become, at least, in part his area of ideas.

Ideas do not develop in a vacuum. As has been partially suggested by the illustration on color and beauty, ideas develop in connection with things. In his daily life an individual comes into contact with hundreds of things. He may handle some things directly, for example, scientific apparatus, his car, garden tools, and machinery of all types. He moves furniture, arranges books in a case, does repairs, plants trees and flowers.

He handles other things indirectly—formulating concepts through reading a book, promoting action in a policy-making or legislative body relative to some idea, and conversing with friends and acquaintances with regard to some thoughts he has been pondering. Regardless of whether things are handled directly or indirectly, they are all productive of ideas. All the things that he handles are part of his environment and are stimuli both toward a practical arrangement of his living process and toward more ideal realization of understanding and satisfactions.

Casual observations may obscure insight to ideas

It is so obvious that an individual's contact with the things in his environment are idea-producing that it might appear superfluous to develop the point. The very fact, however, that things are obvious introduces a real danger in the development of the setting for ideas to develop in the learning situation. The danger is the existence of the casualness characterized by statements such as the following: "Did you see the new car model? It is almost accident-proof." "I was over to Jim's house last night and watched television. I just can't be without it so here I go get me a set." "Did you see the plan for the new super-highway? That will really be the answer to the traffic problem." "With all these new developments the taxes keep going up. When and where is it going to stop?" "We are going to redecorate the house. We got some good ideas from the magazine on that." "Billy was sixteen the other day so I had to buy him a car operator's license." "I spent all my money on a dress for Jane so that she would be outfitted for the prom." "This is Dave's senior year. He plans to enroll in ——— College next year." "We have a new supermarket going up in the next block." "I expect to trade the car in for a new one. We have had it two years."

These and many more casual statements are made day after day by people. The very casualness has the effect of deadening any sense of inquiry about the statements. The existence and easy accessibility of a rather powerful educational medium such as television seems to cause the user to take it for granted. Similarly, more abstract ideas such as relate to freedom, rights of individuals, and morality are also taken for granted.

The superabundance of ideas related to any single statement above lie dormant because the environment abounds with all the things mentioned. Only the philosopher peers into the mysteries of the casual and how it affects human beings. There is an absence of insight and appreciation of the conditions which made these things possible. Even more tragic is the absence of any thought as to the degrees of adversity under which things were developed into their present state of serviceableness. Very late do some individuals arrive at an awareness of a need for rather high grade competences to sustain many priceless gains.

True, individuals read somewhere about an Edison, a Fulton, and others—about how they struggled in the face of real barriers placed in their path. The reading is done casually, however, and the book is just as casually put away. This might be best described as a "so what" attitude. The process is a sort of recounting of a chronology from beginning to end. The trials, emotions, and determination in the face of possible disgrace of the Edisons and others are absorbed in the process of chronology. While it is true that the chronology of an idea from its source to the point of fruition is important, this process brings only a small segment of the most significant ideas into the environment for learning. A great vacuum exists in this type of idea development which either goes unrecognized or is purposely disregarded.

DEVELOPING MORE ADEQUATE TREATMENT OF CONTENT IN ENVIRONMENT

The environment is a reservoir of content. The content has its contemporary meanings. The resourceful and enthusiastic treatment of this content by teachers of wisdom will give strength to living today and will provide the avenues for the past to function most meaningfully in the resolving of today's problems. Whenever one ponders the nature of environmental forces, he soon finds himself studying its roots for identifiable aspects of the present direction of life. Viewed intensively, the environment has a sort of universal substance whose beginnings and endings cannot be defined. The curriculum worker must develop the conditions whereby there is a continual effort on the part of all the staff to relate learning to the continuum of experiences in the environment. This means that there must be readily accessible the thinking of all times and places relative to man's response to the environmental forces. In this connection, it should be emphasized that curriculum workers must free themselves from any delusions about what is contemporary knowledge and what are the real sources of curriculum direction.

The sources of curriculum content and direction obtain from all the disciplines and the whole stream of man's thinking. Both the contemporary and past thinking may be alive or dead depending on the selectivity and treatment of the identifiable elements of knowledge by the curriculum workers and teachers. The disciplines need to be taken out of their compartments and made to function in translated meanings for children and youth. In other words, a careful perusal and appraisal of the concepts derived from the disciplines should reveal a whole field of relationships to the ways and problems of people today.

Typical treatments may further stereotyped conceptions

To focus the discussion on the question of adequate use of content, the topic of "Making a Living in the Country" might be considered. The typical systems of approach to this topic would deal with it in a more or less general or stereotyped manner. Books are produced which have stories about life in the country or on a farm. The books usually show rather expensive houses and barns, some cattle, a horse or two, and ducks, chickens, and turkeys. In the picture of the modern farm will be a tractor, possibly a combine, a hay loader, and certain other tools. Rarely something is even indicated about water, milk protection before the milk goes to the distributors, cultivation of land, and the type of recreation enjoyed by people who make their living in the country. Usually a rather glowing picture is painted for the children in the books and by the teacher. Children read some stories with the guidance of the teacher, record some of the facts in writing, carry on discussion which frequently is quite repetitive of what has been

read, and probably draw and build some models of farms or
life in the country. Later, they might invite in the parents to
show what they have done and learned. The work is usually
portrayed quite profusely on bulletin boards. With some minor
variations, the above is representative of the process by which
the pupil is led into an understanding of making a living in
the country.

It is clear that the above development of meanings with
regard to country living has certain characteristics. First of all,
it portrays quite extensively some of the popular appearances
and conceptions of making a living in the country. The picture
reveals friendly people who seem to have purposes and who are
working ahead on those purposes. The people in the stories and
pictures are happy and busy. The importance of this portrayal
should not be underestimated. It is a picture of good mental
and physical health which are the real attributes of a good life.
Another characteristic which is evident in this process of teaching is that the story of making a living in the country is derived
from written materials only. In other words, the thoughts in
the writings are accepted as synonymous with making a living
in the country. The teacher generally follows the ideas and
sequence of the content. The stories and pictures of the books
are accepted as an ample portrayal of country living.

It is true that the characteristics suggested are all proper and
necessary in the process of teaching. They are inadequate, however, in that they deny the real use of ideas in connection with
content. The behavior aspects which operate in people in the
process of making a living in the country are not considered.
Furthermore, the values which exist in the task of making a
living have not been incorporated in the teaching process. The
stories and pictures in the books might portray a stereotyped
conception of living in the country. There are the nice house,
barn, green fields—all presenting an appearance of immaculate
neatness and order. The members of the story are friendly,
happy and do not exhibit any sign of tension. In other words,
it looks as if the setting had always been there. There is no sign
of problems which are encountered by people in the task of
making a living in the country. There is no indication of the

thought, study, planning, and effort which is behind most operations in the act of living.

Adequate treatment demands intensive analysis of varied resources

An adequate treatment of content necessitates the conditions
for an intensive assessment of the thinking of people both past
and contemporary on topics or ideas under consideration. Many
people have devoted a great deal of study, for example, to the
topic of making a living in the country. The thinking has been
reformulated into principles and relationships of ideas which
in turn have been written down as possible background on
the topic. The studies which have been made are of various
types. There is, of course, the view of the sociologist who thinks
and writes about rural and community living in all its forms.
No doubt he has done considerable research on the topic of
social living as it pertains to the country community. He writes
about the family—its relationships to neighbors and its adjustment to community life. He writes and speaks about the various
agencies which contribute to life in the country. He points out
the interrelationships of various agencies in helping people
integrate their purposes and actions toward better living in the
community.

People, other than the sociologists, approach the whole question of making a living in the country from different angles.
The economist, for example, deals with the role of the farm
producer in the whole picture of the economy. He thinks and
writes about prices of commodities, about "parity," farm subsidies, and price control. The economist further deals with the
matter of farm income and its relationship to other facets of the
economy of a nation. He furnishes statistics about income per
capita, the changing spending habits of people, and other items.

There are many people who think, do research, and write
about the improvement of farm production, better use of the
land, and the whole question of improved community living.
Officials of the Department of Agriculture and the Bureau of
Labor Statistics of the Department of Labor of the United
States Government prepare reports, pamphlets, and other ma-

terials of information about the farm and its workers. The research people, the professional thinkers and writers on rural and community life, and others have prepared a host of materials which are stocked in the libraries and are on sale in all types of book establishments. It should be clear that in view of the thousands upon thousands of ideas contained in these materials that the task of making a living in the country would assume vastly differing and exciting proportions.

The immediate discussion above has dealt mainly with the professional and scientific thought relative to the question of living in the country. The materials produced do not by any means constitute all the ideas which must be used in the approach to the topic. Although a vast amount of thought relative to the topic of making a living in the country is contained in the materials, it would be humanly impossible to use all or even most of it. A wise use of content materials on the topic used would preclude much of it. It is important to be highly selective in the use of the materials. It is more important in the selection of materials to include many alternatives to each idea so that broad insights and understandings may result.

Selection of material demands careful examination of thinking back of ideas. A highly important factor in the selection and use of materials is the analysis of the background of thinking relative to ideas. Every writer in developing an idea reveals much about his thought process which led to the idea. An extremely important aspect in teaching is to make provision for the student to study and analyze the circumstances which produced a certain kind of thinking relative to the evolvement of an idea. In this attempt on the part of the student, much will be revealed to him with respect to the types of experience which go to make up types of ideas. For example, one who was writing in a setting where average yearly rainfall was twenty inches or more would have somewhat different ideas and experiences about making a living in the country than one who was writing in a setting where the yearly rainfall was less than twenty inches. Furthermore, a person writing about life in the country in Connecticut would be influenced by different experiences than one who was living in the state of Ohio. A person living in a shack in eastern Montana on a "dry farm" would reveal somewhat different thinking about country life than one living in a beautiful ranch style home on an irrigated farm in California. The point that should be made is that good teaching expands the ideas, bringing out the various circumstances and experiences which produced the ideas.

Development of meanings necessitates conditions which provide intense points of identification with ideas. To become even more analytic, it is important to trace the types of feelings experienced by people in different settings. In this type of analysis, it is necessary to provide the conditions wherein the feelings envisioned in different settings may be experienced. This is very difficult to do since one cannot jump from one setting to another at will and have realistic experiences with each setting. The different settings producing different ideas must largely be developed vicariously.

The analysis of feelings and experiences vicariously will tax the utmost ingenuity of the curriculum worker. One of the first requisites to the development of conditions where feelings and experiences can be analyzed is to have at hand the writings, reports, pamphlets, and other materials already indicated. The next task is to select out of the materials those that seem to be the most representative of different settings in connection with the topic or idea being studied.

The most descriptive passages should be carefully perused and studied to try to determine the angles or circumstances under which the writing was done. For example, one passage might refer to "dry weather" or "lack of rain" whereas another might refer to "the parched soil with yawning cracks frightful to behold." In the latter passage, the impact of extreme drouth reveals intense feeling in connection with it. One might readily conceive of "dryness' or "lack of rain" as a rather ordinary condition. On the other hand, an expression of intense feeling attendant to the conditions of drouth will tend to produce a realistic identification with the conditions on the part of the reader.

Identification with an expressed feeling on the part of the recipient occurs only when he senses an element of satisfaction or dissatisfaction on the part of the one who transmitted the expression. In other words, when the recipient of the feeling communicated senses the satisfaction or dissatisfaction of the one who communicates it, he is, in a very great sense, experiencing expanded meanings of the feeling. The identification takes place because the recipient has analyzed the feeling experiences of the communicant—how he would feel if he were communicating ideas under the circumstances envisioned. No doubt, almost everyone has heard the question, "How would you feel if you were in his shoes?" Although this question is often asked casually and regarded that way by the receiver, it implies the ingredients for conditions to promote real understanding. The question furnishes a valuable clue to the curriculum worker, the teacher and the children or young people in the development of further conditions to promote learning.

It is clear from the discussion that the perusal and reflection with regard to written as well as spoken communication must be more than mechanical. One has to "read one's feelings" into the experiences and circumstances under which the ideas have been communicated to assure actual reading of the ideas. The teacher must first of all "read his feelings" into the reading that *he* does. Next, he must analyze his feelings in terms of the feelings expressed by the professional writers. Further than that, the teacher undertakes to analyze many of the writings of people in the nonprofessional field—that is, commentators, lay people, politicians, and others. A possible next step is to line up the different ideas relative to the topic under consideration and restudy them in terms of the original sources that were used.

The teacher will probably find that the original sources said nothing about "parity" or "subsidy" or "flexible controls," which are the terms used by the commentators, politicians, and others. The new terms will cause a new speculation in the thinking relative to the topic, for example, of Making a Living in the Country. One will have to be concerned about what the original sources indicated about costs and possible income for living. Then one will have to consider what would happen to the income if all the products would be thrown on the open market. Students will have to think back to the time when wheat, for example, was thirty cents per bushel and the effect of this price on the morale and conditions of living of the producer.

New angles of thought in learning experiences necessitate provisions for new meanings by curriculum workers. The questions which will arise in connection with the added elements to thinking will cause some confusion in the logic and assumed orderliness of learning. This is where the curriculum worker has to bring this thinking into a constructive direction for learning. He must develop the conditions for the development of new angles of thought in the creation of learning experiences.

That means that teachers will need to handle ideas together. Much newspaper reading will have to be done. The speeches made, for example, by the Secretary of Agriculture and others will have to be analyzed to discover the thinking in their proposals. The teacher will have to discover what is meant by maintaining price levels at "70 per cent of parity" and what is meant by flexible farm supports. If the proposals of the present Secretary of Agriculture are different from those of the previous Secretary under a previous administration, the difference will have to be analyzed in several ways in terms of such questions as: (1) What are the relative benefits of the present proposals as compared to the immediate past? (2) How may these proposals affect the feelings and habits of people who have become used to the previous system of control or regulation? (3) What must be done to readjust these feelings and habits to present practices? (4) To what extent will this affect the economy of the communities and nation? One problem here is to indicate to what degree there will be a change in the status of living. Another question that has to be resolved is, What is the basic thinking behind the new system of "price leveling" of farm products?

It is important in the study of the comments by politicians and others to put oneself into the position of thinking as they do so as to understand that thinking. Roles must, perhaps, be played by the student so as to catch the realism of the moment. In other words, the teacher must develop the conditions wherein the children will play the role of thinking characterized by the question of the moment. This is, of course, very difficult to do. The very difficulty, however, constitutes an important challenge to teaching.

In order to fit oneself into the role of thinking characterized by a certain proposal, it is necessary to analyze to some extent the background and philosophy of living of the one who made the proposal. In this connection, it is important to analyze and study the thinking and philosophy of the people who constitute the organization within which the person who made the proposal operates. Then, too, it is necessary to study the motives of both the organization and the individual to determine to what degree they are the individual's motives or those of the organization in control. Now, it isn't probable that any group which constitutes a power organization would make a proposal which would cut too deeply into the established habits and feelings of people. This is especially true in a democracy where the feelings of people can be reflected in the ballot. It might, therefore, be considered an element of courage when one undertakes to change certain habits and feelings honestly because he would not purposely attempt to jeopardize his position. There is, of course, a chance of error. One may make an honest proposal and be quite mistaken as to the results which might ensue. This may, of course, result in the proponent's loss of status with some of his associates. That is one reason for the teacher and children to do everything in their power to give due study and consideration to the motives and feelings of others.

A person who has honest motives, whether they are mistaken or not, should have his feelings respected. The constructive approach to the proposals of such a person is to point out to him several alternatives to his proposals. Chances are that the person with honest motives will admit his mistakes and effectively influence the organization to readjust its operation accordingly. It is probably much more constructive for an opponent of a proposal to point out alternatives to the course of action than to simply oppose the action in the shelter of another organization.

DEVELOPING CRITERIA FOR JUDGING VALUES AND IDEAS

In another part of this book appears considerable discussion relative to the importance of admitting all values into the conditions for learning. The admission of the values does not, of course, set a premium on the importance of each one of the values in carving out a doctrine or course of action for living.

The values, as explained, are to be admitted to the learning situation for the plain purpose of examination and analysis by the teacher and the students. In any examination of values by students, it is necessary to have patterns or criteria by which the values may be judged for acceptance and action. The questions then arise, Who establishes the patterns? and, Where must one seek to discover the patterns? It is important that decision and action with regard to values cannot be kept in the speculative stage but must rather become realities in daily living.

It is imperative for those engaged in the task of analyzing values to set before themselves various alternatives of patterns as conceived in the culture. They might, in this connection, study differing cultures to determine by what values people will live and act. This would seem to be a healthy undertaking but since the students are already creatures of a going culture, it hardly behooves them to decide to change to another culture. A logical step, then, seems to be to analyze and study elements of different cultures to determine to what degree they are common to the culture within which one now lives and acts. In all probability, it will be discovered that a basic value will be identified in all cultures and understood as indigenous to people in the culture. At the same time, it will be found that some questionable values are conceived of as common to all cultures. It will become apparent, then, that there are patterns which are accepted in all cultures by which values may be judged. The big task is to discover those patterns.

Before going further with this discussion, it is important to throw in a note of caution against a seeming dogmatism, that is, the exclusiveness of a pattern of values. Perhaps, this exclusive acceptance of a pattern may be due to a lack of understanding of the relationships of acts to values.

Developing an understanding of limiting criteria

A limitation in value patterns may be illustrated by a hypothetical situation. The situation relates to the ideas of possession and the incentives of people. *A* believes that property is a commodity that belongs to individuals as they acquire it. If a person has worked hard and acquired property, he should be commended for this acquisition. *A* believes that honesty is a good policy. The acquisition of property to him is a perfectly honest act. To him, therefore, honesty and acquisition of property are synonymous as a value pattern. It may be that A owns very little or no property but he has accepted the idea of ownership as a value of high import. It will be noted that A believes in private property ownership as a value. He believes in honesty, too, but the emphasis with regard to his value acceptance is "property." Honesty is taken for granted and may, as a result, stand dimly in the background as a value.

B also believes in the right of an individual to own property. B, however, gives some thought as to the nature in which property is acquired. He reflects on the price, for example, of the property and whether the price represents honest value. While A feels it is all right to sell for whatever the "traffic may bear," B recognizes the ability of the purchaser in terms of the "lows" and "highs" of different economic conditions and deplores a deviation from the true worth of the property. While B goes along with the economic concept that property is worth more at one time than another, there is a floor to price levels which keeps them in the realm of human ability to pay. As might be suspected, B has made a study of the causes of inflation. He, therefore, tries to convince people that there should be some regulation as to prices. As a result, there may be government regulation. In line with B's contention there has been price regulation by government from time to time. A fact with which many are conversant, price regulation resulted in both good and bad consequences in the economy.

Although A and B have rather different views about property acquisition, there are alternatives to both conceptions of value. In fairness to B, it might be said that apparently he identifies with the human angle of property ownership more so than A. On the other hand, it may be that he is looking at his own lack of purchasing ability in the process of acquiring property. In other words, if he had the financial ability to acquire property he might fix the floor of honest value at the level at which he is able to possess property. Is it not possible, then, that he will lose sight of the aspirations for property acquisition of those whose ability to acquire is below that of *his* floor of honest value?

Providing constructive latitude in criteria

C has certain conceptions as to what constitutes the right to live a full life. He, too, as do *A* and *B*, believes in the institution of private ownership of property. He recognizes that there exist degrees of ability in ownership. Some naturally own more than others, due to incentives to own particular kinds of goods or commodities. Besides this, he recognizes that incentives for things are different among people. Some people desire tangible things whereas others feel more satisfaction in acquiring more or less intangible possessions. Intangible possessions might be more education, travel, music, art consumption, and others. *C* points out that intangible things provide a balance in the realization of possessions in the culture. Some people may expend the major part of their resources in acquiring a home and furnishing it expensively. The incentives here are to save and plan for the time when the home may be realized. Others are content with a modest home with modest furnishings but plan and save so they will be able to travel, for example. In the case of those who put their savings in a home, the satisfactions to be derived are those of more comfort and to have something to show for one's labor. In other words, they have tangible evidence of their efforts. Those who choose to expend part or even the major part of their resources for travel will not have any tangible evidence for their efforts, especially not insofar as others can see. They will, however, have the satisfaction of having realized an important desire—that of seeing first hand so that their observations about things may be altered or expanded. Although their realization is intangible to others, generally it may be very real to them. Furthermore, what are conceived of as intangible elements may become really quite tangible when revealed in conversations with others.

Criteria for judging ideas move beyond materialism. Someone has said that as people mature they expand their horizon of ideas or concepts from the material into the spiritual or philosophical realm. *C* accepts this premise with certain conditions. The conditions are that people must not lose sight of realism. In other words, it is important that everyone become conversant with the means of acquiring and maintaining a sound standard of living. That means that the mechanistic functions that are frequently referred to as materialism are a very real aspect of one's living and culture. He does, however, guard against materialism becoming the dominating force in the realization of values. He gives meanings which, although related to material possessions and tangible services, form the basis for other qualities of incentives.

A and *B* represent values which are very much related to the culture. They are, therefore, the basis of many ideas which should be in the conditions of learning. The conditions, however, should not be confined to these ideas. There needs to be provision in the setting for learning of a wide range of potential experiences which give an opportunity for the evolvement of great insight and understanding relative to the role of living. *C*'s thinking represents some of the meanings for the development of this wide range of learning experiences. His thinking, also, establishes the basis for the expansion of meanings beyond his area of action. In other words, *C*'s thinking is the type which would establish the conditions for the learner to go beyond him in the pursuit of ideas. Thus, his thinking sets the stage for the inclusiveness of values in the conditions of learning.

Criteria for judging ideas must be inclusive of all cultures. With the development of the learning conditions which include all values, the stage is set for the approach to insight and understanding of the values of other cultures. As the points of identification are established with respect to different values, the opening wedge to a detection of the cultural influences operative in the values is provided. The art pieces and customs which comprise part of the background of the children and young people will become a phase of the learning conditions. All young people representative of different values have, for example, "nice" things which are highly regarded by them in relating to the culture. As the "nice" things are being appraised, they seem to take on a universal quality.

The universalism of "nice" will become an object of study and analysis. In this process will be derived the criteria by which people in different cultures judge what is "nice." As young people study the criteria, they will ascertain some attributes of "nice" which are common to all cultures. This will tend to develop a mutuality of regard for the "nice" things of all cultures. Furthermore, this approach will tend to affect a sense of appreciation of other meanings in the cultures. It will also have the effect of turning this regard inward to discover new meanings in our own culture.

The development of ideas and understandings relative to cultures was indicated in some practices which the author observed in a certain classroom of ten-year-old children. Many of the children in the classroom came from homes where languages other than English was spoken. The teacher wishing to develop the conditions for intercultural understanding attempted during discussion periods to elicit some responses in the language spoken in the home. He found that most of the children were reluctant to do so; in fact, they seemed to be ashamed to name anything in the second language. Finding that this approach tended to embarrass the children, he decided to try a different one.

One of the first things the teacher did was to secure books which dealt about art facts and customs of different countries. In so far as he was able, he assembled some materials written in the languages other than English represented by the children in the room. He emphasized that everyone in the room had ancestors who came from another country. He indicated further that many of our activities, many of our customs, and many of our objects of worth have either come from, or had their origin in, other countries. He stressed that the books and materials which had been made available contained some interesting stories about the background of our present activities and way of living.

After some study and analysis of people and their cultures, it was decided by the children and teacher to represent in a mural the background of the present behavior and activities of people. Children were encouraged to label the different objects and ideas in the murals in the language of the countries represented. As the work on the mural proceeded, it was discovered that everyone in the classroom had his roots in some other country.

As the mural was being developed, it was decided that two tables should be provided for a display of the "nice" things the children owned and which came from other countries. All the children participated in bringing "nice" things for the display.

As the mural was developed and the display was being extended, more and more exchange of conversation took place between children about the things and ideas represented. Reference to things being "different" and words of other languages being "funny" became less frequent. A greater sense of appreciation about other nationalities became increasingly apparent. Children from the homes where a language other than English was spoken exhibited a sense of pride in labeling things and ideas in that language. There gradually developed a greater recognition of the fact that no one nation has a premium on quality and ideas.

DEVELOPING THE CONDITIONS FOR GREAT THOUGHT

Anyone who has grown into a sense of recognition about how little he knows about the potential knowledge in the universe has demonstrated a quality of humility which might be envied. If, however, he is content to rest in this condition of humility without relating himself to the task of inquiry into that knowledge, he has relinquished his rightful role of responsibility to advance the cause of wisdom. Too many people are content to leave the task of knowledge-seeking to others. Unfortunately, many of these are found in teaching. On the other hand, many teachers and other workers in education have developed that attitude of questioning, critical examination of ideas, and inquiry into the peripheral areas of knowledge which would put them in the vanguard of great teaching. These people are the curriculum workers who, by extending their influence and leadership, will bring about a continuous rise in the quality of ideas which become the environment of learning for children and young people.

Conditions demand sacrifice for ideas. The principles and processes of continuous development toward high quality learning conditions have been discussed at some length in Chapters 1 and 2. Within those principles and processes, some additional factors are involved with the promotion of curriculum practices to bring about the conditions for great thought. One of these factors relates to sacrifice. In our advanced technological state, we have tended to point our major efforts in this society toward the realization of an ever greater sense of security. This, of course, is important. The resourcefulness of people should tend toward the improvement of the welfare of all people. It could be possible, however, that the conception of welfare has become somewhat overbalanced in the direction of security. One would suspect that the condition of security has found a corollary in the gradual rise of a sense of complacency.

It is suggested that this condition calls for the development of leadership toward a study, examination, and a redirection into more substantial channels of inquiry.

The curriculum workers need to develop that leadership which will bring the element of sacrifice into the handling of ideas. The exuberance of present-day living has caused a degree of relaxation in the preoccupation with ideas on the part of too many individuals and groups. In order to penetrate the areas of higher inquiry and understandings about the frontiers of science, the new questions of behavior, the frontiers in the humanistic quest, and the forces on the international scene, it is necessary to *sacrifice for ideas.* Ideas do not come easy. On the other hand, the pursuit of them with others will tend to promote a new sense of excitement about them. As stated before, the curriculum worker has a most important responsibility to develop the conditions for those ideas and areas of inquiry which are beyond the regular dimensions of knowledge to be made accessible to the classrooms. The frontier idea people in the classrooms of the elementary and high schools of the country must be the leaders in the promotion of this sense of sacrifice for ideas.

Conditions necessitate approach to a unity of knowledge. Another factor which must become an operative condition in the schools of this country is that of unity of knowledge. Compartmentalization of knowledge is a repository condition which has no place in the high level approach to ideas. Great thought has been conceived by man for enabling him to approach the ultimate in existence for himself and his fellow men. Change has become a pattern of living, although it has not been recognized as such by those who are content to think of other days. Change has ceased to be a variable concept. It is a constant in life. The operation with respect to this constant cannot be equated with the mastery of subjects. The curriculum tasks essential to the development of ideas in order to be abreast of and to advance beyond the visible peaks of change are to build that subject matter which makes the substance of unity a fact.

Another task of the curriculum worker is to bring about those conditions which will tend to operate so intensively with ideas in the periphery of inquiry that the dehumanization tactics which are still prevalent among men will be gradually reduced. Great thought rises above the tactics of any nation or group. The handling of ideas must not be in terms of the momentary strategical exigencies but rather directed to the higher realms of knowledge which will overshadow the moment.

It is hoped that this whole task of curriculum improvement for a new humanization and a new excitement about great thinking will become a reality in all schools. The approach to this task is the responsibility of all of us.

SELECTED READINGS

American Association of School Administrators, *Building Americans in the Schools*. Washington, D. C.: National Education Association, 1954. A discussion of the schools' responsibilities in bringing about understanding about citizenship tasks.

Anderson, Vernon E., *Principles and Procedures of Curriculum Improvement*. New York: The Ronald Press Co., 1956. Chapter 5. Suggestions for the use of values in the community to develop an environment of ideas.

Association for Supervision and Curriculum Development, *Creating a Good Environment for Learning*, 1954 Yearbook. Washington, D. C.: National Education Association, pp. 150-200. Valuable account of teachers' and administrators' relationships and responsibilities in developing conditions which will help children gain meanings about various factors surrounding them.

Hoffman, Paul G., and others, *Basic Elements of a Free Dynamic Society*. New York: The Macmillan Co., 1951. A condensed record of a round table discussion. Ideas presented which may be critically examined by the teacher and pupils.

Bills, R. E., *About People and Teaching*. Bureau of School Service, College of Education, University of Kentucky, Vol. XXVIII, No. 2, December, 1955. An interesting sketch of perceptual theory and how it has been applied to educational problems.

Brinton, Crane, *The Shaping of the Modern Mind*. New York: Mentor Books, The New American Library of World Literature, Inc., 1956, 261 pp. A remarkable history of western thought which provides excellent background for teachers who are seeking to extend opportunities for the study and development of ideas on the part of youth.

Compton, Arthur Holly, *Atomic Quest. A Personal Narrative.* New York: Oxford University Press, 1956. In this book, Arthur Compton recalls the birth of the bomb. It is a valuable example of the development of environments of ideas.

Dewey, John, *Democracy and Education*. New York: The Macmillan Co., 1916. Chapters 11, 12, and 13 are especially significant in helping teachers work with ideas.

Frank, Lawrence K., *Nature and Human Nature*. New Brunswick, N. J.: Rutgers University Press, 1951. Chapters 2 and 7. Some leads to relationships with the various new environments.

Miel, Alice and Peggy Brogan, *More Than Social Studies*. Englewood Cliffs, N. J.: Prentice-Hall, Inc., 1957, pp. 122-148, 217-259, 372-393. Most helpful suggestions for teachers in elementary schools in developing a knowhow in the approach to ideas.

Muller, Herbert J., *The Uses of the Past*. New York: Oxford University Press, 1952. A series of studies of past societies. The studies can be used as rather enlightening background in an approach to our present-day values and problems.

Stratemeyer, Florence B., Hamden L. Forkner, Margaret G. McKim, and A. Harry Passow, *Developing a Curriculum for Modern Living*. New York: Bureau of Publications, Teachers College, Columbia University, New York. Second Edition, 1957, Chapter 10. Gives ideas about the use of resources of the whole school and the community.

Where Children Live Affects Curriculum. Washington Bulletin 1950, No. 7, Federal Security Agency, Office of Education.

◇10◇

Instruction and Social Class Mobility

A CLASSROOM, IN ORDER TO BE TOTALLY EFFECTIVE, MUST ADMIT all social values equally into the setting for learning. As indicated in a previous chapter, this does not mean that they are all admitted for purposes of learning them. They are admitted equally for consideration and appraisal. The values are equally open to consideration and appraisal by the students, children, and teachers. The conditions which the curriculum must provide should solicit a portrayal in thinking of the feelings which accompany the different social values. These conditions will cause the values to be studied for the purpose of ascertaining their possible consequences in case action should take place. In the consideration of the feelings which accompany the values, alternatives relative to possible action on them would be amply portrayed. In the process of study, discussion and appraisal of the alternatives, decision and choice would be evolved. In view of the setting for study, discussion and thinking, young people and children would tend to detect the dire consequences which may result, for example, in action on an impulse. Furthermore, they would discern the more promising alternatives for action and choice.

VALUES OF SOCIAL CLASSES

The task associated with the admission of all social values equally into the setting for learning is one of considerable proportion for the teacher. In the first place, it presupposes that

250

the teacher understands what the values of different social classes are. In the second place, it requires the teacher to adapt this thinking so that he will operate in terms of the roles dictated by different codes of living. This means that he provides for the conditions of acceptance of all children.

The teacher, in order to be effective with all children, must gain some understanding and insight as to what the different social values are. Many studies have been made with respect to the different social classes and their values, and the teacher should inform himself with regard to these studies and give thoughtful appraisal to their implications for learning. Some of these studies are listed at the end of the chapter. These studies give some indication as to the type of codes which operate in the different levels of social classes. One of the interesting features which is common to almost all the studies is that the members of the different social classes generally agree on the classifications both in reference to themselves and others. One might conclude from this that people tend to move and operate in the class in which they are understood and in which they are able to communicate. Furthermore, individuals will more or less move and function in the group in which they feel most secure even if they are not satisfied with their position in life. Other facts which appear quite clearly in all the studies are: (1) the middle and upper lower classes feel that there is considerable opportunity for social mobility upward, (2) the lower lower classes are more or less resigned to their lot, and (3) the upper class has placed many restrictions to discourage mobility from below.

Detecting multiple directions in the social mobility pattern

Social mobility is a strong incentive for people in our culture. On the whole, the status routes of mobility have been quite clearly laid out with economic status being a strong factor. Those who have climbed the social ladder have not all done so in the same manner. Some have climbed it within a rather shining cloak of respectability, whereas others have used more ruthless tactics. This, of course, suggests that there are different ladders. Figuratively speaking, some ladders tend to be wide at the bottom and gradually become narrower on top. The route of mobility on these ladders is based on the principle of survival of the fittest. Other ladders have been constructed so as not to become too narrow toward the top. In other words, there are certain status elements which are received all the way up so as to provide respectability at the top.

The belief that social mobility upward assumes a more or less definite pattern in our society should be carefully tested. It is important to develop the conditions to take a careful look at phases of the social structure so as to detect the flaws in preconceptions about it. This suggests that, in analyzing the social pattern, too little effort has been made to look horizontally rather than vertically in the implementation of social incentives. It is the purpose of this writer to help develop those conditions of learning which will cause people to analyze the social mobility pattern so as to detect many directions in the social goals available.

In order to develop the conditions which will cause people to scrutinize the social pattern for multiple directions, it is necessary to mention and discuss a few of the codes which operate in our society and culture. For purposes of discussion, one might mention that there exists a code which in practice causes some to view man as more or less in a primitive state of behavior. That is the day-to-day and hand-to-mouth living code. This is characteristic of those in the lower scale of the lower class families. Here the chief concern is to do the things which will provide the daily necessities as well as an occassional "shiny middle class gadget" and a "blowout."

Status elements of middle and upper classes tend to preclude mobility from below. The members of the class which operates on a hand-to-mouth and day-to-day basis are as absorbed in the task of providing for themselves as are members of the upper class. The difference is in the degree of realization. Just as the upper class members strive to realize more than they need, so do the lower lower class members strive for a little more than meager necessities. There is also a difference in the methods which are used by the different classes in the efforts at realization. The middle and upper classes have fashioned the routes of attainment so that their goals are quite definitely realizable. These same routes are the only ones which are recognizable by the lower class members and a small segment will operate accordingly. It is, however, much more difficult for the lower class members to operate for realization in the established route because of certain status elements existing there which are beyond the reach of the members. The status elements are largely economic and in turn produce power realization possible only to those endowed with the elements which produce power. Also included in these status elements are those frequently considered as education—that which makes it possible for the possessor to recognize and use the established tools of acquisition.

The crude explanation here is associated with two commonly accepted values in the culture; namely, that education will help you make more money, and that it takes money to make money. The members who live in the hand-to-mouth group somehow haven't that education and, of course, do not have any money. This group has by and large not accepted the middle class code of "saving for a rainy day." Or, if they have, to them the weather just never has cleared up. Most have, therefore, resigned themselves to the thought that the higher class goals are out of reach.

The result of this is a condition of "internalization" of aggression feelings. This means that the members are "mad" at the world because it seems to them that the world is against them. They have as a rule never arrived at the state of contemplation of their feelings other than that the odds are against them. As a result, the "pent-up" feelings are often released in acts of aggression, even to the point of violence, against members within their groups. In the matter of dispute or differences, "fighting it out" becomes an accepted form of solution. Both adults and youth are aware that their ways are in conflict with many of the values of the culture. Feeble efforts on the part of some of the lower class members to take on or experiment with the "higher" values are met with rejection on the part of the members of the higher classes and with rebuffs and, sometimes, retaliation on the part of their own members. Such efforts are considered as degrading to oneself—the relinquishment of pride.

Status elements within framework of lower classes provide

mobility "peculiar" to its members. Mobility upward in the class structure, insofar as it reflects middle class values, is discouraged in the lower lower classes. Viewed from the same middle class values, however, there is a "circular" or "horizontal" mobility within the lower lower class structure. It is really "vertical" as viewed from the lower class perspective. Speaking generally, this "vertical" mobility assumes a status development system. The most astute "internalizer" of aggressions, for example, draws others, who entertain similar feelings, around him. The feelings are easily communicated to each other as deprivations. The one who is best able to whip the feelings into a frenzied unity is more or less accepted as the status leader. The members, on the other hand, experience a sense of status by being beholden to the leader.

In time, there develops a degree of understanding among the group of some of the operational practices within the value system of the world around them. They ask themselves, What is there in our social arrangement that others might want? Insight relative to this question might be equated to the implications of the thoughts characterized by these statements: "Of course I want to follow a straight course but I will not permit a good thing to slip out of my fingers," "Right is right but a man has to be practical." It is obvious from these statements that advantages may accrue not only to the members of the organized group but also to the other constituents. The "deals" may be a bit "shady" but who has offered anything better? A "delivery of the vote" is a practical arrangement here, especially if the price is right. If this is not a "social good" who has provided an alternative?

The above description of mobility in the value system of the lower lower classes is, of course, not nearly exhaustive; nor is this type of practice and mobility confined to these classes. It is found in other classes and a combination of classes. As a matter of fact, in the pursuit of advantages, mobility takes rather strange and unorthodox directions in the social structure. Indeed, this picture provides some of the greatest potential for curriculum development in the education for social mobility.

Status by upper lower classes assumes a middle class direction.

The codes of the upper lower class are somewhat different from those of the lower lower classes. Perhaps the greatest difference lies in the fact that a much greater effort is made to emulate middle class values. The upper lower class is by no means resigned to lower class standards. The codes have a definite relationship to wants and needs.

In middle class groups, the emphasis is on the satisfaction of needs and a practice of deferral with respect to wants. The idea is to take care of "first things first." For example, middle class families see to it that there is adequate food, clothing, and shelter before they begin to provide for other tastes. In the lower class families, however, there is no such planning and no such deferral of wants. Furthermore, there is no sharp differentiation between necessities and wants which may be classified as luxuries. The lower class families may, for example, provide meagerly in the way of food, clothes, and housing so as to buy TV sets and a secondhand car of the more expensive variety. The TV sets and the car are usually bought on time. The "novel" and easy type of recreation made possible by the television set overshadows any possible pangs of conscience about going into debt that the lower class families might have harbored. The members just "rationalize" themselves out of any slight middle class values of thrift that some of them might have entertained. The thinking is characterized by the statement, "We have just as much right to enjoy television as those folks." The ownership of a used car in the expensive model class, however, represents an aspiration to higher class values. Driving the car gives the owner a certain feeling of prestige, not among the higher class but among his neighbors.

There is developing more and more a certain similarity between some of the values of the upper lower classes and the middle classes, particularly the lower middle—that is, to give in to wants which are in advance of actual needs. For example, the members of the middle classes also buy on time and buy more luxury type items than needed. A difference, however, presents itself in the degree of guilt feelings with which they approach a violation of an abiding value—that of thrift. They tend to compartmentalize their values. In other words, they go ahead and buy the luxury items but accept it as foolish or a "sign of the times." They feel they are living beyond their means but, nevertheless, keep living that way.

Deprivation must be viewed within framework of each social class

The discussion on the lower class code has up to this point established a sort of "slot" within which the members operate. The picture created is more or less one of deprivation, that is, when viewed by those in the middle and upper class positions. The members of the lower class, as far as their code is concerned, may not consider themselves deprived unless they are actually short of food, shelter, or clothing. If they view themselves from a middle class perspective, they will naturally feel deprived. However, their membership in the lower class may be accepted by them as having its positive aspects. Middle class people may spend an evening in the living room playing bridge and poker. At the same time, lower class people may be sitting around the kitchen drinking beer and talking. The question as to which one of the two classes is deprived is not easily answered.

Deprivation of lower classes may be intensified by temporary mobility outside of code. Viewed from a middle class perspective, the intensity of deprivation of the lower class increases and relaxes from time to time due to economic conditions. For example, when there is a threat of war, or when war actually breaks out, the economic condition of most members of the lower class, along with members of other classes, improves during the duration. The consequences of the "high" are, for most of the members, a period of satiation of wants. Of course, some take advantage of the "high" to enhance themselves on the economic and social ladder. The tragedy is that the mobility takes place in terms of the middle or upper class social pattern for which the members are not prepared.

The middle and upper class members know the "ins" and "outs" of their social class pattern. The lower class has been the recipient of a temporary charitableness extended by the upper classes. At the same time, the members seem to forget the positive as well as the negative aspects of their previous status. As a result, when a slump in economic conditions sets in, they lose all sense of security in both high and low classes. They are not only rejected all around but may come to reject themselves. The point of departure is now confused and the nature of deprivation changes to a depression of spirit. As a result, this class finds itself in a peculiar position at the lower end of the ladder which tends to be frightening to the members.

One might say that it would have been better for this group never to have tasted the air of middle class exhilaration. Then the members at least would have retained the respect of other members who either were unable to penetrate the ranks of the middle class or refused the "charity" of it.

DETECTING CLUES TO UNDERSTANDING LOWER CLASS BEHAVIOR IN SCHOOLS

As indicated before, a value which commands a considerable degree of acceptance in the lower class is the use of direct aggressiveness in working toward solving a grievance. "Fighting it out" is often rated highly in settling disputes. The aggression tactics which are used are those which are directed at the person rather than the situation. Frequently, this is precipitated either in a threat short of violence or in actual violence. This is considered as teaching the person a "lesson." Teachers frequently use the same tactics in a less violent manner. They inflict some kind of punishment for the purpose of teaching the child a "lesson." Teachers feel that they must deal with these youngsters in terms of "what they understand."

These tactics do teach the pupil a "lesson" but not the kind the teacher had in mind. These methods will have the effect, instead, of generating hostility in the youngsters toward the teacher and school. The youngsters may grudgingly conform for a time to the patterns of the classroom but, in the long run, nothing has really been accomplished toward establishing better working relationships between the teacher and the children.

Non-acceptant behavior of teacher generates aggression of lower class children

There are several basic factors involved in a pupil's reaction to the teacher as indicated above. In the first place, studies have shown that teachers usually behave in terms of middle class values. Most teachers do not acquire an understanding and sympathy with lower class values because their origin and much of their education have been in terms of middle class standards. Consequently, they will not accept those who exhibit the values. The child reacts with increased hostility toward the teacher when his feelings are never considered, as he behaves according to his values in the classroom.

If the teacher had accepted the child, he would have considered what feelings were operating in the child's behavior. In that event, the child would have accepted a degree of counter-aggressiveness on the part of the teacher. When the child recognizes that the teacher accepts his feelings, he will reconsider his method of response. In other words, the behavior of the teacher may deflate the effectiveness of hostility as a weapon. As the child conceives a sense of recognition from the teacher, it suddenly occurs to him that he has no reason for fighting back. Although the child may have other flare-ups at some of the problems with peer relationships, chances are that they will gradually become more infrequent. It is clear to the child that the teacher does not consider him a threat. This conception on the part of the child is an initial step toward understanding his feelings.

School frequently considered a threat

Another reason for the aggressive behavior characteristic of people who come from lower class neighborhoods is the absence of a mature consciousness as viewed by middle class standards. The people yearn for something different from what they have but are somehow encumbered with those values which receive high esteem: namely, brute strength, lineup with questionable political power, and retaliation against imagined threat. Freedom is conceived as endowed with these values. If you don't "fight" for your rights, "they" will take them away from you.

Schools are frequently considered by lower class children as institutions foisted on them by outsiders. The tragedy is that the behavior of some of the people who staff the schools has too frequently justified this conception. The school is, therefore, categorized as a threat to the values which they have known. So when the youngster goes to the school, he is already set to oppose it. His parents haven't helped him when they refer to teachers as "those who will make you behave." Conceiving of the school as a whole mass of threats to his way of behavior, the idea of giving it a chance is farthest from his thoughts. With all these attitudes toward school smoldering in him, the child usually makes the first move to exhibit how he feels. The teacher, conceiving this as a threat which might grow in intensity as time goes on, makes a countermove which reveals him as fighting back at the child's level. The idea is to meet force with force.

A sizeable element of the population from which this youngster comes either lacks or refuses to acquire an understanding of middle class ways of looking at things. It is reasonable to assume that the child will exhibit a similar attitude. On the other side of the picture, it is deplorable that many members of the school staff exhibit a similar lack of insight with respect to the source of the child's values. It is difficult for many people to conceive that behavior can be dealt with only through an understanding of the components of that behavior.

DEVELOPING AN ACCEPTANT ENVIRONMENT IN THE CLASSROOM AND SCHOOL

As indicated in Chapter 8, in order to positively influence behavior, all the values of children must be admitted into the learning situation. Proceeding in terms of that principle, it is important that the teacher develop an environment of acceptance of feelings in the classroom and school.

An important step in developing an environment of acceptance is to try to suppress all preconceived assumptions based on equating certain human characteristics with readiness for learning tasks. The teacher needs to be open-minded in the approach to individual children. Each one is, then, regarded as possessing human potential. The teacher views learning as the combined power of the differences in individuals as essential to personal and group realization. The curriculum should provide for approaches to the development of an acceptant environment.

Providing conditions for children to establish meanings
about their classroom and school

There are several approaches which may be used to demonstrate the acceptant conditions. With elementary school children, the teacher might take the initial steps to develop a center of interest or understanding relative to the meaning of the caption, THE SCHOOL AND CLASSROOM BELONG TO EVERYONE. As he talks about the caption with the children, he will detect the clues for transferring a considerable portion of the burden of establishing meanings to the children. As children are in the process of searching for meanings, subheadings will begin to appear under the caption. There will be a clarification of such terms as responsibility, usefulness, helpfulness, contribution, expansion, and goal. Soon the children, with the aid of the teacher, will be carving out various tasks which justify the meanings which they have established relative to their classroom and school.

The development of the conditions for acceptance may be continued in the same manner as indicated above with centers of interest to establish meanings about such topics as: The Need for the "Peculiar" Ideas of Every Individual in Deriving Answers to Big Questions, The Right and Duty of Everyone to Tell What He Knows About a Problem Confronting the Group, The Right and Duty to Raise Questions for Understanding or Clarification of an Idea, and The Responsibility and Opportunity for Everyone to Help Plan the Experiences for Optimum Learning.

Conditions should provide for extension of resourcefulness of children. Another approach to the establishment of an acceptant environment is the arrangement by the teacher of a series of appointments with pupils. This should be a two-way proposition. The teacher, serious in his attempts to amass the resources of every child in the promotion of learning, could suggest that he has certain questions with which he needs help. Together with the children, he develops a plan whereby he will spend a stated period of time with each individual in the next two weeks. After the series of conferences, he will make a note of types of information possessed by different individuals. On the basis of the resources existing in the group, he might plan a weekly consultation period with the children.

At the times designated, both teacher and various individual children would be serving as consultants to other individuals or groups on the basis of need in the tasks undertaken. At various times, different individuals who had information and ideas relative to the learning tasks carried on in the classroom would serve as consultants with the other children. This approach would certainly utilize the differences of children in a positive manner. Furthermore, it would demonstrate that each one possesses human potential which serves the group and individual. Finally, it would establish acceptant feelings between children since they would be learning from one another.

Conditions should help secondary youth approach basic issues in learning. The above approach is readily adaptable on a more advanced level to secondary classroom pupils. Since the children are more mature, the approach could be used with even greater effectiveness than in the elementary school. In the secondary school, the consultation sessions could be constituted as weekly seminars. Three or four students would lead out on the particular questions to be studied to be followed by mutual exchange of ideas. There should be no dearth of questions or problems which could receive attention in the seminars, as pupils harbor literally hundreds which have meaning for them. The curriculum should provide for the assessment of the questions and problems of youth in such a manner as to get at basic issues in learning. For example, rather than have a seminar on a question such as dating, there should gradually develop a plan for the discovery of meanings with regard to behavioral science and the rise of different cultures.

Conditions should provide for a wide range of experiences. In order to bring about the conditions for an environment of acceptance, it would be necessary to develop a range of experiences sufficiently wide to enable every individual to acquire meaning and resourcefulness. For example, toward one end of the range of experiences in a seminar on "What Causes One to Behave as He Does," there could be guidance into an examination of the nature of one's likes and dislikes with respect to people. Some young people, assisted by the teacher and two or three pupil consultants, would pursue the values inherent in this question along with the consequences. At the same time, at the other end of the range of experiences, questions relating to a study of behavior through historical, sociological, and psychological sources would be evolved. Some individuals could study both types of questions at different levels of intensity. Some pupils would have a greater understanding and insight relative to the nature of their likes and dislikes than others. Then, too, in the whole process, pupils who possessed greater powers of learning could be resourceful with others. The heart of this approach is to develop an attitude of sensitivity on the part of pupils to the problems of others. An environment of acceptance of one another is virtually guaranteed when pupils care whether others acquire an understanding of questions related to their goals.

Conditions must be designed to eliminate obstacles to acceptant environment for learning

In order to further the conditions for an acceptant learning environment in the classroom and school, it is necessary to consider some of the obstacles which exist. One of the obstacles against the development of acceptance conditions is the preconceived assumption on the part of some individuals that there exists a relationship between socio-economic characteristics and background to readiness and potential with respect to learning tasks. It is highly doubtful, for example, if an environment of acceptance can be established by the assumption of powers to prescribe the educational tasks in terms of general, commercial, industrial, and college preparation. Yet this is a familiar pattern of the curriculum in many high schools all over the country. The lines of demarcation as between the "divisions" are often rigidly established.

Conditions must promote the integration of opportunities in learning. Curriculum workers and teachers who are associated with schools that persist in maintaining rigid lines of segregation of students as between the several "curriculums" might consider questions such as the following: What is the basis of differentiation between the divisions? Isn't there a relationship between college preparation courses and the others?

Isn't the college-bound student also general-bound and industrial-bound? More important, isn't the college-bound student life-bound? Why narrow the opportunities of college-bound students by these restrictions? On the other hand, isn't it plausible for the student in the general course to enjoy the richness of association with students in the industrial and college preparation divisions? By the same token, why deny the college preparatory and industrial course students the opportunity to handle ideas with the general and commercial course students?

It is important that the curriculum design make provision for the integration of opportunities in learning. Channels of communication between curriculum divisions should not only be open but, also, "charged" with compelling impact for students to handle ideas together. There should be centers of learning relative to industry, business understandings, science, the arts, and other areas which cut across subject and curriculum division lines. All children and youth should have the opportunities to become self-seeking in the pursuit of ideas wherever they might be found.

Conditions should eliminate grouping as an obstacle to acceptance conditions. Everyone who has had some experience in working with children knows that some children are able to learn more and faster than others. As a result, there have developed practices of segregating children in terms of "ability to learn." This is known as ability grouping. It is, of course, a violation of the needs and rights of children to expect everyone in a given length of time to learn at the same rate of speed and in the same proportion. Furthermore, this practice violates the principles of uniqueness and individuality of children. At the same time, in the efforts to plan learning experiences in terms of these principles—that is, individual differences and uniqueness of individual children—the results have frequently been as devastating to children's growth and personality as when children were all expected to work with materials and experiences of the same difficulty. We have reference to a grouping of children in the mythical categories of "slow," "average," and "superior." One fallacy in this method of grouping lies in the assumption that teachers can definitely determine the sharp lines of demarcation between the groups. Another fallacy in grouping children on high, average, and slow levels lies in the assumption that teachers know the "slots" where the children fit by using tests which have been devised according to a middle class standard of values.

A third form of questionable reasoning used in this system of grouping is that which is associated with the blanket education phrase "Take them where they are and take them as far as they can go." We would ask: How can anyone determine exactly where children are and how far they can go? Would the children coming from the lower classes be considered as starting far behind the others? According to whose values would the starting point and finish line be determined? Would the route be determined in terms of academic achievement or growth in democratic competences? Would the criteria for determining how far children had come be based on the nature of subject matter skills or on the competences in solving problems of behavior?

A fourth fallacious concept in the high to low grouping plan exists in the belief that children can actually be homogeneously grouped. In the so-called slow group, there remain the individual differences; also in the fast group. Then, if the grouping would be continued into the ultimate homogeneous group, we would be back where we started: that each child *is* the group. This brings us back where we want to be for the purpose of developing the conditions for ideas to evolve through the efforts of all of the children.

DEVELOPING A COMMUNICATIONS LABORATORY FOR MOBILITY IN LEARNING

In the development of class mobility, it is important to provide for a wide range of experiences charged with the stimuli to evolve ideas. The term, center of interest, is used because most elementary teachers are familiar with that term in connection with classroom experiences of children. As the discussion continues, however, the term, laboratory, will be used interchangeably with centers of interest. The reason for using "laboratory" is that it explains more clearly the action conception of a center of interest. The learning situations in a laboratory are usually developed to show elements of cause and effect with special emphasis on what is happening in the situations to matter and people. Thus we speak of the conditions which are developed to charge the learning environment with ideas.

To clarify the discussion relative to the development of a center of interest which contains a wide range of experiences, we have chosen to illustrate an approach to communication which might be used with ten- and eleven-year-old children. We shall call this a communications laboratory. Normally, this would be called a center of interest in language or English. It is assumed, of course, that some work has already been done with the children in reading and sentence structure. No doubt, the children have had some opportunity to write about some topics or ideas in which they were interested. We are not concerned especially with what type of neighborhood these children come from because the range of potential differences, if discovered, is about the same in every neighborhood. It is assumed that the teacher who uses part or all of this type of approach to learning accepts the values of all the children into the classroom for developmental purposes. The range of experiences to be indicated here is designed to give an opportunity for every child to identify with at least some of them.

Conditions must create stimuli and opportunities for communication

In the development of a communications laboratory, one of the first tasks of the teacher is to provide the setting which points up the need for communicating on the part of the child. It is true that the need is present and is partially being satisfied on the part of most children. They talk with their friends, parents, other adults, and the teacher. Many children, however, do not have all the opportunity they should have to convey their thoughts and feelings. Others who have more opportunity also do not convey some of their thoughts and feelings for various reasons. More important, thoughts and feelings need to be conveyed and exchanged by children and teachers so they may gain more ideas about each other, about themselves as individuals, and about the nature of things in the environment. To take the initial step toward providing the setting for the need for communication, the teacher could ask a question or two such as: I wonder what it would be like if people couldn't talk? What are some ways people use to make their wishes known? How do people show their feelings about things? These questions in all probability would give rise to an onrush of comments on the part of children. After a certain period of time, the teacher might suggest that the children present some of their reactions to these questions and others which arose in the process, in drawings, cartoons, or writing.

Teacher helps provide setting to move reactions of children forward. While the children are busy with the questions the teacher could be making plans to take the questions and the anticipated reactions a step further. In the plans, the following ideas might be conceived:

(1) Finding a few pictures representative of the ideas involved in the questions above and putting them on a bulletin board.

(2) Recalling radio and television programs in which much action is involved with feelings, and devising some plans for child response regarding the programs.

(3) Securing a film to be shown to the class wherein feelings are clearly presented.

(4) Showing a film of the silent movie days to illustrate different ways of showing feelings.

(5) Making plans to point up reasons for talking, other than those indicated in the questions.

(6) Devising an approach to show the necessity of using words to convey thought as well as seeking answers to one's questions.

The teacher tries to plan in such a manner as to develop concern about communication in connection with the child's purposes. The plans are designed to minister not only to purposes already conceived by children but also to create new purposes. Not all the plans will be used, especially since the children, with their reactions on paper to the questions, will furnish many leads toward cooperative planning for the communications laboratory.

Children offer clues toward extension of laboratory experi-

ences. After a given length of time, perhaps the next day, the teacher might call on the children to show what they did with the questions. In response to the questions as to how people make their wishes known and how they show their feelings about things, the following representations might be offered by the children:

People just standing and looking at each other.

Showing three or four people making grimaces or gestures to indicate wishes.

A newspaper clipping showing an editorial or letter to the editor of a newspaper.

Two children walking home from school together.

A group of boys at Bill's home on a Saturday afternoon playing games in the back yard and later watching television.

A group of girls at Jane's house practicing for a play they are going to put on at school.

Pictures pointing up the importance of doing things together with friends.

A girl walking home all alone on a deserted street.

A cartoon about a boy and his dog.

A sophisticated cartoon showing a person expressing apprehension as to Russia's intentions.

A group of people discussing a question to reach a decision. The question is indicated in the representation.

A picture of spring or summer together with what it means.

A picture or clipping of a senator talking for or against a proposal.

A picture of the President having a press conference.

The picture and story of a visitor from another country.

A picture and story of picketing in a labor-management dispute.

A picture of boys having a dispute.

The above are by no means exhaustive of the possible representations which children would make relative to the questions. The list, however, gives a sufficient sampling to serve as clues to the further planning of the range of experiences in a communications laboratory for ten- and eleven-year-old children. In addition to these representations offered by the children, the teacher would have submitted pictures, clippings, cartoons, and other items indicating a relationship to the questions. Many of these would be placed on bulletin boards.

Conditions enlarge on cycles of experiences in laboratory

Having offered the representative materials relative to the questions, the next step is to do something with them to encourage further experiences in communication and the development of ideas. One procedure could be the placing of all the materials on a bulletin board and talking about them to discover the ideas children had in mind as they prepared them. This, however, would be difficult to do since there wouldn't be enough space to include them all on the bulletin board. Furthermore, endless discussion about the materials may become monotonous and result in loss of interest on the part of the children. Alternatives to this suggestion would, no doubt, be offered by the children. They might suggest that the materials which seemed to be most representative of their feelings and ideas be placed on the bulletin board or boards with the others to be filed under proper labels in a large carton. Another proposal might be to file all of the materials and examine them further for more ideas and questions to be filed with the materials. After a given length of time agreed upon, the materials could be discussed again by various groups in the light of the new ideas and questions submitted.

Another development which might arise in connection with the various proposals is a sort of self-seeking for answers to other questions which children have. They might generalize that most of the ideas which have been presented in the materials are about feelings. They would probably like to talk about other areas more of a scientific nature. They may wish to know about the nature of air, water, health, electricity, television, radio, space, and other phenomena. Besides, the suggestions of the teacher from time to time may lead to an examination of new areas of ideas.

Teacher and children together "charge" the conditions for expanded meanings. All this time the teacher has been learning a great deal about the values of children. As he observes what has been done with the questions originally raised and what additional ideas have been conceived when the materials are scrutinized a second time, he is in the position to help the children redirect their thinking as well as their organization in the efforts to tackle the next tasks.

In a previous section, some reference was made with regard to what the teacher was bringing to the environment of ideas. In order to further charge the conditions for learning toward concern about ideas and ways of communicating, the teacher could bring pictures and clippings and unobtrusively put them upon a bulletin board. He might state to the children that these items somehow attracted him, and he wondered what meanings they hold for people. One should be careful not to "strain" for meanings for to do so may cause some children to work on someone else's purposes rather than their own. In the event of such a situation, there is the danger of youngsters working on meanings and ideas in such a manner as to rule out any identification with them on their own part. Some of the pictures and clippings which have been put up by the teacher will spontaneously evoke concern and reaction on the part of some children. Other children may view the items in a more reflective manner and come out with some real reactions which will reveal some real identification with the items. Still others may relate to the items in such a manner as to indicate new directions in thinking. An illustration of this approach might be in order here.

Let us assume that the teacher has brought to school the following pictures which have probably been cut out of magazines:

A little girl walking alone in a littered and deserted alley.

A family scene with the father reading a newspaper, the mother knitting, a boy doing his homework, a teen-age girl reading a magazine, and a smaller child playing on the floor with toys. No television set is in evidence in the picture.

A family scene with members intensely viewing television.

A boy sitting on the bank of a stream, all alone, fishing.

A group of boys, too many for two teams, getting ready to play baseball.

A group of boys and girls walking home from school talking and laughing in such a way as indicative of a great deal of energy.

At first, the teacher will unobtrusively observe what children do with regard to the pictures. Some children may not pay any attention to them, having seen them in magazines in their homes. A few might glance at them and make some laughing remarks to their companions. Two or three may spend considerable time studying the pictures thoughtfully. A few others will come to the teacher and make comments or ask questions about the scenes. The different ways in which the children react to the pictures will furnish some clues to further steps in working on the development of ideas. Some of the comments which might be made and which could also serve as guides to the extension of the communications laboratory would be somewhat as follows:

She better watch out walking alone that way in an alley.

I bet the boy who is doing his homework wishes he was the father.

The television show must be a good one as they all look as if they are anxious for what will happen next.

Did you see ———— on television last night?

I bet that boy doesn't get to play.

They should choose up and let the others umpire.

Some of the boys should play half the inning and let the others play the second half.

The boys are teasing the girls.

They are glad that school is out.

They seem to be "razzing" two of the boys.

Could we play ball at recess today?

They ought to clean up that alley.

That family looks very much like ours.

I would rather work with my chemistry set after school than study.

Some of the girls seem mad at the boys.

There will probably be a fight before long.

I don't think they will fight. Most of them are laughing. They don't have anything to fight about.

The boy doing his homework will soon be through. Then he can read a book or do something else. Maybe there is a television set in another room.

I don't believe that boy will catch fish at that spot.

He probably stayed away from school. That's why he is alone. He'll probably get a paddling from his dad when he goes home.

I like to go fishing on the stream below Bill's house. My dad and I went last Saturday.

I get my homework done the first thing when I get home so I can go over to Jane's house and play with her.

I like the kind of things you give us to do for the next day.

One could go on and on listing comments showing the reaction of children to the ideas that they see in the pictures. The above comments, however, are sufficient to indicate some of the values which are operating and the direction the conversation might take as it is carried on further. The teacher, of course, will be in the midst of the discussion as it develops and will supply suggestions and hints from time to time which will help it along toward more intensive degrees of concern about the ideas. For example, in connection with the picture of the little girl walking in the alley, the teacher might raise the questions, "Have you ever been lonesome?" "What feelings does it give you?" Relative to the discussion about the boy doing homework, the teacher might suggest that probably he is interested in what he is doing or that he might be doing some work on his own that wasn't assigned.

The interjection of questions and leads on the part of the teacher has the tendency to take the conversation or discussion into higher stages of thoughtfulness and concern. As children weigh their thinking relative to a feeling about someone else's experience, they at the same time relate the feeling and its consequences to themselves. For example, when children become deeply concerned about lonesomeness and its effects, they may make efforts to keep others from being lonesome. The development of those conditions in the environment of ideas which will produce a thoughtful analysis of the experiences which bring unhappiness to people are extremely important in causing behavior to be extended positively to others. Children must first gain an understanding of behavioral effects on themselves in order to envision the consequences of behavior.

DEVELOPING EFFECTIVENESS IN COMMUNICATION SKILLS

After a period of study and discussion regarding evolvement of social understanding and action with respect to ideas, the teacher might proceed toward the establishment of the conditions for the promotion of effectiveness in communication skills. In the comments and discussion indicated on the previous pages, different words and terms have been used by children in expressing their reaction to possible ideas represented by the pictures. This could lead to the development of a center in the laboratory which might be labeled, *The Center for Better Ways of Expressing Ideas or Meanings.* A group of youngsters might help the teacher tabulate the "feeling" words which were used by the children in the discussion. These words could be placed on cards and filed in alphabetical order. This would give the children constructive and purposeful experiences in spelling and alphabetization. Alphabetization and spelling are useful skills which one should acquire in the process of carrying on research in the laboratory.

Providing for development of a "feelings" vocabulary

At the beginning of the discussion on developing a communications laboratory with children, it was emphasized that there should be a wide range of experiences so that all the children could find meanings for themselves. In terms of this principle, it would be necessary to develop with some children a rather extensive and technical "feelings" vocabulary and, with others, a rather limited one.

The reason for the emphasis on a "feelings" vocabulary is that in order to bring about mobility in communications, it is important that children identify differences in feelings and, hence, differences in people. In the development of this vocabulary it is hoped that children will learn to discriminate between one individual's feeling as against that of another. When a child recognizes that his feeling about an idea does not necessarily make it a fact, he may begin to examine other feelings and reactions. When children begin to examine many feelings about an idea, they will get nearer to the facts in a situation.

The teacher, in the effort to arrange for this wide vocabulary range, might find it necessary to ask the principal and supervisor for help. If practice teachers have been assigned to the room, they should be fully involved in the task of developing the communications laboratory. Another resource for the task of preparing "feeling" words and sentences is the children themselves. Different individuals or groups may be scheduled each day as "assistant laboratory technicians" to prepare card files of words used frequently, words used sometimes, easy words, difficult words, and unusual words. The vocabulary lists should consist largely of words chosen in terms of the ideas which are before the children.

The above procedures could also be used in developing sentences pertinent to the ideas which have been discussed. This does not mean that all the sentences have to be created. Many of the sentences could be selected from readings dealing with points similar to those which are being handled by the children.

In order that children may have the opportunity of working on their vocabulary, it is important that the tools necessary for doing this be provided in the laboratory. There should be available several children's dictionaries, regular dictionaries, and several copies of a good thesaurus. Besides these materials, several textbooks in language should be available as well as handbooks which contain clear and simple explanatory statements and rules about grammatical construction. Other materials which should be in the laboratory or otherwise easily accessible to the children, are newspapers of all types, magazines of all types, and many books about children and their problems as well as books on a varied assortment of topics. The school library should, of course, be easily accessible so that children may do research on their topics and ideas.

Expanding the "feelings" vocabulary into areas of action, facts, and research. We do not wish to give the impression that children should work only on their "feelings" vocabulary. As the "feelings" phase of the communications laboratory is being developed, the teacher will be setting the conditions for vocabulary expansion into the areas of action, facts, and research. What is being done to discover a more extended and better vocabulary to express feelings will also be done in connection with the examination and action on feelings. The teacher and children will be designing ways of approaching an understanding of the feelings. They will be analyzing the feelings in terms of the consequences, thus using intelligence toward promoting choice among the alternatives envisioned. It will be necessary, then, to build a vocabulary of action words as well as words designed to state facts in connection with ideas discovered in a situation.

Developing conditions for effective handling of ideas

It will be noted that little or no reference has been made to the use of grammar. This omission is by no means intended to convey the impression that grammar is unimportant. On the contrary, the omission of any considerable degree of reference to grammar has been done to emphasize the importance of first developing the environment of ideas. Grammar must come as a tool to help the child organize the expression of his feelings and ideas toward situations. It is poor psychology to have children learn all about grammar—such as rules, sentence structure —before there is sufficient substance in the learning environment to make them react strongly to ideas and to develop the desire to express them effectively.

Grammar should facilitate conditions for talking and writing. When the children have arrived at the point where they are identifying with many ideas, it is important to learn grammatical construction. When a child is ready and desirous of expressing ideas at considerable length, he should be led into examining what he is saying and how he is saying it. Of course, it is extremely important that the child should be helped in such a way as not to inhibit his urge to talk and write. In most cases, it is very questionable to stop and correct a child in the midst of the presentation of an idea about which he feels strongly. An interruption of this type might do one or both of two things. First, a sudden interruption of his thought pattern may break the pattern and lessen the effectiveness of the expression. Second, having been corrected by the teacher or some other individual, he may tend to concentrate on the form to the extent that he loses sight of what he really wanted to communicate as well as how he wanted to communicate it.

Rather, the teacher should make observations in notes as to

the type of grammatical improvements that could be made and later have sessions with individuals and groups for the purpose of leading them to identify ways of attacking their language expression and organization problems. In these sessions, the teacher would be prepared to help children recognize their communication difficulties and plan with them on the types of experiences needed to overcome the difficulties. In these sessions, the teacher would also plan to have the children become familiar with ways of using handbooks, language texts, and other materials which would help them toward better grammatical usage. The teacher would arrange for consultation periods with the children two or three times a week. During these periods, the teacher would attempt to answer some of the questions raised, evaluate with the children the progress they are making, and clarify grammatical as well as other meanings with the children.

Teacher and children examine ways of communicating ideas. Although this chapter is designed to emphasize the importance of developing an environment of ideas to promote effective learning, we must always recognize that ideas, in order to survive as well as serve people, must be handled in communication. By "handled," we mean that they need to be presented in an organized and effective manner. In the consultation periods indicated above, the conditions are provided whereby children will have an opportunity to devise their particular systems for improving their skills in speaking and writing. Concentrated attention will be given to sentence structure, composing paragraphs, and devising outlines for the communication of ideas.

The consultation periods, which are in reality teaching periods, are used to consolidate the ideas into usable patterns of thinking. Furthermore, although the teacher has been accumulating data on children's ways of looking at ideas as they dealt with the pictures made available as well as the questions in the files, he gathers additional information about children as he works with them in the consultation sessions. The ways in which children express their feelings tell much about the values which they hold as a result of their everyday experiences. It is important, therefore, to constantly charge the environment with those elements which induce concern on the part of the children with regard to the expression of their behavior. Having gathered considerable meaning from the "helping" materials in the laboratory and the conditions provided in the consultation sessions, children will begin to question certain ways of communicating ideas. We would increasingly hear such comments and questions as the following:

"Why isn't it better to say it this way?"

"If we're going to tell something, we might as well learn to tell it right so we don't always have to ask someone else or refer to the handbook. That will save a lot of time."

"I don't think those words tell exactly what I intended to say."

"I used to say things in a rather funny way."

"Boy, does that man butcher the English language."

"I don't think I use words strong enough to express my feelings about that point."

"When one gets mad he gets all mixed up in what he is saying."

"I found some rather expressive language in a book I picked up last night. Could I read a few sentences from it?"

"I found some books which had good answers to this question. Would you help us decide how much of this I should use in writing the answers?"

"Sometimes I read something about a thing and never think anything more about it. Then I will read what someone else said about the same thing and keep thinking about it. What is the reason for the different feelings?"

"Sometimes when I get angry at someone, I tell him off. Afterward I am sorry for it."

"When you tell someone off it just makes him madder at you."

"When someone says something to you in a fit of anger, it is probably better to ignore it at the time. Later, when he cools off your answer may do more good."

"I get too much in a hurry when I write and do not think through what I am saying."

"When I get an idea I don't have time to think how I'll write. I want to write it quickly before I forget it."

"I guess if we try to use good language in practice, later it will come easy."

"You explain it better than the book. I wish you had written one of these books."

The questions and comments above reveal several facts about the behavior of children as well as about the environment in which they are working. It is quite evident that the conditions are such as elicit conversation in a very relaxed manner. Children are making their comments and asking questions in a casual way. The nature of the comments are outgoing. There is no sense of holding back. Yet, at the same time, there is considerable evidence on the part of the children of concern about their practices in writing and oral expression. One does not, however, get the feeling of the strain and attrition which often prevails in learning conditions.

Mental hygienists have pointed out time and again that good mental health is more apt to prevail in conditions where the atmosphere is relaxed and where unproductive tension is at a minimum. Mental hygienists also contend that the conditions for learning must lead toward concern about what needs to be done with ideas which people have. The conditions for learning must provide for time and opportunity for children to think through their ideas in a relaxed manner. At the same time, the environment must be sufficiently charged with the questions which develop a compulsiveness for learning relative to the questions. Children have the right to a type of discipline which helps them recognize if, in the pursuit of ideas, something is happening to them, and what it is that is happening.

As children are working in connection with the fulfillment of their plans in the communications laboratory, the teacher periodically and frequently evaluates with them whether they are doing their task with more facility than they did the previous week. "Ann," for example, may have become conscious of a stereotyped system in her writing and expression. She has the opportunity of consulting with the teacher about it. The teacher provides some guide lines for Ann's thinking. Then, Ann is encouraged to take time to think about these guide lines and how they pertain to her use of language. She examines some of the handbooks and other materials. She talks with some of the other children about ways of changing some of the expressions without becoming dramatic. Ann will have further opportunity in the laboratory to examine some of the specimens in a possible expanded center of interest under a caption such as DIFFERENT WAYS OF SAYING IT.

She may even record alternative forms of her original stereotypes and gain some guidance toward improved expression. She may type the forms and see how they look in print. Again, she returns to the teacher with her findings about herself and, also, some new ideas she has acquired with regard to writing and speaking. She is encouraged to discuss her discoveries with other children for the purpose of helping them find ways out of possible writing and speaking difficulties. The efforts of relating some of the ways in which Ann improved certain forms of expression will evoke response on the part of other children which will prove of further help to her. This process could eventuate in a plan for better use of many resources for self and group development in communication skills.

Ann, of course, typifies what should take place in varying degrees with every child in this classroom or school. The process of the communications laboratory, as described in the previous sections, clears the way for fluid social living and development of competences. The conditions for learning are such as facilitate class mobility. Everyone views each other as possessing potential to move in understanding from one step to the next one. Each one is conversant with what the other one is trying to do. Each one helps the other in reaching goals which are successively visualized and draws strength from the insight provided in the process. A lower floor of standards does not exist. Nor are upper limits established. Rather, the efforts are designed to cause movement continuously forward. There are, of course, points of consolidation of gains and a leveling off, but there is no upper end to achievement.

PROMOTING CLASS MOBILITY IN LEARNING WITH YOUTH

Although designed for elementary school children, the laboratory for class mobility in learning described in the previous sections may be carried on in a more advanced manner with youth of secondary schools. The curriculum must be developed in such a way as to provide a range of experiences sufficiently wide to enable young people from different social classes to find meanings for self and group realization. In this connection, a most important principle of curriculum development is that the experiences which youth have should be initiated in terms of the perceptions which they have acquired about phenomena in their living environment.

Conditions for learning must encompass meanings with which students live

In the approach to the task of curriculum improvement, teachers should in the beginning consider what their commitments are with regard to education for social mobility. One of the commitments could very well be to develop the conditions wherein youth who live under different codes of values may have the opportunity to identify with the learning experiences.

To illustrate how all youth may identify with experiences, we have taken a typical unit, namely, "The Struggle for Life," which may be found in many biology textbooks. The overview of the unit would tell about all living things being constantly engaged, from birth till death, in a struggle for life. At times, people must struggle against organisms of other types in order to remain alive. Furthermore, all plants and animals must depend on energy to carry on their fight for life.

As young people approach the study of the unit, in all probability, there will be considerable discussion about the differences in the organisms engaged in the struggle. It will become clear that some organisms are better equipped than others to engage in the struggle. Some organisms are incapable of coping with the forces about them and gradually die out. Others, in contrast, are highly successful in the struggle. In this manner, the whole unit is discussed at considerable length in the textbook. At the end of the unit or chapter are usually a number of questions which, when answered, help the student to recall the material of the chapter. The questions run somewhat as follows: Are animals independent or dependent? What is meant by *matter?* What is meant by the *balance of nature?* Explain what is meant by the term *adaptation?* There are also some directions about lists and definitions. There may be some supplementary questions designed for "extra credit."

As one carefully considers the unit with the questions indicated above, he could find many great facts and meanings, both scientific and cultural. The questions indicated above, if followed verbatim, will not, however, produce a sufficiently wide range of experiences in thinking to enable all students to identify with some of them. This is especially true if they attempt to see themselves in "the struggle for life." A study of the questions relative to the topic "The Struggle for Life" would reveal a scientific fact, namely, the survival of the fittest. As this fact is studied further, questions such as the following would arise: What is meant by the fittest? Does it mean physical superiority? Does it mean greater knowledge about one's surroundings? Is "fittest" related to size in people? What determines the qualities which produce the "fittest"?

As these questions are studied and discussed in the laboratory of learning, the resources for answers and greater enlightenment are gradually assembled. Many other facts about the struggle for life will be revealed. Experimentation will be introduced relative to animals and plants. Planting will take place in different types of soil. Differences of growth in individual plants as well as groups of plants in the varied types of soils will be recorded. Soils will be examined to determine the respective nutritive elements present. Scientific truths derived from the experiments will be recorded and discussed.

It is clear that a considerable range of experiences will be provided by the development associated with the questions and experimentation indicated. The range, however, is not wide enough to provide for identification on the part of all students. The development of experiences as described above is important and is typical of many science classrooms. Although many learning experiences are taking place, it is doubtful that they are of sufficient magnitude, intensity, or variety to encompass the meanings represented by the different codes with which the students live. The facts are developed in a rather confined area of meanings. The process of inquiry and the pursuit to understandings is somewhat rigid. The textbook is the chief resource. The resources which are brought to the situation by the pupils and teacher suffer rather strict limitations with regard to possible meanings.

To illustrate an expanded environment of ideas to make possible greater class mobility in learning, it is necessary to return to the topic "The Struggle for Life." In order to develop the conditions for meanings in the laboratory with which all pupils may identify, the teacher might begin by suggesting *what is necessary to exist.* The caption WHAT DOES ONE NEED TO EXIST may appear as a center of interest in the laboratory. As discussion and study continue on this topic, some students will turn the questions inward to themselves. This might bring forth the question, Do I have more than is necessary for existence? Other questions and comments which will, no doubt, arise are somewhat along this line:

Life would be very dull if one just had enough to exist.

Is the struggle for life the same as the struggle for existence?

What are the things which make us happy or unhappy in the struggle for life?

The struggle for life means more possessions. Everybody wants things and will plan to get them.

I would value friendship more than possessions, I think.

As one gets more possessions he makes more friends.

People work to satisfy their needs. Many of these are possessions.

A farmer tills the soil so that he will have a crop. He sells the produce to get money to buy things for himself and his family.

My dad works in a factory. His wages are not enough to get the things we need. My mother has to work to help make a living. Dad says that, if his job paid what it should, my mother wouldn't have to work.

As people acquire more possessions, or the things they need, they have a better outlook on life.

Some people have so much. Others barely have enough to make a living. Why does this difference exist?

Getting things is not the whole story. Things give you some security, but you are still not safe. For example, the people of the United States have, perhaps, more possessions than the people of any nation —yet the spending for defense is at an all-time high for peacetime.

Man, in his struggle for life, seeks more than goods. He seeks security and peace of mind. He seeks entertainment, friends, and knowledge.

As one struggles for life, when is life realized? What are the goals
one should have? What must a person do to reach the goals of life?
In what ways has the struggle for life changed over the last hundred
years?

In what ways does our struggle differ from that of other cultures?

Does acquisition of the means for life hold as much meaning to the
people in Samoa, for example, as in our own culture? In what way
do our values differ from those of the eastern cultures?

What are the sources in your experience which caused you to be
elated? Were you ever elated over the discovery of a new idea?

The number and quality of ideas one has acquired make a difference
in the struggle for life.

*Settings for learning must provide meanings indigenous to
individual and group codes.* The above questions and comments
are by no means exhaustive of the topic at hand. They do, however, serve to illustrate the expansion of experiences and meanings so that all students may have a degree of self-realization.
The questions and comments indicated above, as well as others,
would be developed with sub-questions, cartoons, graphic representations of facts and ideas, and ample supply of books,
pamphlets, yearbooks, films, pictures, and other types of research materials. In other words, many of the big questions
would become core questions around which would be portrayed
all types of relative facts, ideas, and principles.

This portrayal or visualization of facts and ideas would represent various communicative avenues through which pupils living with different values would perceive meanings. Furthermore, the experiences which students would have in building
the various communicative avenues in connection with the
centers in the laboratory would develop and establish many
competences and values relative to mobility in learning. One
competence, for example, that would be developed is that of
communicating meanings indigenous to groups living under
various codes of values. One group might think of the struggle
for life as a striving for the "better things." Another individual
or group would conceive of the struggle as "ekeing out of an
existence."

Still another conception of the struggle for life on the part of some individuals might be represented by the statement, "To get ahead is a dog-eat-dog system. You have to outsmart the other fellow." Various characterizations of the struggle would be represented by such status terms as "Big Shot," "In the swim," "Top Dog," "Connections," Fair-haired Boy," and others. Perhaps a more salutary meaning might be conveyed by an individual or group that thinks of the struggle for life as "That effort on the part of individuals to create and expand incentives the pursuit of which will reveal to many the positive excitements which can be realized from living." This, of course, would be challenged by others as they begin to survey the nature of incentives, and under what conditions they are available.

One competence, that of communicating in terms of meanings indigenous to various codes of values, has been indicated. One value, among others, which would have a great chance to be established in a laboratory of learning such as described in the previous pages, would be the recognition that highly useful meanings are the attribute of everyone, regardless of his social class or the environment in which he has formed his values. A corollary to this value is that the answers to one's questions take on new and more effective meanings when sought through communication with all classes. As one conceives of the possibilities of learning in a laboratory such as has been described, it becomes obvious that many other values and competences will be developed.

Mobility in learning demands unified approach to knowledge. We have tried to show how mobility in learning might be developed with secondary school pupils. It will be observed that, whereas we began with a unit in biology, namely, The Struggle for Life, the conditions for learning which were indicated lead into the whole question of behavior, social meanings, and other areas. The scientific facts and principles will have to be pin pointed as the process of learning continues. One would certainly be amiss, however, with regard to the development of meanings, to confine youth to science learnings alone. In other words, in order to bring about the utmost realization of meanings to youth regarding the struggle for life, it is incumbent on the teachers to develop a curriculum which will cause the student to draw from all the contributing disciplines. Thus the student will see relationships and gain a greater degree of unity of understanding in the approach to all learning. The idea of the development of relationships in knowledge and the expansion of meanings is discussed in every chapter. The curriculum worker and teacher will tend to effect a clearer direction for the realization of mobility in learning by providing the conditions for a unified, rather than an atomistic, approach to knowledge.

SELECTED READINGS

Bush, Robert Nelson, *The Teacher-Pupil Relationship*. Englewood Cliffs, N. J.: Prentice-Hall, Inc., 1954, pp. 103-127. A study of teacher-pupil relationships. The section referred to describes the interests and social beliefs of teachers and pupils.

Davis, Allison, "American Status Systems and the Socialization of the Child," from *Personality in Nature, Society, and Culture,* ed. by Clyde Kluckhohn and Henry A. Murray. New York: Alfred A. Knopf, 1949, pp. 459-471.

Havighurst, Robert J. and Bernice L. Neugarten, *Society and Education.* Boston: Allyn & Bacon, Inc., 1957. This book presents an excellent picture of the child, the school, and the teacher in the social structure. Especially recommended is Chapter 2, "Mobility in the Social Structure."

Hollingshead, August B., *Elmtown's Youth.* New York: John Wiley & Sons, Inc., 1949. Deals with the impact of social classes on adolescents.

Horton, Paul B. and Gerald R. Leslie, *The Sociology of Social Problems.* New York: Appleton-Century-Crofts, Inc., 1955, pp. 207-274. A good description and discussion of social class problems.

McGuire, Carson, and George D. White, "Social-Class Influences on Discipline at School," Educational Leadership, Vol. XIV, No. 4, January, 1957, pp. 229-236.

Miel, Alice and Peggy Brogan, *More Than Social Studies.* Englewood Cliffs, N. J.: Prentice-Hall, Inc., 1957, pp. 339-372. Valuable suggestions for promoting the conditions toward democratic social interaction.

Mills, C. Wright, *White Collar.* New York: Oxford University Press, 1953. Discussion about the old and new patterns of the middle class. Especially revealing is the rather complete statement of the work, status, and success pattern of the class.

O'Brien, Robert W., Clarence C. Schrag, and Walter T. Martin, *Readings in General Sociology.* Boston: Houghton Mifflin Co., Second Edition, 1955, pp. 333-359.

Stendler, Celia Burns, "Children of Brasstown," *The Bureau of Research and Services*. Urbana, Illinois: College of Education, University of Illinois, 1949. A study showing the awareness of children of the symbols of social class. A very interesting study about class differences which should furnish many clues in developing conditions for social mobility.

Whyte, William Foote. *Street Corner Society*. Chicago: University of Chicago Press, Second Edition, 1955.

⋄11⋄

Basic Considerations in the Approach
to Intangible Meanings

A CONSIDERABLE PART OF ONE'S LIVING IS TAKEN UP WITH A speculation on intangibles. In the efforts to unravel the intangibles for a degree of meaning, individuals are frequently confronted with frustrations and tensions. This condition becomes all the more acute if the intangibles appear rather abruptly to interfere with the continuum of one's living. For example, an individual may have held the same position for many years and have established rather firm roots in a community. He knows his neighbors, participates with satisfaction in community affairs, and views with intensive concern the shifting fortunes of his friends and neighbors. In other words, as a result of experiences together, there exists a common basis of understanding. Even more important are the habitual experiences of his children with the other children of the community. They go to school together, play together, and are associated with each other in the customary activities of the community. As so often happens in this period of technological change and development, this individual may be transferred to some other position miles away from his familiar surroundings.

SOME INTANGIBLE ELEMENTS OPERATIVE IN
RELATIONSHIPS BETWEEN PEOPLE

As the family is getting ready to move to the new location, many emotionally charged experiences are taking place. All the

activities incident to leaving a home, with its familiar surroundings and memories of happy and significant occasions, produce
a more or less jarring effect on the feelings of the family. The
anticipations regarding the new home, friends, and surroundings are not without their traumatic qualms. The parties, good-
byes, and other final events take their toll of tears. The preparations to move, however, are not without their happy moments.
As the members of the family talk about getting ready for the
new experience, they try to anticipate the excitement in moving into a new or different home. The children think about the
new friends they will meet in entering a different school. They
are looking forward to continuing their relationships with the
members of a new church home. Then, too, the plans and
preparations for moving might have brought to the members
of the family the realization of their need for each other.
Among other pleasurable events is the increased appreciation
of friends and the opportunity to continue the warm effects of
friendship through communication.

As the family arrives at the new location, the members will
again be faced with all types of somewhat novel experiences.
One person will try to compare the qualities of the new home
as against the one he left. Another will notice certain differences
in the present neighborhood as compared to the one in which
they have lived for so long. The children probably enter the
new school with mixed feelings. They may envision it as a
threat and find themselves being cautious about making new
friends. After several days at school, they decide that the change
to a different school was not as difficult as they expected. They
write letters to their friends they left. At times a nostalgic
feeling produces a degree of lonesomeness and sadness.

One could go on and on with this illustration relative to the
impact of changes on feelings. It will be observed that many
intangibles as well as tangibles are operative in the illustration.
The fact that the family had to leave because the father was
transferred to a new or different position is a tangible one to
the older members. It may also be so to the younger members
if carefully explained. It is very difficult if not impossible, however, to understand the feelings of lonesomeness, regret, and

fear at becoming established in a new home a considerable distance away from the present home. These feelings are intangible to a rather high degree. There are so many intangibles involved in all the activities of moving away. The physical move itself is a tangible fact. The feelings of all types which are connected with the experiences of tearing up roots, leaving friends, re-establishing new roots, and sustaining a level of stability contain many intangible elements.

There are, of course, many other intangibles which children encounter every day. Any new experience may carry a degree of intangibility. Intangible feelings are present in the peer relationships of children, in the difficulties with school work, in the relationship with the teacher, in connection with family problems, in unwanted experiences. The feelings accompanying anger, fear, and remorse are fraught with intangibles. The experiences of rejection and acceptance engender feelings which are difficult to understand by the child and the adult.

THE TASK OF THE CURRICULUM WORKER

The curriculum worker is confronted with many tasks in the approach to the development of meanings relative to intangibles. One of the initial tasks is to charge the conditions for curriculum change in such a manner as to elicit reflective questioning on the part of the participants as to the vacuity of understanding regarding intangibles. One approach may be the consideration of various intangible feelings which people have in different situations and the ways in which they attempt to resolve the feelings. Another approach is for teachers to determine to what extent their own activities are thwarted by intangible feelings. For example, teachers may have gone to considerable effort in developing what they considered well-laid plans to produce certain understandings on the part of children. As the plans are carried out, they will encounter many unforeseen difficulties, some of which will be understood and others not. They find themselves "at sea" about certain problems. The changes in children which they envisioned do not occur. This may cause the teachers, and the children, to become discouraged. Frequently, nothing is done to advance toward the sources of discouragement to discover new meanings relative to them.

Providing avenues toward meanings about intangibles

The task of the curriculum worker is to develop the conditions whereby teachers will relate the questions implied above to themselves. How many times have they experienced feelings which they could not understand? What efforts had they made to discover meanings with respect to these feelings? Isn't it true that perhaps a major portion of the activities of people are the efforts to resolve intangible elements? These and other questions would lend at least a partial clue to the task of extracting meanings from intangibles. Teachers need to shift their thinking back and forth, between children and themselves, in developing meaning with respect to intangible questions. Only as they recognize to what extent their personal and group activities are involved with intangible elements, will they begin to understand the difficulties children face in resolving intangible questions.

Evoking meanings children and young people hold about themselves and others. A task which the curriculum worker faces is the development of the conditions which will evoke meanings which children and young people entertain relative to things and ideas. In other words, the curriculum should make provisions for discovering relationships of ideas and their meanings in action. It should establish a variety of avenues for building a degree of sequence to the meanings already held and providing for alternative routes of thinking.

In order to develop meanings with respect to intangibles, it is necessary to discover what meanings children and young people have regarding status, peer relationships, family, friendship, and other phases of social interaction. It is also important to discover how they regard themselves and how others regard them. A revelation of the nature of fears and elements of insecurity in children and young people would lend further clues to the effort on the part of teachers to develop meanings about intangible questions.

Having suggested the importance of the discovery of some meanings and feelings which are entertained by children and young people, a next step is to consider the techniques to be used for this purpose. There are, of course, many tools and techniques which are being employed by teachers in acquiring an understanding of children. Some of these are sociometry, personality tests, anecdotal records, informal interest inventories, personal interviews, and individual diaries. These tools all serve a purpose in giving clues toward developing meanings about intangible elements in a child's feelings. It is important to emphasize however, that they serve only to give clues and not final answers. In fact any answers, at best, will be relative. In the approach with children and young people to an extraction of meanings from intangible elements, it is important that any use of such tools as listed above should be made part and parcel of the whole process of instruction. They should not be used in isolation from the process of learning. An isolated use may be warranted in certain kinds of research, but in the attempt to clarify meanings with respect to intangibles such use would be artificial. Sociograms and other tools should be employed only after the process of analysis of intangible questions is well under way.

In the establishment of conditions for learning to develop meaning about intangible elements, it is important to begin with tangibles because they can be observed and touched and are thus related concretely to the child's activities. The child has some of the most satisfying experiences with things that he can handle and manipulate. Educators are mindful of this fact when they recommend supplying a classroom of young children with blocks, paints, large paper, toys, aquariums, and play apparatus. Frequently pets are brought to school and handled. Excursions are made to see the furnace in the school and children are shown how the fire makes the building warm. Those things that cannot be brought to the classroom are observed in other places. Consequently, field trips are planned and organized so the children can see a grocery store, a train, a tractor, a bulldozer, and other tangible things.

INTRODUCING INTANGIBLE ELEMENTS

The whole succession of activities indicated above is involved in the process of becoming acquainted with the environment. Children are becoming acquainted with those things in the environment that can be seen and touched. If a teacher stops at this point, one could hardly say that he was using tangibles to give meaning to intangibles. The teacher has a deep concern at all times as to what is happening to the children in the process of the many activities with which the children are occupied. The teacher gets many of his clues as to what is happening from the manner in which children engage in play and the comments they make.

Intangible elements revealed as children "play" their conception of things

Some clues as to what is happening may be derived from observations, such as children's conceptions of a bulldozer. This machine is observed as pushing big piles of dirt from one place to another as needed. The machine, however, cannot operate alone. Accordingly, the man who operates the machine is, no doubt, regarded as strong, admirable, and one who helps people. The children go back to the classroom and play at bulldozing —perhaps with a toy bulldozer. One will say to the other, "Jim is a good bulldozer man. See how he handles it!" or "Here, let me show you how the man did it." These and similar play patterns give some simple clues as to what different children regard as good. The child who says, "Jim is a good bulldozer man," may point out certain characteristics about Jim which reveal something about the child's values of good. The teacher takes note of this as well as the appraisals of Jim by other children. This series of appraisals may be followed by a careful consideration together of why the children regard Jim's performance as good. Good, to be sure, has some tangible connotations as revealed by the children's comments and reactions.

The intangible concepts of good, however, began to appear in the second comment noted on a previous page, namely, "Here, let me show you how . . ." The child may really want to show or he may just want a chance with the toy. He may be the class "showoff." No doubt, he will have pals who will go along with him in spite of ineffective performance. These pals admire him and not his performance. They see something strong in him. These observations contain intangible elements which can be capitalized on by the teacher. This same child or another one may be using the bulldozer toy so long that others

will say, "Why doesn't he give us a chance?" Then, when the
teacher says, "Bill, don't you think you better share the bulldozer with others?" he might answer, "Jim used it longer than
I have. He wasn't letting others run it."

Using children's conceptions to approach meanings in intangible questions

This poses a tough problem to the teacher. Evidently, here
good is interpreted by some children as sharing or taking turns.
No doubt, children have been told that they should take turns
so as to give everybody a chance. Why take turns? Why should
people give other people a chance to experience something
which they have experienced? These are intangible questions
for children. Without trying to give answers as to what to do
now, several alternatives might be developed to provide the
conditions for what might be called a higher level of learning
which is concerned with value-building.

In the initiation of the setting to develop meanings with
respect to sharing, many questions would arise in addition to
those mentioned above. Some of these questions might be as
follows: Should you always share with others? Shouldn't you
share just some things? Is one who doesn't share selfish? Should
one share his clothes with others? Is sharing the same as trading
something for a few days? What good does it do you to share
or trade?

Developing the setting for analysis and simple abstractions.
In order to develop meanings with respect to these questions,
it is important to develop situations wherein children might
have the opportunity to arrive at decisions through analytic
thinking. This could be done by setting aside one section of a
bulletin board and providing captions to cover the questions
mentioned above. The captions might read as follows: WHY
SHARE? THESE ARE THE THINGS WE SHARE. WHEN DOES ONE TAKE
TURNS? THESE ARE THE THINGS WE DO NOT SHARE. Boxes could
be placed below the captions to which the children could bring
pictures, ideas, and books to supply meanings. At a stated time,
agreed to by the teacher and children, the contents of each box
would be considered. The time when this is done might be
called THE PERIOD FOR SHARING TO GET IDEAS AND MEANINGS.

During this period and subsequent periods the children will exhibit their resourcefulness with respect to meanings first, by what they bring to relate to the topics, and second, by the thinking which may turn to a new area of inquiry. In other words, this type of setting for learning could provide the impetus to an elementary level of thinking about abstract meanings. For example, it might be brought out that sharing is the same as being kind and generous. It might also be brought out that one can be generous to a fault. Then, if there are some things one should not share, one would have to be selfish. The exhibition or harboring of some types of selfishness, therefore, would be a promising form of behavior. To be selfish in the individual acquisition of knowledge and the development of ideas might make one a valuable member of the class. Certainly, we want to foster that type of attitude which has to do with the individual search for ideas over and above learning tasks undertaken by a group.

Extracting certain tangible meanings from intangible feelings. The thoughts on sharing which could develop in the process of analysis by the children and teacher would open up a new direction of study. One element of this direction would be the practice on the part of children to work as individuals to study ideas and formulate them so well in their minds that, when they communicate them, the sharing conditions will be more pleasant and satisfying than if the ideas had been presented in haphazard fashion. Each child, then, will somehow experience a somewhat greater reward in terms of a heightened sense of satisfaction. Philosophically speaking, the feelings still remain in an intangible state. For the child, however, the feelings reveal tangible meanings. By defining them as better, more exciting, and, perhaps, worthwhile, helpful, and valuable, he is a recipient of real meanings. In other words, although the concept of one process being more worthwhile than another still remains in an intangible state, the fact that the child recognizes a difference in quality between the processes presents to him some tangible meaning.

A continuation of the pattern of approach indicated will, as the child grows older, tend to develop the practice of assessing the relative merits of different ways of realizing one's purposes or goals. The child may also begin to observe that the meanings with regard to such terms as sharing, selfishness, and satisfaction are relative depending on the circumstances. Furthermore, the attitudes which are developed relative to the terms will be in line with tangible meanings.

Returning to the illustration in connection with the bulldozer, two additional intangible elements might be introduced. One is the goal or objective involved with the moving of dirt, and the other is the element connected with the idea of helping people. It will be noted that a tangible concept on the part of the children is that the bulldozer is a machine that moves dirt from one place to another. The fact that this moving of dirt is for a purpose such as preparing to build a house or other structure remains an intangible as far as young children are concerned. That the dirt might be moved to prepare the terrain for the development of a lawn remains an intangible concept in the mind of the child.

It is impossible for small children of kindergarten and early elementary age to grasp the sequence in such a complicated process as building a house or preparing to make a lawn. It is difficult for a child to view a house or lawn and think of a bulldozer as having something particular to do with it.

FURTHERING EXPERIENCES WITH CHILDREN

As the teacher considers the approach to the clarification of intangible meanings, he might draw upon the leads given by children as they relate their concepts about the experience of seeing the bulldozer in operation. He might take the bulldozer situation into a number of different relationships. He and the children may begin the development of a record of the sequence of ideas in the form of an "experience chart." The teacher might initially place on the chart some of the experiences suggested by the children. These would probably be simple and short sentences as statements and questions and, perhaps, a drawing or two. Being alert to opportunities for the promotion of learning experiences, the teacher would probably arrange to have pictures of bulldozers as well as the type of work they do. Depending on the maturity of the children, he would also have some words and sentences attractively displayed on cards, on chalk trays, or pocket charts. These words and sentences, describing the bulldozer and its work, would not be arranged in sequence. The words and sentences would be arranged on the experience chart by the children to fit the situation as they saw it. The teacher would purposely have seen to it that the supply of cards would be limited. He would want to determine at what stage the children were approaching a recognition of concepts which required additional words and, hence, meanings.

Providing stimuli for extended experiences with small children

Some other approaches would be to have available several charts so children could work in small groups, or to bring in the bulldozer operator as a resource person. Still another approach might be through the different kinds of work done by the parents of the children. Different occupations could be portrayed on a large chart or on several small ones.

While the experience chart is being developed by the children, the teacher is especially observant relative to the ideas which they introduce to the situation. As ideas appear which demand additional word and sentence cards, the teacher evaluates with the children the progress being made. Frequent leveling-off periods are helpful in establishing meanings, especially with young children. The teacher might consider with the children what they have done and hint at some of the value-charged ideas indicated on the chart, such as the words and sentences which describe bigness, hard work, growing up, being safe, and caring for what one does. The teacher will write on the chart additional words and sentences as suggested by different children. All in all, there is an extended discussion between the children and teacher of the relationships in the situation. During this time, the teacher is already setting his sights to possibilities for new experiences through the thinking which is taking place.

At this time, it might be well to approach the meanings with respect to the larger objectives of the bulldozer operation. To do this, it would probably be helpful to make another trip or two to the site of the bulldozer operation to see what had happened. Chances are that some other types of operation would now be taking place at the site they originally visited. Perhaps men are preparing the molds to pour cement for the foundation of a house. Perhaps some men are planting grass seed and raking it in. Thus, there develops another sequence in the experience. Now the teacher and children can probably begin to talk about the steps in building a house or the making of a lawn. Gradually, the experiences are taking on sequential and extended relationships. Some intangibles in the minds of children are taking on new meanings. Whereas on the first visit they witnessed the moving of dirt, now they are beginning to see some reasons for the moving of the dirt.

Providing conditions for extended experiences with older children

If experiences of the type indicated should be carried on with older children, say in the nine-to-twelve age group, the matter of how fast the bulldozer moved the dirt might be explored. Furthermore, the question of how long it might have taken people using shovels to do the same thing might be developed. Whereas years ago many men would have had to work hard several days to move the dirt, now one man operating the bulldozer can move it in a very short time. Intangible questions which could be used would be such as the following: What effect has the bulldozer had on the ways of working? What effect has the bulldozer had on technological advances? Has the use of the bulldozer given a different meaning to the occupation of "ditch digger"? How many men would it take to do the job of moving dirt for a project that is now done by one man with a bulldozer?

There would, of course, be other questions relating to man-hours of labor, wages, people being thrown out of work, and the role of the machine in this society. Many aspects relative to the development of meanings about intangible concepts discussed in the previous sections could also be used with older children.

CONSOLIDATING MEANINGS AND VALUES

During the consolidation and talking-up period, several value situations may be pointed up by both the children and teacher. Some of these may be that growing up is necessary for certain kinds of work, that the worker is paid for his work, that he uses the money to care for his family, that workers in a family help each other with the housework, and that there is much work that needs to be done. Other value concepts may relate to finishing a job before another is started, planning how to do work, and helping to lighten tasks as much as possible. Higher value concepts may relate to preparing oneself to do better work, training people to help others, and learning to do more complex jobs as one grows up.

Establishing conditions for examining alternatives toward goals

More intangible value concepts may emerge from a consideration of some of the meanings about happiness. These concepts may come about as a result of a discussion on what types of work the children like to do best. In this connection, the point that people cannot always do what they most like to do will arise. The pursuit of this question with the assistance of charts, pictures, and books may evoke a recognition of satisfactions enroute to the goal. The satisfactions are viewed in terms of the consequences which are involved in the goal of accomplishment. At the beginning of a task, a fruitful discussion and evaluation of alternatives might point up many understandings relative to values. One alternative may be to plan for an extended task. Another will be to plan for tasks which can be completed within an hour or so. Still another might be trying out at a task to see if it could be done within a certain length of time. In connection with these alternatives, innumerable value concepts would be in competition. The merits of each alternative should be fully appraised. In all probability, numerous consequences of failure to complete the task will be examined in thinking. A choice will be made. The fact that the choice is based on consequences envisioned makes the choice one that is highly regarded by the children. This fact, together with the other values which assume the form of real meaning to youngsters, constitute directional learning products. The choices assume meaning by virtue of the high regard placed on them by youngsters and are directional in that the approach to the merit of the choices is through an analysis of the consequences through which the choices are made.

Children develop routes to new and higher level meanings

At this point it is important to caution readers against the conclusion that the teacher is *the* leader in value direction. The teacher is one of the leaders. The leadership resides in the exciting concern by each child for new routes of meaning in the experience with thinking. One route may relate to the problem of growing up before one can do certain tasks. In the pursuit of this question, different children make observations with respect to themselves—changes which have occurred to them as they talk about growing up. Some children are excited about telling what their mothers let them do now that they are growing up. They also talk about what they and their parents do together. Other directions with regard to value concepts are apparent. Some children may tell about how hard their parents have to work and how careful one has to be to do things right. Still others may indicate different kinds of work, such as sweeping the floor and doing one's arithmetic. They are regarding both manual and mental occupations as work. Some are recognizing that thinking is work. Thus the value concepts are being shaped, altered, and again reshaped on a higher level of meaning.

It is clear that the value concepts have taken direction far beyond the bulldozer. Furthermore, what are seemingly intangible experiences in thinking are definitely assuming tangible characteristics in that they are satisfying and productive in the feelings accompanying pride, excitement, and concern.

VIEWING THE CONSEQUENCES OF PLANS

Frequent reference has been made in this chapter and the preceding ones to a study of consequences in connection with learning experiences. Almost every child of school age is able to view the consequences of a contemplated plan or act. The habit of viewing the consequences of an act or a plan gives quality and tangibleness to experiences. It is important, therefore, to provide the conditions wherein children will consider undertakings in terms of the consequences which may be entailed in the tasks.

Environment for planning must provide for many alternatives

In developing the conditions for the study of consequences relative to a plan, choice is necessarily involved. It is essential to provide for alternatives both with respect to the plan and the process of carrying it out. In any classroom the teacher has one definite responsibility to promote learning—to provide for an environment of ideas. He may initiate two or three ideas as a result of a picture, the reading of a story, or an event which has occurred in the community. Following the initial efforts of the teacher, the resourcefulness of the children will expand on the ideas. An illustration which is fitting is one related to how different children play. Depending on the degree of artistic ability the teacher has, he might draw a picture or a figure representing someone at play. He might identify this as a child in the classroom. Following this, some talk may arise with regard to different games or how children play. This will, no doubt, evoke several artistic attempts on the part of children to represent acts of play. Thus the ideas about them are expanded. Soon children will come forward with different ideas about play such as: "Look at Mary—she looks almost like a wheel as she skips rope," "Jane is very good at hopscotch," and "See Jimmy as he dribbles that ball," and so on. The teacher might suggest that it would be a good idea to show how children play in the block where they live. Since children come from many streets and roads, they might want to show "how we play in our neighborhood."

At this point, the children are anxious to get at the job of showing how they play—the different games, the places, the sandlots, the empty blocks, and so on. The question arises, "How is this going to be done?" It is impossible to predict how the children are going to plan their community at play. It is probable that they will venture to suggest many ways to do it. The teacher would be in the midst of the planning, taking note of the alternative proposals. Someone will suggest that all the blackboards be used. Another will suggest that the members of a group living on the same street do theirs first, then another group show their methods of play, and so on. As the different plans are proposed, someone may ask what should be put into the pictures or figures representing play. Questions may arise as to the problems with neighbors—consideration for lawns, shrubbery, and others. Should these be represented in the pictures?

After it has been determined what will go into the drawings, the question arises as to how long this project will take. Some feel that it could be done in one day if some other subject was postponed. Others contend that the project is too extensive to be done in one day. It would make the drawings mean too little to them. Still others feel that enough time should be allowed so that the groups could have time to think about the ideas which should go into the drawings. They want more time for planning.

Another group of children emphasize that the drawings should be planned so that they tell a story. This story could represent safe and unsafe ways of playing, portray consideration for the rights of neighbors, and suggest the use of areas which are free from sidewalks, pedestrians, and travel. Then, too, the story should have in it more than pictures. The suggestion is made to have a large book prepared by the groups which would describe the idea each group of pictures was to represent. One group of youngsters advocates the development of groups of pictures representing different blocks of children at play and which could be used with an opaque projector. Still other children suggest that something important should be done with the mural or story after it is finished. They feel that it might be a good idea to show it to parents and city officials who might use the ideas in exhibiting a need for more places for neighborhood play.

Examination of possible consequences produces new directions in plans

The question of ideas in the story might be seriously considered. The story might deal with a portrayal of "The Story of Our Town," or "A Challenge for Action on Recreation," or "Consideration for the Rights of Parents," or a consideration of the question, "Do All Citizens Do Their Part?" The nature of the choice of topics, of course, would depend on the age level of the children. The story might have all of these titles in the whole book prepared by the children. If all the titles are accepted in the making of the project, there would be many alternatives with regard to each title. For example, in the title "Do All Citizens Do Their Part?" the development would have to go beyond that of recreation. Whereas citizens may be delinquent in contributing to the development of recreation, they might be willing to support an improved school program of recreation. That would possibly be an alternative to be considered in the use of that title. In the title, "Consideration for the Rights of Parents," the matter of consideration for the rights of children would be an alternative.

All the titles would have to be viewed from many alternatives, and the consequences carefully weighed in developing the story. In considering the possibility of including the title, "A Challenge for Action on Recreation," careful study would have to be made as to whether there exists a need for recreation out of proportion to other needs. Then, too, it would be necessary to determine whether the city had a responsibility for the recreation in a block, or whether that responsibility rested with the people in the block. The question which would arise then is: To what extent does the responsibility for the provision for recreation lie with the city and to what extent is it local? There would, of course, be many other alternatives which would be appraised as to consequences in the process of making decisions. The above, however, illustrate the problems which youngsters would face in the development of their project.

THE TEACHER'S ROLE OF LEADERSHIP

The teacher has a wonderful opportunity in connection with the resourcefulness of the children to vitalize ideas, replenish evidences of vacuity, and enrich and elevate the direction of planning and action. He is definitely a member of the group and is at the forefront of the efforts at decision. The teacher exemplifies his leadership by being one who experiences along with the children. His role is that of a liberator for responsibility. He does not have a captive audience. If he did, he would have to keep the children in line with *his* purposes; otherwise there would be bedlam.

Developing compelling conditions for ideas

The teacher should provide the conditions which will have the impact to promote an excitement about ideas on the part of children. Children will then augment the conditions into ever wider ranges of learning experiences. The teacher, of course, stops for leveling-off periods and an evaluation of what has been done and a regrouping for successive tasks. In these periods, efforts are consolidated, new sights are indicated, and new directions are established.

Promoting opportunities for appraisal and testing of consequences in learning. From time to time, the teacher is alert to the "pay-off" observations. Different reactions exhibited by children reveal to him their appraisal of what they have done. Many of these appraisals will be made by children during informal conversation opportunities with the teacher and among themselves. Since the teacher is an accepted member of the group, he will make observations as to the satisfactions and disappointments which will have resulted in the process. Someone will say, "Wasn't that a good idea that Billy suggested?" Another will add, "Yes, it really made our work show up." Still another will say, "I think we tried to do too much with some things," "We had too many cartoons," "We should have read more about the way other children play." Another will counter with, "This is the best thing we ever did," "I think it helped when we stopped and planned out the pictures with the ideas which we had talked about," "We always have tried to do things before we had all the ideas together." The comments are endless, but the ones indicated illustrate the testing of consequences in leading to decision on subsequent plans.

The teacher will also arrange for more or less formal evaluation sessions. At these sessions, there is a reappraisal of the decisions which were made and a re-examination of the consequences for future decisions. The decisions which were made are appraised as to constructiveness and faultiness. They are also appraised in terms of satisfactions and dissatisfactions with respect to goals attained. The satisfactions and dissatisfactions are, in turn, spelled out into descriptive phrases showing resourcefulness in meanings attained.

The important point to remember when developing a plan

in accordance with choice through a study of consequences is that the tendency to action on impulse is removed. The behavior pattern which is being established in the conditions for learning is a search for better answers through experience in thinking. The objective is to develop concern as to how well the goal envisioned has been reached. An impulse carries a high degree of concern about a problem which is faced. Action on the impulse will often have the effect of causing a confused disturbance which because of its gross unpleasantness will be rejected. In other words, the recipient gets to the place where he doesn't want to have anything more to do with it. This is indeed an unfortunate consequence because the result is a loss of the opportunity of recognizing the intelligent, as well as the unintelligent, elements in the impulse. The trouble in this condition is that the impulse wasn't sufficiently examined for the consequences involved.

The teacher has a responsibility to develop the conditions wherein the impulse will be looked at to ascertain the elements of strategy in terms of possible effects on the people toward whom the impulse is directed in action. To illustrate, sudden action for bigger and better opportunities for recreation may fail to take into account what plans and action are already in the making by the good people of the community. Perfunctory planning may turn out to be bursts of enthusiasm which are quickly dissipated. As a result, the learning experience is "thin," the product is baseless, and the ends are losses as far as value concepts are concerned. The best that can be done after such an unfortunate development is to start all over again and adapt the new experiences to choices in view of the study of possible consequences.

It might be said that the appraisal of contemplated action in terms of the consequences which may result is, perhaps, the best assurance of real self-discipline. It behooves the teacher, therefore, to exercise the greatest intelligence and ingenuity in making provision for those conditions which will develop that degree of concern which causes inquiry and thinking on the part of the youngster before action is taken. Under these conditions, there is a high probability that tangible results will be achieved.

Providing tools for implementation of intelligent behavior

The discussion in the previous pages is related to an examination of impulses and plans in view of the consequences which may ensue in connection with action on those impulses and plans. The action as a result of this examination and appraisal is assured of a degree of improvement in the quality of living. The discussion has dealt to a considerable extent with the development of intelligent behavior.

Intelligent behavior cannot be a reality without the necessary tools for its implementation. Youngsters must be able to read, communicate, and write in order to make their experiences more fruitful. The conditions designed to analyze and appraise learning in terms of the consequences must, of necessity, be made more replete with resources than the usual course of study in reading. The readings which youngsters must use in connection with, for example, the topic "The Story of Our Town" have to come from many sources and to be pursued with varying degrees of intensity by the different individuals. Here is, indeed, one of the greatest challenges which the teacher has faced to improve the reading skills of youngsters. In order to examine the consequences of practices with regard to the development of this topic, it is necessary to find out what other towns have related as "Their Stories." The youngsters are intent on producing a good product. As a result, they must rise to the demands for a good product and must therefore examine and understand what other books say about other towns. There exists, then, a real purpose for reading and the children will demand help with the skills of reading. It is assumed, of course, that there has been a degree of mastery of reading skills depending on the ages of the children. It is essential, also, that there be regular developmental reading periods to strengthen reading skills.

In addition to the regular opportunities for the development of skills in reading, there now is presented a real opportunity for the teacher to make an extra special effort to help youngsters refine and strengthen their reading abilities. It is obvious, therefore, that the conditions for learning must be such as will encourage the use of many books of varying degrees of vocabulary difficulty. As a matter of fact, the whole process of planning has included books, pamphlets, visual aids, and other materials in setting the conditions for the story contemplated.

LEARNING EXPERIENCES MUST BE REALIZED IN ACTION

In the illustration presented in the previous pages, one other aspect should be included—that is, the development of decision as to what will be done with the finished product. It is true that this type of decison has been part of the whole process of planning, but there has to be some definite decision on what the work of the children will accomplish. The trouble with too many learning experiences is that they stop short of realistic action. That, in fact, is the case with the major portion of learning carried on in the schools. It stops short of potential realization. The learning remains in an intangible state.

Action needed to produce tangible meanings and realization

This fact dictates that the conditions for the study of consequences be such as will push into the realm of action so that the innumerable feelings of satisfaction and accomplishment inherent in the undertaking will become tangible products. Many alternatives will readily be envisioned and the consequences of these can be carefully considered for decision.

Any one of the topics mentioned in the illustration on the previous pages has meanings for varying degrees of action. Taking the topic "Consideration for the Rights of Parents," some of the action possibilities are as follows: Development of an interview technique which children can use with parents; enlisting the aid of parents in the development of the topic; coming to an agreement on a statement of responsibilities of children and parents regarding home life; and making a survey of cooperative efforts between parents and children. Any one of the above action possibilities when undertaken should have the effect of giving satisfactions as well as providing a feeling of real accomplishment to both parents and children. These possibilities are charged with behavioral content which should generate deep concern for what otherwise might be passed over as ordinary uninteresting tasks. Action with the topic, "Consideration for the Rights of Parents," could clearly lead to such

questions as "Am I doing my part?" "Am I open-minded in
my thinking about the feelings of others?" "What is real
sacrifice?" "Is it a good idea to postpone the fulfillment of my
wishes?" "What are our rights?" "What is meant by respect
for one another?"

These questions would indicate real concern on the part of
children as to consequences and, in all probability, could lead
to much decision and understanding in terms of a higher order
of values. An inference which can be made and which is really
intended in the discussion is that action need not be overt
to be considered action. An act in the process of fulfillment
produces other action such as is indicated above—that is, the
development of a greater sense of understanding with regard
to one's behavior. The action then results in a changed attitude
or a new value. That becomes the product. In other words,
the changed feeling is a tangible satisfaction which operates in
subsequent action. For example, the question of rights may be
introduced by children in their discussion with parents. Rights
initially viewed by children, and demonstrated in thinking and
action, exhibit intangible concepts. As they view the question
of rights with parents, a higher sense of mutual understanding
will be generated. This, then, is truly a high type of realistic
action.

In the previous pages, the discussion with regard to "The
Story of Our Town" and the many related topics has dealt with
the tangibles which are realizable on the basis of consequences
in connection with the tasks of learning. The discussion has
indicated the implementation of the task through the tools of
learning, such as reading. An effort has been made to point
up the importance of the tools in the constructive accomplish-
ments of tasks undertaken. More important, a way has been
indicated to develop the conditions wherein the tools of learning will take on more intensive meaning for children. A further
attempt has been to indicate products of learning and the
promotion of realistic action in connection with the products.
It has also been emphasized that realistic action is accompanied
by behavioral ingredients which are manifested in the strengthening or the generation of new values. It is contended, further,
that action need not be overt but rather is inherent in pro-

ducing constructive feelings of satisfaction in children. The products resulting will in turn become attitude patterns in subsequent action.

This chapter has dealt at length with some of the general considerations and procedures in the approach to meanings about intangibles. An effort has been made to indicate the conditions in the curriculum which initiate the content and process toward an ever-increasing recognition of meanings about phenomena in the environment. The procedures relative to the handling of ideas by teachers and children have been described. Many suggestions have been made about the sequential development in understanding. Provisions in the curriculum for leveling-off periods and consolidation of meanings have been emphasized. It is hoped that the discussion of theory, the description of processes, and the analysis of ideas within various avenues of direction will prove useful to curriculum workers.

◦12◦

The Intangibles of Anger and Fear

MOTHER ASKS JANE TO PUT THE BOOK DOWN AND HELP HER CLEAN house. Jane, in a fit of anger, slams the book down and stomps out of the room. A ten-year-old boy falls off his bicycle. He cries and kicks the bicycle. Bill wants to play first base. The other team members feel that Tom plays that position better. Bill becomes angry and refuses to play. Two adults almost come to blows over an argument. Two little boys have a fight on the playground. The teacher talks to them about it and they tell him they didn't know why they fought. A few days later one of the same boys, in a fit of anger, hits another boy. Again he says, "I don't know why I did it. I guess I lost my temper."

These and other incidents of anger and some of its consequences occur almost every day in one form or another. Frequently, the perpetrators do not exactly understand why they did it. Sometimes they are sorry later over what they did while angry. Somehow they hadn't thought of any other way to resolve a difficulty. Anger, of course, is also used in many other ways. It produces certain effects and is used to fulfill certain purposes.

What is significant about anger is that it is often used as a device without seeking to understand its ingredients. It is clearly an intangible which needs to be carefully regarded by the curriculum worker in developing the conditions for understanding behavior and its processes. An attempt will be made in this chapter to indicate some of the elements of anger which furnish clues to curriculum improvement.

Many incidents could also be indicated about the intangible

308

of fear. Fear is operative in the feelings of people. Sometimes it can be used as a constructive force. At other times it can become devastating in its effects. The intangible of fear will be dealt with later in the chapter.

EXAMINING ANGER AS AN EXPRESSION

Anger is a form of expression. This expression ranges all the way from simple indignation to extreme aggression. Extreme aggression may result in violence. In all the relationships and interaction between people, anger as an expression is present in one form or another. It is often used by demagogues to promote their power over others. It has been used throughout history as a weapon to incite people to action against something or someone, or in the perpetuation of a cause which has some common appeal. On some occasions, anger may be classed as a weapon of righteous indignation to preserve or perpetuate a sound principle. At other times, it may be used as a means to establish some form of questionable power. In its extreme form, it may cause an individual or group to inflict harm or pain on others. In view of the range of potential which anger possesses, it is important that conditions be established which will cause children and adults to examine it critically.

Using experiences of people to appraise anger and its effects

There is perhaps no experience involving people having to deal with each other in which indignation and anger is not expressed by someone at one time or other. It is quite simple, therefore, to draw upon the experiences of adults and children in developing the conditions for a critical appraisal of the cause and effect of anger. An introduction to the study of anger may be called forth by a simple casual question or comment which may be dropped by a child. Such a comment may be "He always gets mad when you work with him," or "Why are my parents angry when I do not hang up my things?" or "Why does someone always have to start a fight?" These comments and questions would in turn evoke many others. The alert and discerning teacher will, of course, supply additional questions and illustrations related to the topic of anger. He will also include in the conditions for the study of anger clippings of news items, articles and advertisements from magazines which point up the issues of conflict in the problems of people. The idea of pointing up issues of conflict is used directionally with respect to the whole question of behavior. Problems of anger are, of course, involved with the whole question of conflicts. People take on different forms of behavior in the attempt to resolve conflict.

ANGER AND CONFLICT RELATED

In order to develop the conditions for learning with respect to the question of anger, it is necessary to introduce the whole question of conflicts which exist in a social group of any type. Anger and indignation are frequently involved in conflict. In order to simplify the questions relative to anger and conflict, it is necessary to indicate the feelings which operate in these elements of behavior. The feelings, of course, are varied and many. They might generally, however, be considered in connection with satisfactions and dissatisfactions. Both feelings are involved in anger and conflicts in different ways, according to the circumstances surrounding a situation.

Assessing the elements of aggravation in conflict

Anger is usually an expression of the feeling of dissatisfaction. An individual or group may harbor deep dissatisfactions with regard to an action or a condition without others being aware of that feeling since it is not expressed. The dynamics, therefore, which potentially exist in the dissatisfactions lie dormant. The dissatisfactions then remain dissatisfactions. This condition has the further effect of inducing a form of unresolved conflict in those who are harboring the dissatisfactions. This, in turn, may induce mental disturbances in the personalities of the individuals. At times these disturbances may reach serious proportions and, in the attempts at their resolution, may come out in an explosive manner with attendant destructive consequences. Retaliation entering in as defense or punishment will create new conflicts and disturbances in individuals. In the effort to resolve the new disturbances, the individuals keep compounding the unresolved conflicts.

All the efforts at resolving the disturbances are directed toward inner satisfaction of the ones who are disturbed. This satisfaction is dangerous in that it is a satiation of a disturbance regardless of the consequences. The forms of expression toward resolution, then, may be misunderstood and viewed as threats to security by those to whom the expression is directed. Thus unresolved conflict continues between two groups of individuals and the intermittent attempts at alleviation of dissatisfaction may, instead, increase it. In other words, the wounds are aggravated with no hope of being healed. Conflict rages apace until the one overcomes the other. Extreme aggression frequently is a factor in this method of approaching conflict. It is a tragic commentary on human relations that the above description of the attempts at a solution of conflict is still characteristic to a large degree of present-day society.

Conditions for the alleviation of aggravation in conflict

An attempt has been made to analyze the efforts of resolving conflict where the attendant conditions are those of aggravation. It is clear that the conditions were such as would use anger as a medium of expression. It was implied, also, that the conditions for expressions of dissatisfaction were relatively absent, thus causing the potentiality which exists in true expressions of feelings to be submerged. Obviously, the conditions which did exist were those of suppression, "leaving well enough alone" and "being satisfied with your lot." For fear that the discussion may be misunderstood, it is emphasized that the reader view the conditions presented in connection with the alleviation of conflicts with a discerning attitude.

Peace is always desirable. Living in the full knowledge of the brotherhood and good will of one's fellow men should be in the forefront of all human motives. In order to promote peace, brotherhood, and good will, however, the environment must be free from the conditions which suppress and deny the expression of the human spirit. The conditions must be such as will invoke expression of indignation relative to a dissatisfaction. The conditions must, at the same time, provide the alternatives of the object toward which the expression of indignation is directed. The consequences of the expression must be clearly portrayed both as to the object and the alternatives.

The alleviation of dissatisfactions may reside in the alternatives. The alternatives may invoke other forms of expression which have the effect of reducing anger and indignation to a thoughtful consideration of the consequences. Residing in the consequences may be those values requisite to a refining and strengthening of that to which the individual gives expression.

Conditions for analysis of anger may alter initial feelings. It might be said that when the conditions for a true analysis of anger are developed, the dissatisfactions for which anger serves as a medium of expression take on meanings different from those initially conceived. This is especially true when the causes of anger are portrayed in the conditions for learning. These portrayals, derived largely from the experiences of children and the observations which they have made, will point up causes which might range all the way from ridiculous origin to those more fundamental. Many of the portrayals will be derived from readings and pictures. Some of the ridiculous causes of anger would grow out of such situations as a boy kicking a bicycle because he fell off it, a rumor about somebody being "mad" at another, and that someone else was chosen for a part that he wanted in a play. Some of the more fundamental causes would be the portrayal of anger at a reckless motorist, the action of a "bully" designed to inflict pain, and the effort of one person to pick a fight with another.

Conditions should provide for intense meanings of behavior to potential users. It is important to point out that the ridiculous causes of anger may be very serious in the effects on the person who displays the anger as well as on those to whom he directs it. It follows that this type of anger cannot be dismissed by the recognition of the ridiculousness of it. A dismissal is, in effect, an encouragement of the negative potential of this state of behavior. A clear-cut effort must be made to provide for those conditions which will present the full impact of this behavior to the ones who are using it as a means of expression. The conditions must lead to a clear portrayal of the consequences inherent in this behavioral expression.

It is significant that the conditions for learning with respect to any form of behavior be established in anticipation of the behavior which people employ in various media of expression.

It is important, therefore, for the teacher to take cognizance of the behavior displayed by people and the observations of behavior indicated by youngsters. The conditions for appraisal may be represented under the caption TYPES OF EXPRESSION EXHIBITED BY PEOPLE TO INDICATE SATISFACTION AND DISSATISFACTION. Under this caption would be presented both those forms of anger coming under the label of ridiculous causes and those forms resulting from fundamental causes. All types of resources would be used: observations of anger displayed in everyday life; all kinds of newspaper clippings representing indignation; magazine articles with forceful portrayals of expression either for or against an issue; commentaries and speeches on the radio and television.

Besides these resources, case studies and situations representing indignation would be developed by teachers and pupils. Various situations would be portrayed through role-playing and dramatic representations. Cartoons depicting forms of anger and indignation might be selected from magazines and newspapers. Youngsters might wish to portray types of behavior in drawings, cartoons, and the writing of playlets. Various forms of music in which the artist expresses anger or indignation might also be used.

All in all, the different elements of expression would help to clarify meanings with regard to feelings held by children in their attempts to react with respect to situations encountered. Thus the intangibles with regard to feelings take on rather tangible meanings, especially in connection with the consequences which are visualized. This would have the effect of inducing reflective thinking which would hold the impulse and accompanying intangible feelings in restraint. This is important since intangible feelings are those that one cannot understand. Consequently, thinking will tend to ameliorate the impulse implicit in the feeling and direct it into a more constructive form of action than would have been the case if action had been immediate. The decision, then, based on a careful appraisal, a clear "look at," and a form of thought-testing of the consequences, will be one in which there emerges a set of values which are either new or refined. Subsequent thought and action will then take off from a more refreshing and enlightened base. The intangibles have become tangible with respect to one's motives and action. In other words, the participating agent has a clearer view of himself—his potential for constructive action.

FEAR AS AN INTANGIBLE ELEMENT OF BEHAVIOR

Fear is for the most part an intangible concept both for children and adults. Of course, when one says that he is afraid the feeling seems very real to him, but when one ponders the whole question of fear as operative in his life, he isn't so sure about its meaning. Fears for some people result from superstitious beliefs held. Other people are beset by fears which arise from real or imagined threats. In children, fears may have developed as a result of early experiences, such as loud and sudden noises. A child may fear a dog because of its loud bark or because of having been bitten by one. Then, too, children may have taken on some of the fears exhibited and fostered by parents and other adults. All these fears are very real to children in terms of their feelings. The impact of the feelings is, however, not actually understood.

Effects of fear on children

Studies on child development have presented fear as a real problem with emphasis on its prevention. The accent of these studies is in the direction of eliminating some of the disturbances which hamper the smooth and harmonious growth of the child. In terms of this discussion, the above hypotheses are wholeheartedly accepted. It is clear from many studies that fears are a real detriment to wholesome development. As a matter of fact, the whole growth process may be seriously affected if fear becomes a controlling factor in behavior. Overcautiousness resulting from fear may seriously endanger inquiry into natural causes and consequences.

Fear may interfere with the development of confidence on the part of the child in his approach to tasks. Sometimes fear limits him even before he gets started. Some children do not try their best, because they are afraid of failure and perhaps ridicule. As a result, their abilities may never be discovered and developed.

School sometimes contributes to fears. The traditional organization of the school has contributed to the perpetuation of fear in children. This organization, borrowed largely from the Prussian system, continues more or less to foster a lock-step arrangement of hurdles which the child is expected to overcome. These hurdles appear in preconceived standards associated with uniformity in quantity and quality of "coverage" and performance, rigid marking systems and report cards, grouping of children as to ability, measuring progress largely by standardized examination, and fragmenting the continuum of progress through the several years on the basis of grade levels. Under this arrangement, the teacher is able to use fear as a motivating force. This form of motivation is the threat of failure to "pass," low marks, and other ways which contribute to child fears. This whole system has taken its toll in engendering and multiplying fears in children. When carried to an extreme by teachers and parents, the system may bring about complete disintegration in a child's personality and emotional stability.

General tasks of curriculum worker. The curriculum worker and other staff members must develop the conditions which will intensely portray the effects of fear. The curriculum task is tremendous in its proportions since it must penetrate the basis of the whole school structure. It is hoped that school people will have the courage to make provisions in the curriculum to transcend confining conditions in the school structure so that children will be freed for responsibility in learning. Furthermore, it is hoped that the conditions for curriculum improvement will be such as promote the impact for needed change in the structure.

RESOLVING FEAR

As indicated before, the thinking and acts of people are very much involved with intangible elements. One may do something over and over without ever giving any thought to the reason for the activity. Dewey, in a discussion on making an act mental, states in part:[1]

[1] John Dewey, *Democracy and Education* (New York: The Macmillan Co., 1916), pp. 35-36.

Repeated responses to recurrent stimuli may fix a habit of acting in a certain way. All of us have many habits of whose import we are quite unaware, since they were formed without our knowing what we were about. Consequently they possess us, rather than we them. They move us; they control us. Unless we become aware of what they accomplish, and pass judgment upon the worth of the result, we do not control them.

It is important that children become aware of the meaning of those feelings which exist in an intangible state, such as an imagined fear. The conditions for learning must embody those factors which will cause them to analyze those feelings which have become habitual and for which they cannot account.

Conditions for resolving should carry factor of acceptance of fear

In dealing with the question of fear, certain factors must be present in the conditions for learning and action. One of the factors which should initially become a definite working element in the conditions for learning is the recognition that it is perfectly natural to be afraid. Children should be given an opportunity to tell about their fears, different objects and phenomena which have made them afraid at various times. They should be encouraged to use drawings, cartoons, socio-drama and other media to represent their fears. Books with stories about being afraid should be made accessible. If anxieties are evident, the conditions should lead the child into looking at them in a relaxed and unashamed manner. As the different representations of fears are observed, one will find that some children are afraid of the dark, some fear animals, some are frightened by loud noises, some are apprehensive about what parents might think about their fears, and others fear the threatening attitude of some children and adults.

As these subjects of children's fears are brought into the conditions in an atmosphere of freedom of expression, there will be an early tendency to face the fears and try to ascertain some degree of meaning about them. Furthermore, since it becomes clear that fears are natural and nothing to be ashamed of, children will be more inclined to seek the aid of the teacher and others in resolving them than if it is regarded as ridiculous and silly for hiding them. The more children talk about their fears in an open manner, the more they will tend to seek meanings about them.

Conditions must promote analysis of fears by learner

Another factor which should be present in the conditions for learnings is a sense of encouragement to analyze one's fears, to try to determine what feelings they give to the child, what anxieties they engender. Here, again, all the children should have the opportunity to portray these feelings by means of drawings, cartoons, sociodrama, and other means. Extreme care should be taken not to pick the child who has an overwhelming fear of some element to play out that fear in a formal role. The role-playing designed to provide clues for the analysis of fear situations should be done either by volunteers or by children who are not especially disturbed by fears. If a child who has a fear of the dark is asked to play a role in such a situation, the fear already held may be accentuated rather than lessened. The important task on the part of the teacher here is to discuss with the children the feelings which have been represented by their drawings, cartoons, and role-playing, bringing out some of the changes which occurred in these feelings. The discussion will reveal, no doubt, that many of the children either have controlled, or are in the process of controlling, their fears. Some of the causes of their fears will also be made apparent by the portrayal of them. The teacher's task becomes one of patient observation of the changes which are taking place in children relative to their fears. In tactful ways, he can help the direction of these changes through counsel with children and conferences with parents.

Conditions must provide for ways of living with fear

Any number of studies have shown that fears are learned. The paramount task, then, of the teacher and others is to redirect the learning toward positive changes in children with respect to their fears. As one approaches the redirection of fears, it is important that the conditions of learning contain another factor and that is the development of ways of living with fear. Fear will always be present in our society. Almost everyone

experiences elements of fear from time to time. Lee speaks of
the positive use of fear by stating:[2]

> Our task is not the elimination but the utilization of fear. Is there
> anything that teachers can do to provide children with immunity
> against the destructive contagion, so that children are moved to
> action rather than paralysis, so they face up to rather than retreat
> from the difficulties?

The curriculum should have provisions for the development
of those conditions which will lead children to exercise discriminative thinking relative to the effects of fear. Let's take,
for example, the fear of loud noises. The conditions for analysis should portray the sources of noises of all types. By this is
not meant that these noises should be created. Rather, the
experiences with loud noises should be recalled in conversation,
discussion, and through other representations such as children's
drawings and facts on bulletin boards. It would be noted that
some of the experiences were unpleasant and others were not.
Furthermore, in recalling the effects of the noises it, no doubt,
would develop that all, or almost all, were relatively harmless.
The point to be made about this whole process is that people
have to live with certain loud noises whether they like it or
not. In the study of this question, however, much progress
could be made by each individual toward evaluating his feelings and establishing some meanings relative to them. In other
words, it is hoped that some steps would be taken by each individual to view his feelings intelligently.

With older children, the whole question of noises could
eventuate in a study of the nature of sound and its effects on
people. Man in the process of his development has created
sound to serve his purposes in communicating and providing
aesthetic experiences such as music. Further study could be
made of the efforts of people to eradicate loud noises. Noise
abatement programs are in effect in many cities and laws have
been passed by many states to prohibit the sale of fireworks
indiscriminately for celebration purposes. At the same time,
fireworks displays are planned by organized groups for public

[2] Irving J. Lee, "On Being Afraid of Being Afraid," *Childhood Education*
(Washington, D. C.: The Association for Childhood Education International,
January, 1952), p. 197.

enjoyment. A study and discussion of these measures will contribute much to the development of meaning about fears and how to live with them.

In viewing the purposes and actions of people, it appears that fear may be at the center of most of the problems with which people are confronted. On the one hand, fear is frequently conceived of as preventing or retarding necessary action. On the other hand, it is important to point up the things which should be feared as people approach various situations. It is accepted that one fears certain acts of people —reckless driving, for example. If, however, one decides that nothing can be done about recklessness, he is escaping from fear. He refuses to live with it and acts as if it didn't exist. As people escape from responsibility relative to fears, they are contributing to the perpetuation of the effects of fear. The impotency occasioned by irresponsibility tends to create a hopeless insecurity on the part of individuals.

Use of fear must be made an object of study. Fear can become a controlling force of one's living unless the use of fear itself is made an object of serious study. In line with this thought, it is important that acts which tend to promote fear become a prominent phase in the setting for learning. In dealing with these acts, one has to resort to a testing of possible consequences which may ensue in their pursuit. The environment for learning must, therefore, be developed by teachers and pupils so as to show the whole field of consequences entailed by practices which develop fear. Out of the consequences may emerge those plans and procedures designed to reduce or eliminate the practices which engender fear.

A statement frequently made by a high school principal at educational meetings attended by the writer was as follows: "What one does is not as important as that one cares." It seems that the thinking in that statement is at the center of the whole problem of learning. Facts are very important, but what one does with those facts reveals whether real concern has developed in connection with the learning of the facts. In order to develop concern about facts with secondary school pupils, one must be sure that the facts are strongly identified with those concerns which have meaning to youth. The facts then must be presented in such a way as will have real impact on the sensitivities of youngsters. In order to do this, the element of fear as a relative factor must be introduced. Fear here has the effect of emotionalizing the meanings brought out by the facts which have accrued in the efforts to create a strong learning environment.

Viewing possible consequences of fear-producing acts may give tangible meanings. In analyzing a practice which is regarded as questionable, fear may be a factor in promoting alternative practices. This has the effect, also, of showing tangible indications with respect to intangible acts. To illustrate, recklessness is an intangible often viewed as being fun or adventure. The one who is reckless is more or less unaware of the possible consequences of the practice. Recklessness may be a means of expressing a form of bravado to establish status with pals. The tangible quality here becomes satisfaction over status. The intangibles are the consequences which may ensue in furthering status. If recklessness, however, is viewed in terms of its consequences, there will be many tangible conceptions which alter the original conception of satisfaction. In fact, the original quality of satisfaction may become one of dissatisfaction. It will become clear that if the original quest, that is, status through recklessness, is pursued, that many dissatisfactions may occur as indicated by the facts. Thus the limitation, dissatisfaction, is beginning to be a factor in the thinking about what is apt to happen under certain conditions. Tangible meanings are becoming apparent. Fear then becomes a logical element in ascertaining the consequences of possible acts.

As has been indicated in the above discussion, fear is an element in emotionalizing meanings brought out by the facts. One fears to take certain measures because of the danger involved. As recklessness was first viewed by the agent, fear was not present as an element. All that was present in the thought was a sensuous form of satisfaction. Fear had to be introduced through a careful gathering of facts and an intensive analysis of the facts through graphic and dramatic portrayal of them. Then and then only did the full impact of contemplated acts become visible to the agent.

Curriculum must promote competences to
remove cause of fear

As indicated before, individuals may become so overwhelmed with fear that they escape from any attempt at approaching its causes. This often happens when organized forces are at work in a community to "leave well enough alone" or to stifle action because of the money cost involved. This happens also where law enforcement becomes lax due to vested interests of individuals who have "connections" with unscrupulous enforcement bodies. The curriculum worker must enlist the many resources which can be instrumental in approaching the meanings of fear and its effects. The curriculum must provide the conditions wherein young people may gain an understanding of the power which can be wielded by elements in our society that capitalize on the fears in people. The environment of learning must be charged with those stimuli which will promote competences designed to remove the causes of fear. Strange as it may seem, here is a paradox which operates in the interest of the community—that is, fear is employed as a means of removing the causes of fear.

The discussion in this chapter relative to the intangible elements of anger and fear is not nearly exhaustive of the meanings associated with these topics. It is hoped, however, that the curriculum worker and teacher may find many of the ideas useful in the development of learning experiences with children and young people. It is felt that within these intangibles reside the dynamics for the promotion of greater realization and action on the part of people. The curriculum must have the ingredients for the release of the dynamics.

·13·

Clarifying Intangibles
with High School Youth

NO DOUBT, MANY ADULTS ARE IMPRESSED, AS THE WRITER IS, WITH the questions which high school pupils raise from time to time concerning purpose, behavior, conformity, and other intangible concepts. The questions are probably raised most often in a setting away from the preoccupation with the activities and subject matter of the school. In this setting, young people tend to feel release from preconceived patterns of approach to meanings.

At times the questions are raised in the classroom in connection with various areas of study. This happens especially in those situations where the curriculum provides for real latitude in the approach to ideas. This condition tends to develop through the efforts of those curriculum workers and teachers who view learning as ideas which go beyond the bonds of any compartments or confined subject areas.

CONFUSED RELATIONSHIPS AS TO SOCIAL ROLES

Some of the questions which high school pupils ask and the comments they make relate to their role in society. Some young people are concerned about how and where they fit in; others about what contributions they should make. Frequently, young people ponder the matter of their behavior and its relationship to that of others. Some of their thinking is implied by the question, Why is my behavior not acceptable when others do the same thing? The question of conformity and non-

322

conformity becomes a matter of great concern to many young-sters. They might be in a quandary over the question of how to reconcile their biological drives with the standards established by parents, church, school, and other institutions and agencies. They experience the impact of contradictions and surprises relative to the behavior of people around them. They view with considerable concern and apprehension the lofty verbalizations relative to constructive behavior and the exhibition of weakness when put to the test. The picture which they carry of a healthy society becomes somewhat blurred in its perspective as they read about and witness glaring violations in "high" as well as "low" places. Young people find themselves foiled in the attempt to preserve a wholesome equilibrium in the compartmentalized value system with which they have to live. The dilemma into which they are thrust by the necessity of the many contradictory roles they have to play may have devastating effects on their values.

Young people begin to think about the meaning of success. They wonder if success has come to be considered as getting ahead regardless of how it is done. They view with no small concern such statements as "People who are educated are in the higher income brackets," "If you work hard you will get ahead," "There is plenty of room at the top." They recognize, too, with considerable apprehension, that for the most part the thinking in these statements is based on material possessions. Some youth ponder the sense of dedication with which these statements are offered as against a spiritual truth embodied in the words MAN CANNOT LIVE BY BREAD ALONE.

Difficulties in establishing a balance in peer relationships

Young people find themselves disturbed from time to time over the compelling force of peer relations. They become so wrapped up in group thinking and action that they lose all awareness of themselves as individuals. They appear to be caught and carried along in the swirl of group activities. Their whole sense of values seems to be absorbed in creating roles which will conform to group expectations. The domination of the group has been so effective as to cause the individual to lose sight of any potential that he might have capitalized for self-direction. As this process goes on, the individual discovers that he has difficulty in standing alone on any problem or issue. Furthermore, when he is away from his crowd, he doesn't know what to do with himself. Parents, too, become confused over the whole question of peer relationships. They cannot see why their son or daughter never wants to do things by themselves or within the family. Perhaps the parents, too, have their groups and cliques and are unaware of themselves as individuals. The whole question resolves itself into a confused process of relationships with the power and impact of peer groups. Parents are disturbed because their teenagers never want to be alone. Teenagers are disturbed because their parents are disturbed. Furthermore, the disturbance of the teenagers is accentuated by the injustice of the parents' attitude in view of their identical behavior with their adult peers. Both youth and parents must examine values.

Curriculum must help youth unravel anxiety as to purposes. The many questions which young people are asking and the many problems which give them much concern are fraught with intangible elements. The anxiety which is prevalent in the minds of the young people as a result of these questions is very real and tangible. However, the unraveling of the components of this anxious state necessitates the development of conditions for the extraction of meaning with respect to the intangible elements involved. The curriculum must be designed to unravel the components of anxiety so that youth may establish a sense of balance and direction with respect to their purposes. Henry, in a discussion of the foundations of general education, gives a clue to the conditions which may make some provision for clarifying the intangibles with which youth are confronted. He states:[1]

> General education adds a new dimension to liberal education by attempting to see to it that the very process of education itself does not impair the self; to see to it that in liberating youth from provincialism we do not uproot youth from a sense of community; that in releasing them from superstitions and pointing out the false assumptions built into them over the years, we do not leave youth

[1] George H. Henry, "Foundations of General Education in the High School," *What Shall the Schools Teach?* (Washinngton, D. C.: Association for Supervision and Curriculum Development, 1956 Yearbook), pp. 164-165.

with nothing to believe; that in having youth understand the separate parts of an object, a movement, a culture, a body of knowledge,
we do not rob them of the fuller meaning of it.

Youth may lose their identification when absorbed in their
peer relationships. With their intense involvement with the
peer group, they come to regard themselves somewhat less than
what they really are as individuals. As the curriculum provides
the conditions for individuals to look appraisingly at the compulsiveness of their peer relationships, it is expected that some
sense of release will be effected. With this release should come
a degree of recognition on the part of individuals as to their
potential and resourcefulness apart from the peer group. The
curriculum must make provisions for this to take place in such
a manner as not to effect a reasonable relationship with peers.
Peer relationships serve to fulfill an important need of youth
for companionship. The curriculum must provide further conditions which have to do with the responsible application of
the potential and resource powers of the individuals. If this
provision is lacking, a form of open rebellion may accompany
the sense of release from peer control. Thus the self may be
impaired by the very process intended to produce a greater
degree of self-awareness.

*Curriculum must help establish meanings about controls
in society*

The curriculum worker might approach the task of identification of individual powers on the part of youth by portraying
the various types of control by which people live. One of these
types is peer compulsiveness. Another is custom, which
may be related to peer relations. Another type is parental
control. Society exercises many controls through the various
conventions which have grown up. In the portrayal of controls,
the limitations imposed on the individual are discussed and
studied. The picture about controls which is represented exhibits those elements which provide positive direction to individuals and those which thwart the development of individual
powers. In connection with the portrayal of controls, many
readings are made available so that youth might gain greater
insight about the thinking underlying man's behavior with

respect to controls and freedom from some of their damaging effects. Meanings will gradually become apparent to youth, regarding intangibles, as generalizations such as the following are analyzed and studied:

Permitting a group to do one's thinking is an abdication of responsibility and self-regard.

The peer relationships become valuable when they influence constructive imagination and individual initiative.

When freedom is conceived as "doing what one pleases," the freedom of others is severely limited.

To give vent to unbridled impulses is to extol ignorance as a virtue.

Whether to conform or not to conform must be decided on the basis of carefully considered principles of behavior.

An intelligent approach to whether or not one should act on an impulse or idea is the experience through thinking of the possible consequences which may ensue.

Blind conformity to the code of one's peers closes the door to creativity.

Extreme submerging of thought to the dominant influences of a group may cause a sense of loss in self-regard.

A loss of self-regard produces an impoverished learning environment.

The above list of generalizations is by no means exhaustive. It would be added to by both the students and teacher as the reading and study proceeded.

Curriculum must bring disciplines and other resources to bear on meanings for youth. It is necessary to emphasize again that all those engaged in the process of curriculum development need to give careful attention to the clues which structure the conditions for learning toward the examination and appraisal of the questions which youth are asking. The curriculum must also provide the direction toward an intensive penetration of the historical, sociological, biological, psychological, and philosophical resources with respect to the questions. Let us take, for example, the question of role expectations of individuals in different situations. Suppose somebody suggests that one should say exactly what he thinks in every situation in which he is involved. This suggestion would be in line with the principle of consistency of behavior. In history, however, would be found some clues as to the behavior of individuals or groups which defy this principle. Much of history is a record of diplomatic and undiplomatic behavior with respect to the roles that different individuals pursued on vital questions. Diplomacy has frequently been evaluated on the basis of timeliness and prudence in statements that were made.

Sociology would contribute much to an understanding of the question of role expectations. Relative to the suggestion of overt expression of one's thinking, sociology might provide a resourceful note of caution. The sociologist would consider the role expectations of the group, and suggest that an individual who initially indicated a different role might jeopardize his effectiveness with the group. The biologist would certainly fulfill an important function in contributing to a knowledge of role expectations. An understanding of the nature of the nervous system and how organisms respond to stimuli would help materially in the analysis of roles.

Psychology would give some very important clues as to overt expression of thinking. The psychologist might suggest that saying what one thinks at certain times might be viewed as a threat by another person. Statements which are made in connection with a situation should tend to maintain the equilibrium of individuals. On the other hand, the psychologist would maintain that at times it is important for individuals to divest themselves of what is bothering them. This might call for the individual's freeing himself of certain inhibitions by stating what he thinks. The philosopher would view the statements in terms of a pursuit of truth. He might contend that in certain situations it is more important to hold a thought in abeyance so as to free the conditions toward the evolvement of ideas. Perhaps it is better to compromise on an idea so that more influence might be exerted in the development of a higher principle of truth later.

Curriculum must stimulate ideas about roles of people. We have given only a few excerpts of how the disciplines might contribute to an understanding of the roles which people must play in their daily association with others. The curriculum must develop the conditions whereby the learning environment is charged with questions which create a compulsive pursuit for ideas about the roles of people. A center of interest might be established in the school for the purpose of developing competences needed in the fulfillment of the various roles which people perform in their relationships with others. The questions and issues which would be developed in this center would be such as to establish meanings relative to roles which are performed in different compartments of values and those which retain a degree of consistency in those compartments. At times, the center of interest on roles would become a laboratory in which different roles might be tested for consistency. For example, one might play the role of "peacemaker' or "harmonizer" consistently in various situations and then have the effects appraised. Another role which might be examined for consistency is that associated with the maxim, "Honesty is the best policy." The enacting of the above and other roles would give rise to some interesting and valuable meanings to youth about intangible situations operative in their society.

THE SCHOOL MUST ENCOURAGE INTELLIGENT ACTION ON YOUTH'S PROBLEMS

Much of the criticism directed at education is that the school today has a tendency to try to deal with too many social problems, spreading itself all over the place, and not studying intensively any one problem. Along with this line of criticism is the charge that the school, in trying to venture into so many problems, loses sight of some major responsibilities—those of developing literacy, good habits of study with respect to subject matter, and competency in oral and written communication. Another phase of the criticism leveled at schools is that they are trying to change people and the world by means of the classroom. In other words, it is pointed out that schools try to take over the role which belongs rightfully to the home, church, and other agencies. The criticism is partly justified, but for the most part it is not based on facts. In the first place, most high schools are devoting the major and, in some cases, almost all attention to the so-called solids—English, Latin, mathematics, and a science such as chemistry, and history. Very few high schools have directed their efforts toward clarifying the intangibles of behavior involved in social problems of youth.

High schools which are approaching an intensive study of a problem such as indicated in the foregoing discussion on questions of youth are relatively few in number. Could it be that the blanket criticism which demands that schools attend to their job of instilling "basic fundamentals" has engendered such fear in school people over the years that the real problems facing youth have been put aside? It is always good to have criticism if it is based on an intelligent examination of all elements of a situation. Then criticism will tend to point up fear of consequences to be avoided. On the other hand, if a critic lumps the panacea for all ills as the mastery of the regular high school subjects to the exclusion of any attempts by the school to do something intensive with regard to youth and community problems, he evades the issue. He also impugns the motives of the school as a responsible community agency devoted to the development of good citizens. What is needed is more criticism calling attention to community needs and the inadequate efforts of certain schools in doing their part in acting on the needs. Citizens should act to encourage teachers and youth to develop clear-cut approaches to deal with the crucial problems of the community.

Learning conditions must relate subject areas
to people and behavior

In the development of understanding of behavior, it is necessary to provide the conditions which will help teachers to see their subjects in relation to the culture which they are perpetuating and improving. It is necessary that they view critically questions such as the following: Is history a story of the past which might be viewed as a *fait accompli,* or is it a living story which shows the growing skills and understandings which have accrued to men in their action on situations and events? Is history a series and sequence of events or is it an ever-enlarging conception of man's insight into his behavior in relation to his fellow men? Isn't it important to clarify in terms of man's present-day behavior what he has learned from the past? In the history of political institutions, isn't it just as important to depict time-lines of positive as negative acts of men in their efforts to perpetuate the qualities of democracy to relate to the chronology of events? What have the great thinkers contributed to an understanding of the cause and effect of the behavior of people?

Teachers must pursue ideas about social reality. To attempt to develop concern with respect to these questions requires not only great teaching, but that the teacher renew and redouble his efforts to gain greater insight and understanding of present-day society and the people who live in that society. What is implied in the questions presented above relative to history is implied equally in questions which the teacher must ask himself about his subjects of Latin, biology, literature, mathematics, and others. All of these subjects, to a considerable degree, deal with man's behavior in his environment, his action in that environment in terms of his behavior, and the nature of his thinking when his behavior is at odds with the environment. The subjects all deal with those resources which are available and those which man must devise in order to raise his stature as well as that of his fellow men in the pursuit of truth and happiness. The subjects are open-ended, that is, they provide avenues of release for the human being to seek to understand himself in relation to the forces which are operating on him.

Learning conditions must engender compelling need for pursuit of ideas. In view of the discussion about behavior and its elements, it is important that all subjects be related to the development of an understanding of the ways in which people can work together to improve their environment for the good of all. It is important that the points of identification of the individual with his environment be sufficiently and intensively portrayed in the conditions for learning to engender a compelling need in the learner to act intelligently on them. With reference to the discussion in the preceding sections relative to the questions youth are asking, it is essential that they establish some goals in resolving them. There is danger, however, that when they approach a fulfillment of those goals that they will regard the task as completed. They might view it as the completion of a requirement even if they had a big part in establishing the requirement. It is proposed, therefore, that the incentives for learning proceeding from the questions evolving from the various areas of study be expanded into an ongoing and intensive pursuit of ideas about the whole problem of behavior of people.

Learning conditions should provide unifying approach to understandings. In the previous discussion it was suggested that the questions of youth could be approached in several ways. One way was to utilize the various disciplines in seeking answers to the questions. This would be done through treating the content of the several subjects in such a manner as to point up its relationship with the roles performed by people. Another way would be the development of a center of interest or laboratory for the study of the roles of people in their relationships with others. This method could also be used to develop meanings about questions of youth other than those pertaining to role expectations.

Still another way in which the whole question of behavior of people could be approached is by unifying the resources of the various subjects into areas such as Communications, Social Relationships, and Behavioral Sciences. One aspect of communications would be the development of such skills as reading effectively and discriminately, speaking with ease and fluency, writing with some degree of clarity and power, and listening both effectively and appreciatively. Another aspect of the area of communications would be the provision for an intensive portrayal of discourse in terms of roles of people in their relationships with others.

To illustrate, a person may be quite disturbed about a proposal made by some individual. The proposal, together with the various statements, which could be made by the disturbed person, are indicated on a bulletin board or brought out in discussion. A question which might develop is: What type of statement might be most effective in having the proposal altered? In considering that question, the teacher and students are considering what type of statement might represent the role which the disturbed person could pursue for the best results. In the analysis of the inconsistency of roles with respect to beliefs and values, an effective type of communication might be the raising of questions such as the following: Could it be that in our effort to be agreeable we frequently say things that we don't believe? Why is it so difficult in some groups to say what you think? What might we do in our group to get more members to express their opinions? Shouldn't we give just as much attention to what an individual who is speaking is not saying? What are some of the ways in which writers and speakers communicate by inference? Why is it that if *A* and *B* are present in a group, you always know what *B* is going to say after *A* has spoken? Why is it that in a meeting any number of people who at the beginning will not say anything will come forth with all kinds of statements after two or three individuals have spoken? Is it true that few people actually have courage to say what they believe is right? What is our responsibility in promoting individual thinking relative to questions which involve our values?

As one views these questions, he might be somewhat overwhelmed in thinking about the resources which should be provided in the process of seeking answers. One faces the task of making available reading materials from the various subject areas. Literature of all types must be perused by youth to approach a sense of understanding relative to the tangibles involved in the questions. Related to the questions, for example, is a statement by the philosopher, Whitehead, regarding the cleavage between youth and their elders. He says:[2]

> I think it came from their parents having lost their own belief but going on insisting on the dead formulae of conduct in order to keep their children "good," when they no longer believed in these formulae themselves. The children eventually found it out, deceived their parents in turn, and it resulted in deceit all round. . . . Their children, in those years between eighteen and twenty-four, when one is experiencing for the first time vital necessities, emotional and physical, were left in total ignorance of the social consequences of certain types of conduct.

These are samples of resources which might be used. Other resources would be drawn from studies in history, economics, sociology, and any number of fields. Great thinking, both by

[2] *Dialogues of Alfred North Whitehead,* as recorded by Lucien Price (New York: Mentor Books, 1954), pp. 59-60.

present writers and lecturers and those of the past, would be used to pursue answers relative to the questions.

ESTABLISHING CONDITIONS OF RELEASE TOWARD "SINCERE" PURSUIT OF IDEAS

It is necessary to expand on the above discussion to clarify the role which school subjects should serve in relation to individuals who are particularly involved. The curriculum must be designed and developed in such a manner as to show the relationship of subjects to people. What other purpose is there for a subject than to function with the individual to clarify his roles in effective living? Certainly, his performance should transcend a static sense of sufficiency with subject matter mastery. The individual should have the opportunity to relate himself to subject matter in such a way as will establish routes to new meanings. Furthermore, in his relationship in the instructional setting he should be put in the position of discerning his roles with other individuals. Other individuals then, in a sense, become subject matter.

Behavior resulting from distorted concepts of knowledge[3]

Too frequently the main effect of so-called mastery of a subject has been to set the individual apart from others, to give him certain satisfactions, and to regard the verbal knowledge of subject matter as a terminal objective. Little thought has been given to the idea that the subject is a means to greater effectiveness in promoting service and understanding on the part of individuals and groups of individuals. On the contrary, those who have mastered the subject matter often tend to flout this brand of erudition in an egocentric manner. In other words, the attitude is exhibited somewhat as follows: "I am good, I have been told I am good, my marks prove it, so why shouldn't I make the most of it?" Humility as a factor is absent. The exhibition is one which may be characterized as pedantry.

The exhibitor of this conception of knowledge has either equated verbalization with ideas or is ignorant as to the true

---

[3] The writer had originally planned not to include the discourse which follows. However, after discussing it with some college students who had recently graduated from high school, he was constrained to include it in the manuscript.

nature of ideas. In other words, he "knows the subject" but has few ideas.

To the one who has been oriented to this confined concept of knowledge, learning is considered something apart from one's daily activities and relationships with people. He unwittingly operates under the philosophy that what *is* doesn't matter and that events just happen. The relationships between people and the trend of happenings in local, national, and world affairs are treated in a detached manner from learning or knowledge. The process of learning is one of exclusiveness of reality. Meaning remains in a very intangible state.

Instructional practices bolster false conceptions about knowledge. It is disturbing that the above type of behavior relative to knowledge is still respected and admired. It is reflected in the instructional practices in many classrooms. These practices bolster the false values which are associated with the equating of learning with "knowing the subject." The "knowing" of the subject is frequently conceived of as that which is in the textbook and the responses to examination questions developed largely from the book. If the performance of the student to examination questions is consistently high, he is considered as one who "knows" the subject. The questionable value being established here is that good memorization on the part of the student to respond effectively to the examination questions is considered knowledge. This is hardly a valid criterion in determining whether one is possessing knowledge.

The greatest calamity which might occur in connection with the above practices is the building of false values in young people as to what constitutes knowledge. As youth observe the narrow preconceived patterns in which learning is pursued, they begin to regard knowledge as a sort of "package" which they will receive if they conform to the patterns. Knowledge becomes a kind of "veneer" or "façade." This "coating" is developed through the process of "parroting" the sequence of the book and the instructor and perhaps a few other sources. The youth remains ignorant as to what is behind the "coating." He is interested only in making sure that he gets it. To him it has been demonstrated that possession of the "coating" pays off.

Those who do not attain this position will tend to cower

under the impact and regard the "exposition" either with awe, disgust, or resignation. Since no other doors are open, the hopes and aspirations of so many are dashed to the ground. The channels to discovery and realization of potential are closed. This condition is indeed representative of a fatalistic design in educational direction.

Tasks of curriculum worker in promoting "sincere" pursuit of ideas

The conditions indicated pose weighty problems for the curriculum worker. It is his responsibility to bring about the conditions which will provide a sense of release on the part of teachers to seek out many routes to ideas. As was described in Chapter 1, the curriculum worker must become a learner with teachers in the handling of ideas together. They must together ascertain what constitute limiting factors in the conditions for learning and how these may be eliminated.

Parallel conditions to those indicated above should be developed in the classrooms with young people. Teachers and young people must handle and test ideas to find tangible meanings.

The conditions must carry that sense of release which will elicit a compulsiveness on the part of youth toward the analysis of facts for relationship and meanings.

The curriculum worker must help teachers clothe the subject with a new dignity. Instead of regarding it as a narrow pattern of sequential development, it will be used as a springboard to an ever-widening range of learning experiences. Instead of using the subject to confine the thinking of students to its content, it will provide a release toward higher levels of inquiry. To illustrate, instead of giving students an examination based on the subject, the teacher might find it a much better practice to suggest for an examination that the students spend an hour or two developing questions to which they would like to find answers. This practice would not only point up what the students had learned, but would also show their attitude toward inquiry and how thoughtful they had been in their efforts to discover real meanings and understandings. The practice would also give the teacher some new clues to the conditions needed for more extensive learning relative to the subject.

SELECTED READINGS FOR CHAPTERS 11, 12, AND 13

Anderson, Marian, *My Lord, What a Morning*. New York: Viking Press, 1956. An autobigraphy by Marian Anderson which tells much about her learning process under rather difficult conditions. Very valuable in an approach to depth of understanding with young people.

Association for Supervision and Curriculum Development, *Creating a Good Environment for Learning*, 1954 Yearbook. Washington, D. C.: National Education Association, pp. 150-200. Valuable account of teachers' and administrators' relationships and responsibilities in developing conditions which will help children gain meanings about various factors surrounding them.

————, *Growing Up in an Anxious Age*, 1952 Yearbook. Washington, D. C.: National Education Association. Deals with the tensions and stresses of the present age.

Cunningham, Ruth, and Associates, *Understanding Group Behavior of Boys and Girls*. New York: Bureau of Publications, Teachers College, Columbia University, 1951. Provides innumerable leads to teachers in helping boys and girls with an approach to intangible meanings with respect to behavior.

Dewey, John, *Experience and Education*. New York: The Macmillan Co., 1956, pp. 53-86. Meanings about freedom and purpose which should help guide the thinking of teachers in working with intangible questions.

Fromm, Erich, *The Art of Loving*. New York: Harper & Bros., 1956. Author attempts to demonstrate, through the concepts of distinguished individuals, the principles of unity in diversity and permanence in change. This resource should help the teacher and curriculum worker approach some meanings about intangible concepts.

Lane, Howard, and Mary Beauchamp, *Human Relations in Teaching*. Englewood Cliffs, N. J.: Prentice-Hall, Inc., 1955, pp. 165-201, 247-266, 280-297. These sections are helpful in teaching for the clarification of roles in group living.

Miel, Alice and Peggy Brogan, *More Than Social Studies*. Englewood Cliffs, N. J.: Prentice-Hall, Inc., 1957, pp. 300-339. Valuable helps in building socially useful meanings with children.

Sargent, William, *Battle for the Mind*. Garden City, N. Y.: Doubleday & Co., Inc., 1957. A rather striking analysis of the different approaches to mind control.

Stanley, William O., *Education and Social Integration*. New York: Bureau of Publications, Teachers College, Columbia University, 1953. Furnishes some guiding principles to educators in approaching a degree of clarity and direction in the confusion and conflict of our times. Chapters 1-6 inclusive and 11 and 12 are especially valuable.

◦14◦

How Communication Develops
Social Understanding

IN THE APPROACH TO AN UNDERSTANDING OF THE FACTORS IN-
volved in effective communication, it is necessary to look at
the function of language in the conveying of ideas. Language
is a medium of communication. The use of language, however,
does not always mean that communication has taken place.
Words and sentences may have been spoken. Whether an idea
has gotten across to the intended recipient of the words and
sentences is another matter. In other words, has meaning been
conveyed? If the recipient reacted to these words and sentences
with understanding, communication had taken place. If he did
not react in any manner, the conveyance of words and sentences
had about the same effect as if they had been spoken to a recep-
tacle. Unless care is taken, children in a sense become "recep-
tacles" of words and sentences. Teaching sometimes assumes a
"pouring in" process. True communication is a much broader
term than language. It is concerned with the human interrelatedness of meanings.

Language, to become a conveyor of ideas and meanings, must
not be at or even to a person but must be interpersonal. It
becomes communication when it operates with feeling which
touches a chord of commonality. Communication must carry
with it more than words. A twist of the eyebrow, a facial expression, a gesture with the hands may be a form of communication. Furthermore, a person is usually able to detect by the
appearance of faces in the audience whether communication is

taking place. Almost everyone has had the embarrassing experience of launching out at a group with what he considered
were some well-thought-out words, to be met by a stony silence
when he had concluded. Obviously, he had not succeeded in
communicating. His efforts for the most part were nothing more
than a fruitless audition. Communication takes place only
when that which is communicated is related to the experiences
of those to whom the communication has been directed.

The structuring for effective communication will have to be
such as will give an opportunity for the meanings which children bring to school to function in a natural setting. In the
process of working together, the effects of various forms of communication could be examined and evaluated for improvement
of the media of the communicants. The structuring might well
be built around concepts which have the quality of universality.
Such concepts would be those related to the terms, nice, good,
caring, neighbor, growing, creativity, musical aspects of a culture, and others. In an atmosphere of this type much social
understanding and action would result from the potential inherent in differences in the patterns of values held by participants.

COMMUNICATION FOR CONSTRUCTIVE SOCIAL UNDERSTANDING

In the effort to provide a better working base for a dynamic
approach to the problems of people, it is necessary for curriculum people to work constantly to improve the conditions for
constructive social understanding. The curriculum must provide for the conditions which will develop learning relative to
the following questions: What are the qualities which must be
studied and observed with respect to language so that individuals and groups may become more resourceful in communication for social understanding? How must people communicate
in order to understand each other? One of the factors which has
to do with the development of quality in communication is
that related to the indigenous characteristics of language of cultural and socio-economic groups in a neighborhood or community. Another factor is that of language in relation to social
mobility and status. Still another and very important factor

with regard to communication is the relation of language to different occupations. Extremely important in communication is the factor of identification with the problems of people. Then, also, there is the language of youth—forms of codified expressions sometimes developed by youth groups to serve their particular purposes. Youth, in their attempts to break away from conventions as well as to resolve some of their problems, go through a period of inventing expressions of their own.

Indigenous qualities of language to promote communication

Indigenous qualities of language represented by national origin of individuals or groups must be considered in the development of communication patterns. The belief, however, that national origin alone gives the communication of a group its indigenous quality may be faulty. The indigenous characteristics may, in some cases, be a result of racial or religious discrimination and, in others, social stratification. The indigenous characteristics may be accentuated by the isolation of a group. The group may have settled or banded together for protection from the impact of established or misunderstood class levels. The members of the group may be reacting to the conception which goes with being on the "other side of the tracks." It is necessary, therefore, in order to communicate effectively with groups, to go behind what appears to the observer as the indigenous qualities and discover how people in those groups communicate meanings to one another.

One should be mindful of the limitations imposed on understanding by thinking of people in terms of groups. The thinking which automatically associates this and that individual with a pattern of behavior as representative of a certain group is a dangerous form of stereotyping. Also, thinking of an individual's behavior as being representative of a group is a stereotyped form of thinking which acts as a closure to the route of social understanding. Everyone, of course, draws from the resources of a group in the process of formulation of ideas. However, either the group as a whole, or individuals within the group, have values and attitudes which are common to other groups. When one labors under the stereotyped conception that an individual typifies a group, he thereby refuses to accept the principle that each individual has personal worth and potential.

The school cannot labor in confined boundaries typified by preconceived standards of learning, but must extend itself to all individuals and groups to gain real insight into the interrelationships of cultures. It must see the operative values in those cultures—what holds meaning for the people in those cultures. The meanings, of course, which are real to the people in particular groups or neighborhoods are reflected in the school by the children who come from those areas or segments of population. Then, in order to communicate with those children, a single standard of communication cannot be thrust upon them. A single standard would have many elements outside of their realm of values and would thus carry no real meaning for them. It is important, then, that the communicative patterns of these children provide for a comparatively free field of operation in the learning experiences planned with children. The conditions for learning must carry a wide range of meanings within which identification is possible for every child.

In diversity of meaning lies potential strength. A springboard for communicative operation is the acceptance of the principle that in diversity of meanings lies potential strength. The operation will proceed with experiences based on that principle. The problem can be put in another way. When one thinks of language in connection with meanings as indigenous to a group, he must think of meanings as indigenous to him and his group as against the other groups. Then there is no standard form of meanings as all are indigenous to each even as individuals. By virtue of application of this principle to thinking, the indigenous aspect is really removed and common understandings emerge with respect to the values which hold meaning to the groups and individuals who are working together. The indigenous aspect of one group or individual is understood by the other groups and individuals and, consequently, the base for communication has been effected.

As each group and individual becomes conversant with meanings conceived by other groups and individuals, the channels of communication for effective social understanding are extended. The fact, then, that others are different will not be a deterrent to action with understanding. The fact that each group or individual has ties to a certain group does not confine his area of understanding or operation to that group. To put it more strongly, the members of a group will fail in responsibility for greater effectiveness in understanding by confining their communication to the group locale.

Communication in local bounds must produce interconnections with broader area. In the broad conception of human relationships, communication in the local area is a training ground for intercommunication with other and broader areas. How people communicate with their immediate neighbors and friends is a true index as to how they will communicate with the nation and world.

Localization often degenerates into a type of "smugness" indicated by such statements as "Let's mind our own business and let them work out their own problems," or "They are just different so we better leave them alone." This type of thinking is a resignation to a form of divisive philosophy that thrives on the thought that an individual cannot work with people who do not believe as he does. Those persons who advocate this philosophy believe that a development of understanding with other groups is an encroachment on their domain. The philosophy of human relations respects the rights of all individuals and groups to work out their problems. The same philosophy, however, recognizes that a loss to real progress occurs when the approach to problems by one group is not communicated to other groups. Again it is emphasized that in difference lies strength when resolved into constructive social understanding and action. Too much sameness in beliefs is a deterrent to resourcefulness because no new values are evolved.

Language often a vehicle of social mobility

Language is often conceived of as a vehicle of social mobility. This conception has considerable connection with the whole problem of stratification in society. Every so often one hears the remark, "He is a good fellow but he does butcher the English language," indicating a value which relates goodness to good English. What is not recognized in this conception is that this "good fellow" must really be communicating himself as otherwise he wouldn't be called "good." This remark is just another way of saying, "Too bad, he is a good fellow but he doesn't really belong with us."

The language of social mobility, unfortunately, is frequently conceived of as something apart from effective communication. It operates in a vacuum with no real relation to feelings, but rather in terms of status or class. This concept does not accept the principle that each one has worth as a person. On the contrary, this concept operates on the questionable practice of using one's language characteristics as a basis for acceptance or rejection.

Conception of a "hierarchy" of use restricts language as communicative art. Language too frequently has been divorced by a "language hierarchy" from the art of communication among men. This "hierarchy" has created an ivory tower of language facility, a place high in the clouds of bombust, where participants seem constrained to deport themselves in the patterned demeanor of an inner circle of communication. Consequently, language has been held apart from the pattern of communication of the "rank and file." It has been divested of the true service that it should render as a communicative art to be used by all people. In view of such a conception of language, its use as a resource of real strength in promoting social action and understanding becomes negligible. To say the least, the fraternity of English in our own country haunts countless children, youth, and adults as an ogre of awesome design. It should not be so and, thanks to those who have conceived of language as a universal instrument of communication, it is becoming a medium for the promotion of understanding.

Language is learned and experienced. Gradually, more and more people are becoming aware of the fact that language is learned and experienced, not inherited. This awareness is making communication an instrument of human relations in which the participants emerge more effective communicants. This awareness has also brought about the realization that language becomes a communicative art relative to the meanings which are of daily concern to people in their environment. Now people can learn to be more effective in the use of language by talking about prices, conservation, the city water system, the playgrounds, Billy's pets, Mary's illness, father's job, and other items which are of real concern to them.

In an atmosphere where communication really functions in every situation, the "language of the street" will have as important a spot for social understanding as the language of the "coming out" party. To be sure, action with regard to common problems will result more effectively if the stage is set for communication between the two groups. Consequently, the teachers should come to realize that perhaps their greatest responsibility in reconciling the factor of social mobility with respect to language is the development of communicative conditions for cooperative insight into mutual problems. The structuring which leads to these conditions must encompass the working relationships of teachers and adults in the community as well as those of the children.

Interrelationships of language, occupations, and the culture

The factor of communication with regard to the language related to different occupations can be very rewarding to social understanding. Teachers should more and more become conversant with the relationships between the work which people do and the nature of society and the culture. A study of this relationship would have a tendency to cause teachers to become more analytic in their approach to the understanding of how values are bound up with the occupations of people. A study of the formation of values in terms of occupations of people would also give teachers a greater sense of realism as to the make-up of a culture—its origin, growth, changes, and meaning in the destiny of man. When a culture is laid bare for examination, its elements become specified. A very important specification is the work which people do. Man's beliefs, hopes, aspirations —in fact, the whole constellation of specific patterns of values —are largely shaped by what he does. The greater part of his living is devoted to the pursuit of purposes to improve his livelihood and that of his family.

In his efforts to carry on the operations of making a living, man has daily contact with others. He discusses his purposes, plans, successes, failures, and hopes with his friends and neighbors. He finds that he cannot live alone. Not only does he find it necessary to communicate and plan with others for greater realization of goods and services, but also for the satisfaction it is giving him. In other words, feelings develop which are stronger than just a mechanistic design of transaction involved in cold occupational relationships. The feelings are varied and many. An individual may be concerned about his neighbor's success, the efforts at price manipulation by a group, or the buying capacity of customers in the face of unemployment. Then, too, he may be interested in hours and wages, his relationship to his employees, the beautification of the city, the opportunities for his and the neighbor's children for wholesome recreation, and other factors which go to make up his community.

The matter of people's occupations becomes a whole system of interrelationships with others. Interest and concern is expanded to what other people are doing and what success they are having. A person who believes in improving his community will be concerned with the success and prosperity of people in other occupations. He will cooperate to bring about the success and prosperity of all because that will set the stage for growth, opportunity, and a fuller life for him as well as others. Thus his values are being built and rebuilt on the basis of new outlooks and understandings.

Teacher must gain understanding of workaday world. The teacher has a great stake in the interactions of people engaged in various occupations because the values and meanings of those interactions are being reflected by the children in their thinking and doing. The living of children is bound up with the occupations of their parents and other adults. The teacher must be a sympathetic and understanding cooperator in the feelings which children hold relative to the workaday world. He cannot fulfill this important role unless he can communicate with the workaday world. The experiences which children plan with the teacher are anchored largely with the occupations of the community. The teacher is constantly a learner along with the children in studying, analyzing, and developing designs for improvement in this culture.

Providing conditions for communication with occupational

and professional groups. Communication too frequently takes place within professional and occupational categories—that is, the farmer talks with other farmers, the merchant gathers for conversation with other merchants, insurance people talk together, teachers go around only with other teachers, and so on. In view of the categorical communication situations, a structuring for intercommunication would need to be developed around several conditions. In the first place, opportunities for common gathering places for the evolvement of new thoughts and ideas must be provided. The gatherings must be focused on a common interest which not only relates occupational interests but evolves common issues and problems. For example, people in all walks of life are interested in the welfare of their children, so the school or classroom could be a common gathering place not only to discuss problems related to their children but also to consider the interwoven problems of the community.

Various groups could meet in the local areas of a city or town and work on problems related to all the people. In this manner, people would become more conversant with the various value patterns of their culture and the type of behavior inherent in those patterns. People will begin to work on the questions of where they are, where they wish to go, and how they can get there. The same process should take place with children—in fact, their experiences should be interrelated with the total scheme of communication.

The teacher must identify with the problems of the people

The profession of teaching makes it incumbent on the teacher to constantly practice the skills involved in effective communicative processes so as to become a dynamic agent in the promotion of social understanding among groups of people. This, of course, calls for much initial social engineering in the creation of the setting which will cause social action. It is essential, therefore, that the teacher identify himself with people engaged in various occupations and professions so as more fully to understand the problems involved in these occupations and professions.

True identification develops from a sense of need for greater resourcefulness. Too often identification takes place on an artificial level. In other words, the person feels that he has to do something because it is being done and is considered good practice. This is the sort of identification which goes with wanting to be a "good fellow" and a "good mixer" and is usually characterized as "fitting in." The motives involved in the artificial type of identification are usually associated with a desire for status.

A teacher may try to identify himself with the community because he feels that the administration wants it or that it is what he thinks is being done. This sort of practice is worse than no identification at all because it fails to interrelate or bring about true intercommunication. True identification takes place only when the one who identifies has sensed a real need for human resources to help bring about action designed to promote better understanding. He thus improves the quality of living. True identification is not approached from a crusading angle nor is it conceived from the standpoint of status satisfaction. It really follows from a sense of release in a cooperative process toward an objective. The purposes have been arrived at together with others and the planning is directed toward the fulfillment of the purposes. In this process, the isolated conception of occupation and profession becomes transformed into a more comprehensive conception of people working together toward common goals. The status structure between occupations is, thus, minimized.

Identification takes place with people rather than with what they do. There develops a respect for personality, an acceptance of people for themselves. Thus people and what they do becomes a unity. The identification with children proceeds in the same manner. The teacher becomes identified with the values which children bring to school through the learning experiences which are carried on together. The values are largely tied up with the work of parents and neighbors. The learning experiences are planned with children in such a way that understanding will develop toward effecting, among other things, respect for all work and a modification of values in view of felt needs. Thus real intercommunication takes place on the basis of understanding and needs.

Language of youth

In the matter of communication for social understanding, it is important to recognize the language of youth. Insight into the forms of communication of youth in informal situations is essential in influencing understanding and constructive action with them. An extreme form of communication of youth is the language of "gangs." This language is a type of expression developed in connection with a code of revolution against conventions. In order to understand the code and its inception it is necessary, of course, to go behind the scene of gang patterns to find the causative elements of "ganging." An opening to the importance of developing communicative channels with gangs is suggested by some points expressed by Gist and Halbert relative to the cause of gangs:[1]

> Ganging is a natural process. Whether the activities of a gang are perverse or constructive depends upon the character of the habitat of the gang—upon the culture patterns predominating in the region and upon the sequences of situations that arise in the natural history of the gang. The gang is a form of adjustment that boys, and even girls, make whenever their family or neighborhood do not satisfy their major wishes in a conventional way.

Sociological literature gives abundant evidence that spontaneous group formations such as gangs or cliques, far from being isolated or rare phenomena, occur quite generally. As a matter of fact, they occur in one form or another wherever individuals experience various sorts of deprivation or lack of a stable social identity. As a result, the individuals develop a form of social identity among themselves as an effort to meet their needs for intercommunication. The problem for the teacher here again becomes one of identification with the needs of the youngsters.

True identification cannot be effected without developing and strengthening the channels of communication with the groups. This must be done by structuring the working atmosphere in such a manner that the youngsters will feel safe to communicate their problems and feelings. A good illustration

[1] Noel P. Gist and L. A. Halbert, *Urban Society*, 2nd ed. (New York: Thomas Y. Crowell Co., 1941), p. 212.

of this was observed by the author in a school situation several years ago. A group of boys and girls in a sixth grade drifted into some gang operations which had their inception from the study of history, hero stories, and movies. The ringleader of the gang was a boy who felt that there was discrimination against him.

After a few days of operation, the teacher called the members of the gang together and sought to determine the reason for this type of behavior. After several attempts on the part of the teacher to evoke some response, the leader, with a satisfied ego, described a rather highly organized system of operations against another group in the classroom. He told about the meeting places of the members, their territory of activity, and how the attacks against the other group would take place. Upon being questioned how girls were used in the gang, the leader replied, "They were used to carry messages." It developed that a complete system of communication by code had been worked out.

The teacher was at first rather dumbfounded with the problem. He planned at once, however, to do something about it. Rather than stop the operators of the gang, he worked on another type of approach. He planned with the children to study and do research on the communication services of many organizations. Resource people were brought in to help with the study. The teacher and the children studied signal systems of Indians, people of the deserts, and people of the jungles of Africa. They studied about communication and intelligence services of the armed forces. They read and discussed mystery stories. On the basis of this study and research, the teacher and the children planned a code which they could use in communicating in the classroom about their work. Before the children arrived at school each morning, the teacher would place on the board some "mystery language" which had something to do with the plans for the day. The children would spend some time decoding this "language." To say the least, this was a novel form of opening exercise.

As this project continued, many experiences in communication developed. One of these consisted of writing about things in regard to which children held strong feelings. Many of these writings were kept confidential for guidance purposes; others, which dwelt on topics of general concern, were considered as editorials and were included in a newspaper which was developed as a result of this gang experience.

This was an excellent approach by a teacher to identify himself with the problems of children and to help them do something about them. It might be well to note in passing, that the leader of this gang experience later became editor of the official student newspaper of a prominent university while he was a student there.

THE LANGUAGE OF FEELING

True communication for understanding has a language and that is the language of feeling. That feeling plays a most important part in communication is indicated by excerpts of remarks by parents in their evaluation of a "parent and teacher night" conducted in connection with a workshop at the University of Connecticut. The excerpts of remarks follow:

"It was a very friendly group. I enjoyed the friendly atmosphere. It was more friendly than I expected. I did not feel that it was necessary to have refreshments."

"The meeting was very worthwhile. I liked the discussion groups. Miss Tracey's group was especially valuable because we were all grouped together. We benefited by the comments of all."

"We did not feel a part of the whole group and felt that we were missing some important contributions in other groups about us."

"I was pleased that the meeting was concerned with curriculum rather than P.T.A. services as so many meetings are."

"It was a wonderful interrelationship between parents and teachers. Everything was very informal and all the participants seemed so much at ease."

"From the parents' point of view it would seem that the meeting was an excellent starting point or meeting ground. They had a chance to get the feeling that they were an essential part of the school at the very outset."

"I was very sorry that we couldn't keep our group discussion going longer. We didn't have nearly time enough. All contributed very well. The program was very valuable and should be continued every two weeks."

"It was a wonderful experience. If it could only continue indefinitely!"

"The evening's experience proved to be a wonderful setting for communication. Almost every remark by the parents emphasized a satisfaction over the fine feeling which prevailed in the groups."

There is no intention to create the impression that communication for understanding is based solely on emotional considerations. It is necessary, however, to state the fact that feeling and thinking are closely related. Frank, in a discussion on the education of the emotions, expresses the relationship quite clearly:[2]

> An educational program designed to foil the demagogic dictator leaders would be a program of emotional education that would, by provoking repeated emotional reactions in controlled situations of adequate provocation, create a gradually rising threshold of susceptibility to these destructive leaders, just as training of soldiers, firemen, policemen, nurses, and others dealing with emotion-arousing situations are trained to act in definite patterns that inhibit or reduce the emotional response. Emotional susceptibility is greatest when the emotion is denied, repressed, or evoked by an experience for which there has been no preparation. Acknowledgment of the emotion, acceptance of the excitement, and the pressure of impulse to action, and training in handling the situation effectively, as the fireman or soldier, eliminates the emotion or reduces it so that it merely reinforces the learned pattern of action.

Learning to cause one's feelings to reinforce a pattern of action stems from the opportunity to communicate feelings. The teacher must first of all examine his own feelings to understand to what extent they have been repressed and denied, and to what extent they have been evoked by unwanted experiences. The curriculum worker should bring about the conditions where children will have the opportunity to use feelings in positive experiences. The feelings, then, will be used to serve a pattern of intelligent action.

PEOPLE MUST DETERMINE THE COMMUNICATION IN A DEMOCRACY

One of the attributes of a democracy is that the people determine their way of life. This attribute remains in the verbalistic stage unless implemented with ways and means toward its

---

[2] Lawrence K. Frank, *Society as the Patient* (New Brunswick: Rutgers University Press, 1948), p. 317.

realization. This implementation must be supplied by all the people. It requires thought, effort, insight, and the learning of new skills of understanding. This means that people, first of all, must develop the communication facilities which will cause interaction in thinking, feeling, and effort toward evolving the issues concerned with their needs. Secondly, they must build the machinery which will be used to facilitate the action in resolving the issues which have been evolved. In the third place, people must constantly evaluate the machinery of communication which has grown up over the years to determine its effectiveness in reflecting the values held by people.

In the approach to a discussion of the agencies or machinery of communication, it is important to consider two observations. One, the common conception held with regard to the news paper, radio and television is that they are agencies which are beyond the reach of the average citizen. Two, the communication policies of these agencies are wholly determined by the owners, directors and program sponsors. Both observations are, of course, partly true. Unfortunately, in too many cases the observations could be almost totally true. The important issue with regard to these communication agencies is to what extent the people exercise a voice in determining the quality of the communicative material transmitted. In a democracy, the people evolve the manner of solution of their problems. Since communication is a medium of interaction to promote common understanding with regard to problems, the people must determine what that communication shall be.

Important communication develops casually

It is difficult for people to conceive that communication of thought which becomes public opinion has its origin in the most simple and casual sources. Perhaps the most important type of communication is that which takes place casually among people in informal situations such as "street corners" or at parties. It is remarkable as to how quickly casual conversation spreads. The reason for the spread is that in situations of this type people really reveal their innermost thoughts. They are not on guard. As a matter of fact, they are sometimes too much off guard, which may cause serious consequences. Sometimes people are misunderstood and, as a result, are misquoted. The misunderstanding which does develop in these instances may be due to a lack of perceptiveness as to the trend of the conversation on the part of some member who was present. In other words, communication had not been established with all the parties involved.

Setting the informal stage for the development of public opinion. There are clearly several guideposts which must be observed in setting the conversational stage for the development of public opinion. One of these is an effort to know the people with whom one is conversing—and that is more than acquaintanceship. It is a type of knowing which comes from the art of putting people at ease so that they will become ebullient with interests and ideas.

Another guidepost is the practice of a form of behavior which seeks to discover the bases of interaction of people. One way to do this is to project an idea for consideration. The process, however, may become impaired when the one who projects the idea or the one who opposes it may do it so dogmatically that the base of interaction is threatened or destroyed for the time being. When people feel themselves threatened, involvement will be lacking. The process, to be effective, must rather proceed on the basis of discovering self through others. In order to cope with a situation or to bring out the thinking on a problem, the approach must be toward finding out what meaning the situation or problem holds to those who are involved. This has the effect of bringing out the facts, which will go far toward the evolvement of a common idea.

Rumor becomes a factor in evolving communication. It was indicated above that misquotings arise out of a situation where the conversational conditions for communication have not been clearly established with some of the members present. The fact that one has been misquoted may not be harmful unless the misquotation is magnified into a rumor. Rumor proceeds easily in loosely contained groups. Closely knit groups which operate in a sense of trust and seriousness can easily "spike" a rumor in the evolvement of the facts. As a matter of fact, groups of this type can be far more effective in setting in motion the machinery of communication of factual evidence than ever so many individuals denying, affirming, and arguing alone.

Communicative groups have their beginnings in almost every place where people gather to pass the time in amiable conversation. In the rural areas these are the Saturday evening shopping crowds, in urban areas they are the groups in the luncheon clubs, the hotel lobbies, the scout committees, and others. This is where opinion may be evolved to influence not only local action but also policy formation on a regional or national level. In fact, steps to the promotion of international policy can very well have their beginning on a local level.

Up to this point, the local level of opinion evolvement has been stressed. This may be derived from informal "pass the time of day" groups or semi-organized groups such as luncheon clubs, forums, P.T.A.'s, or discussion groups. In many communities, there are attempts to combine the "spots" of thinking into a workable mass so as to give a basis for patterns of action. The community coordinating council is one type of organization which tries to do this. It attempts to organize the thinking into a body of opinion which reflects the desires of the people in a community. Each person has the opportunity, then, to observe his contribution to the whole. The group then is in a better position to give weight to its influence in further communication to the proper agencies to initiate action toward the fulfillment of its purposes.

Involvement of everyone most important in opinion formation

The necessity of involvement of everyone in the process of opinion formation cannot be overemphasized. In a democratic society there is no exact over-all structure for the development of opinion relative to the problems of the people. This is a condition which is in accord with the nature of democratic institutions. There are, of course, organized bodies all over the country, many of which in a sense are designed to develop opinion in behalf of the problems of people. Most organizations, however, have special objectives and interests which may not reflect the thinking of the people as a whole. Many of these organized groups, through various types of pressure tactics, may try to make their special objectives appear as representative of the people. This would have the effect of making the "trees" seem more important than the "forest." At various times, these efforts have been quite successful in influencing the thinking of people.

The potential of latent thinking must be channeled into opinion formation. At most, this condition carries only a limited involvement of people both in terms of numbers and degrees of feelings. In the absence of a communicative thread to gauge latent thinking, government could become a rule of the minority. Latent thinking is inaudible. Yet, it has great potential for action. The discovery of feelings is important in this latent area. How do people really feel about what is happening? What would they do if they only felt they could do it?

The fact that these questions so frequently cannot be answered by various groups was revealed rather clearly by an illustration of what happened in a midwestern city. In this city of forty thousand people, an important Board of Education election was coming up. Every P.T.A., every luncheon club, and the central bodies of labor had pledged themselves in favor of the incumbents who were up for re-election. On the day of election, however, the incumbents were overwhelmingly defeated. Everybody seemed amazed at what had happened. The fact was obvious that these groups had not reflected the thinking of the majority of the people. What became even more obvious was that the lines of communication had not penetrated into the thinking of those who made the real decision.

Communicative machinery should provide for inclusiveness of thinking. A very good example of failure to gauge the thinking of people was the election of Harry Truman as President of the United States in 1948. An overwhelming majority of the newspapers and practically all the public opinion polls had all but conceded the election to Thomas Dewey before election day. Somehow, the latent thinking had not been gauged. The inadequacy of the communications process had been brought into sharp focus.

No doubt, much has been learned from this by those who operate the communicative machinery. An inference which might be made from the above example is that communicative processes are often confined to established operation centers and few attempts have been made to open new centers. Much valuable opinion and thinking is communicated only among the members that "understand." It is a sort of guarded "top secret" that does not find its ways into newspapers, the air waves, and other more or less formal accepted media of transmission. From time to time, communicative media should be examined for inclusiveness of the thinking patterns of people. In order to approach a state of involvement of everyone in opinion formation, it is important for the communicative media to tap those centers of thinking which operate in channels outside of the accepted ones.

It is interesting to observe the relationships of communication to the structure of a social system. Gardner shows the effect of status, prestige, and the "rung of the ladder" or the "room at the top" concepts on communication in his discussion of the factory as a social system.[3] He speaks of the processes of communication vertically in the structure. The following describes some significant phases of the processes:

> Because of the nature of the man-boss relationships this movement up and down presents certain problems. In many cases concern over what the boss wants leads to over-reaction to his commands, or to misinterpretations of unimportant comments or requests. The big boss inquires about maintenance costs. The subordinate wonders if he thinks they are too high and the shop finds there is a sudden clamping down on all maintenance work.
>
> This same concern also affects upward communication. The subordinate is always trying to anticipate what the boss wants to know. He is reluctant to pass up unpleasant news and quick to pass up good news. He is prone to gloss over and put a favorable slant on bad news or to find an alibi for what may look like his failures. He is constantly alert to his superior's moods, watching for the favorable time to present some request or to put forward some new idea.
>
> Thus in the line we find a channel of communication that works by fits and starts, which is apt to modify or distort what passes through, and what may constitute a complete blockage. And, as a result, we find that the man at the top is apt to be quite well insulated from the bottom so that he has only a partial and highly

[3] Burleigh B. Gardner, "The Factory as a Social System," *Industry and Society*. William Foote White, ed. (New York: McGraw-Hill Book Co., Inc., 1946), pp. 13-14.

interpreted picture of what goes on. And, at the same time, the ones
below are aware of this insulation and feel helpless to break through.

Gardner's description of the problems inherent in this vertical system of communication which, incidentally, is not peculiar
to the factory, reveals an important fact which has been implied
from time to time in previous discussions—that is, only the
thinking which is considered safe will be communicated. In
order to conform to the status structure and the conditions of
stratification, the operator in the system feels constrained to
communicate in terms of the value pattern inherent in that
structure. The real thinking will be held in reserve as far as
this particular system is concerned but will find its way gradually into the communicative network of another "crowd."
This ultimately results in cleavage patterns which apply pressure tactics for change. Thus there arises the labor-management
strife which has characterized an important chapter in industrial development. The important task of the educator is to
study the background and operation of the processes of human
relations so that new insight and understanding will be developed in a foundational approach to the intercommunicative
process. This means that the communicative machinery must
be converted into a system of interaction wherein the true feelings of people will be openly displayed and appraised by the
people themselves.

Much has been said regarding communicative machinery in
general and the various directions communication can take.
The discussion has dwelt on the specific organs of communication, such as newspapers, magazines, radio, and television.
These organs are, perhaps, more effective than any other device
as instruments of education. Much of what has been communicated through these media is constructive; some might be
seriously questioned.

In any event, these organs of communication must be considered as having the greatest implications for social understanding and action. Certainly, they must reflect the thinking of the
people to a high degree since they have become such powerful
vehicles in the molding of opinion. Yet, how powerful and effective have they really been in causing action on the problems in

a democracy? Certainly, as effective as the people have caused them to be.

THE TASKS OF THE CURRICULUM WORKER

The foremost task of the curriculum worker in promoting communication for social understanding is, of course, the development of conditions wherein learning experiences relative to many of the various items discussed take place. Many of these have been implied, especially in the first half of the chapter. Thus it is important that the content and process of the curriculum should be carefully examined for the communicative approach to the indigenous characteristics of people, the relation of language to social mobility, the communication of occupational and professional groups, the identification with the problems of people, and so on.

In the approach to effectiveness in communication for social understanding, ideas relating to the following questions should be handled with teachers, children, and young people:

What are the various characteristics indigenous to groups which are reflected in children?

How are forms of expression related to values?

In the approach to communication in terms of the indigenous qualities of people, what are the conditions which bring about a consonance in direction as between diversity and commonality?

What are the conditions which will promote identification with the language and meanings of occupational and professional groups? How may literature in high school classes be utilized in developing insight relative to the communicative operations of these groups?

Since in a democracy there are no regularly established channels for the evolvement of opinion, how is the thinking of the people ascertained?

How can the base for communication toward opinion evolvement be broadened?

What are the conditions that need to be developed in schools to channel the latent, "undercover," "top-secret," and other more or less unobtrusive thinking of students into idea evolvement?

What are some of the factors involved in the development of inclusiveness of thinking in schools?

What type of laboratory conditions might be established to test the effects of various aspects of communication?

These and many other questions might be handled in such a manner as will promote dynamic conditions for the development of competences in communication for constructive social understanding. The conditions for the handling of ideas with teachers and children should provide for the use of all the media of communication as regular resources in the learning environment. Television, newspapers, recordings, magazines, reports and other materials should be used as resources not only to contribute ideas to units of learning but also to develop competences for the critical appraisal of the resources.

All types of ideas and roles associated with communication should be experienced and tested. Motives of people and organizations should be critically appraised. A center of interest might be developed to experience the motives of different editorial writers and various commentators. Opportunities should be provided for children and young people to editorialize on ideas about which they have strong feelings.

These ideas are not nearly exhaustive. Perhaps the most important task of the curriculum worker is to help establish the conditions which will promote an excitement about new dimensions of inquiry regarding the whole field of communication. Under stimulating conditions, questions far in advance of any indicated would probably be examined.

SELECTED READINGS

Anderson, Howard R., *Approaches to an Understanding of World Affairs.* Twenty-Fifth Yearbook of the National Council for The Social Studies. Washington, D. C.: National Education Association, 1954. A most useful guide to the study of world tensions, ways of living in the modern world, and approaches to teaching for an understanding of world affairs.

Anderson, Vernon E., *Principles and Procedures of Curriculum Improvement.* New York: The Ronald Press Co., 1956, pp. 39-67. Useful suggestions on the development of group process skills in curriculum study.

Benne, Kenneth D. and Bozidar Muntyan, *Human Relations in Curriculum Change.* New York: The Dryden Press, 1951, pp. 66-294. Ideas by many authorities on the use of groups and group methods in promoting curriculum change.

Brogan, Peggy and Lorene K. Fox, *Helping Children Learn*. Yonkers-on-Hudson, New York: World Book Co., Chapter 2. Deals with the meaning of language; also how language skills are learned.

Frank, Lawrence K., *Society as the Patient*. New Brunswick, N. J.: Rutgers University Press, 1948.

Gardner, Burleigh B., "The Factory as a Social System," *Industry and Society*. Edited by William Foote Whyte. New York: McGraw-Hill Book Co., 1946. Shows the operation of different communication systems in various organizations.

Lane, Howard and Mary Beauchamp, *Human Relations in Teaching*. Englewood Cliffs, N. J.: Prentice-Hall, Inc., 1955. Section I, pp. 3-58. Significant helps in teaching for social understanding.

Language, Meaning and Maturity. Edited by S. I. Hayakawa. New York: Harper & Bros.

Lee, Irving J., "Why Discussions Go Astray." Interesting statement on the points of breakdown in group discussions.

Roethlisberger, F. R., "Barriers to Communication between Men," pp. 61-66. Gives some valuable clues to resolving the question of how communication is possible when people do not see the same things and share the same values.

Rogers, Carl R., "Communication: Its Blocking and Its Facilitation," pp. 53-60. A paper on the use of psychotherapy in facilitating communication.

·15·

Establishing Conditions
for High Level Thinking

COMMUNICATION IS ALWAYS INVOLVED IN VARYING DEGREES WITH both the process and content of thinking. Man is by nature gregarious because he has the facility to communicate. In some of the discussion in other parts of this book, reference has been made to conversation as being satisfying to people. As suggested, communication may range all the way from "small talk" to rather intensive discussions on crucial problems. In the latter type of communication, individuals and groups gain the greatest satisfaction out of "getting somewhere" evolving decision. Important elements in this form of communication are discovery of new ideas, reconstruction of thoughts into a new direction, and an appraisal of what has been discovered or reconstructed.

DEVELOPING CONDITIONS FOR HIGHER LEVELS
OF THINKING

There is need for great responsibility on the part of curriculum workers to affect the conditions for the discovery, reconstruction, and appraisal of ideas which reach beyond the usual patterns of thinking. In order to facilitate movement and direction toward a higher level of thinking, it is extremely important that the communicants operate in a sense of release relative to rigid beliefs and values. Beliefs and values must serve as guides to action in thinking. They must liberate and stimulate the mind to enter into the many ideas which have occupied the thinking of men.

Perhaps even more important is the establishment of conditions which will not only capture in children the curiosity of the moment but will arouse and expand it. Provisions must exist for the nurturing of curiosity about things and ideas. The provisions should have the stimuli for many questions and the development of routes toward intensive inquiry.

Curriculum procedures must help teachers to identify with tasks

It is usually assumed that teachers like to work with children who have enthusiasm about ideas, who have a desire to learn about things. Yet, frequently starved conditions for learning exist in schools and classrooms. Sometimes the procedures and the content in the learning environment would suggest that curiosity, enthusiasm and questions are the exception rather than the rule.

In order to utilize and expand the immediate curiosity of children toward a sensitivity to, and a love for, ideas and knowledge, it is important that curriculum improvement conditions be established wherein teachers will be helped to have similar experiences. The conditions should contain focal points of contact with the curiosity of teachers toward ideas and things. Provisions should be made for teachers to reflect on certain past satisfactions which they have had, to recapture some of them, and to experience a pursuit of ideas incident to their present curiosity.

To illustrate, many teachers have always wanted to do something to satisfy a curiosity or to see a more or less concrete fulfillment of some hypotheses about ideas which they have had from time to time. Somehow, however, they were always either too busy or were too hampered by preconceived patterns of doing things or by rigid policies laid down by school authorities. Then, too, they may have refrained from following through with ideas which they entertained because of the lack of encouragement or the absence of conditions for the venture. The curriculum worker should be conscious of these voids as he works with teachers. Just as a teacher would capture the curiosity of the child for the furtherance of meanings and a sense of inquiry relative to the curiosity, the curriculum worker should utilize the curiosity of the teacher in helping him expand his area of inquiry and pursuit of ideas.

All possible efforts should be made to provide the setting where the teachers might follow through with their ideas. The setting might be in the form of a workshop, where some teachers may inaugurate new approaches to science, others may represent ideas about social relationships in graphic form, and others may work with color combinations to point up a state of feeling. Still others in this workshop may wish to develop some experimental materials toward establishing arithmetic meanings, some may want to develop open-ended questions about new scientific ideas with some illustrative clues, and some may wish to provide for children some seat-work exercises which will provide avenues of approach to peripheral areas of inquiry.

The conditions for the handling of ideas relative to curiosity, and hypotheses which are entertained by teachers, can be carried on both with elementary and secondary teachers. In general, there is really no difference as to the method used except that it must be followed through on the basis of different levels of maturity. In both elementary and secondary divisions, however, it is important that the emphasis be on making things happen. As stated before, the learning conditions should provide a sense of release, the removal of limitations to thinking and higher inquiry. The avenues for the pursuit of ideas should be broad, containing many side roads for the testing and appraisal of alternatives. The conditions should contain elements of impact for the generation of inquisitiveness on the part of young people. The structure must of necessity evoke questions and provide the machinery for following through toward answers.

It is hoped that those who pursue in some manner the conditions described will gain a better understanding in relating learning experiences to the traits, sensitivities, and indigenous characteristics and habits of children and young people. The utilization of the curiosity and meanings which children and young people hold should automatically expand their interests, increase and intensify their questions, and elevate their areas of inquiry.

Curriculum workers must help overcome negative thinking

If one observes closely the practices in institutions and agencies which are involved with the activities of human beings, he will be impressed by the large amount of effort which is exerted in preventing action. In ever so many schools, the administrators, counselors, and teachers spend a great part of their time in preventing things from happening. Counselors and other guidance personnel in a school system are occupied much of the time with disciplinary measures of the preventive type. Administrators periodically meet with teachers and other personnel to develop policies and rules regarding the overzealousness of youth. Welfare agencies devote a great deal of time in checking cases of delinquency and the circumstances attendant thereto. Over and over, matters dealing with steps to prevent this or that are brought to our attention. Many newspapers, bulletins, magazines, and books deal with efforts and plans to keep certain things from happening. It even appears that some organs of communication would be hard put to function if there should be a dearth of violations or an absence of human frailty with regard to rules and conventions.

The occupation with the negative aspects of processes extends to governmental administration and organization. Judging from the coverage given by newspapers, magazines, and other media of communication, the governor of a state has to devote a considerable portion of his official duties to keep certain proposals from becoming actualities. Furthermore, most of the offices connected with the affairs of government must give a large proportion of their time to the detection and prevention of certain acts which may impair the conceived mode of governmental functions. Many in high places frequently devote a lifetime of service to duties connected with prevention.

It is not the intention to speak derogatorily of the preventive functions of schools, administrative and welfare agencies, and the governing bodies. These functions are essential in the effective operation of institutions. It is necessary, however, for people to view with some degree of concern the vast degree of effort which must be expended toward preventive measures. Although realism dictates that certain acts and proposals must constantly be detected and stemmed in order to preserve an equilibrium in living, it is equally important that other acts and proposals become actualities if life is to be realized in its fullness. In other words, life is involved with initiatory and activating processes as well as with those that are terminal and preventive. The elements of causation give meaning, strength, and purpose to living. One of the greatest differentiating factors between animal and man is that man has the gift of creativity; that he has the potential to cause things to happen.

Effects of communicative stagnation. It would appear, as one looks at the practices of many schools and other institutions, that their members are so occupied with preventive efforts that they haven't stopped to ponder the causative basis of those efforts. They have viewed their act of causation in a negative way; that is, to cause things *from* happening without going to the source of those things. Thus the thinking which has been conceived in their communicative attempts has been largely terminal. Responsibility as well as insight with regard to the needs of children and young people has been obscured in the task at hand. To be sure, there has been communication, but it has been largely related to action designed to perpetuate established beliefs and patterns *per se*. It has been designed to enforce a pious allegiance to the status quo.

Under the above conditions, communication is related to a clinging to beliefs and patterns—a maintenance of rigidity. The existing scene of operation of people is excluded from these conditions.

Curriculum workers must penetrate focal points of stagnation. In the preceding pages, it was contended that there needs to be a broad base of operation toward higher levels of thinking. It was emphasized that in order that there may be real stimulus toward higher thinking, the mind has to be liberated to draw on all the resources of knowledge which have been provided by man. The beliefs and values should guide action in thinking about the situations which should be anticipated in a changing culture and world. In view of the tremendous amount of time and effort which is expended by people in preventive functions, it is important that conditions be developed wherein the resources of knowledge might be reconstructed so as to deal adequately with the anticipated changes.

In order to understand the future, it is first of all necessary to understand the present. There is a woeful lack in the school organization and the curriculum in providing for an understanding of the present. When people devote as much energy toward preventive measures as has been indicated, they have become so involved with the problems attendant thereto that they begin to view them as axiomatic. The school organization and curriculum is accordingly designed to promote order and system on the basis of past experience rather than on the knowledge of the contemporary scene. Consequently, people become more or less blinded to the meanings and potential in the present.

The curriculum workers must carefully assess the ingredients residing in the process of containment of communication and thinking. As they ascertain some of the focal points of penetration for the release of communication, they must help teachers carefully build the routes for ways out of the pattern. While the routes must of necessity disturb the people in the process, their sense of equilibrium must be maintained. To both disturb and preserve the state of equilibrium necessitates the development of insights relative to the scenes of action with which people are involved. Perhaps they are involved blindly and complacently. To arouse some attention and some new angles of perception relative to their involvement necessitates conditions for questioning and study of the objects of involvement. It is hoped that these conditions will be approached in the sections which follow.

DEVELOPING UNDERSTANDING OF POTENTIAL IN THE PRESENT SCENE OF ACTION

To provide for an upgrading of the quality of thinking and to promote a dynamic approach to an understanding of the evolving possibilities of the future, it is important that conditions for learning be established which will point to meanings of the potential in the present scene of action of people. In these conditions for learning, the ingredients for the interpenetration of ideas regarding these meanings must be provided. Also, it is most important that the conditions contain those resources which will serve to promote responsibility on the part of participants to move into higher levels of thinking and action.

The setting must provide the incentives to go beyond what is already known. Furthermore, it must contain the ingredients or elements which will lead children and young people to approach questions on the basis of unity of knowledge. That means that many resources from the various fields of thinking, both past and present, must be made accessible to students. It also means that the conditions for learning will liberate the child's mind and intensify his efforts in pursuing answers to his questions. His search for meanings must not be confined to subjects or restricted assignments but, rather, needs to be abetted by provision for wide reading, frequent analysis in group discussion, and periodical evaluation as to logic and direction.

Living content of communication must be identified and portrayed

The content for communication toward higher levels of concern and thinking may initially be that which is embodied in the problems of people in the contemporary scene. It is most important that the conditions be established whereby teachers may arrive at some means of simple identification with the living content in the contemporary action of men. A necessary parallel is the establishment of conditions for learning with children which will provide the ingredients for insight and understanding with regard to the problems of people, their purposes, motives, drives, conflicts, and aspirations. It is important that the picture pointedly portray the immediate scene of communication.

One of the sources for a graphic portrayal of the problems of communication is the newspapers. To illustrate somewhat in detail the living content of communication, the following headlines are taken from a metropolitan and state daily newspaper:[1]

GOVERNOR SEES NECESSITY FOR STATE ORGANIZATION

RESERVE BILL PASSAGE IN SENATE SEEN

90 DEATHS LISTED, TOP LAST YEAR'S

THREE EMPLOYEES ACCUSED OF LOOTING SUPERMARKETS

KEEP YOUNGSTERS OFF HOT STREETS: HELP CAMP FUND

$1 MILLION CAR FACILITY PLANNED ON ASYLUM STREET

PRICE SPIRAL INDICATED BY WAGE HIKES

MEASURE TO CUT MEDICAL CARE FOR SERVICE FAMILIES

EDEN AGREES ON PROPOSAL FOR RUSSIA

GIRL ON PONY HURLED HALF-MILE BY TORNADO

PAY INCREASES BOOST AIR FORCE ENLISTMENTS

NEHRU TALKS IN BELGRADE; BACKS FREEDOM FOR ALL

CLOSE HAIR CLIP SPARKS CONTROVERSY

STRIKE-BOUND COPPER MILLS ARE PICKETED

PARTIES COME THROUGH ON PLATFORM PLEDGES

STATE HOSPITAL INMATES NEED RECREATION SHOES

Concern about local problems intensified. It will be seen that most of the headlines listed deal with local incidents and problems in which many people in a community have a high degree of concern. There are, of course, many other items in the daily newspapers covering the problems of the communities of a state. Needless to say, there is a great deal of communication regarding the problems covered by the content under the various headlines. People discuss these problems as they meet each other on the street, in the hotel lobby, at luncheon clubs, with neighbors in the evening, and at meetings called for the purpose of promoting action on the problems. Let's take, for example, the headline STRIKE-BOUND COPPER MILLS ARE PICKETED.

In connection with this issue, there are many meetings of labor groups and management groups separately, and other meetings where the two groups try to arrive at some solution together. Frequently, rather spirited communication takes place in these meetings regarding such matters as the cost of living, security benefits, business conditions, health and welfare,

[1] The Hartford, Conn. *Courant,* Sunday, July 3, 1955.

profits, and human relationships and understanding. Usually, advertisements are carried in the newspaper by both the labor and management groups stating their respective positions relative to the controversy. In these advertisements appear many facts pertinent to the problems as seen respectively by labor and management.

Since the whole community is more or less affected by the issues relative to the strike, people talk about the problems involved at the dinner table, in neighborhood gatherings, and in other places where people come in contact with each other. Editorials appear in the newspapers in all parts of the country with regard to the strike. Letters to the editor are published stating positions pro and con relative to the controversy. Commentators discuss the issues of the strike on radio and television broadcasts. The tensions developed by people in connection with the strike may be reflected in the behavior of children in school. Their concerns vary in terms of the occupations of their parents. Those children whose parents are employed by the copper mills exhibit one type of concern. Other children will entertain varying types and degrees of concern.

The conditions for communication toward concern and learning which must be established with regard to local issues should, of course, provide opportunities for ascertaining the facts in the issues. They should further provide insight relative to the emotions, fears, and other feelings involved in the issues. Then, too, it is of the utmost importance that the conditions for learning provide for a basic study of the conflicts of people and the thinking which gives rise to the conflicts. Finally, present in the conditions should be the alternative values which are basic in the approach to a solution of the conflicts.

INVOLVING TEACHERS AND PUPILS IN CURRICULUM FOR HIGH LEVEL THINKING

In the process of curriculum development for the promotion of high level communication, it is necessary to provide the setting for teacher involvement. The structuring which would be necessary in providing for this involvement would be the same, on different levels, as that provided for child and youth education. Many resources on behavior should be accessible to the teacher, both in its raw manifestations and the basic thinking which produces it. The conditions must bring to bear a unity of understanding regarding the behavior which operates in the variety of efforts of people to solve the problems incident to their needs. Under these conditions, the teacher should conceive of a sufficient number of elements to identify himself with the roles of people and their problems. The impact of this experience in thinking will, to a considerable degree, clarify to the teacher the process of behavior of people in different situations. The experience will contribute to the synthesis of ideas in his own mind respecting the methods of communication which are productive in different situations.

Involvement of teacher, pupil, and others equated

Since the structuring for teacher involvement in curriculum improvement is essentially the same at different levels as child and youth involvement with learning experiences, the discussion which follows will relate to both. Furthermore, it relates to all those who are directly concerned with the promotion of curriculum improvement toward high level communication and thinking. That includes curriculum consultants, supervisors, principals, and, in many instances, parents and other citizens. These are all workers in curriculum and thus are learners together.

It is also necessary to indicate that the discussion is directed both to those who work with children in the elementary and those who work with secondary school pupils. The material and methods are appropriate to a wide range of levels, granted that the approach is in terms of maturity levels of pupils.

Identifying problems of people in a local question

Let us recapitulate the conditions for high level thinking experiences, using local issues as the content in the conditions. Taking the specific illustration indicated by the headline STRIKE-BOUND COPPER MILLS ARE PICKETED, how would the conditions for insight and understanding be developed with respect to this issue? First of all, it would be necessary to clarify the topic so that the problems in it could be recognized. It is clear at once that a strike prevails, and that the mills where the strikers are employed are being picketed. No doubt, there will be communication among teachers and children as to the reason for the strike and the picketing of the plants. The group will try to assess the feelings of the people engaged in the strike. The members will try to view the strike from the standpoint of the workers, members of the management group, and the people of the community. They will try to ascertain the type of communication which is taking place in terms of the feelings of the people involved.

At this point the study of the issue or controversy should be made to clarify and define the facts and problems which are immediate and tangible. The communicative efforts of the teachers and students together and in separate groups should portray the picture of the issue as it now exists: the variety of emotions and concerns exhibited by the various groups, the meetings which have been held, together with the results, the tensions prevailing in the community, and other ways in which people are reacting in this state of disquietude.

Expanding the thinking on local problems into realm of conflict. A second stage of the conditions for learning and communication with respect to a study of a local question is the expansion of the thinking into the realm of conflicts of people. At this stage, it is necessary to bring to bear the thinking of other times and places through a study of history and literature. At the same time, it is essential that the teachers and students should try to gain understanding about the nature of behavior and the forces shaping it through a study of much of the literature in sociology, psychology, anthropology, philosophy, biology, and other areas. All these sources of knowledge must be made graphically accessible to the students.

The treatment of much of this material in research and communication in relation to the conflicts of people will produce the method of teaching. Method grows out of research and communication directed to a unitary approach to the understanding of, and action on, conflicts and behavior of people. The student, beginning with a study of local issues, should be identifying with the factors which are common as between the behavior exhibited in the issues and the present thinking as well as that of other times and places regarding man's behavior in resolving conflict. Thus there will develop a synthesis of knowledge which will provide some sense of direction toward an elevated sense of understanding and further inquiry on the part of the student.

Using contemporary resources. Although all the stages in the conditions for learning are related and interwoven, for purposes of emphasis, a third condition to develop study and research with regard to a local controversy is the envisioning of action toward resolving the present level of conflict. This means that the conditions for communication with respect to strikes, picketing, and other elements of conflict must be replete with the literature dealing with the thinking on the contemporary scene. Accessible to students should be literature on the problems of labor and management; books on group dynamics, human relations, morale and welfare; materials on the standard of living; and others. Portrayed in the conditions, also, should be the alternative plans of action resulting from research and the considered thinking of the group engaged in the study. The research and the process of communication should reveal patterns of behavior which would serve as guides to decision between the alternative plans of action.

Providing dynamic resources for high level thinking

In connection with the conditions for the development of higher levels of communication, a few general suggestions relative to dynamics of curriculum improvement are in order. First of all, the teacher should have ample opportunity to gain an advanced understanding of the use of the disciplines through a program of general studies. It is important that during this period there should be many opportunities through seminars and other arrangements for the teacher to relate his studies to people and their behavior. Certainly, meanings should be clarified so that the teacher will tend to expand learning opportunities within the context of these meanings. The teacher should develop similar opportunities with students. Arrangements should be made for students to handle ideas together in seminars and other learning centers. Much time should be devoted during the period of involvement with the general studies in helping students with difficulties which they may have in reading, communication, and in ways of approaching the subject matter.

Relating fields of knowledge to living issues. A second stage in the curriculum conditions for high level communication should give teachers and students an opportunity to do two things—to gain knowledge, skill, and understanding in a special subject or area and to gain a deep appreciation of the other areas and how they might be used to contribute to a unity of understanding. During this stage, the student would study intensively such an area as biology, history, English, mathematics, and some of the other sciences. Again, the subject should be treated in such a manner as to relate to human behavior and natural and physical phenomena. One of the best approaches in the preparation for carrying on a program of unified studies with children is to develop a clear understanding of at least one subject or area of study. To have an intensive understanding of a specialized subject or area means that the student recognizes its interrelatedness with other fields of knowledge. In addition to a special preparation in at least one subject, a period of time in this second stage should be devoted through seminars or some other organized block arrangement to enable the student to use the arts, humanities, and sciences in developing insight and understanding relative to issues of living and behavior.

A third stage, and this might be integrated with the other stages, is the development of the opportunity for the student and teacher to translate the thinking derived from the studies, communication, and research into meanings as to one's roles in the pursuit of present activities and, also, their use in higher areas of inquiry. Of course, this is being done all the time in the process of learning, but it needs a place of particular emphasis so that the student and teacher will push beyond convenient terminal points.

Characteristics of a program for high level thinking summarized

An attempt has been made to present a general picture as to what might be some elements of a program directional in the approach to higher levels of thinking. It is not contended that the plan is unique. On the contrary, many teachers and schools are either working on the problems of promoting high level experiences or have evolved most promising programs. The program briefly described above has certain characteristics which it is believed will make it more effective than most programs in improving the conditions for high level thinking. One of these characteristics is that the methods are repointed with content. Nowhere are methods developed apart from content. A second characteristic in the program is the emphasis on the treatment of the subjects and areas of learning in such a manner as to interrelate with the behavior incident to the problems of people. The conditions for learning suggested are those which will give sufficient clarification to basic thinking to bring about an identification of the student with that thinking.

A third characteristic of this program is the development of the conditions for the student to become involved with the various disciplines and areas of learning in such a manner as to give meaning and strength to his purposes. Communication then will draw from all thinking, past and contemporary, in evolving higher levels of decision and action. A fourth, and very important characteristic in the program indicated, is the provision of many seminars for intensive study and communication regarding the various problems of people in the society in which we live.

Conditions for high level thinking with young children

In developing the conditions for learning with children, it is important that several points be emphasized. The conditions should, first of all, be geared to the developmental levels of children. The books and materials should carry meanings within the understanding levels of children.

A second consideration in promoting learning and communication with children is to develop in the classroom conditions a type of realism which does not seriously disturb their equilibrium. For example, if the burning issue in a community is a strike, it is certain that a considerable degree of tension exists in the families that are involved. It is important that caution be used in dealing with a local issue which has been productive of tensions. The role of the classroom and school is to develop the stage for calmness and calculated concern in thinking in a controversial atmosphere.

Development of new and expanded needs. A third factor to consider in working with children is the provision for the development and expansion of concerns about local issues which have meaning for them. Although it is very important to consider and study the immediate needs and concerns of children, the conditions for learning should make provision for a clarification of the interrelatedness of the concerns to other and new concerns. It is essential for a teacher to help the child with his felt needs and purposes. It is even more essential for the teacher to help provide the alternatives to these needs, thus setting the stage for a recognition of, and identification with, new and expanded needs. This will have the effect of strengthening the thinking of the child to communicate with others toward evolving a more sharpened look at his own values as well as those of his fellow pupils. A fourth factor in developing the conditions for learning and communication with children has already been implied in that they should parallel those with which the teacher is involved in his own preparation.

Provide "charge" for basic thinking. A point to be emphasized is that children, even in their early years of school, should have the opportunity to do basic thinking with regard to behavior involving conflicts, emotions, needs, purposes, aspirations, and their role in living. It is as true with children as with adults that a great part of their thinking is involved with themselves—their proposed acts and plans and the consequences of them. In view of this, it is extremely important that this thinking have a prominent place in the conditions for learning in the school and classroom. It is felt that if the four considerations indicated are observed in the development of the conditions for learning for children, that the opportunity for constructive communication and decision on the part of children will, to a great extent, be served. There is, of course, much more to the problem of promoting learning with children than has been indicated. Many aspects of the conditions for learning for children, however, are implied in the next chapter and further discussed in the other chapters. It is hoped that some answers will be provided in those discussions.

•16•

Human Relationships
in High Level Thinking

IN CONNECTION WITH THE IDEA THAT THE SPRINGBOARD FOR higher levels of communication may be through local questions and problems, it is highly essential to view and study many aspects of the behavior of people involved. Frequently, controversies arise over what might be conceived as simple local problems. Controversy with regard to a local issue often is precipitated by the manner in which a proposal was introduced. The proposal under discussion may be considered a good one by most of the citizens, but the method in which it was presented by an individual or group of individuals may have led some to question the motives of others. In other words, either the proponents did not wish to clarify certain items in the proposal, or their attempt failed to establish true communication. The inception of the whole problem, then, of communication is related to the behavior of the communicants. Individuals daily meet other individuals and groups either under informal or formal conditions. In these contacts, they discover much about the needs and wants of people, together with their efforts toward satisfying them. By engaging in simple communication with people, one may find out a great deal about how they regard themselves as well as how they regard others. At the same time, one communicates elements of his own self-regard as well as how he regards others.

376

EGO-INVOLVEMENT AN IMPORTANT FACTOR
IN COMMUNICATION

It is apparent that in any form of communication between individuals there exists a degree of ego-involvement. Sherif and Cantril, in dealing with the question of ego-involvement, make this observation on how one regards himself:[1]

> In spite of the relative similarity of the norms to which an individual in a given society or a group may be exposed, the content of any individual's ego, what he regards as himself, is a rather distinct constellation of social and personal values that vary not only in their number and nature but also in the intensity with which they are held.

The components of the ego are tied up with the individual's possessions, his politics, his language, his manner of dress, and most everything else which he calls his. In order to understand another individual, one must learn much about the components of his own ego. As one becomes more familiar with one's ego, the initial conditions are provided for communication and social understanding.

Involvement may lead to recognition of needs

Communication between individuals and among groups is facilitated when there develops a feeling of mutual understanding. Mutuality does not come about by itself. The conditions for it begin to develop when individuals take a look at their own behavior as well as the behavior of others. A valuable approach in helping others to know themselves is to develop the conditions where individuals will try to analyze their own feelings, purposes, standards, values, goals, ambitions, and ways of doing things.

The teacher must seek ways to understand himself in working out situations with others. His involvement with others will, at different times, cause him to feel elated, restricted, gratified, supported, disturbed, or insecure. As he tries to examine his experiences in his involvement with others, he will have some clues as to the behavior of others. Everyone will

[1] M. Sherif and H. Cantril, *The Psychology of Ego-Involvements* (New York: John Wiley & Sons, Inc., 1947), p. 117.

have to somehow clarify to himself the causes of different feelings. In doing so, each one will recognize some of his needs as well as the needs of those with whom he is trying to communicate.

Developing a new equilibrium. Dewey speaks of a need as representing any disturbance which an individual feels so keenly about that he wants to resolve it in order to achieve a new equilibrium.[2] The movement toward the restoration of equilibrium is search and exploration. The recovery is fulfillment or satisfaction. It is indicated here that a need is a disturbance of equilibrium. A disturbance may continue when there has been no attempt to bring it into focus. It can be brought into focus in connection with involvement in a situation. That means that one must look analytically at the feelings in connection with that involvement. As the disturbance is involved, the values within which it was felt might be challenged. This will have the effect of causing the needs to emerge. In resolving the needs, a new value pattern begins to take shape.

Discovering more about disturbances. As an individual observes his own disturbances, he becomes more conscious of the disturbances which must exist in others. This will tend to give him a greater sense of sympathetic appreciation of others in their attempts to resolve disturbances. As one begins to understand his disturbances, he may have the clues which will help him develop the conditions wherein they may be resolved. The acts of understanding and resolving of behavior do not follow one another. They develop simultaneously. Similarly, understanding the disturbances of others does not necessarily follow an understanding of one's own disturbances. Rather, as one begins to understand his own feelings, he is at the same time beginning to understand the disturbances of others. The clue, which might be used to initiate an analysis of one's own behavior, is the disturbing effect observed as the result of expressions on the part of one or more individuals. If the expression was disturbing to several people but failed to disturb one or two individuals, an attempt might be made by both those who

[2] John Dewey, *Logic* (New York: Henry Holt and Co., 1938), p. 27.

were disturbed and those who were not to analyze the reason for the contrasting effects.

As one analyzes his own disturbances and also tries to analyze the absence of disturbance on the part of others in connection with some thought or idea communicated, he may find one or more of the following elements present: He might have misunderstood what was intended in the communication. He may have discerned some angles in the communication which escaped the others. Perhaps the communication was intended to cause him, rather than the others, to be disturbed. Possibly he said something which was disturbing to the communicant and the others present, whereupon the communicant, sensing support from the others, drew upon his resources to reciprocate in kind. Perhaps the one who was communicating was using language to serve a particular function; that is, to cause a disturbance in the person to spur him into action with respect to an idea or proposal.

Deviation from predictable behavior may be resourceful

As the one who is disturbed over the communication which has taken place begins to examine his feelings, he will find that the skill of communicating involves more than just serving as media for simple relationships. Perhaps the communicant, in saying what he did, either did or did not behave in a predictable way. Certainly, his expression or response did not conform to the anticipation of behavior as conceived by the one who was disturbed. In other words, the communicant, in this case, had deviated from the pattern of behavior as it was usually conceived by the one whom he had disturbed. Chances are that others were disturbed too. They probably were not ready for this new approach either.

Much has been said and written about ways of communicating in a group. Some thinkers on group process urge that communication be developed so as to move the thinking of the group forward. Every group, however, has one or more unpredictable communicants whose action may sidetrack the discussion. This action is frequently frowned upon by other members. In some cases, action of this type on the part of an individual is unwarranted. He may have purposely wanted to provoke unpleasant dissension. This individual may be trying to maneuver himself into a certain questionable status position. On the other hand, the thinking which he attempts to convey may carry a sense of quality which should receive due consideration. It is somewhat depressing to find that, in some groups, the majority of individuals behave in such a predictable manner that any deviation regardless of quality may be met with rejection. Chances are that they do so with complete regularity in every other situation. To them progress may be equated with the preservation of the status quo. This condition is phrased quite aptly by Embler in a publication on language:[3]

> The moment we say that the human being is a machine, at that moment we shall believe that the human being can be conditioned to behave in a perfectly predictable way with admirable regularity. Then it is that we shall have made ourselves something less, ever so much less, than we are.

To behave in a predictable way at all times indicates that one is resting on a certain plateau of ideas from which he is reluctant to rise. He has more or less opportunistically landed at a certain haven of thought that he considers sufficiently safe and pleasurable for himself. He will do everything to espouse the merits of this condition to others. Needless to say, too many others will accede to the lure of this reposing state. He and the others will reside in mutual communication at this place for too long a time. It is questionable whether real quality in thinking will result in this condition.

SIMPLE AND INDISCRIMINATE EMOTIONAL IDENTIFICATION MAY RETARD THINKING

In the process of communication as well as in the process of thinking, there exists a high premium on fitting in with the crowd. The speaker who is well received is the one who conveys ideas which are for the most part already believed by the audience. Furthermore, in order to be assured of widespread reception, the speaker must communicate in language which is popular. The reader will, no doubt, recall the many times he

[3] Weller Embler, "Metaphor and Social Belief," *Language, Meaning and Maturity*, S. I. Hayakawa, ed. (New York: Harper & Bros., 1954), p. 138.

has heard individuals refer affectionately to a speaker in such phrases as, "He speaks the language of the people," "He speaks in the language that we can understand," "His talk leaves no doubt as to where he stands." If one were to question further, he would, no doubt, discover that the individuals who made these references were already identifying favorably with almost all of the ideas that the speaker had presented. People who run for public office are well aware of the importance of communicating in the language which is either generally popular or indigenous to a particular group.

Emotions must be operative in conditions for communication

Language symbols, to have popular effectiveness, must be identified with the simple emotions of people. Frequently, however, emotions have been left alone in the processes of learning; that is, they have been turned inward—away from the state of truth. As a result, the emotions have not been viewed intelligently. The process of education, as carried on in the schools and colleges, has often lacked the conditions which will set the stage for an analysis of the emotions on the part of the instructors and students. Too frequently, any thought or symbols of thought which venture beyond the realm of simple emotional identification either fall on deaf ears or must struggle for existence. Most of the literature produced for the layman is written in the popular language with which his emotions are involved.

Curriculum must provide understanding of emotions. Provision should be made in the curriculum for the development of learning experiences which will enable children and young people to better understand their emotions. Furthermore, the curriculum should provide for the conditions which will promote understanding of the use of emotion in communication. Thinking is related to feeling and feeling is bound up with emotions. When a person reacts to an issue or idea, he usually tells how he *feels* about it rather than how he thinks about it. Emotions may be powerful factors in the establishment of working relationships between people. Some people are drawn to others because of the *warmth* which they exhibit in human relations. Kindness is a great influence in learning and in everyday social relationships. Children and young people respond to kindness under all conditions. Love and kindness are most powerful factors in promoting the conditions for learning.

The conditions for communication of ideas relative to the emotions should occupy a most important place in the classrooms of every school. A high level understanding and use of the emotions will open up many new areas of inquiry. Questions relative to emotions which could well arise and be dealt with are exemplified by the following: What is the basis of our feelings toward others? Why do we like or dislike certain qualities in people? In what way are different types of music and rhythm involved with the emotions? What is meant by certain people possessing *"warmth"*? How is love related to human needs? What are some of the meanings of love? Are feelings of uncertainty related to emotions? What are some of the practices in schools which affect the emotions? What can we do in our classroom to promote a better understanding of emotions in relation to caring, kindness, sincerity, and human regard? In what way may "emotional outlets" be dangerous? Under what conditions may the use of emotional responses provide great meanings?

These questions are, of course, not nearly exhaustive of the whole area of emotions. The wise use of emotions relates to such issues as "integration," international relations, world tension, economic recession, and scientific advances. Curriculum workers need to deal with the issues of emotions both in promoting the conditions in schools which will lessen their dangerous impact, and as accompanying tools for the development of attitudes and direction in high level thinking.

CURRICULUM MUST BROADEN BASE FOR COMMUNICATIVE BEHAVIOR

The curriculum must provide the avenues for the active handling and expansion of ideas in thinking and action. As stated before, beliefs and values, if clung to tenaciously, will solidify thinking in a static groove. Beliefs and values must guide action to higher levels of thinking. In other words, beliefs should provide the impetus for the mind to inquire into a wide area of knowledge.

As one makes discriminative observations of the conditions

which exist in the contemporary scene, he is struck by the more or less complacent attachment by people to a regularized pattern of behavior. This has influenced to a great extent the ways in which the tools of communication are used. The common patterns of word magic applicable to various groups and age levels of children and young people have not caught the discriminative attention of teachers and curriculum workers to the degree that is needed.

Conditions for communicative skill must go beyond standardized procedures

The patterns of word magic have reached a sort of standardized state. Children are supposed to use a certain vocabulary. Older children are supposed to use more words of increasing difficulty. Still older children are required to identify with the previously learned vocabulary and go farther. Secondary school pupils are led along certain channels to an acquisition of additional words in their vocabulary. Thus the process goes on and on. The idea of vocabulary development has, in many instances, become confined to degrees of gradation. Educational literature has a word magic which is designed to channel immediate and uncritical reactions toward this or that system, particularly the type indicated above.

It is necessary, at this point, to clarify further relative to the above discussion on word magic. The gradation of vocabulary in terms of developmental levels of children and young people is, of course, necessary. The idea, in most respects, has a sound psychological basis, especially as it relates to the mechanics of reading and vocabulary development. The system of standardization and gradation indicated, however, if pursued by itself, out of context with environmental relationships, contributes little to needed competences with regard to the patterns of word magic which exist outside of the school. The system is beautiful, it is neatly developed through research in reading, but there exist few connections or insights relative to the word magic which is perpetrated outside.

Conditions must include vocabulary patterns of many groups. The patterns of word magic outside of the school pattern are found in various groups. For example, musicians have their own expressions and use of words. An outsider will find some difficulty in understanding them. The same is true with other groups such as the "rock-and-roll" group, lower class groups, various occupational and professional groups, and so on. A good way to test for oneself whether the language or communication patterns of the schools are related to outside groups is to observe a group of secondary school age people on a playground or at a dance; better still, in a skating rink, pool room, or bowling alley. It is doubtful whether much similarity in patterns will be detected.

Most writers and producers of popular literature channelize their thinking in terms of the groups indicated above. They relate the symbols to the human behavior which prevails in the everyday relationships of people.

Rapoport[4] suggests a crucial need for an understanding of the far-reaching relationships between human behavior and the use of symbols when he points out that:

> Both word magic and demagogy aim to channelize the reactions of people to symbols, so as to make responses automatic, uncritical, immediate. Such reactions make possible gigantic sales volumes unrelated to the quality of the product; they make for persistent hostilities among groups, they make wars inevitable.

Conditions must assess "word magic" mediocrity for communicative direction. The responsibility for the perpetuation of a form of complacent thinking through a common pattern of word magic lies with the people, the schools, and the writers. In connection with the responsibility for the present state of word consumption by the public, it is necessary to refer again to the lack of conditions in educational institutions and in other learning situations to bring about, on the part of the learners, a discriminate analysis of the values which they hold. In spite of the fact that more people go through college today than ever before, the sales of literature catering to rather common tastes continue in gigantic proportions. Somehow the sense of discrimination which would distinguish between the word and the object is grossly lacking or inadequate in the consumers of written material.

[4] Anatol Rapoport, "What Is Semantics?" *Language, Meaning and Maturity,* S. I. Hayakawa, ed. (New York: Harper & Bros., 1954), p. 16.

The approach to reading on the part of a great proportion of the public might be characterized as lethargic rather than discriminative. Many honest writers, having ventured once or twice into the realm of thought elevation without reasonable success, have succumbed to the pattern dictated by the sales volumes. Many more writers, not without remunerative success, have been content to perpetuate the mediocrity occasioned by this demand. The impact of this demand must become glaringly apparent to those people who are engaged in the task of developing the conditions for the redirection of values toward a regard for quality in communication and toward constructive ends.

In view of the vast indiscriminate reception of the written work on the part of the populace, it is more significant than ever that there should be concern about the conditions which have promoted it. The fact that the responses of people to symbols have to a large extent been automatic and uncritical has great implications for the role of education. Curriculum workers and teachers should promote insight and understanding about the power of symbols and how this power is shaping or "regularizing" the patterns of the thinking of people. The role of education should extend to the question of words and their relation to behavior. Embler,[5] referring to the danger of words, states: ". . . our behavior is a function of words we use. More often than not, our thoughts do not select the words we use; instead, words determine the thoughts we have."

The questions which loom large are those of doubt as to the position of man's relationship with the symbols. Is his relationship to symbols one of elevation of resourcefulness in thought and action or one of enslavement to them? Does he, in the course of reading a selection, maintain a discriminative attitude and sense of mastery, or does he permit the magic of words to reduce him to a benign and maudlin creature? Judging from the huge sales volumes of literature of doubtful quality, it appears as if too many people have fallen before the onslaught. Those who are enlisted as purveyors of these ministrations discover that the meaning of the expression "let sleeping dogs lie"

---

[5] Weller Embler, "Metaphor and Social Belief," *Language, Meaning and Maturity*, S. I. Hayakawa, ed. (New York: Harper & Bros., 1954), p. 125.

makes remunerative sense. It becomes increasingly clear that education is confronted with a tremendous responsibility.

Conditions for communicative competences must provide indigenous meanings. As the curriculum worker approaches the question of the relationship of the symbol to behavior and its influence on communication, it is necessary for him to assess the whole process of reading and vocabulary development. Along with the developmental process of reading and vocabulary, there must be ample provision for the portrayal and analysis of words and meanings of the many groups in the environment surrounding the school. The objective here is to develop the competences of communication for higher levels of thinking. A corollary of this objective is to develop those competences which will be used to develop higher levels of thinking within the framework of communicative patterns and meanings indigenous to the various groups. Since the conditions for these competences are described in considerable detail in Chapter 14, they will not be discussed to any great extent here.

The conditions to develop competences which will serve to promote higher level thinking in many groups should, first of all, enable children and young people to analyze all types of values. It is again emphasized that all values must be admitted into the conditions for learning. Centers of communication could be established in the classrooms or school where the forms of communication of different groups would be clearly portrayed for appraisal and analysis.

Questions such as the following would be considered: What is meant by words determining the thoughts we have? What are the provisions we can make in this room to discover how different people and groups communicate? As you read different novels, what effects do they have on your feelings? As you read different stories, do you often get the feeling that something has been left out? As you observe "commercials" on television, what is your reaction to the nature of responses envisioned? Do you get a feeling of certainty relative to the product described? Have you ever observed a "commercial" that was difficult to understand? As you think about the "commercials," what do you envision as the thinking back of them? Which should come first, words or thoughts? How is word magic related to demagogy? Can word magic be used to develop as well as relax tension?

These and other questions would tend to give clues to an intensification and expansion of the conditions for the development of competences for high level thinking. Editorials, news items, television, and many other communicative media should be examined and studied in order to become more conversant with the design, process, and psychological bases underlying the media.

SEEING ONESELF IN THE SCENE OF COMMUNICATION

We have indicated the importance of understanding oneself as a factor in facilitating communication. The importance lies in the study and analysis of the elements of disturbance experienced in immediate interpersonal relationships. In the discussion on the previous pages, stress was placed on viewing certain types of disturbance as a productive device for action on some idea or proposal. From this followed a digression into language and literature not unrelated to the individual in his immediate social setting. In speaking about the relationship of man's behavior to word magic, it seems logical that we must come back to the individual and his role in the scene of communication. Since symbols are basic in human relationships, it is essential that we make some further observations about individuals in the scene of communication.

An individual usually communicates ideas within the bounds of his understanding. The bounds are determined largely by what he reads and by the people with whom he communicates verbally. He is kept more or less within the bounds by the forces of immediate social control—a status quo pattern of communication. In his few efforts to communicate about some matters which are on the fringe area of his conception of things, the channels have usually been blocked by the incapability or reluctance of fellow communicants to enter into this area of inquiry. Frequently, this reluctance is punctuated by censure for the one who dares to disturb the equilibrium of the group. This has the effect of causing those who attempted to penetrate the bounds of security in understanding to withdraw into what appears to them an innocuous state of thinking.

As this pattern continues, more and more individuals of potential courage retreat into the safety zone of communicative equilibrium. Communication in this attenuated atmosphere may gradually reduce itself to a state of utter vacuity. As a result, there exists a plateau of thinking and communication characterized more or less by mediocrity which is nourished by a literature designed to perpetuate this level of aspiration. As the individual comes to recognize this condition, he will have the initial clues toward a higher communicative equilibrium. The curriculum must provide the conditions for learning whereby these clues are ascertained for redirection in communication.

ACTION TOWARD A HIGHER COMMUNICATIVE EQUILIBRIUM

The conditions for the development of action toward breaking out of the bounds of communication established by a stationary plateau of thinking are implied almost at every step in the discussion on the previous pages. These implications relate to the quality of education. In order to go beyond a confined area of thinking, it is necessary to operate under the conditions which produced the thinking so as to experience the components of it. It is important for the participant to observe the nature of communication as it operates in the confined area. It is even more important for the participant to help develop the conditions which will bring about an analysis of the communicative relationships which prevail in the bounds of this state of equilibrium.

Curriculum must help individual examine his role

The curriculum must bring about the conditions which portray the component parts of this plateau of thinking in such a manner as to develop concern on the part of the participants to seek insight with regard to their own behavior in this environment. This should have the effect of raising certain evaluative questions such as the following: Why do I behave as I do under these circumstances? Are we suppressing ideas which bother us in order to maintain a smooth equilibrium of the group? What seems to be the nature of the experiences which are essential in conforming to this pattern of thought? Has the practice of sensitivity to feelings developed to a point where potential individuality is treated as a liability?

When an individual begins to ask questions of the type indicated, he is taking the initial steps in relating himself to the pattern of understanding in which he operates. He is beginning to examine the actual role he is playing in the group and testing it against the possible role he should be taking. He is at the same time taking stock of the disturbances he experienced on different occasions in connection with the actual communicative role he took in his group. He is taking a careful look at his disturbances to ascertain the component parts. When he does this, he is trying to locate some of the causative factors of his disturbances.

One cause of his disturbances may have been the feeling that while the members of his group were always talking they never got beyond rehashing the same ideas. Another cause of his disturbances may have been encountered in connection with the dim view taken by the members toward some efforts by certain individuals to redirect the line of thinking. He is probably concerned about the state of communicative vacuity which has come to exist as a result of the confining thought attitudes of the members of the group with which he associates.

Conditions should provide resources to penetrate communicative pattern. As an individual is more or less seeing himself with respect to the role that he is assuming in the group with which he communicates, he is making careful observations as to what is happening to the other members. He wonders if it might be possible that some of the other members are also examining the parts which they are playing in connection with what is taking place in the group. At the same time, he is thinking of ways to charge the communicative environment in such a manner as to promote concern on the part of the other members with regard to the state of inaction which has beset the group as a whole.

A step he might take is to raise some questions about some of the materials he has read. He might follow through by raising other questions about his lack of understanding of what is taking place, for example, on the national and international scene. This could lead to a discussion on some of the questions and problems involved in national and world affairs and their relationship to the people of the local community. There may be a question or two about the similarity or difference of channels of communication as they prevail on the local scene and how they operate on the national or international scene. The members of the group might observe that when people speak about national or world affairs they somehow consider them as distant or detached from the local scene. Furthermore, they might have noticed that when people talk of national and foreign affairs, they usually consider any real understanding of that category as being the task of someone else. Accordingly, they relinquish all sense of responsibility to those "who know about these things."

During the past few years, the writing on national and world questions has been turned out at an unprecedented rate. Comparatively few people are conversant with this important literature. Many behave as if world problems do not exist. Curriculum workers must take it upon themselves to charge the learning conditions with those stimuli which will induce concern on the part of the learners regarding the gross lack of understanding of world problems and related topics and issues. This means that a study of history as such is far from sufficient in promoting an intelligent approach toward world understanding.

There must be a determined analysis of world questions through local as well as world channels of communication, both verbal and written. Many of the materials written by thinkers on government and politics should be accessible in the learning environment of students. Also easily available should be materials on social psychology, anthropology, economics, and other subjects. Books and articles about the progress of science throughout the world must be read and analyzed along with the other materials mentioned, for the purpose of understanding the function which all people have to promote communicative relationships with other peoples. The conditions for the promotion of understanding of communicative relationships should be replete with newspapers from every country in the world. These should be portrayed in such a way as to bring about a studious insight into the issues which produce the differing modes of behavior communicated by leaders in the various countries of the world.

Curriculum should provide for intelligent approach to changes. The events in recent years show a glaring degree of evidence that changes are taking place at such a fast pace that it taxes man physically and mentally to keep up with them. One of the major tasks of the curriculum worker is to develop the conditions which will help young people become intelligent about the nature of changes and their responsible role regarding them. The vast majority of people are content simply to be consumers of change and make no attempt to see the social and moral implications in it. The curriculum must make provision for the stimulation of constructive change. It should provide the impetus for young people to seek and discover roles in areas beyond the familiar circles of communication. The graphic accessibility of ideas about people and places should develop an excitement in young people to take learning far beyond the "package" conception of education. The conditions need to place youth in an active working relationship with new meanings in science, the nature of behavior and the approach to social relationships.

IDENTIFYING THE NEW POSITION OF MEMBERS IN THE COMMUNICATIVE PATTERN

In the previous pages, an attempt was made to explore the possible roles an individual might pursue in enhancing the forward movement of communication, both written and verbal. He was pictured in a state of speculation as to what he might do to penetrate the status quo of a plateau of communication. He was shown in the role of evaluating the effects of his attempts to remove some of the confines of thinking of the group with which he associated. He was also trying to gain insight with regard to the behavior of the other members of the group.

Although he met with certain types of resistance, it is doubtful that he had any intention of retreating from the situation and "leaving well enough alone." He was disturbed, not because of the seemingly negative attitudes of the other members, but rather over the fact that his own behavior was ineffective in the situation. This very recognition, however, gave him insight about his behavior.

It is hoped that this insight would lead him to strengthen his resources of knowledge about people through reading, observation, self-evaluation, and considered thinking. His observations, as well as his analysis of people's reaction to ideas, revealed much to him which would be rewarding in his efforts to exert some degree of influence with others. He was acquiring a knowledge of certain elements of behavior. This revealed to him, for example, that people usually resist what they do not understand. Furthermore, he reasoned that people will avoid ideas which they regard as threatening to their status feelings. By the same token, individuals frequently show antagonism to those whom they regard as a threat to their sense of security. People are extremely reluctant to be involved in communication which is outside of their pattern of thinking. They like to do the customary thing.

Using the saturation point in communication to enter new ideas

The individual who is making a resourceful approach to an understanding of the types of roles people customarily take in communicating, is discovering ways of behavior which will furnish some clues toward effecting a degree of change away from the closed pattern of thinking. He is discovering that although people are prone to follow a customary pattern of thinking and communication, they reach a point of saturation in the process. In other words, the inbreeding process approaches a state of vacuity. Then something must happen. When a process reaches this point, there has to be a decision about redirection or a new point of departure in communication. When people have talked so long about a certain issue that they become exhausted from sheer boredom, they are receptive to almost anything that is different. There is, of course, a danger in this indiscriminate receptiveness in that an unscrupulous demagogue may introduce a design of such deterioration in thought that it will be difficult to repossess even the process which was exhausted.

When a line of communication has been exhausted by the

members, a real opportunity is presented for the development of a more resourceful approach as well as a new outlook toward idea formation. In the first place, the exhausting process could be analyzed to determine what brought about the saturation of ideas. This, in itself, would provide some of the conditions for a new direction of communication. Secondly, the process has to be reconstructed in such a manner that the elements which produced the saturation are absent. The pattern must be different. In the third place, it is well to retain those elements of the original process which analysis revealed as being constructive. As participants identify some phases of the customary procedures in the reconstructed process, they will approach it with some degree of security.

Responsibility must accompany introduction of new ideas. When reference is made to an individual becoming resourceful with a group toward a new plateau of thinking and communication, we also have in mind every other individual in the group. Since individuals make up a group, it follows that the group will be operating on questions of concern about issues only to the extent that the questions are introduced by the individuals. The degree of concern will vary in direct proportion to the manner in which the questions were brought to the group. For example, an individual may raise a question about a situation and, at the same time, accept no real responsibility in developing insight with regard to the question. If other individuals do the same thing, it is doubtful whether much real concern about the situation will be awakened in the group.

When anyone brings a question to the group, it is expected that he has been doing some basic thinking in connection with it. Furthermore, it will heighten the attention of the members of the group if the one who raises a question will show some conviction and understanding regarding it. Thinking about the question may be further intensified if the questioner provides a portrayal of the issues in the question with some background or documentation. This will also have the effect of creating a desire for further insight on the part of the other members as well as the questioner.

Frequently, there is too much talking in groups about an issue without people knowing much about it. It is important to have sources at hand so that ideas may be clarified through some degree of research and documentation. If a question does not produce sufficient interest on the part of the members of a group to seek out the related issues through analytical thinking and reading, not much concern about it has been developed. If a question fails to bring about further questions, considerable reading, and analytical thinking, the members have not related themselves to the question.

Intensifying the approach to analytical thinking about questions

The development of concern and analytical thinking may be illustrated in connection with some questions about the nature of prejudice and class distinction as it prevails in groups of people. Numerous books have been written on prejudice and how it operates in thinking and action. It is often said that to be prejudiced is to be human. Also, quite frequently the point is advanced that it is important to personality growth to recognize that one has prejudices and is able to identify them. When one denies that he has prejudices, he either is closing his mind to them or they have become such an integral part of his personality structure that he does not realize that they exist. Suppose, for example, that someone in the group, which is trying to analyze prejudices, has read the magnificent novel of South Africa written by Paton. This novel is the story of a young white South African police lieutenant who violates one of the strictest laws of that country governing the relationship between white and black. We shall suppose that the one who has read the novel submits this question to the group: In assessing the patterns of conduct of people in their relationships with each other, could it be that the dynamic factors in those relationships grow out of the prejudices held by the individuals? After several attempts on the part of different members to approach an analysis of the question, the one who submitted it might refer to the opening words of the novel written by Paton as follows:[6]

[6] Alan Paton, *Too Late the Phalarope* (New York: Charles Scribner's Sons, 1953), p. 1.

"Perhaps I could have saved him, with only a word, two words, out of my mouth. Perhaps I could have saved us all. But I never spoke them."

Following this quotation it would be necessary, of course, to relate more about the story: that is, who spoke these words, the circumstances which prompted the words, the characters in the story, and a few other high points. In all probability the question raised was given some direction by the quotation and other parts of the story related by the member. This would prompt the other members of the group to raise further questions and also to read the story for themselves.

Promoting analytical communication by expanding relationships in a concept. The conditions for real concern with regard to the question on prejudices which was submitted above might be established rather promptly. Much reading, as well as careful maneuvering on the part of the members, will keep the question in focus. The elements introduced into the question by the maneuverings of the members serve to enrich the conditions for a more intensive understanding of the nature of prejudices of people. In assessing the patterns of conduct of people in different situations, the part that prejudices play will be analyzed according to some plan arrived at through definition. It is possible that this plan will include a portrayal of different types of prejudices as well as positive and negative effects of prejudices. The members will try to determine the inception of prejudices. They will peruse the thinking of various people who have written on the question of prejudice to determine how prejudice is often used to promote the power of some individual or group of individuals. They will attempt to analyze how consequences of prejudices vary in relation to the patterns of values prevailing in different groups.

It is impossible to begin to predict all the types of study and action which will develop as a result of questions which might be raised about the nature of prejudices. It is hoped, of course, that there should develop some new ways of looking at one's own prejudices. This would introduce some new values in understanding which would be useful in one's associations with others. Certainly, some new insights about the use of prejudices in positive action would be developed. Above all, it is hoped that the concern with regard to the devastating effects of prejudices may lead to the removal of some of the barriers of communication and to an elevated sense of truth and understanding.

SUMMARIZING THE ELEMENTS TO BE ENVISIONED BY THE CURRICULUM WORKER

As has been indicated before in this discussion, thinking and communication have become more or less stabilized on a certain plateau characterized by automatic and uncritical responsiveness. Change is taking place all around people and yet they scarcely realize what is happening. Here and there, some individual attempts to translate the seeming imponderables into meanings which have some relationship to the values of people. In the effort to point out these relationships and meaning to people, he is at first met with a form of ennui. People take one look at the process, get a glimpse of the responsibility entailed in the route to understanding, and withdraw again into the well-worn ways of illusory calm and serenity. Some say that people are so basically lazy, that they want only to follow patterns which have been automatized. The word 'lazy,' however, connotes a symptom and cannot, therefore, be accepted as a logical explanation of automatized patterns of action.

The curriculum must make provisions for young people to seek out the foundational elements of these patterns of behavior. It is important to visualize the conditions under which these patterns continue to flourish. It is, however, extremely difficult to visualize the conditions until the elements which constitute the plane of automatized thinking are brought into bold relief by analytical experience and study within groups. Later, the elements must be reanalyzed as they become a part of the conditions for learning.

Some of the suggestions which have been made in the previous sections of this chapter are quite fundamental and should illuminate the thinking relative to the causative elements of a confining plateau of communication. The suggestions emphasized that people behave in terms of the values that they hold. People will operate in connection with ideas that they understand. They tend to reject what is not in terms of their customary ways of behavior. They feel threatened by new and involved ideas. They hesitate to jeopardize the safety and satisfaction in the status feelings which accrue to them in the established routes of communication. Although they sense the usefulness of innovations, they fail to accept—or refuse to understand—the effects of change in their environment. They tend to refuse admittance to their plateau of thinking and communication any ideas which may disturb the equilibrium of the communicants. Although they are consumers of the results of ideas, they, in effect, deny that the ideas are finding inroads into their values. Although the ideas may actually be operating in their physical environment, people frequently fail to identify them in connection with their patterns of thinking or action.

From time to time responsible and courageous individuals break out of the static equilibrium. This has been illustrated in the previous pages where an individual discovers a role of responsibility in a group by which he produces action toward an extension of the area of thinking. This role is discovered only after he has gained some insight about the components of a static situation. It is hoped that the direction out of a static condition which has been discussed will provide some insight and courage to curriculum workers and teachers who might attempt to move groups into a higher level of thought and communication.

◦17◦

Curriculum Development for
Higher Levels of Thinking

IN THE PREVIOUS CHAPTERS, INNUMERABLE SUGGESTIONS POINTING
to the dynamics of curriculum development are embodied in
the discussion on the conditions and processes for higher levels
of thinking. It is hoped that the discussion relative to the conditions designed to give a clearer understanding of the problems
of people might help teachers and other curriculum workers in
their efforts to provide dynamic learning experiences for children and young people. Certainly, the description of the conditions for learning with respect to local issues and problems
should provide useful situations for the development of critical
thought and inquiry on the part of youth. It is hoped that the
suggestions for moving thought out of static plateaus to higher
levels of abstraction and new and promising states of communicative equilibrium may be rewarding in an expanded area of
living.

The school, of course, has a major responsibility in providing
the conditions and refining the channels toward higher levels
of inquiry and understanding. In the preceding chapters many
suggestions have been developed relative to the promotion of
these conditions with young people. In this chapter, an effort
will be made to provide some direction with regard to the
major tasks of curriculum workers in promoting higher levels
of understanding and more advanced competences in thinking.

DEVELOPING HIGH LEVEL CONCEPTIONS OF LEARNING

The curriculum should provide ample opportunity for children and youth to analyze together their conceptions regarding various situations so that their values may be moved to a new point of equilibrium and constructive understanding. This means that children should identify securely in their operations with new meanings. They should be helped to assess their feelings concerning situations against the facts which are made available in the conditions for learning along with the consequences of proposed action on the feelings.

Analyzing feelings relative to learning experiences

Many examples about the analysis of conceptions and the assessment of feelings against facts are given throughout the book. To keep before the reader, however, the importance of feelings in the development of higher levels of thinking, some examples are in order here. People are always mindful of the experiences which make them feel good. They are constantly striving for satisfying experiences. Children and youth, of course, assume pretty much the same pattern as adults and people in general. Outside of requirements essential to the accomplishment of certain tasks, they gear their activities largely around goals which are envisioned as producing feelings of satisfaction. In the process of reaching their goals, children and young people are very conscious, also, of those experiences which have not been satisfying. They do everything to avoid feelings which might be referred to as "lows" or "in the dumps." They are always looking for the "highs" or the "walking on clouds" type of feelings. They want feelings of elation, of exuberance, of excitement. Thus the quest for the "highs" goes on.

It is perfectly natural for people to desire experiences which will make them feel good. Certainly, one should do everything possible to avoid ugly experiences. Sometimes, however, the pursuit of satisfying experiences may become such an obsession that it is engaged in at all costs. The quest may proceed without regard to consequences. The pattern of seeking satisfying experiences or for the "things that make one feel good" may become so firmly established in the child in the process of growing up that he may lose all sense of reality. This pattern, furthermore, will have the effect of gradually reducing the responsibility for intellectual inquiry. The pursuit may be associated with a pattern of acquisition so simple as to insulate the mind against any serious basic and high level powers of application.

Examining distorted conceptions of learning. Some of the practices in schools contribute to a rather low level pursuit for satisfaction. If learning proceeds on the basis, for example, of an attitude which equates hard tasks with monotonous drudgery, it is contributing to a rather questionable approach to high levels of thinking. Other practices which may contribute to a pursuit of satisfaction regardless of consequences may be characterized by the following directions which are sometimes given to children: "When you have finished your work, you may read the new books on the reading table," "When you have finished your seatwork you may do something more interesting," "On Friday afternoons during the last period you can do what you want to," "When you've finished your art work you may do something more interesting," "This course is no fun, let's all understand that."

An illustration which is apt is an experience the writer had when he was a supervisor in a school system several years ago. He had discussed with a principal the idea of improving learning by developing the conditions where the children would participate in planning some of the work they would need to do in acquiring some competences in communication. The principal did not display much enthusiasm over the idea but agreed to work with it. Sometime following this discussion, the principal called the supervisor to come and see his class in action during the last period of the week. The supervisor, glad to comply with the request, went to the school and was entertained by a play that six or seven children had developed. Most of the children in the room were participants only in the sense of listening. Although the children enjoyed the performance, they displayed a sort of release characterized by an unnatural form of hilarity. The principal said, "You wanted more participation by the children so here you have it. We do this every Friday afternoon at this same time."

This type of display represents a fallacy in learning. There was no real learning intended in this situation. It was planned for Friday afternoon so that it would not break into the "important work" which was carried on for most of the week. The planning had been perfunctory because no real value was attached to it by the children. That the activity was considered a rather unnatural break in the sequence of experiences was made apparent by the children as their behavior revealed a more or less sharp release of pent-up feelings. To them this was not to be construed as learning. It was fun which, to them, provided an escape from elements of unpleasantness. Furthermore, the fact that this "release" always came on Friday as a sort of special occasion was further proof to them it really was not a part of school.

One might say that the attitude behind this whole process contributed to a dissipation of learning; that is, the activity not only was considered as something apart from learning but, also, enjoyment was regarded as unrelated to work or constructive achievement. This type of practice represents an attitude which places learning and satisfaction on opposite ends of a pole; also there is the idea that enjoyment and pleasure are special privileges which have no relationship to the process of learning.

Using interests of children to develop a demand for ideas. As indicated previously, another practice which contributes to rather low level goals and practice is represented by the statements: "When you have finished your work, you may read the new books on the reading table" and "When you have finished your seatwork you may do something more interesting." These directions are still given frequently in many classrooms. The "reading table" is frequently stocked with what are usually considered pleasure reading types of materials. A rather emphatic distinction seems to be made between work-type reading and reading for pleasure.

Relative to this attitude one might ask: Is the reading which the pupil does at the reading table less valuable or productive in ideas because it is thought of as pleasure reading? Is not there an integral relationship between the skills that he has acquired in so-called work-type reading and his enthusiastic approach to the books at the library table? Does he stop thinking when he approaches the reading table or when he does "something more interesting"? Why would it not be just as logical to say to the children, "When you have finished working at the library or reading table, you may work with some of the other reading which we have planned"? Or, would it not be just as logical to say to the children, "As you work with some of the interests which you have indicated, will you take note of some new things you learned about the interests? Were other interests discovered in the process of working with your regular interests?"

It is important to use the interests which children have to point up other interests and needs. Following this, the teacher and children might plan the experiences which would give meanings and establish competences relative to their interests and needs. This practice would tend to develop an aspect of the conditions which increasingly demand a type of communication among the teacher and children designed to produce a higher level of thinking. The conditions would create the necessity of resources of all types. By virtue of the expansion of interests, the process would demand much more than talk. The communication responsibilities would make it necessary for the individuals to reinforce their thinking more and more with study and research in connection with books, pamphlets, visual materials, resourcefulness of others and experimentation. The teacher would constantly work with the children to analyze and assemble the books and other resources in terms of the questions which have arisen in their study, research, and communication activities. As the teacher and children work together in this learning environment, they will increasingly establish levels of acquaintance with new interests and advanced ideas. Together they will consolidate the meanings at a new level of understanding. They will thus have attained extended areas of competences.

Developing conditions for the testing of perceptions of facts

The conditions and process indicated above might be illustrated by two different approaches to the study of Mexico and its people. The study might have its inception either at the reading table with the new books or with the regularly planned program of reading. A typical approach to the study of Mexico would be to read some books and make observations as to how living in that country is different from living in the United States. Children would read about the homes of Mexican people. They would read and talk about their occupations, their recreation, their holidays, religious customs, and so on.

The discussion, readings, and activities in this approach are designed to draw attention to the differences of Mexican living as compared to that of people in the United States. Some culminating activities productive of murals, notebooks, oral and written reports usually close off the study of Mexico and its people. The questions which present themselves are: What have the children really learned? Have the values of children moved to a new point of equilibrium and constructive understanding? Have the children assessed their feelings relative to the facts in the situation? Have they had the opportunity to analyze their feelings in terms of the consequences? In view of the above questions, has the communication which has taken place in the typical approach indicated produced a higher level of thinking? It is extremely doubtful whether the process involved in the approach has produced any real sense of value analysis or understanding on the part of children and teachers. What then needs to be done?

Experimentation to derive high level meanings. The curriculum must be designed to develop the conditions wherein the ingenuity of the different people will be tested. Furthermore, it must provide for an identification on the part of the learners with the values highly regarded by different people. Although the topic chosen for this illustration appears to be in the realm of the social studies, in order to test the ingenuity of Americans and Mexicans, for example, it is necessary to venture into some scientific experimentation. The subject of this inquiry might be the homes of people in rural Mexico. The homes are built largely with an earth product, adobe. The children and teacher might discuss the whole question of ingenuity and decide on a procedure of testing it with regard to houses. It seems plausible that the teacher and children might discuss the reasons for the types of houses in which many of the people of rural Mexico live. It is necessary to study some facts relative to people and houses.

Wherever people live, they will attempt as far as possible to provide shelter which will be comfortable. This necessitates the study of those elements which contribute to discomfort as well as those which create comfort for people. Some natural causes of discomfort, for example, are extreme heat in summer and extreme cold in winter. In the winter time, on the other hand, people make an effort to secure heat for comfort. At this point, it is important to acquire some facts about climate. These facts and others provide the conditions for children to assess their feelings in terms of the facts, that is, the children will tend to alter preconceived notions and approach a new point of understanding. They will think about, discuss, and study the efforts of people to provide for the alleviation of discomfort.

In connection with the study of Mexico, it is hoped that thought, discussion, study, and analysis will provide the procedure to test the ingenuity of the Mexican people with respect to simple housing. At the same time, chances are that the children will test the ingenuity of American people with respect to simple housing. Perhaps, to make the test, they will improvise miniature adobe and frame houses in the classroom. The houses will be put in a place where they will be subject to the same temperature. With thermometers the children might ascertain which of the two types of houses will be cooler in the summer and warmer in the winter.

Arriving at high level generalizations. In all probability, the thermometer readings show that adobe houses are warmer in winter and cooler in the summer. A discussion of the readings would lead to the development of reasons and meanings relative to the facts about shelter and climate. Questions such as, Why is an adobe house cooler in summer than a frame house? and, Why are adobe houses found only in certain regions? would be considered. The discussion relative to questions could lead to a study of the sun's rays and their action on sundried earth as compared to frame materials. Furthermore, children in their quest for meanings would find that a reason for the extensive use of adobe houses by Mexican people is that this product is more available than lumber. This would be discovered from a study of parts of Mexico as well as the southwestern part of the United States.

Other possible generalizations which might develop are as follows:

Mexican people are fully as ingenious as people of the United States in providing shelter suited to the climatic conditions.

Adobe serves the same purpose as insulation.

Some materials are greater conductors of heat than others.

One sign of intelligence is the use of the resources at hand to facilitate and improve life.

The acquisition of facts by themselves should not be viewed as a finality in the process of learning.

When an individual draws conclusions on the basis of his perception alone, he limits the conditions for self-understanding.

It should be noted that the possible generalizations indicated above which might be arrived at by children contain both simple and abstract elements. The testing of the ingenuity of the people who have created different types of shelter, may easily bring about in the establishment of some rather simple concepts or understandings. The conditions for the development of these concepts, however, provide the basis for study and inquiry on a higher level. From the study and experimentation might come ideas, for example, about the extent of conductivity of heat in different types of materials. Thus will develop a greater concern and occupation with scientific meanings. Facts would not be viewed as a finality of learning but rather as points of contact in thinking with new facts. For example, an understanding of the qualities of nonconductivity of heat or cold on different materials has led to the development of improved products for people.

The conditions which have been described and the illustrations which have been indicated are, of course, not nearly exhaustive of the provisions which the curriculum must make to enable children and youth to move to new points of equilibrium and constructive understanding. It is hoped, however, that the discussion has served to point up some responsibilities and opportunities of curriculum workers in developing the conditions for learning which will help children to gradually identify with, and pursue, a higher level of meanings.

FACILITATING EFFORTS OF CHILDREN AND YOUTH TO SEEK MEANINGS

The curriculum should be developed in such a manner as to facilitate the efforts of children and youth to seek meanings. Children should be helped to learn ways of achieving results meaningful to them in the most efficient manner. One of the first essentials in embarking on achievement is to discover what is interesting to different individual children. Then, too, it is important to find out what common interests are held. It is important to know what the ideas are with which children and youth identify. It would, however, be a serious mistake to act upon interests alone. To have children work on their interests indiscriminately might be an invitation to chaos. To illustrate, suppose someone said that his interest was in hot rods. To proceed on the basis of this expressed interest without considerable redirection might be a step toward the negation of real educational values.

Helping children understand abstract relationships of simple meanings

Some interests must be viewed as symptoms of values a child holds. The hot rod type of interest might be classified as being in the symptomatic category. That does not mean, however, that this expression of interest should be eliminated as a possible source of meanings. Viewing the interest in a positive way, the teacher's task is to develop with a youth those conditions which will cause him to seek deeper meanings with respect to it. The conditions for seeking meanings could, for example, lead into a rather intensive analysis of the behavior associated with "hot-rodding." The interest, then, may be dealt with in connection with cartoons, news stories, and the various consequences resulting from the behavior associated with this so-called sport.

To develop practices on the part of young children to seek meanings, it is necessary to make provisions in the school and classroom for these practices to occur. For example, a developmental arithmetic center might be established in a classroom. The teacher might give some initial suggestions for such a center. His initial efforts could be the clue to children to develop many features in the center for expanded meanings. One feature of the center might provide for the development of meanings with respect to the use of symbols with number groups. The center might contain boxes of bottle caps, checkers, or buttons which could be used for grouping of numbers into various combinations. Children might consider the meaning of nine things. The following question might get some thinking started: Are there different ways of showing nine? The children would get nine bottle caps and try to arrange them in different ways. Other questions and comments which might arise are: Can we make as many groups as we want to out of the caps? You cannot make many bunches because there aren't many caps. I count four caps and five caps. Is that nine? Are six caps and three caps nine caps? Four and five together and six and three together each make nine.

Facilitating opportunities for children to approach meanings differently. There would be other comments and questions. Some children would discover that they would arrange the groups in many ways and find that each time they could count nine altogether. At this point, the teacher might introduce into the arithmetic center cards which have the number names both written and as symbols. The teacher could suggest to the children that these cards might help. Before he points out, however, how the symbols might be used, he should let children talk about the cards and how to use them so that they might have the thrill of discovering some ways of using them by themselves.

Chances are that some of the children will find out how to use the cards to identify the groups they have made; others will use a set of cards to indicate the two or three groups and the total; still others will use the cards in place of bottle caps entirely. Thus different children are discovering different ways of using the cards. Some learn quickly to use the symbols represented by the cards without the aid of the caps. These children are probably ready to enter into the stage of learning which requires the use of more abstract meanings of numbers than some of the others. The other children will probably have to approach the abstract meanings more gradually. The teacher, of course, makes use of all these clues in furthering the understanding of arithmetic.

As children talk about what they are doing, they are gradually learning more and more ways of representing the meaning of a certain number. As they are acquiring more advanced meanings with respect to numbers, it follows that they will need to communicate these meanings in their own way. Whereas, they first might say that four caps and five caps are the same as nine caps in connection with grouping the caps, later they might indicate that four (4) and five (5) mean the same as four caps and five caps, so they can save time by just recording 4 and 5 are 9. The important point here is that children are figuring out meanings through the conditions provided, resulting in a greater understanding of number relationships.

In all probability, the identification with meanings by the children will be more intensive than if the teacher had gone through the meanings step by step. The teacher, of course, had given some direction to the meanings by virtue of the development of the arithmetic center with the children. Then, after the children have dealt with the meaningful materials and devices in the center, the teacher will, no doubt, help clarify and unify some of the meanings which have been discovered by the children.

Developing conditions for approaching more advanced meanings. The next steps which might be taken in connection with the arithmetic center are in terms of the clues which the children have provided by communicating their understandings. New devices which might be used with more advanced approaches to number meanings are made a part of the center. It is extremely important, of course, that the center be continuously expanded so that a wide range of opportunity is provided for the fulfillment of the potential strengths of all the children. For example, the center will include devices to represent thinking relative to fractions, the relation of ones and tens, simple forms of measurement, and so on. The nature of the ability of different children in their thinking with numbers should be carefully observed by the teacher so that guidance and clarification might be given at the proper time and place. Every effort should be made to encourage children to talk with one another about new discoveries and to demonstrate their thinking for the class. By approaching this responsibility, children will experience both a satisfaction and a sense of seriousness in the tasks which they undertake. At the same time, within this responsibility, they will gradually take on a higher mode of communication because of the new interests that are being developed and the new learnings with which they have identified.

The curriculum should provide the conditions for seeking meanings on the part of older children as well as youth of secondary school age. The illustration in reference to a laboratory of communications indicated in Chapter 6 indicates some ways in which opportunities may be provided for children, ages nine through fourteen, to seek meanings. In fact, a more advanced laboratory in communications would serve efforts toward self and group realization for meanings among youth and adults. In the succeeding section, an attempt will be made to point out some of the conditions which might be developed for youth to come to a better understanding of some new meanings about their existence.

THE CURRICULUM MUST HELP YOUTH FIND NEW AREAS OF USEFULNESS

One of the questions which faces youth as well as adults today is: What are the new areas of usefulness which must be conceived in today's practice of living? One of the major objectives of education is that youth develop the arts and practices of effective citizenship. This means that youth must develop competences which will enable them to understand contemporary life and occupy resourceful roles. If this objective is to be realized even in part, it seems essential to develop the conditions wherein youth as well as adults will increasingly become aware of what skills and knowledge are needed for the practice of effective citizenship tasks. More important than that is to gain an understanding of the problems which people will have to face in the pursuit of citizenship roles today. Youth must have an opportunity, therefore, to discover what is important in the task of total living.

Developing conditions for youth to seek new roles of usefulness

It is essential that the learning environment be charged with those elements which will evoke concern and action on the part of youth to seek roles in new areas of usefulness. Questions such as the following might provide some direction: What acts are usually considered as important to success? What are the areas of usefulness as now conceived? What are some areas of usefulness and importance which have been overlooked? What is meant by being socially adjusted? What constitutes a reasonable and balanced horizon of wants?

As you view the new developments in science, what do you envision as possible new roles for young people? To what degree is science considered an instrument of survival? One frequently reads about the efforts at superiority in scientific advance. When writers and speakers make statements about superiority in scientific advance, what are the criteria upon which they base their thinking? In your estimation, in what areas of living will surprises be occasioned by scientific innovations? What areas of knowledge are most instrumental in influencing the changes in living? There are, of course, many other questions with which youth would be concerned, but the above constitute a rather broad base for higher communication relative to the meaning of one's existence.

Clarifying concepts as to what is important. Assuming that a center of learning relative to these questions might be established in the school, one of the first steps is to bring into the setting a consideration of the acts which are usually regarded as quite important. An example of such acts would be the following: Be neat and systematic. Be punctual in your tasks. Conform to the rules set down. Be agreeable. Work hard.

These items have been stated so often that they have become equated with success and responsible action. For example, the first task approached by a businessman or executive as he comes to his desk is to clear it, to answer letters, take care of routine items, and to follow through with the details. To work hard is considered axiomatic with success. It is important to be agreeable so that things will go smoothly. There is danger in becoming so devoted to habitual acts that the extent of their importance may never be questioned. Perhaps these habits are not as important as usually considered. Perhaps a more constructive way of looking at these items is that it is important to consider them, follow through on them, and then get at the more important tasks. In other words, let's be punctual, clear the desk, and tend to other minor details so that we might get at the real areas of usefulness.

Developing conditions for seeking new roles in home and family relations

To illustrate further with respect to new and more important areas of usefulness, one's responsibility in connection with the home might be analyzed. Frequently, a youth views his responsibilities in connection with his home as requirements. He will try to do his part in conforming to and contributing to the smooth functioning of the home in terms of the rules and regulations established by his parents. In doing his part, however, he finds that there isn't much to the task. He finds that there isn't much to do to conform to the requirements set down by parents. Actually, his responsibilities with the home are rather meager. As a result he does not actually come to grips with the real meaning of home and family living. In the development of the conditions for learning about the meaning of one's roles, it is important to include those ingredients which will develop a perception of new and expanded areas of usefulness with respect to the home. These ingredients might relate to such questions as the following:

How might one become more useful in the development of the well-being of one's home life?

What are the assets accruing to us out of family sacrifices?

What are the expenditures which we incur which may come under the category of liability items?

What are the pressures which are instrumental in causing us to incur liability costs?

How may we develop a new sense of direction relative to those acts which we perceive as liabilities?

How may we get parents involved in the development of some expanded meanings relative to home and family living?

In connection with the first question, the discussion would revolve around the question of what can be done to give aid and comfort to the family as a whole. In other words, are children and youth asking for more than their fair share of attention and service from the parents? The discussion and study would lead to possible ways in which youth might be more useful and contributory to family stability and resourcefulness than just doing what is expected. A careful rethinking and reappraisal of family living on the part of youth would tend to strengthen the bonds of mutual action in the family group. Youth, under the conditions of a center of learning charged with meanings about family life, would have the opportunity to form new insights and understandings as well as carve out new areas of usefulness relative to the family group. The teachers, students, and others who work with the curriculum must provide these conditions for learning.

Helping youth to see the assets of family relationships. As suggested by the questions on assets derived from the family, young people will become conscious about items which are usually taken for granted. As young people are growing up, they frequently lose sight of the sacrifices which are made by parents to provide for their well-being. If the actual sacrifices are broken down into tangible meanings, chances are that young people will develop a greater sense of appreciation of what their home means to them. Furthermore, an identification with these meanings will tend to develop a greater concern for the problems of family life and the responsibilities which are entailed.

Some of the assets which accrue to youth, and which are usually taken for granted, are clothes, incidentals for recreation, and items for furthering opportunities, such as music, travel, education. In these assets may also be considered insurance policies which are purchased for the protection of the family, investments which are made tangible by figuring out what they mean in dollars and cents. The impact of the meanings should become more intense if those who are planning to attend college will figure out the cost. More and more, as young people analyze the assets which come to them from the family, they will tend to realize the sacrifices which are made by parents in their behalf. Furthermore, meanings with respect to their debt or responsibility to the family as a whole will be pointed up with greater and greater intensity. Going further, when young people begin to conceive of the unselfishness of their parents in the sacrifices, their gratefulness will increase which, in turn, will tend to intensify a mutual responsibility in family functions.

The discussion with regard to the assets which young people derive from the family group has dealt more or less in terms of material considerations. As young people work with the center of learning on family development, they will gradually perceive more and more assets of a moral and spiritual nature. They will dwell on phases of happiness resulting from home and family living. They will analyze other elements of family living, such as the bonds of affection which keep the family together, the examples of teamwork which prevail in family functions, and the great moral and spiritual supports contributed by the combined wisdom which is inherent in the family group as a cohesive body. As the members deal with the many questions which have evolved about the family as an operating unit, they will come to attach greater importance to the role that each one must play. Thus the family will function more effectively for each and every member. They will come to recognize that one must give as well as receive, that one must be creative in the family endeavor as well as be a recipient of the creation. The facts and ideas relative to family development will indeed become responsibilities of a moral and spiritual character.

Helping youth assess liabilities which may be incurred in family relations. As the youth deals with the assets resulting to him from his home and family, he will also consider the liabilities which he may be incurring, both from his point of view and that of his parents and other members of the family. Although the family as a whole will consider the need for balanced living, there are certain costly practices which may be unnecessary. Some of these may be certain social events, unduly high expenditures on dates, and expenditures based solely on peer pressures. Young people will, under carefully developed conditions for learning, try to resolve such questions as the following: What are the things we do because of peer pressures? What would it mean in dollars and cents if we succumbed to all the peer pressures? Does adjustment mean that we must do what others do? What is a reasonable approach to the question of emulation of peers? How can we begin to influence a redirection of the peer concept of values?

Conditions for understanding related aspects of home and family living. The development of answers to the above questions will require much basic thinking, reading, and research on the part of young people as well as adults. The teacher, in aiding this thinking and study, must become involved with the whole problem of peer relations of boys and girls. He will need to become conversant with the pressures and forces which operate in the culture of these young people as well as those which operated in the cultures of people of other times and places. He must make himself conversant with the literature which reveals great thought on societal forces and the family. He will need to read and discern the thinking of sociologists and anthropologists on family life and youth problems in different cultures. He will need to become aware of and to digest the thinking of psychologists on peer relations and the culture. Furthermore, he will need to become aware of the type of literature and studies which can be used by the young people.

The center for the development of new perceptions about home and family living should take on expanded meanings as youth become involved with the studies, research, and literature related to the question of social forces, peer pressures, social values, and the behavior demanded by different cultures. Youth can be helped to become very resourceful with the center of learning on family living. They will be encouraged to bring to the center all the types of readings, for example, which have been conceived by them as contributing answers to their questions. It is important, of course, that the learning conditions be sufficiently free so that this will be done. If all values of youth are to be admitted into the instructional setting for appraisal and examination, it means that all the vicarious sources from which youth receive answers are admitted for the same purpose.

The author, in his association with young people, is impressed with their great potential for new areas of usefulness and thinking. Too frequently the program of the school has been organized with a complete unawareness of this potential. It is the responsibility of the school to provide those conditions which will cause the potential of young people to evolve into new directions of effectiveness. The development of the educational setting with the stimulating ingredients for positive fulfillment of the powers of youth should be the heart of the curriculum task of all staff members in a school. If the conditions for learning contain the stimulating effects for the evolvement of high level communication among young people about such questions as indicated on the previous pages, a most constructive step has been taken toward a dynamic curriculum for youth.

Analyzing peer relationships for new areas of usefulness

Following through with the questions relative to liabilities resulting from peer relationships, what are some of the ideas which may develop as young people study and communicate their thinking on the questions? In the first place, it must be recognized that peer relationships are extremely important to young people as well as adults. Even if one does not perceive matters the same as his peers he, nevertheless, finds it necessary to go along with them in various situations. A certain feeling of security is established by functioning in terms of the wishes of the group. In the second place, it is recognized by individuals that it is necessary at times to go along with the group so that they will become sufficiently established with it to exercise influence toward new areas of thinking. Everyone is at different times consciously playing roles. He may be playing a role to identify himself with his peers. He may be playing other roles to test the reactions of his peers to them. He may assess the reactions carefully and come out with a role which may preserve the equilibrium of his peers and, at the same time, establish direction with respect to new anticipations of behavior. In other words, several people in the group may have wanted to break out of the confines of the thinking of the peer group and found their opportunity in the new direction established by the role performed by a discerning and courageous individual of the group. This has already been discussed to a considerable extent in Chapter 16. A possible step in the development of a new sense of direction is an exploration of proposals for action on the questions studied.

Conditions for analyzing liabilities of peer relationships. An initiatory step to action on the liabilities of certain peer relationships is to locate the problems inherent in them. After the problems are located, they should be analyzed carefully to determine the reasonable and unreasonable actions of the peer group. An attempt would be made to discover how the unreasonable actions became a part of the peer role; also to point out how these actions have led to expenditures which were unnecessary and which worked hardships on at least several members of the peer group.

The young people might plan to bring the whole question out in clear perspective. One phase of the planning would be to list, in connection with various situations and activities, those actions which are necessary and warranted for each activity and those which are superfluous and superficial. For example, they might feel that it is necessary for a boy to buy an inexpensive corsage for his date as well as to see that she is escorted to the dance. Some individuals might also decide that it would be nice to have something to eat after the dance. They might feel that it is unnecessary for a boy to take his girl to an expensive dinner before their date and to own a car for the purpose. In other words, they will try to arrive at some budget for different activities which will not work a hardship on youth or their parents and, at the same time, enable them to carry out the requirements of the activities in a respectable manner. They will attempt to influence against the superficiality which is exemplified in excessive expenditures.

It is hoped, of course, that the planning indicated above may result in a more basic study of superficiality, for example, and the forces which operate to bring it about. The conditions for learning should be sufficiently charged with questions and literature to bring about some of this basic study and thinking. This would necessitate reading and studying of literature on the high school student's level in the fields of sociology, economics, anthropology, and social psychology, as well as other areas relating to the forces which influence practices in social behavior.

Conditions for developing new directions in peer relationships. A period of study of the literature, interspersed with occasions for the communication of thinking relative to the literature, could result in action designed to build values on the basis of realistic meaning to youth. With the conditions provided for the assessment of values regarding peer relationships, some real meanings might become clarified relative to the constricted practices prevailing in the peer group. One meaning which might become apparent is that a certain confined pattern of behavior in the peer group is usually that of adherence to particular social class values. As a result of this clarification, a possible form of action may develop which might be characterized as a "sense of humor" practice. This means that certain peer practices may be viewed as ridiculous since the practices are impossible of attainment by some of the members because of economic factors. In other words, as these members would strive to approach the plane of living of others, they would come to realize that if the attainment appeared in sight, the other group would have moved beyond. Then the process would have to be started all over again. It is obviously impossible to emulate certain members of the group. Furthermore, the values achieved would fall far short of a preconceived importance of them. The burden of evidence, then, as to the true values would be in another direction than the original constricted values apparent in the peer group.

The redirection which could very possibly take place would be toward a new concept of values of the peer group. This redirection would be away from class consciousness. In the action accompanying the new direction, the emphasis could very well lead to the establishment of study and discussion centers for the improvement of competences of all young people. They may, for example, wish to help the teacher extend the opportunities for the development of understandings and competences in the areas of science, arts, the humanities, economics, language, and social and human relationships.

With the involvement of their parents in the effort, they may use the funds they would normally expend for unnecessary luxuries toward the equipping of a school and community center for the study and understanding of science in the present society. Other students may wish to do the same with the arts. Still others might make plans to develop a center for youth economics. Some may wish to bring together the books and materials which deal with the study of the incentives of man.

Analyzing wants and needs toward new areas of usefulness

The efforts which would be made in the development of the various centers of learning together with the understandings and knowledge emanating from the efforts could very well lead into a center of a unified study of wants and needs. Young people would develop a list of wants and assess them against their needs. In arriving at these wants and needs, they would deal with such questions as the following: When thinking about wants, what criteria should be developed with regard to limitations? What are our needs as compared to what we would like to have? Will the determination of our wants have an effect on others? If so, in what way and to what degree? How might we develop the means whereby the human aspirations of all would be integrated? How does the principle of sacrifice operate in the pursuit of our wants?

In connection with the study and thinking about these questions, the wants and needs might be considered in relation to a time table of realization. The wants and needs might be distributed into (a) those immediately realizable, (b) those realizable over the next few years, and (c) those realizable in the more distant future. In each case there would, also, be a description of the means proposed for realizing the wants. The wants could further be categorized into those which have to do with financial returns, such as jobs and certain economic and technical competences, and those with more intangible rewards, such as the study of art, travel, aesthetic consumption, sacrificial type responsibility, community service skills, and some professions.

As one views the questions above and the conditions which might develop as a result of the study and thinking relative to both the questions and conditions, he can indeed be hopeful with respect to the level of communication which would follow. Youth, in the process of dealing with the questions and centers of learning indicated, will be obliged to carry the communication of their thinking and observations far beyond and above the routine confines of peer group perceptions. It is assumed, of course, that the teacher will have opened the channels to the literature which will provide background for young people in their efforts to communicate effectively about the questions. With the resources which youth already bring to the questions and conditions for learning, the involvement which is provided with the literature cannot fail to definitely raise the level of communication into higher levels of thought and understanding.

Helping youth understand the inevitable search for need fulfillment. In connection with the center of learning about wants and needs, a youth will try to come to an understanding with himself on what it is that he is seeking. The question of happiness will be fully digested in the process of study and communication. The problem of man's pursuit of the ultimate good could come in for a good share of philosophical analysis. The possible consequences of different means of realization of wants might be analyzed and appraised. The problem of selfishness in people will be studied and discussed openly and freely. A clearer concept of the meaning of sacrifice will be established. In all probability, there would come out of this study and communication many altered conceptions on the part of youth in regard to the real purposes of living and the means chosen for the attainment of the purposes.

Developing understanding of roles in national and world problems

As youth study and communicate their thinking and understanding relative to the meanings of home and family living and man's existence, an infinite number of related learnings will be encountered by them. As they proceed to establish thinking as to ways of realization of their purposes, they will have to face up to the barriers which exist. Furthermore, they will have to become conversant with the means already designed to facilitate greater realization on the part of people. They will, for example, have to identify the great price which is exacted for the maintenance, defense, and perpetuation of freedom and democratic principles. They will need to clarify for themselves the sacrifices that people are making in maintaining a greater national defense program than ever before in history. The bulk of the national budget goes for national security. In connection with this fact, youth will need to gain increased knowledge and understanding about what people in high places are doing to promote peace and good will among nations.

Youth should, no doubt, become greatly concerned about the nature of foreign policy; its effects in ameliorating aggressive practices and the burden imposed on people because of the atmosphere of distrust. It should become increasingly clear to youth that theirs is a tremendous responsibility in helping devise the channels of communication and understanding which will tend to lessen the tension that distorts man's powers and means of resourcefulness.

Developing understanding of government problems as related to youth. Other related learnings which youth could encounter in connection with the study on home and family living are the questions of government subsidies, social security, scientific and social research, and others. They will need to become conversant with the reasons for government subsidies, for example, and the issues involved. They will need to become acquainted with the basic meanings of such terms as per cent of parity, soil bank, crop control or restriction, and so on.

The question of social security would become a clearly integral phase of the home and family center of learning. Young people should have ample opportunity to become conversant about how they now are, and will be, affected by the social security laws. They should also learn how the social security measure was brought about and what efforts have been made over the years to strengthen it as a phase of human welfare and protection. The curriculum should provide for the conditions which will lead to an expansion of learning on the history of pension and security movements all over the world. It should further change the conditions for learning with questions about the motives involved in social security, the relation of individual initiative to security, the provision of incentives through social security, and the broader issues of the whole program.

Discovering new areas of usefulness in scientific and social research

The curriculum should have definite provisions to enable youth to discover the nature of the scientific and social research which has been done and which is being carried on for the advancement of human welfare and understanding among all people. The research, for example, on atomic energy has given rise to many vital questions which must be resolved by people. Youth must now prepare to face the tremendous responsibilities, both political and social, which are involved with the development of nuclear energy.

It has been contended time and again that the time and attention given to scientific research is infinitely more than that given to research for social and human understanding. The present-day curriculum of the schools must develop the conditions for learning which will clarify to young people the need for both the scientific and social research. The laboratory for communication should contain those ingredients which will tend to develop in youth the powers to understand the relationships between science and social meanings. Teachers have an obligation to make available to young people an ample supply of books, films, slides, and other materials on scientific and social research. A phase of the communications center of learning should be devoted to the gathering and development of sources of information on nuclear energy, research carried on in various scientific and social areas, government policy on atomic energy, and the nature of changes which will be brought about as a result of the research and policy. The center should make contacts with personnel engaged in research of types mentioned and work out some plan whereby their resourcefulness will be utilized wherever possible.

The librarian and other staff members of the school should make every effort to organize the services of the library in such a way as to function integrally with the centers of learning which are developed, such as home and family living, mathematical understandings, man's quest for understanding through scientific research, the role of social research in promoting human welfare and understanding, man's efforts to promote security and peace, and many others. These efforts will help provide the impetus toward a level of communication on the part of young people which is productive of thinking and action associated with the tremendous responsibilities occasioned by a changing society and world.

SELECTED READINGS FOR CHAPTERS 15, 16, AND 17

Association for Supervision and Curriculum Development, *What Shall the High Schools Teach?* 1956 Yearbook. Washington, D. C.: National Education Association. Chapters 5 and 6. Gives high level ideas about general, special, and vocational education in the high school.

Barraclough, Geoffrey, *History in a Changing World*. Norman: University of Oklahoma Press, 1956. A revolt against the "parochial" type of history. A rather scathing indictment of the type of history that centers on Europe and in a meaningless fashion.

Brogan, Peggy and Lorene K. Fox, *Helping Children Learn*. Yonkers-on-Hudson, N. Y.: World Book Co., Chapters 3 and 7. Valuable suggestions for developing meanings in arithmetic. Interesting ideas are provided about the meaning of creative living.

Dewey, John, *Logic*. New York: Henry Holt & Co., 1938. Chapter 2. Discussion on biological natural foundations of inquiry.

Frankel, Charles, *The Case for Modern Man*. New York: Harper & Bros., 1956. A thoughtful and exciting book about ultimate values and the promise of modernism.

Hayakawa, S. I., Editor, *Language, Meaning, and Maturity*. New York: Harper & Bros. Parts III, IV, and V. Intensely valuable points developed relative to language and thinking.

Hugh-Jones, E. M., Editor, *The Push-Button World: Automation Today*. Norman: University of Oklahoma University Press, 1956. Will automation emancipate men so that they will no longer be slaves of their own machines? This publication is a helpful resource to lead into new areas of thinking in this technological age.

Kenworthy, Leonard S., *Studying the U.S.S.R.* Brooklyn, N. Y.: The author, Brooklyn College, 1952. A bulletin designed to aid teachers in the approach to the study of the U.S.S.R.

——, *Asia in the Social Studies Curriculum*. Brooklyn, N. Y.: The author, Brooklyn College, 1951. A brief statement of the importance of the study of Asia together with a bibliography for teachers and children about Asiatic countries.

Lane, Howard and Mary Beauchamp, *Human Relations in Teaching*. Englewood Cliffs, N. J.: Prentice-Hall, Inc., 1955. Section II, pp. 87-165. Important discussion on the development of meanings in terms of contemporary needs; pp. 266-280, suggestions for using group discussion and role-playing.

Lapp, Ralph E., *Atoms and People*. New York: Harper & Bros., 1956. Story by a physicist turned publicist about the great need for the peaceful use of atomic energy. Mr. Lapp has contributed measurably to the layman's education on this subject. An excellent resource for developing conditions in the classroom for communication toward higher levels of inquiry.

Mead, Margaret, Editor, *Cultural Patterns and Technical Change*. A manual prepared by The World Federation for Mental Health. United Nations Educational, Scientific and Cultural Organization, 1953. A survey designed especially for workers in the Technical Assistance program. The survey contains many suggestions for communication to relieve tensions in working relationships between peoples.

Miel, Alice and Peggy Brogan, *More Than Social Studies*. Englewood Cliffs, N. J.: Prentice-Hall, Inc., 1957. pp. 259-300. Useful in developing communication tasks with elementary school children.

Mumford, Lewis, *The Transformations of Man*. New York: Harper & Bros., 1956. Penetrating discussion of the development of man. Fundamental questions relating to the destiny of man and the alternatives he faces today.

Schools on the Threshold of a New Era, Official Report. Washington: American Association of School Administrators, National Education Association, 1957, pp. 110-123. An address by Norman Cousins, at the National Convention, A.A.S.A., Atlantic City, N. J., on the creating of a *great idea*. The thoughts embodied in this address could serve as a springboard of communication toward higher levels of thinking.

Smith, B. Othanel, William O. Stanley, and J. Harlan Shores, *Fundamentals of Curriculum Development*, Revised Edition. Yonkers-on-Hudson, N. Y.: World Book Co., 1957, pp. 529-651. Highly significant treatment of theoretical curriculum issues.

Smith, Dora V., *Communication, The Miracle of Shared Living*. New York: The Macmillan Co., 1955.

Sorokin, Pitirim, *Fads and Foibles in Modern Sociology and Related Sciences*. Chicago: Henry Regnery & Co., 1956. Criticism of backward theories and crude methods of the social scientists in approaching an understanding of the group behavior of human beings. Sorokin's interesting chapters on "testomania" will "shake" some proponents of testing. A provocative resource for thought about approaching learning through "epidemics" of systems.

Teaching World Understanding. Ed. by Ralph C. Preston. Englewood Cliffs, N. J., Prentice-Hall, Inc., 1955. Excellent guide to curriculum development in world understanding.

Wiener, Norbert, *The Human Use of Human Beings.* Boston: Houghton Mifflin Co., 1950. Chapters 3-8, 11. Intensely interesting and valuable discussion on a new point of view with respect to communication. The contents should be very helpful to the curriculum worker as he works toward the development of high quality handling of ideas in communication.

Woodbury, David O., *Let Erma Do It:* The Full Story of Automation. New York: Harcourt, Brace & Co., 1956. A rather comprehensive "compendium of information" on automation. This edition should be a valuable resource in the development of higher levels of thinking with youth.

•18•

Developing a New Sense of Stability in Learning

IN A DISCUSSION OF STABILITY, IT IS IMPORTANT TO CONSIDER SOME limiting concepts regarding it. One concept of stability is that which is equated with the quality of being agreeable. One is considered stable if he gets along with people. Stability is often conceived of as a quality of adjustment to a group. Stability in behavior of an individual is often measured by the degree to which he conforms in various group situations. Stability is frequently described in such terms as "fitting in," "mixing," "having tranquilizing qualities," and "going along." There are, of course, many other concepts of stability but the above are sufficient to show some limitations with respect to this condition.

ESTABLISHING CONDITIONS FOR A NEW SENSE OF STABILITY IN LEARNING

It is, of course, rather difficult to say what constitutes stability. What may be considered stable behavior by one individual may not hold true with the meanings attached to it by another. As one views the concepts, as indicated above, however, it should become apparent that several qualities which might establish a heightened sense of stability seem to be missing. There is no mention of the important aspect of uniqueness. The factor of differences is absent. Individual worth somehow fails to be valued. The question of dealing with conflict seems to be avoided. The tenor of the concepts would tend to disregard tension as a factor in stability. Because of the absence of these qualities, the concepts indicated appear to limit the conditions for the development of what we choose to refer to as a new sense of stability.

The new sense of stability as considered in this discussion means the taking on by an individual of those attributes which will function in establishing a sense of oneness with an invigorated environment. He will work to establish the conditions where tension and conflict become operational factors in learning and understanding. He will assess the ingredients of tension for those elements which provide motivation for the dynamics of human existence. This means that he will think and act beyond "escapism." He will act on the principle that it is more comfortable to face discomfort than to retire from it.

Using tension, uniqueness, differences, and other qualities as stabilizing elements

In the above framework of meaning, tension in a sense becomes a stabilizing element in a higher dimension of operation. This equation of tension with stability may be likened to a pilot who is propelling his ship at a comfortable draught depth in an uneasy sea as opposed to one who attempts to bounce erratically from wave crest to wave crest, uncertain as to when he will hit, how he will hit, and the devastating consequences which might ensue if he does hit.

Requirements in the new sense of stability are the conditions for the accentuation of the qualities of uniqueness, differences, personal regard, social sensitivity, curiosity, and enthusiasm for new ideas. These qualities will be present in the establishment and pursuit of goals.

Maintaining equilibrium without crystallization. The qualities must carry those elements of consonance among individuals which will help sustain their sense of equilibrium. At the same time, the state of sustenance will be nourished by a sufficient number of tensional items as to promote continuous and directional change. This condition will tend to prevent the state of equilibrium from becoming crystallized at any particular level.

Providing for resourcefulness in higher dimensions of mean-

ings. Individuals who approach the charged conditions indicated will experience a sense of comfort and satisfaction in a gradually expanding network of ideas. Learning becomes equated with excitement about ideas and their application. The channels of communication will be both lengthened and broadened so that the differences in people will have a free flow of resourcefulness for high level meanings.

The handling of ideas beyond the regular confines of meanings will become a familiar condition in this conception of stability. Research, experimentation and analytical study in this framework of a new sense of stability will become a regular aspect of the learning experiences of all children from beginning elementary years on up. In other words, research and experimentation will be the rule rather than the exception in connection with the pursuit of meanings.

With older children and secondary school youth, the conditions for discovery, testing, analysis, and inquiry with respect to ideas will be well within the realm of "surprises." The conditions must contain that impact which will take children and young people into the higher dimensions of understanding relative to the concepts of space, matter, human adaptation, incentives of people, status, and human behavior.

In this new sense of stability, while differences and other qualities will tend to be accentuated, the individual will seek to ascertain and understand the perceptions of others. As he does this, he will establish a relationship with others sufficiently consonant with their goals generally to elicit their support of his goals even though they are different. He will be acceptant of ideas other than his own for appraisal and examination. He will strive to develop the conditions where all values will be brought into the setting for analysis. He will constantly strive, and enlist the aid of others, to bring about the conditions for freedom of inquiry. In these conditions, open-mindedness and novel approaches to thinking will be highly valued.

Many individuals, teachers, and some school systems are doing some very effective work in promoting the conditions to develop meanings beyond the regularized patterns of learning. Workers in curriculum have the responsibility of expanding the possibilities for the realization of a new sense of stability in learning. There are many avenues of approach which may be conceived in proceeding into this task. Many of these have been suggested in the preceding chapters, such as the approach to intangibles and the analysis of values.

Somewhat more novel directions and areas will be dealt with in the discussion which follows.

ESTABLISHING CONDITIONS FOR REALISTIC DIRECTION IN THE CULTURE AND SOCIETY

In the development of the conditions for the attainment and maintenance of a new sense of stability in learning, it is important to build many meanings with children and youth relative to the problems in the establishment of realistic direction in the culture and society. It is necessary for curriculum workers to provide the resources and bases for an intelligent approach to novel ideas and, at the same time, seek to maintain a related thread of perspectives resident in the cherished elements in the tradition. The heritage must be constantly re-examined for the purpose of bringing out the many elements of richness which have hitherto been viewed only as placid reminders.

Penetrating deeper layers of the heritage for meanings

It is important to penetrate deeply into the layers of meanings residing in the great documents of this and other nations. For example, very little is still being done about handling the ideas which reside in the welfare clause of the preamble of the Constitution. It is doubtful if sufficient consideration has been given to questions such as the following: Is it possible that the thinking about the welfare clause of the Constitution has come to be equated with complacency and security? Does the welfare clause have any relationship to the principle of sacrifice? In what way is welfare related to the conditions of freedom of inquiry? These questions should reveal great possibilities for a depth of thinking compatible with a new sense of stability.

Maintaining responsibility for discriminative selection from heritage. In the process of transmitting the heritage, care must be taken that the handling of ideas relative to the shifting contemporary scene is not restricted by outworn aspects of the tradition. The development of vision into the peripheral field of inquiry should be positive and unmistaken. A new sense of stability in learning demands not only the open-ended conditions for inquiry into high level meanings but, also, a discriminative responsibility toward selection on the basis of pertinence and appropriateness. High level meanings must function in the establishment of high level competences in individual and group performance.

Promoting insight to limiting factors in the culture

In the approach to a new sense of stability in learning, it is important for the individual to gain much insight and understanding of the ways of the culture. Especially significant is the development of a new perspective relative to the factors in the culture which are usually considered as limitations.

A factor which obviously places limitations on an individual is the differentiation in achievement, economic and otherwise. The first thing that one must understand is that differences of this type are prevalent in the culture. Another fact that must be made apparent is that there are no ready answers as to why these differences exist. A third consideration is that it is perfectly natural that differences in achievement exist. No amount of rationalizing will make it otherwise. Rationalization as to one's place in the scheme of things may in effect constitute a self-inflicted limiting process. Rather, a more stable sense of direction may be found when one positively works toward the improvement and fulfillment of the potential peculiar to him as an individual. To illustrate, individuals soon recognize that some people "do better" than others. They find, too, that some have more economic resources at their disposal than others. Some students, for example, have at their disposal one of the family cars or cars of their own, whereas others have to get around the best way they can.

The "less fortunate" youth observe the estimation that the culture puts on economic resources. Riches are all around them. They begin to assess their lot. They wonder why some "have" and others "have not." The apparent limitations may stalk them at every effort they make. If one adopts the "what's the use" attitude, however, he will tend to further limit his potential. Without seeming to rationalize, it is suggested that a careful study of the apparent limitations may lead to a clear recognition of significant routes to goal realization.

Approaching insight to differences in people. The curriculum worker and teacher have important responsibilities in connection with the understanding of differences in people. Certainly, provisions should be made to develop the conditions for learning which will unravel some of the intangibles in the differences. One phase of these conditions is the portrayal and study of the many differences in people. The routes that these differences take in the culture need to be visualized in such a manner as to enable youth to choose intelligently between them in terms of values they have accepted. Youth would be discovering, for example, that choices for potential achievement are not limited to one or the other extreme but are accessible on a wide front. Curriculum workers and administrators should make every effort to enlist the powers of children and youth to make accessible to all the potential resources of education. Any practice which limits the fulfillment of the potential powers of children will weaken the fabric of democratic institutions.

The study of the differences in people and a growing insight by youth into the ways in which the differences function provide innumerable clues for the establishment of goals. When working with the children, it is important for the teacher to promote not only competences in reading, writing, and other areas, but also an intensive understanding of the purposes of people in the workaday world. When children are reading a story about packing up and going for a visit to "grandfather" on his farm, they should be learning more than the story tells. They could be learning, for example, how "grandfather" started his farm, how large it is in acres, what it produces, the work that needs to be done, and whether he is doing it all himself. They could be learning further about how farming has changed as a result of inventions and research, and how and why the standards of living have changed from the time when grandfather was a young man.

The children should learn something about the difficulties which "grandfather" faced on his farm from time to time, that there were "ups and downs" as between productive and lean years. The children will learn, too, that there are other farms different than the one they have been reading about. Some of these farms will have more buildings than others, some are large and some are small. They will begin to raise questions about why the farms are different. They might wonder whether the individuals who have large farms are happier than those who have small ones. Do more extensive possessions make for more happiness? Why are some people who possess little just as contented as others who possess much? Do some people seek a share of contentment in other things than what they are doing? These and other questions which could be raised by children will tend to establish meanings about differences and individual realization.

Studying more advanced questions about differences. In the approach with older children to the study and analysis of differences in people, it is important that the conditions provide for a rather forceful portrayal of purposes and incentives which operate in the culture. Situations would be developed which show, for example, the purposes that different individuals have in wanting to "get ahead." Some may want to "get ahead" so that people will look up to them, whereas others wish it so that they may provide better opportunities for members of their families to fulfill various objectives they have. The whole question of incentives would be studied. Questions such as the following would be examined: What are the factors involved in man's quest for something different or for more than he has now? What has been the nature of the incentives which have brought about the acts of men represented by different events over the years? What seem to be the controlling incentives of men today?

The children would consider differences in their own purposes and incentives. They would try to analyze why they are willing to do some tasks and unwilling to do others. The conditions for this type of analysis could be promoted by indicating on a blackboard or bulletin board all those tasks which seem pleasant to do. Then they would try to determine why these tasks were pleasant. They could use the same procedure with tasks which were considered unpleasant. To go deeper into the development of understanding about incentives, they could develop at least two other categories about tasks. They could portray the tasks which were pleasant but, perhaps, not too useful and those which were unpleasant but extremely useful. They could also indicate the criteria which are used by the culture in judging usefulness and vice versa. Then, too, they could consider tasks which are important but which they could not do at their age. Books and other resources should be made available to add impetus and greater meaning in this approach to an understanding of incentives. This study should give some meaning as to the role of children in this culture. It would also tend to give them a degree of stability, especially as they begin to understand themselves in relation to their environment.

EFFECTING A REASONABLE BALANCE BETWEEN INDIVIDUAL AND GROUP BEHAVIOR

The curriculum is often broadly defined as the process of inducting the young into the ways of the group. A refining of this definition would, no doubt, take into account those experiences which the individual needs to comprehend the purposes and functions of the group and his role in it. The group has, sometimes within broad and sometimes with narrow limits, more or less determined its purposes and goals. The purposes and goals of the individual are expected to coincide more or less with the limits established by the group.

Viewing the social make-up of groups

By and large, the rules, ideals, esthetic objects, and values of the group are established by the culture. For example, the monogamous conception of family is rather firmly entrenched in the American culture. The fact that the family is a primary institution in the American culture and many other cultures would usually not be brought under question in any group. That is not to say, of course, that changes brought about by science and technology have not had their impact on family life.

Many groups have created certain standards which may not be based on the fundamental rules and principles of demo-

cratic institutions. The members of the groups are schooled in
these standards just as if they were the values of democratic
institutions. People began to relate themselves to certain groups
in such a way as to assume a stratified picture. Many studies
by sociologists and anthropolgists have revealed that members
of a community tend to classify one another generally as
"upper," "middle," and "lower." Each of these classes is sometimes further divided into two substrata: upper upper, lower
upper, upper middle, lower middle, and so on. In interviews
with research workers in the studies, it was found that a person
is more apt to speak of another individual or family in such
words as "our kind of folks," "people like us," "we poor folks,"
and the like, depending on his position on the social scale. The
words reveal the social scale as associated to a large degree with
socio-economic status. Other factors which figure in the more
or less intangible classification on the social scale are amount
and type of schooling, family connections, possessions, type of
profession or occupation, and so on.

Developing conditions for social mobility

The curriculum of democratic institutions must develop the
processes of induction into group living which provide for
social mobility. One's birthright would be severely restricted
if he was inducted into the slots of a socially stratified order.
It is, of course, natural for each individual to want to be with
other individuals so as to enjoy that sense of security which
comes from being in a group. The curriculum, however, must
provide for those understandings which promote inclusiveness
rather than exclusiveness relative to groups. This means that
the individuals of a group, while performing certain functions
as a group, recognize and draw strength from the potential of
individuals in all groups. This means, furthermore, that the
affiliation of individuals with groups will be based on factors
quite different from those operating in stratified groups.
Finally, and most important of all, it means that the curriculum
must provide for those conditions which will strengthen and
dignify individual integrity and initiative.

*Providing conditions for meanings and values beyond the
group.* In order to bring about the above conditions relative

to group and individual behavior, it is necessary for the curriculum to provide for many meanings in connection with such terms as riches, goods, sportsmanship, being agreeable, incentives, and courage. Riches, for example, must be conceived as meaning more than possessions and ownership. Riches could relate to ideas, to love, to service, to art and travel. Sportsmanship and being agreeable are often equated with going along with the ideas of the group, even if it means the suppression of individual thought. On the contrary, sportsmanship may frequently be exhibited in espousing an unpopular cause or idea, without withdrawing from the group. At times real integrity is exhibited in not being agreeable to the wishes of the majority with regard to an issue. Great courage has been shown by men throughout history when they had to "stand alone" on important issues in the face of ridicule and persecution. Frequently, it requires great courage on the part of young people to contend for the testing of ideas in terms of consequences before accepting or rejecting them. Too frequently there is a premium on conformity to an idea rather than the examination of it in thinking. One is often more nearly assured of the plaudits of the group if he "goes along" with an idea, regardless of his own individual thinking about it, than if he questions the idea.

Testing issues for directional elements. The curriculum must develop the conditions where issues and ideas are examined as to reasonableness, workability, and promise for individuals as well as groups. The conditions must contain those ingredients which will help develop an attitude on the part of children and youth to discriminate between ideas. Provisions must be made for young people to gain insight as to which ideas can be treated casually and which need to be tested for possible consequences.

An illustration of the treatment of ideas is the preparation for a camping trip. Six or seven young people desiring to camp out a short distance from needed facilities will find that only casual preparations are necessary. If, however, they desire to "pack in" in the mountains far removed from facilities, the preparations need to be anything but casual. In the latter case, the arrangements must be very carefully planned. A casual suggestion by a group to camp out will need to be reconsidered in thinking by individuals. The thinking by individuals will, of course, eventuate in group decision as to the plans for the camping trip. By the acceptance or rejection of various ideas advanced by individuals, the group reaches consensus on a plan which will in turn give satisfactions to individuals. A further element of this plan is that it requires much greater responsibility on the part of each individual for himself as well as for the group than would be necessary in casual preparations. There has to be a reasonable balance between individual and group behavior.

GAINING INSIGHT AS TO REALISTIC, IMMEDIATE, AND FAR-REACHING NEEDS AND RESPONSIBILITIES

The question of development of intelligent insight as to immediate and far-reaching needs and responsibilities has to do with the establishment and fulfillment of immediate and remote goals. The question is also related to a so-called "dream world" and the actual world. It is always important to develop experiences with children which will give some immediate satisfaction and which are related to short-term goals. Many of the experiences, however, should be of such a type as will evolve some generalizations or understandings which will serve as a new departure or beginning to somewhat more remote goals.

For example, nine- or ten-year old children may be experimenting on the movement of air. At first, they may keep records on the direction of the wind over a period of a week. They may make little windmills and put them up to show both the direction and velocity of the wind. The records will show that the direction and velocity of the wind may be different on the different days of the week. Thus they have established a learning or understanding that the direction and velocity of the air movement varies from time to time. This could be considered the fulfillment of a short-term goal. To do so, however, would be restricting the possibilities for further learnings. Consequently, the curriculum should provide for the conditions for further goal establishment and fulfillment. The children might, through their questions and thinking, be led to more advanced experiences having to do with the relation of the air movement to weather and the need for certain types of shelter and clothing. They might decide to examine the velocity of the wind with more precise instruments. They may set up an experiment to show the relationship of velocity to power.

Developing conditions for relationships between immediate and far-reaching meanings

In the approach to the study of the movement of the air as indicated above, it would be somewhat unrealistic for many children to start with an experiment showing the relationship of velocity to power. The goal would be vague and confusing. In order to avoid the possibilities of vagueness and confusion on the part of children, the approach is on a short-term goal basis. This does not, however, preclude the development of a range of experiences so that those children who gain insight more quickly than others might go into the more advanced experiments and ideas. The possibilities in this process are unlimited and far-reaching. In other words, with the development of meaningful approaches from the beginning and the establishment of resultant learnings, many children in the elementary school will gain some rather advanced scientific concepts. They will gain some advanced meanings about natural phenomena and the environment.

The question of immediate and far-reaching needs and responsibilities frequently become quite a problem when working with youth in the secondary school. Many of the studies have been prescribed and designed for youth regardless of their needs and interests. If the students try to ascertain the reasons for the studies arranged for them they are frequently told that they are needed for preparation for college, that the studies will do them good someday, and other similarly vague answers. Seeing no relationship between their needs and the subjects they are required to take, many students become disinterested in school. This disinterest will manifest itself in various forms of behavior not conducive to sound learning.

Clarifying relationships between short-term and long-term goals. The conditions for curriculum development must contain those elements which enable students to relate subjects to both their immediate and future needs. This means that there must be provision for the development of short-term as well as long-term goals on the part of students. The curriculum must provide for the establishment of general as well as special needs and must show the relationship between them. It must also provide for the development of expanded meanings in the pursuit of a goal. There must be a clear indication of the means whereby the thinking of the past is integrally related to the thinking of the present. The teachers, students, parents, and other curriculum workers must exercise a keen sense of discrimination in the selection of materials out of the vast heritage of knowledge which will be most pertinent in the furtherance of learning in terms of the goals which have been established.

To illustrate the conditions which must be established for the development of the understandings and competences on the part of students regarding both their short-term and long-term goals, it is reasonable to assume that they are preparing for various occupations or professions. One will choose the profession of law, another medicine, another industrial arts teaching, still another engineering, and so on. Each one of these and other professions and occupations will require an extended period of preparation before actual practice can begin. The decisions to prepare for the professions or occupations would be long-term goals.

As these decisions are made, there may develop a type of confusion on the part of students relative to their short-term and long-term needs and goals. For example, the student who chooses the profession of medicine as his long-term goal may question whether the study of some of the literature in his English courses would contribute to this goal. Thus he would question the prescription of the short-term goal of some knowledge of the literature designated as part of the English courses. His questions might be well taken; that is, there may not be any visible connection between what he is required to study and his goal. In this connection, the curriculum workers have a very important responsibility. They must see to it that the curriculum makes provision for the analysis of the competences and understandings needed by the individuals who are making great contributions in the various professions or occupations.

The conditions must be developed which will clarify the values held by people in these various callings. Some of the values may be inimical to constructive direction. For example, some individuals who have become doctors may entertain rather restricted meanings regarding the social demands on them. They may have some technical knowledge about the body but very limited knowledge about the relation of human beings to each other and to the environment.

Selecting and treating content to serve short-term and long-term goals. The curriculum needs to provide for the extended meanings which are involved in the preparation for any profession or occupation. It must provide for the development of general knowledge and competences regarding people as well as special insights relative to a profession or occupation. It must provide for the development of those learning experiences which will help the student identify meaningfully with them.

Needless to say, the curriculum worker must be selective in the development of appropriate content. He must, furthermore, promote the conditions which will cause the content to be treated in such a manner as to give immediate satisfactions to students in the form of understandings with which they can identify. That means that the material must be related to human motivations, incentives, communications, and the natural and social phenomena within which people live. A doctor must become an educator, a psychologist, a worker who understands people—their hopes, motives, aspirations, and values. The same holds true in preparation for the other professions and occupations. The short-term needs and goals, then, are those which enable the student to know much about himself —his role in the environment in which he lives. The short-term needs and goals also become the long-term ones as one gradually gains knowledge about people—their incentives, values, motives, and their conception of role expectations in the groups in which they live. These conditions will tend to develop greater intelligence with regard to the approach to immediate and far-reaching needs and responsibilities in terms of realistic demands.

DEVELOPING AN UNDERSTANDING AS TO THE RELATIONSHIP AND SEQUENCE OF IDEAS

A type of competence which is contributory to a sense of stability in children and young people is the ability to see the relationship of one idea to other ideas. When a child is able to do more with an idea than to memorize or repeat it, he rises above the idea. In other words, he has the competence of control; that is, seeing relationships between ideas. He begins to control his learning rather than being subjugated by it. The illustration in the previous section relative to experimentation about the movement of air is appropriate here. As a child experiments with the movement of air, more and more ideas are gradually opening up to him. He will, as he proceeds with his experimentation, find that air is related to water and various elements. He will find that air gives life and may, under certain conditions, cause death. He will gain insight as to the relation of air to transportation. He will discover many other things about air.

Affecting sequence through relating of ideas

It should be noted that the relationship between ideas establishes the sequence of ideas. Frequently, instruction is carried on as if the whole sequence of a subject is the content in the textbook. The subject is taught chapter by chapter until the textbook is completed. Workers in curriculum should study the ways in which ideas grow out of other ideas, establishing a sequence quite apart from any textbook arrangement. The sequence, thus, will take place as the learner thinks through his ideas. The student should not be held to the sequence of the authors of textbooks, especially in those subjects dealing with social questions. Even in subjects dealing with history, the sequence is not all-important. It becomes less important as the student begins to deal in relationships of ideas. The relationships of events precipitating the Civil War, for example, will frequently take on more expanded meanings as students try to visualize and interpret the different factors operating in the events. An even more pronounced deviation from textbook sequence will take place if one approaches the study of history from the contemporary world setting. A vast array of intangibles are encountered which just do not seem to tie up neatly with much of the past. When the past is used in connection with this approach certain phases are selected which may span a whole segment of historical chronology to give meaning to the thinking which is operating on the present scene.

Relating ideas within and between subjects or learning areas. The curriculum must provide the conditions whereby the subjects will be used in a more resourceful manner than is characteristic of teaching in many classrooms today. The importance of subjects can be greatly elevated by treating the content in such a manner as will show the relationship between ideas. The true value of subjects can be enhanced also by bringing together the content of other related subjects to develop a unity of knowledge with respect to ideas. In other words, when the preoccupation with ideas and questions germane to contemporary problems is at the heart of the school program, compartmentalization of content within subjects will severely limit potential understandings on the part of the students. The curriculum must essentially be designed to intensify the importance of subject matter by freeing the processes of learning from the constricting features characteristic of isolated subjects.

A good illustration of the treatment of content so as to develop the relationship of ideas is the topic of automation. This topic can be adequately developed in science only as science draws on history, biology, social science, psychology and a host of other areas. The topic by no means needs to be confined to science. It can be dealt with adequately in the areas of English and social science as the teachers of those subjects draw on other fields of study and resources. Perhaps the most effective way of dealing with this topic is to approach it by itself irrespective of any of the subject areas. This can be done when a school develops the curriculum in terms of unified studies or centers of learning.

One of the centers, for example, could be devoted to social understanding or a visualization of contemporary problems. As the students would work on the topic of automation, they should be able to arrange with the teacher for time to study related subjects such as chemistry, physics, history, mathematics, and others. These subjects would be used to answer many questions relative to the problems of automation. They would also be used to develop competences needed in the areas affected by automation.

It is hoped that through the development of the conditions whereby the student may be freed from the sequence of the textbook and led into an understanding of the relationship of ideas that a greater sense of stability will result. It is felt that, as students develop sequence in terms of expanded meanings, subjects as such will take on increased importance as resources. It is further felt that the curriculum must make provisions for content of subjects to be treated in such a manner as to open up areas of understanding which will go beyond the limitations of subjects. This will result in the individual's control over ideas to use them in new relationships and understandings.

BUILDING ATTITUDES FOR INQUIRY, RESEARCH, AND ABSTRACT MEANINGS AND CONCEPTS

In the previous sections, the importance of freedom of the student from the limitations of the sequence established in textbooks was discussed. Furthermore, the development of the relationship of ideas was stressed as an important factor in enabling the student to rise above the system of facts set out to be learned. It is felt that these conditions will contribute to the development of an attitude of inquiry and research. When a student has attained the enviable position of exercising some control over ideas, he will begin to adopt an attitude of inquiry regarding the relationship of knowledge. In the case of children in the elementary school, the attitude of inquiry and research was illustrated in the study and experimentation about the movement of air.

Promoting research and inquiry with children and young people

It is apparent that the curriculum might make provision for the expansion of ideas into many directions from the study of natural phenomena. The same provision might be made in

connection with more strictly social ideas. Children might be
led into a sense of inquiry relative to the conditions which
produce varying degrees and types of behavior. They might
recount, for example, their degrees of satisfaction and dissatisfaction with the different types of activities in which they
participate throughout a day or several days. As they recall
with the teacher the periods of satisfaction and dissatisfaction,
they might portray the feelings in the form of drawings or
cartoons. Having done this, they might proceed to list the
reasons, as they see them, which have produced the feelings.
Next, the children might try to determine in what way they
contributed in producing both the feelings of pleasure and displeasure regarding certain tasks which they encountered.

*Examining the results of inquiry and research for high level
meanings.* As children are doing this type of social research,
the curriculum workers should develop the conditions which
will lead them into an examination of their feelings in connection with the tasks undertaken. At the same time, the conditions should give the teacher some leads into making certain
tasks take on more of the elements which produce satisfaction.
In connection with some of the tasks where satisfactions do not
readily happen, some reasons could be established with children which would provide some insight relative to this condition.

As the teacher and children discuss the tasks which do not
seem to give satisfactions, other satisfactions might result from
a knowledge, for example, about the deferral aspects of some
of the tasks; that is, the postponement of realization of goals.
Children will be led into an understanding that many of the
tasks which people undertake are not satisfying in themselves,
but lead to satisfying results. For example, it is doubtful whether
an individual enjoys the drudgery which is involved in the
task of building a stone wall. However, as the wall begins to
take shape, he experiences certain satisfactions. They are
perhaps associated with the esthetic, such as beauty and harmony. The individual has visualized some degree of satisfaction
in his preparation of the plans or blueprints of the wall. He
knows, however, that some pain is involved in carrying through
with the plans.

Some satisfaction will result as the task is proceeding. He is satisfied, for example, that the drudgery associated with the task of building the wall has not prevented him from proceeding toward completion. Seeing the stone wall taking shape will give him satisfaction and spur him on in his efforts to complete it. Furthermore, the satisfaction involved in making progress outweighs the displeasure incurred in the hard work necessary in building the stone wall. The degree of satisfaction in the process becomes so related to the end in view that the original feeling of drudgery disappears as an entity in his thinking. The whole process has had the effect of elevating his sense of regard for himself. He has risen above the task. He has approached a new sense of stability.

Sifting out some false meanings about values. The example given above, of course, shows some real constructive tendencies relative to the feelings which are involved in undertaking various tasks. On the other hand, the value-building elements which are potentially present in such a task may be severely limited by the nature of the process itself. One may become so involved with the work that it becomes an automatic process. The tasks may approach the point of "busy work." He might become so wrapped up in everything he is doing that he is unhappy when he isn't doing something. There is a danger of becoming so absorbed with his tasks that he ceases to think about them. In other words, he becomes a happy automaton.

Many classrooms are suffering from similar conditions. Operating on the idea that children should be kept busy so they won't get into mischief, classroom instruction often becomes a series of "busy work" tasks. Experiences are designed to keep children working with no provision for evaluating what they are doing and what is done to them. This practice lends allegiance to the questionable belief that work is a virtue in itself—that by working, he is doing good.

There is no intention here of speaking derogatorily about work. On the contrary, the attitude which stresses the dignity of work should be highly valued indeed. To regard work, however, as a value in itself, with no thought as to its nature and contribution to human development, may be lending strength to a myth. The practice of keeping children busy may prove to be a façade for a lack of imagination or an inadequate conception of the nature and direction of learning.

Work, as indicated in a previous illustration relative to satisfaction and dissatisfaction about tasks, is closely allied with behavior. If work becomes such an obsession with one that he neglects to think about its merits, behavior takes on the characteristics of innocuousness. Work, then, in a sense may result in a release from thinking. Furthermore, it may take on a rather vacuous materialism; that is, one can conceive of only a single goal, acquisition of possessions. Life becomes confined to such activities as will serve this one purpose alone. Behavior in this condition operates in a rather constricted area of values. One does things for himself without any thought as to his responsibility in the broad area of human relationships. Furthermore, the individual has hardened his attitude in such a manner that he values the things external to the self. He has closed the door to any meanings which his tasks might disclose about himself. The question of what the process does to him is beyond the realm of his thinking and understanding. If unforeseen consequences occur which may be baffling to him, they are passed off as "something that just happens."

Helping children and youth experiment with different approaches to abstract meanings. In view of what might happen in an autonomous absorption in tasks, it is clear that an understanding of one's behavior takes on considerable significance. It is important, therefore, to develop the conditions in the curriculum which will help children to analyze their behavior relative to the many tasks which they undertake. Provisions should be made for children to note their feelings of satisfaction and dissatisfaction with tasks. Next, they should be led to determine the reasons for the feelings. They will not be able in some instances to ascertain the reasons for the feelings because the meanings involved will be intangible or abstract.

The curriculum must provide for the development of the attitude that one does not rule out of consideration those elements of living which he does not understand. Children will then be led into a careful analysis of both the tasks which produced satisfaction and those that did not. As they note certain elements which caused them to feel satisfied with certain tasks, they will try to apply the elements to those tasks with which they were experiencing dissatisfaction.

Let us say, for example, that children find the written drill on addition in arithmetic as rather dull. At the same time, let us assume that they find it rather interesting working in the arithmetic corner where they make groups which equal eleven in different ways. For example, they are given several boxes of eleven bottle tops, each of which they group into such combinations as seven and four, three and eight, five and six, and so on. Then the teacher might suggest that as they work on addition combinations on paper they might take different numbers such as fourteen, eighteen, and twenty-three and group them in terms of equivalents rather than totals. Instead of having eleven and seven equal eighteen, they can have eleven and seven equal six and five and seven, or thirteen and five, or three and fifteen, and so on.

In other words, as they go from the simple and concrete concepts of number to the more abstract, they can use the satisfying experiences they had with grouping objects in the groupings with symbols. Also, instead of thinking of different number combinations as totals, they will think in the more abstract realm—conceiving of one combination of numbers as equal to different combinations.

As children think of their behavior in connection with various experiences, they will tend to become more selective in their choice of tasks designed to gain certain competences. Rather than do things just to be busy, they will begin to analyze the tasks in such a way as to gather new meanings as they approach their goals. They may recognize, too, that there is no one way of proceeding in the attainment of purposes. They will experiment with different approaches to the solution of problems. They will more and more arrive at the attitude that their thinking as individuals might be refined and strengthened by the thinking of other individuals. The curriculum workers must help individuals gain a recognition of the power and the worth of the thinking of other individuals in the realization of their purposes. Under these conditions, individuals will also tend to value the opportunity of contributing to the realization of the purposes of their co-workers.

As children experiment with ideas relative to natural and social concepts, they learn much about themselves: their needs, purposes, incentives, and motives. Many questions will arise, of course, which cannot be answered. It is hoped that they will seek to redefine the questions which are baffling to them. They may experiment with ideas in terms of the new definitions. As children try to face up to many questions and test ideas relative to the questions, they approach the realm of abstract thinking.

The discussion in this section has dealt mostly with developing the conditions to promote inquiry and research with the elementary school children to lead to abstract thinking. The same principles can be applied in a more advanced manner with secondary school children. Certainly, the analysis of feelings of satisfaction and dissatisfaction regarding tasks would be even more applicable to young people in the secondary period of learning than in the elementary.

The curriculum should provide for unlimited opportunities to develop laboratories for inquiry and research relative to both natural and social phenomena. Much of the literature of both the past and present could be treated in such a manner as to necessitate laboratory conditions to delineate for meanings the types of behavior inherent in the content. The laboratories for the understanding of scientific principles should deal not only with chemistry, physics, biology, and other subjects, but should be equipped and extended to promote inquiry and research into the new frontiers of science, into the cross-currents of scientific endeavor and its effect on human beings. An example of this is the study of the science of behavior, namely, what causes people to change, what motivates their purposes, and what may produce degrees of "brain-washing" and tendencies toward mental vacuity.

The resources to be used in the study of the science of behavior are extant in the environment as well as the literature in the various fields of learning. A condition of partial mental vacuity, for example, can develop when more and more people resign from thinking about issues which must be solved. When individuals tend to escape responsibility in facing up to problems, their effectiveness in any subsequent situations may be reduced. The curriculum should help students gain an understanding and direction relative to the components of different states of behavior associated with responsible thinking. The components of the different states of behavior should be portrayed in such a way that teachers as well as students might discern the operational effects in the approach to vital questions.

An attempt has been made in this chapter to trace some of the meanings associated with the development of a new sense of stability in learning. It has been suggested that the search for meanings must not be contained by any artificial arrangements. Inquiry into new scientific and social developments must not be postponed or reserved to this or that year in the continuum of the educational sequence. The conditions for inquiry must have the impact for activation at every age level and in every area of learning experiences.

The base for the pursuit of ideas into higher dimensions of abstraction must be broadened to include more and more children and young people. At the same time, there must be present those ingredients which intensify the efforts of students to relate higher level meanings to themselves. In other words, they will find stabilizing elements in the relationships of abstract meanings. They will feel a oneness with the new level of meanings. They will be comfortable with the excitement about ideas.

SELECTED READINGS

Ambrose, Edna and Alice Miel, *Children's Social Learning*. Washington, D. C.: Association for Supervision and Curriculum Development, National Education Association, 1958. Shows many implications of research. Especially significant are Part II: Interrelationships of Environment and Social Learning and Part III: A School Environment Which Facilitates Selection of Democratic Social Learnings.

Barnett, Homer Garner, *Innovation: the Basis of Cultural Change*. First edition, New York: McGraw-Hill, 1953.

Bossing, Nelson L., *Principles of Secondary Education*. Second edition. Englewood Cliffs, N. J.: Prentice-Hall, Inc., 1955. Discusses the importance of the task of secondary education in our democratic society. Especially helpful in establishing a new sense of direction in learning are Chapters V-VIII which deal with the nature of our society, the problems that youth face, and the task of the school.

Bridgman, Percy Williams, *The Way Things Are*. Cambridge, Mass.: Harvard University Press, 1959. Deepens the domain of science and increases the scope of human clarity. Teachers should find this book a real source in trying to understand why one is usually driven to simple approaches to tasks.

Brinton, Crane, *The Shaping of the Modern Mind*. New York: Mentor Books, The New American Library of World Literature, Inc., 1956. pp. 242-262. Valuable to the teacher and curriculum worker in pointing up problems and discontents which are reflected in the roles of people and, hence, youth.

Broudy, Harry S., *Building a Philosophy of Education*. Englewood Cliffs, N. J.: Prentice-Hall, Inc., 1954. A discussion from the viewpoint of classical Realism. Author maintains the ideas of structures in the universe that are normative in the approach to the good life. Although representing a certain point of view, the book furnishes much direction towards the conditions for curriculum improvement. Especially recommended are Chapter 3, The Structure and Dynamics of Personality, and Chapter 5, Reality and Knowledge; also Part II, which deals with the values in education.

Chase, Francis S. and Harold A. Anderson, *The High School in a New Era*. Chicago, Ill.: University of Chicago Press, 1958. Analyzes the new demands to which the high school must respond and how it might adapt itself to the new conditions. Especially significant with respect to a new sense of direction in learning are Parts II and III.

Galbraith, J. K., *The Affluent Society*. Boston: Houghton, Mifflin, 1958. Questions conventional thinking on economics.

Goffman, Erving, *The Presentation of Self in Everyday Life*. Edinburgh: University of Edinburgh, Social Sciences Research Centre. Monograph No. 2, 1956. An analytic approach to the presentation of self. Excellent for teachers in working on values of people.

Huxley, Julian, *New Bottles for New Wine*. London: Chatto & Windus, 1957. Considers man's "new vision" based upon enlargement of knowledge. Holds great meaning for a new sense of direction in curriculum development.

Hymes, James L., Jr., *A Child Development Point of View*. Englewood Cliffs, N. J.: Prentice-Hall, Inc., 1955. This little volume provides some extremely helpful suggestions to teachers in promoting an exciting environment for learning.

Jaspers, Karl, *Man in the Modern Age*. Garden City, N. Y.: Doubleday & Co., Inc., 1957. Although this book was written in 1931, the author feels that it is more pertinent in the present scene. Especially recommended is Part V, What Mankind Can Become.

Jersild, Arthur T., *In Search of Self*. New York: Bureau of Publications,

Teachers College, Columbia University, 1952. Recommended are pages 29-49 and 83-129. This book is an effort to locate the role of the school in promoting self understanding, based on much research data. It should help provide the conditions wherein one might receive great clarification about one's behavior.

Lerner, Max, *America as a Civilization*. New York: Simon and Schuster, 1957. A bold analysis and interpretation of American life. Especially recommended for curriculum workers are Chapter 1, Heritage; Chapter 3, People and Place; Chapter 4, The Culture of Science and the Machine; and Chapters 7-10, dealing with social class, the life of an American, values, character, beliefs and opinion.

Maslow, Abraham H., editor, *New Knowledge in Human Values*. New York: Harper & Brothers, 1959. Fifteen outstanding scholars question the adequacy of the values that presently govern our society. An excellent resource for the teacher and curriculum workers who are seeking to develop new dimensions in thinking with young people.

Mead, George Herbert, *The Social Psychology of George Herbert Mead*. Edited, and with an introduction, by Anselm Strauss. Chicago: University of Chicago Press, 1956.

————, *Wind, Self and Society*. Edited, and with introduction, by Charles W. Morris. Chicago: University of Chicago Press, 1934.

Meyer, Agnes E., *Education for a New Morality*. New York: The Macmillan Co., 1957. Attempts to show a relationship in thinking between science and humanism and to indicate the conditions for the "new urban industrialism." Valuable to the curriculum worker in his efforts to promote ideas for approaching the future.

Preston, Ralph C., *Teaching Social Studies in the Elementary Schools*. Revised edition. New York: Rinehart & Co., Inc., 1958. Especially recommended is Chapter 8, Units Emphasizing Regions and Cultures.

Rasey, Marie I. and J. W. Menge, *What We Learn from Children*. New York: Harper & Brothers, 1956. Excellent leads for the teacher and curriculum worker in the approach to handling ideas in new dimensions in learning.

Reichenbach, Hans, *The Rise of Scientific Philosophy*. Berkeley, Calif.: University of California Press, 1951. pp. 117-327. How we can find our way through this world without resorting to unjustifiable beliefs. Scientific information indispensable to world view is rather clearly conveyed. Helpful in providing ideas for a new sense of direction.

Riesman, David, *Individualism Reconsidered*. Garden City, N. Y.: Doubleday & Co., Inc., 1955. Develops some new dimensions of meanings relative to individual resourcefulness.

Rugg, Harold and William Withers, *Social Foundations of Education*. Englewood Cliffs, N. J.: Prentice-Hall, Inc., 1955. Especially recommended is Part V, The Intellectual Revolutions: The Great Shift in Thought. Brings together a broad range of materials, some of which are new to the curriculum. Stressed is the need for people to understand their conditions, problems, and responsibilities in times of transition and cultural confusion and strain.

Vidich, Arthur J., *Small Town in Mass Society*. Princeton, N. J.: Princeton University Press, 1958. Valuable observations on shifting power structures in a community.

Ward, Barbara, *Five Ideas That Change the World*. New York: W. W. Norton & Co., 1959. Sheds light on the shifting dynamic forces which are shaping direction of events. Points to new needs in democracies.

Whitehead, Alfred North, *Science and the Modern World*. New York: Mentor Books, The New American Library of World Literature, Inc., 1925, Eighth Printing, January 1958. Deals with aspects of Western culture as influenced by the development of science. Recommended especially are Chapter 9, Science and Philosophy, and Chapter 12, which emphasizes a sense of release toward greater meanings.

Index